Judicial Cooperation in European Private Law

JUDICIAL REVIEW AND COOPERATION

Under the general editorship of Fabrizio Cafaggi, Hans Wolfgang Micklitz, Dominique Hascher, and Torben Melchior, this Judicial Review and Cooperation series is a forum for monographs and collaborative volumes on the role of the judiciary in present day Europe. Each of the books in the series will appeal not only to an academic audience but will also engage policy makers and practitioners concerned with judicial practice in Europe.

Titles in this series include:

Regulating Judicial Activity in Europe
A Guidebook to Working Practices of the Supreme Courts
Edited by Network of the Presidents of the Supreme Judicial Courts of the European Union

National Courts and EU Law
New Issues, Theories and Methods
Edited by Bruno de Witte, Juan A. Mayoral, Urszula Jaremba, Marlene Wind and Karolina Podstawa

Judicial Cooperation in European Private Law
Edited by Fabrizio Cafaggi and Stephanie Law

Judicial Cooperation in European Private Law

Edited by

Fabrizio Cafaggi

Professor, Scuola Nazionale dell'Amministrazione, Rome, and Director, Center for Judicial Cooperation, EUI, Florence, Italy

Stephanie Law

Senior Research Fellow, Max Planck Institute Luxembourg for International, European and Regulatory Procedural Law, Luxembourg

JUDICIAL REVIEW AND COOPERATION

Edward Elgar PUBLISHING

Cheltenham, UK • Northampton, MA, USA

Published by
Edward Elgar Publishing Limited
The Lypiatts
15 Lansdown Road
Cheltenham
Glos GL50 2JA
UK

Edward Elgar Publishing, Inc.
William Pratt House
9 Dewey Court
Northampton
Massachusetts 01060
USA

A catalogue record for this book
is available from the British Library

Library of Congress Control Number: 2016959932

This book is available electronically in the **Elgar**online
Law subject collection
DOI 10.4337/9781786436696

Printed on elemental chlorine free (ECF)
recycled paper containing 30% Post-Consumer Waste

ISBN 978 1 78643 668 9 (cased)
ISBN 978 1 78643 669 6 (eBook)

Typeset by Servis Filmsetting Ltd, Stockport, Cheshire
Printed and bound in the USA

To Ester, forever. Fabrizio

Contents

Contributors

Fabrizio Cafaggi is a Professor at the Scuola Nazionale dell'Amministrazione and the Director of the Master's Program in Behavioural Sciences and Public Administration, Scuola Nazionale dell'Amministrazione and LUISS, and Part-time Professor, European University Institute.

Aurelia Colombi Ciacchi is a Professor at the Law Faculty of the University of Groningen (The Netherlands), Endowed Chair 'Law and Governance', Academic Director of the Groningen Centre for Law and Governance.

Fernando Gómez Pomar is a Professor at the Universitat Pompeu Fabra, Barcelona, Spain.

Mónika Józon is an Associate Professor of Law, Sapientia, Hungarian University of Transylvania.

Stephanie Law is a Senior Research Fellow at the Max Planck Institute for International, European and Regulatory Procedural Law, Luxembourg.

Karolina Lyczkowska is a lawyer working for DLA Piper Spain.

Marek Safjan is a Judge at the Court of Justice of the European Union, Luxembourg.

Anthony J. Scirica, the Honorable, is a judge at the United States Court of Appeals for the Third Circuit.

Christiaan Timmermans is a former Judge, Court of Justice of the European Union, Luxembourg.

Abbreviations

AFSJ	Area of Freedom, Security and Justice
AG	Advocate General
BVerfG	*Bundesverfassungsgericht*: German Federal Constitutional Court
CESL	Common European Sales Law
CISG	United Nations Convention on Contracts for the International Sale of Goods
CFR	Charter of Fundamental Rights
CRD	Consumer Rights Directive
CSD	Consumer Sales Directive
CJEU	Court of Justice of the European Union[1]
DCFR	Draft Common Frame of Reference
DGT	*direction générale de la traduction*
DRD	*direction de la bibliothèque, recherche et documentation*
ECHR	European Convention of Human Rights
ECtHR	European Court of Human Rights
ESC	European Social Charter
EU	European Union[2]
ICJ	International Court of Justice
MS	Member State
OMC	Open Method of Coordination
pCESL	Proposal for a Regulation on the Common European Sales Law
pCRD	Proposal for a Consumer Rights Directive
PECL	Principles of European Contract Law
TEU	Treaty on the European Union
TFEU	Treaty on the Functioning of the European Union
UCTD	Unfair Contract Terms Directive
UKSC	United Kingdom Supreme Court

[1] Following the Treaty of Lisbon, the term Court of Justice of the CJEU has been employed; for consistency purposes, the term CJEU is used throughout this text to refer to the Luxembourg Court, even in reference to cases heard before the Treaty entered into force in December 2009.

[2] For the same reason, namely consistency, the term 'Union law' or 'EU law' is employed throughout, regardless of whether the law referred to came into force prior or subsequent to the Treaty of Lisbon.

Table of cases

Case Law of the Court of Justice of the EU

Case C-188/10 *Melki and Abdeli* EU:C:2010:363 .... 230, 231

ECtHR Case Law

EU Member States' Case Law

US Case Law

1. Judicial dialogue in European private law: introductory remarks

Fabrizio Cafaggi and Stephanie Law

OVERVIEW OF THE TEXT

This text contributes to the ongoing debates surrounding the development of European private law (EPL), paying particular attention to European consumer law. It is oft said that EPL in general, and especially as it relates to consumer protection, is in a constant state of flux. It is currently undergoing substantive, procedural and institutional transformations, which shape its scope, content and formation, interpretation, application and enforcement of its norms, as well as the tools and mechanisms for its development. This book examines the impact of judicial dialogue on EPL development and the regulation of private law relationships.[1] To this end, it offers novel insights from a range of perspectives related to the role(s) played by the national courts, the Court of Justice of the European Union (CJEU), and the European Court of Human Rights (ECtHR). The book aims to facilitate the better understanding of how EPL develops and how its direction is shaped not only by judicial dialogue, to the extent that it exists, but also by a shift to institutional dialogue. The evolution of EPL is shaped by a number of transformations, including adjustments to the allocation of tasks between the European and national courts, the erosion of procedural autonomy (largely resulting from CJEU case law and from the increasing involvement of the EU legislature in matters of enforcement)[2]

[1] On the impact of EU law on private law relationships, see Dorota Leczykiewicz and Stephen Weatherill (eds), *The Involvement of EU Law in Private Law Relationships* (Hart 2013) and Arthur S. Hartkamp, *European Law and National Private Law* (Intersentia 2nd edn. 2016), and on EU more generally, see Juan. A Mayoral and Marlene Wind, 'Introduction: National Courts Vis-À-Vis EU Law. New Issues, Theories and Methods' in Bruno de Witte *et al* (eds), *National Courts and EU Law: New Issues, Theories and Methods* (Edward Elgar Publishing 2016)

[2] Transformations are taking place both at the substantive and procedural level; in the latter context, the role of judges – and in particular, their *ex officio*

and the growing role of European and national regulators in the actual enforcement of European private and consumer law.[3] By analysing these dimensions of change, the book also aims to identify future avenues of research and facilitate the further advancement of the field.

These transformative developments generate fundamental questions concerning the shape, scope and character of EPL, the mechanisms engaged in the making of EPL and the tools used to advance its evolution. Drawing insights on the foundational endeavours of the EU legislature, and the role of the national courts and the CJEU in interpreting, applying and enforcing EU law (often provoking legislative change in the Member States), the book explores the shifting power relationship between legislation, adjudication and regulatory enforcement and examines the influence of this development on the Europeanization of private law.

Each chapter initially examines the development of EPL from the perspective of the relationships that exist between the courts and that evolve via judicial cooperation; they also identify the basis and character of such cooperation. Others go further and encompass an analysis of the scope for this cooperation to extend beyond the judiciary, that is, to engage the European and national legislatures, administrative and alternative regulators and dispute resolution facilitators that are typically responsible for law making, interpretation and enforcement. To this end, the contributions also aim to identify the relative influence of each mechanism of law making and enforcement.[4] Judicial dialogue, while highly relevant, is of course only part of the picture. Indeed, the analysis undertaken suggests that not only judges but also regulators are engaged in dialogue and that cooperation between them often concerns matters relating to enforcement. The book therefore identifies the existence of a shift from judicial to institutional dialogue and highlights the need for its better understanding, in order to incorporate all actors – beyond courts to encompass also regulatory bodies – relevant for its application and enforcement into the multilevel structure of EPL.

The contributions also examine the impact of these mechanisms of

---

powers, their ability to request the reformulation of legal arguments and to seek evidence, to define and allocate the burden of proof, and to design effective, dissuasive and proportionate remedies – is key.

[3] See Bruno de Witte and Hans-Wolfgang Micklitz (eds), *The European Court of Justice and the Autonomy of the Member States* (Intersentia 2011).

[4] See, for previous comprehensive analyses, Roger Brownsword, Hans-Wolfgang Micklitz, Leone Niglia and Stephen Weatherill (eds), *The Foundations of European Private Law* (Hart 2011) and Leczykiewickz and Weatherill, n. 1.

development, and particularly of judicial dialogue at the national level[5] and across different fields of EPL depending inter alia on the character of the system of private law in the relevant Member States, the mechanisms for the implementation and transposition of Union legislation and the character of integration that is subsequently advanced therein.[6] We can identify key sets of evolutions and transformations from these perspectives; these are analysed in depth via a collection of diverse contributions, which facilitate a transatlantic enquiry (Scirica), examine the rationales underpinning the engagement of national courts with the CJEU (Gómez Pomar and Lyczkowska, Józon) and the methodological approaches behind the preliminary reference procedure (Timmermanns), touch upon the constitutionalization of private law and examine the impact of fundamental rights discourses on private relationships, including the impact of the Charter of Fundamental Rights (CFR) on the boundaries, functions and development of European private law (Safjan and Colombi Ciacchi), and the foundational concepts (Law), and enforcement of consumer law (Cafaggi).

(i) The Making of European Private Law and Judicial Dialogue

At the outset, it is necessary to set out the rough analytical – normative and institutional – framework to position the research questions examined in the book. This framework consists of two main component parts: the first, the relevant conceptualization of private law, and the second, the conceptualization of cooperation and dialogue. Beginning with the former, it is prudent in the context of a study of private law and of course in light of its Europeanization to acknowledge its character and its place in the field of EU law. For the purposes of the text a broad understanding of private law is adopted; it is understood to encompass those rules that regulate the relationships of private parties in a multilevel system.

As noted above, EPL seems to be in an almost constant state of development; initially rather modestly affected by legislative endeavours and the political processes underpinning European integration, an increasingly large body of secondary EU law affecting private law relationships and private autonomy has ensured that national private laws have been considerably transformed by EU endeavours in recent years.[7] The EU

[5] That is, across different legal traditions and cultures.

[6] Concerning, for example, whether the national system transposes European private law legislation into a civil code, into individual pieces of legislation, some parts into a consumer code and others into another specialized body of law.

[7] See Stephen Weatherill, 'The Elusive Character of Private Autonomy in EU Law' in Dorota Leczykiewicz and Stephen Weatherill (eds), *The Images of the*

norms that regulate private relationships are predominantly substantive in their nature. Since the 1980s, the EU has legislated in the core of private law for package travel, unfair contract terms, consumer credit and consumer rights, e-commerce, product liability, IP rights, financial markets and investment protection, among other substantive private law interests. However, the EU has also made limited inroads into national civil procedures.[8] In terms of remedies, the EU has legislated for injunctive relief for consumers, the enforcement of IP rights and ADR and provided recommendations on collective redress, and has of course legislated for cross-border civil procedure, establishing regimes that aim to facilitate mutual trust as well as autonomous European civil procedures.[9] This is one trend among others that has begun to undermine the principle of national procedural autonomy.[10] Indeed the correlation between rights and remedies and the principles of effectiveness also makes it impossible to preserve the conventional allocation between the EU (rights) and the Member States (remedies).[11]

The chapters deal 1) with issues arising in the development of substantive and procedural private law via the legislature and CJEU, which

---

Consumer in EU Law: Legislation, Free Movement and Competition Law (Hart 2016) 29.

[8] While the Union has competence to legislate for cross-border civil procedure in Arts 67 and 81 TFEU, traditionally a distinction has been drawn between substantive and procedural private law, and it is difficult to identify a competence basis for any possible future harmonization of national civil procedures. It should be noted that this has not been identified as a definitive step but as one option in the Commission's regulatory REFIT of the consumer *acquis*. See European Commission, 'Evaluation and Fitness Check Roadmap' (Available at: http://ec.europa.eu/smart-regulation/roadmaps/docs/2016_just_023_evaluation_consumer_law_en.pdf; Last Accessed: 14.06.2016).

[9] Including the Brussels and Rome regimes, the European Order for Payment and the European Small Claims Procedure, amongst others.

[10] It is worth noting that the foundations, existence and viability of the principle has been called into question, partly as a result of this line of jurisprudence of the CJEU; see, for example, Michel Bobek, 'Why There Is No Principle of Procedural Autonomy of the Member States' and Adelina Adinolfi, 'The "Procedural Autonomy" of Member States and the Constraints Stemming from the ECJ's Case Law: Is Judicial Activism Still Necessary?', both in de Witte and Micklitz (eds), n. 3, 305 and 281. See also, on the role of the national courts in the implementation of EU law, Bruno de Witte *et al* (eds), *National Courts and EU Law: New Issues, Theories and Methods* (Edward Elgar Publishing 2016).

[11] See Walter van Gerven, 'Of Rights, Remedies and Procedures' (2000) 37 *CMLR* 501.

directly fall within areas of EU competence[12] and 2) those that might rather be deemed to cross the boundaries of its field of competence.[13] The trigger for much of the discussion comes from the greater role that has seemingly been attributed to both the national and European courts and also the significance attached to the mechanisms that underpin these functions, including the preliminary reference procedure.[14] Recent years have seen an increase in the number of questions referred to the CJEU by the national courts for a preliminary judgment on the interpretation of a rule derived from EU law or a finding on the compatibility of national and EU rules.[15] The increase in the number of references extends the possible scope for dialogue between the national courts and the CJEU. In Figures 1.1 and 1.2, a steady incline in the number of questions referred and cases completed by the CJEU is identifiable across all subject areas and in relation to consumer protection specifically.

The starting point of analysis is the following: the national courts and the CJEU have long had a role to play in the development of EPL as the rules governing private relationships have typically been enforced in national courts; a private party normally brings a civil action for compensation to redress the harm arising from the breach of those private law rules by another party to that relationship. The nature of enforcement is typically individual, judicial and private.[16] The significance of judicial

---

[12] That is, the Union's use of Art.114 TFEU for the completion of the internal market.

[13] An example of the latter arises in respect of the CJEU's identification and development of procedural requirements by which national courts are bound and which have required amendments be made to national procedural rules. The case law of the CJEU is cited in section iii below.

[14] On the role of the preliminary reference as an instrument of judicial dialogue, see Opinion 2/13, EU:C:2014:2454.

[15] According to the General Report of the CJEU, and the most recent of 2015, an increase from 302 'new' preliminary references in 2009 to 436 in 2015. (Available at: http://curia.europa.eu/jcms/jcms/P_192323/; Last Accessed: 13.04.2016). Of course, references come from different Member States, and from some more than others; while, as noted Spain, and certain Central and Eastern European Member States are particularly motivated in their engagement of the Art.267 TFEU procedure, the Supreme Court of the United Kingdom (and previously as the House of Lords) has twice considered it unnecessary to refer to the CJEU for an interpretation of the meaning of key terms under the UCTD: *Director General of Fair Trading v First National Bank* [2001] UKHL 52 and *Office of Fair Trading v Abbey National plc and others* [2009] UKSC 6.

[16] Olha O. Cherednychenko 'Editorial – Public and Private Enforcement of European Private Law: Perspectives and Challenges' (2015) 23 *ERPL* 481.

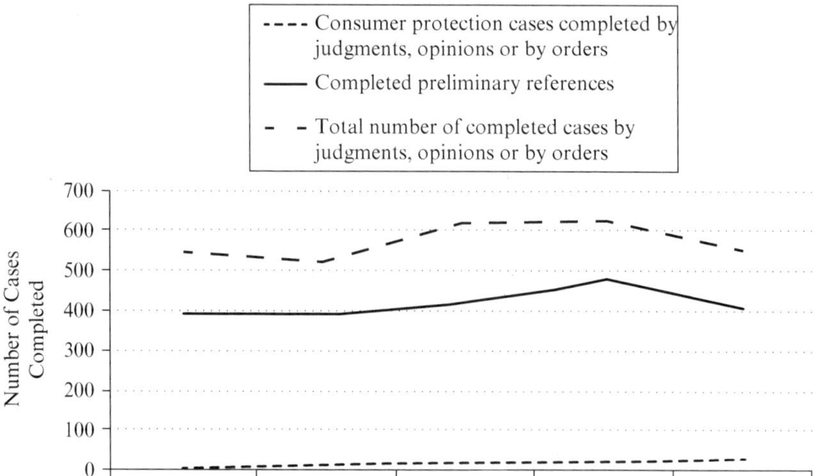

2011	2012	2013	2014	2015
4	9	19	20	29
388	386	413	476	404
544	523	620	624	554

Figure 1.1 Cases completed by judgments, by opinions or by orders, 2011–15

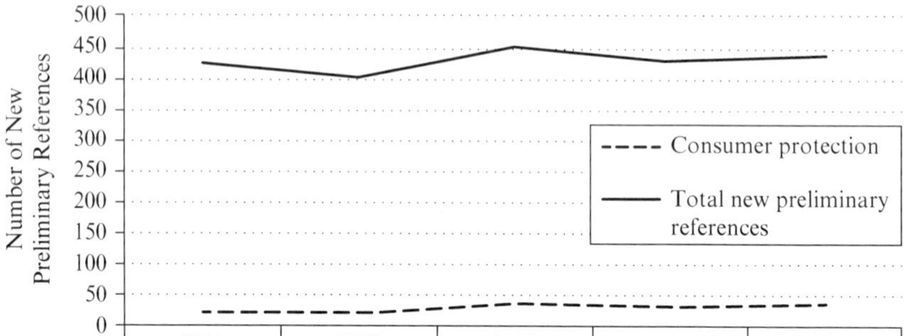

2011	2012	2013	2014	2015
21	22	34	34	39
423	404	450	428	436

Figure 1.2 Preliminary references, total and concerning consumer protection

law making has therefore long been underlined.[17] This book therefore begins from the perspective of the importance of judicial dialogue, including conflicts and cooperation, the function of various judicial techniques as a means to promote dialogue and the role of national courts as agents of European legal integration.[18]

The use of the Art.267 TFEU preliminary reference procedure has triggered vertical dialogue between the national and European courts. The duty to submit a preliminary reference – established in the Lisbon Treaty – has recently been correlated to the existence of conflicts that arise between courts within a single Member State and between Member States. The CJEU promotes horizontal dialogue between national courts by harnessing the preliminary reference procedure as a mechanism that could resolve potential conflicts arising from divergent or conflicting interpretations of EPL norms given by national courts.[19] As such, it is legitimate for a court, for example, the French *Cour de Cassation*, to make a preliminary reference if it realizes that it is giving a divergent interpretation of an EU rule from the Hungarian *Kuria*, the German *Bundesgerichtshof* or the UK Supreme Court, This innovative use of preliminary references could promote a more intense horizontal dialogue among national courts in light of the guidance provided by the CJEU. The use of the preliminary reference procedure as a mechanism in the enforcement of EPL rules may therefore lead to the judicial governance of divergences in the interpretation of EU legislation.[20] This process contributes to the further modification of the conventional distinction between rights (EU) and remedies (Member States), illustrating the weaknesses of multilevel architectures that do not account for conflicts and interactions.

Judicial dialogue is stimulated by the application of the principles of

---

[17] Including, for example, the fundamental rights dimension – namely, the constitutionalization of private law – that emerges from the increased focus on adjudication; see Hans-Wolfgang Micklitz (ed.), *The Constitutionalization of Private Law* (OUP 2014).

[18] Anne-Marie Slaughter, Alec Stone Sweet, and Joseph H.H. Weiler (eds), *The European Court and the National Courts–Doctrine and Jurisprudence: Legal Change in its Social Context* (Hart 1998) and Alec Stone Sweet, *The Judicial Construction of Europe* (OUP 2004).

[19] Case C-160/14 *Ferreira da Silva e Brito and Others* EU:C:2015:565, in which the Court holds inter alia that where there are conflicting decisions between lower national courts, a court or tribunal against whose decision there is no judicial remedy, is obliged to refer to the CJEU in line with Art.267(3) TFEU.

[20] See Fabrizio Cafaggi, 'The Making of European Private Law: Governance Design' in Fabrizio Cafaggi and Horatia Muir Watt (eds), *Making European Private Law: Governance Design* (Edward Elgar Publishing 2008).

equivalence and effectiveness in the enforcement of EPL, and particularly of consumer law, within the national courts.[21] Against this background, judicial dialogue has expanded the application of general principles of EU law to private relationships beyond the specific intermediation of EU legislation;[22] that is to say, the CJEU has provided for the direct applicability of EU principles, for example of non-discrimination, to private parties.[23] These developments of rights and remedies in consumer law therefore find parallels in the horizontal application of fundamental rights.[24] Moreover, and in line with the application of the principles of effective and equivalent protection, judicial dialogue has provided a mechanism for the development of not only the substantive but also the procedural dimensions of consumer law.[25] In particular, the development of procedural law is increasingly driven by the application of the CFR and Art.47 thereof. While the horizontal application of fundamental rights clearly influence the evolution of EPL, it remains unclear to what extent the CFR itself impacts its boundaries, content and functions.[26] The CFR – binding as primary law, post-Lisbon Treaty – has been engaged by the CJEU and is generating changes in substantive national consumer law, and in the related rules of civil procedure, for example, in order to ensure, in light of Art.47 CFR, the right to an effective remedy and to a fair trial; this right may be invoked on the one hand in favour of consumers, and on the other, in favour of professionals.[27] Moreover, the right to be heard

---

[21] See Takis Tridimas, 'The ECJ and the National Courts: Dialogue, Cooperation and Instability' in Anthony Arnull and Damian Chalmers (eds), *The Oxford Handbook of European Union Law* (OUP 2015) 403, Nina Poltorak, *European Union Rights in National Courts* (Kluwer 2015) 39 *et seq*., de Witte and Micklitz, n. 3.

[22] See Arthur S. Hartkamp, 'The General Principles of EU Law and Private Law' (2011) 75 *Rabels Zeitschrift für ausländisches und internationales Privatrecht* 241.

[23] See Case C-144/04 *Mangold* EU:C:2005:709; Case C-555/07 *Kücükdeveci* EU:C:2010:21 and Case C-441/14 *Dansk Industri* EU:C:2016:278.

[24] See Chantal Mak, 'Rights and Remedies – Article 47 EUCFR and Effective Judicial Protection in European Private Law Matters' in Micklitz (ed.), n. 19, 236 and Verica Trstenjak, 'General Report' in Verica Trstenjak and Petra Weingerl (eds), *The Influence of Human Rights and Basic Rights in Private Law* (Springer 2016) 3.

[25] See Simon Whittaker, 'Who Determines What Civil Courts Decide? Private Rights, Public Policy an EU Law' in Leczykiewicz and Weatherill, n. 1, 89.

[26] Micklitz, n. 19 and on the shifts in consumer law in particular, Hans-Wolfgang Micklitz, 'The Consumer: Marketised, Fragmentised, Constitutionalised' in Leczykiewicz and Weatherill, n. 8, 21. See also, Trstenjak and Weingerl (eds), n. 26.

[27] See Case C-119/15 *Biuro* EU:C:2016:987, discussed further below.

and the right to a defence are transforming the role of the collective action at the national level and thus the relationship between individual and collective redress.[28]

Notwithstanding this evolving space for judicial cooperation and dialogue, little research has been undertaken either on the mechanisms and techniques of cooperation and dialogue, or on the impact of CJEU jurisprudence in the legal system of the referring court and across other systems.[29] The increase in the number of preliminary references is one of a number of trends underpinning the contributions to the text. It coincides with other developments that shape EPL and European integration and which call for an investigation into the existence and character of interdependences in the European space.[30] These include the enlargement of the EU, the shift in the harmonization policy of the Union legislature from minimum to maximum to targeted maximum harmonization and the expanding role of regulatory bodies in the enforcement of EU law. It is submitted that the role and influence of courts and the increasing relevance of national regulators in the monitoring and enforcement of consumer law necessitates[31] a reconsideration of the dynamics of institutional dialogue or trialogues between domestic and European actors, and particularly

---

28 See Case C-312/14 *Banif Plus Bank* EU:C:2015:794 and Case C-381/14 *Sales Sinués* EU:C:2016:252.

29 Which might depend on the relevant area of private law and the way in which this is regulated for in the national legal systems, for example, whether there is a civil or a consumer code, or whether Union legislation (generally, directives) are transposed via individual pieces of national legislation.

30 On the one hand, we can consider the interdependence between EU law and national private law and how best to understand the interdependence between the two in private law relationships; see Carla Sieburgh, 'A Method to Substantively Guide the Involvement of EU Law in Private Law Matters' (2013) *ERPL* 1165, who advocates a particular role should being attributed to fundamental rights and especially the CFR in understanding these interactions. On the other, we can analyse this interdependence in light of the spillover effects that emerge from the interactions and transformations that derive – at least initially – from the launching of the preliminary reference procedure and the relationship that is (re)established between the national court and the CJEU, and which affect not only courts in the referring and other Member States but the national legislative bodies and administrative enforcement agencies.

31 This issue is even more important given the reform of Regulation 2006/2004 on Cooperation between National Authorities Responsible for the Enforcement of Consumer Protection Laws. A proposal for a new regulation was published in May 2016. See European Commission, 'Proposal for a Regulation on Cooperation between National Authorities Responsible for the Enforcement of Consumer Protection Laws' COM(2016) 283 final.

between judges and regulators exercising relevant advisory functions.[32] The examination of the processes and actors engaged in enforcement is not without conflict however.[33] Institutional rents are eroded unevenly given the different choices made by Member States when identifying enforcement bodies, the instruments available to them and their objectives. While judiciaries obtain power over national executives, they also cede some of their newly-acquired powers to independent regulators.[34]

---

[32] Consider for example, the French *Commission des clauses abusives*, established by L. 822-4 of the Consumer Code, which can examine standard form contracts and recommend the removal or amendment of clauses which are unfair, i.e., which essentially create an imbalance against the non-professional or consumer. The Commission can also hear references from a judge for a determination on whether a contract term is unfair. Its recommendations and opinions are published online at http://www.clauses-abusives.fr/ (Last accessed: 25.10.2016). A similar body exists in Belgium (see http://economie.fgov.be/fr/spf/structure/Commissions_Conseils/Commission_clauses_abu/avis/#.WBBeeEYuNkU (Last accessed: 26.10.2016). In the Netherlands, standard contract terms are drafted per sector by trade associations, having been determined *ex ante* to be fair. In the UK, the Competition and Markets Authority, which replaced the Office of Fair Trading in 2014, is responsible for assessing mergers, markets and the regulated industries, with competence to enforce competition and consumer law. It does not assist consumers directly but has a role to play educating businesses on compliance; it aims to promote competitive markets, and compliance with consumer protection law via the provision and dissemination of information, advice and education, dialogue, warning, undertakings, penalties and then through civil and criminal actions. It can apply – per Part 8 of the Enterprise Act 2002 – to the courts for an enforcement order in light of a violation of consumer law, and following the Consumer Rights Act 2015, can impose enhanced consumer measures on businesses (which can include training, monitoring of compliance, and voluntary redress schemes). Other bodies also have a role to play in regulating unfair terms, either via an injunction (to prevent a business from using, proposing to use or recommending the use of a term that appears to be unfair) or via an enforcement order (which may also provide redress to consumers who have suffered loss (including monetary compensation)); these include the Chartered Trading Standards Institute, the Trading Standards Services, and others, under the Unfair Terms in Consumer Contract Regulations 1999.

[33] See Richard A. Posner, 'Regulation (Agencies) versus Litigation (Courts): An Analytical Framework' in Daniel P. Kessler (ed.), *Regulation vs. Litigation: Perspectives from Economics and Law* (University of Chicago Press 2010) 11, who examines the relationship between common law judging and administrative regulation as mechanisms of social control, identifying the methods used in each and the overlap between the two. In relation to consumer enforcement see Fabrizio Cafaggi, 'The Great Transformation: Administrative and Judicial Enforcement in Consumer Protection: A Remedial Perspective' (2009) 21 *Loyola Consumer Law Review* 496.

[34] See Cafaggi and Muir Watt, n. 22.

(ii) Instruments and Objectives of Judicial Dialogue

This introduction aims specifically to ascertain and map existing and emerging patterns, mechanisms and techniques of institutional dialogue and cooperation, which are further examined in each of the contributions with a focus on the relevant area of EPL. In terms of its character and aims, judicial dialogue and, moreover, 'judicial cooperation in civil and commercial matters', is multi-faceted. These strands of interaction might be vertical, for example arising between the national and European courts,[35] or horizontal, between the national courts, on the one hand, and between the CJEU and the ECHR,[36] on the other. Dialogue might occur between courts and legislatures, or courts and regulators, giving rise to trialogues or even tetralogues.[37] It can be understood to have varied objectives, which may diverge depending on the perspective adopted, that is, of the national or European courts, of legislatures, academics, civil society bodies or individuals.

Dialogue may aim promote communication or 'conversation' not only concerning the content of European private law norms, that is, their

---

[35] Typically that which emerges via the preliminary reference procedure. See Tridimas, n. 23, 403.

[36] Which arises when cross-references are made between the two courts.

[37] Consider the facts in a recent case, which brings to the fore the significance of the EU's experimentalist governance approach, in this context, in the telecoms sector: Case C-28/15 *Koninklijke KPN and Others* EU:C:2016:692. The national regulatory authority had previously issued a decision implementing a recommendation of the European Commission that was subsequently overturned by the national court on judicial review; the court's decision required the authority to depart from the recommendation. In light of a consultation procedure established under the relevant directive, the national authority notified the Commission, which initiated an investigation considering that the judicial decision constituted a barrier to the functioning of the market. The case referred arose from a subsequent decision given by the national authority, again implementing the Commission's recommendation; the national court requested clarification on its discretion to provide for a decision against the national regulatory authority and the Commission's recommendation on the basis of national legal and factual concerns (namely, the nature of the Dutch market). Both the A-G and Court held that the national court could depart from the Commission's recommendation (but that this should be done in limited circumstances) and 'only where it considers that this is required on grounds related to the facts of the individual case, in particular the specific characteristics of the market of the Member State in question'. As such, the national court can overturn the decision of the regulatory authority, thus giving it the role of a de facto regulator (see the comments of Marta Cantero on the AG's Opinion: http://eulawanalysis.blogspot.lu/2016/05/testing-eu-experimentalist-governance.html. Last Accessed: 22.10.2016).

interpretation, but also in relation to the factors that shape their application (in particular, procedural rules). Indeed, the use of the preliminary reference procedure, and the dialogue to which it gives rise, has been a powerful instrument of legal change in EPL and has emerged as a driver of innovation of both substantive and procedural rules as engaged and utilized at the national level. To take an example: the national courts have long been empowered to police market practices using preventative and repressive measures to deter and stop unfair behaviour; however, the role of the national judge applying national law which transposes EU law may differ from that of the national judge who applies purely domestic law.[38] Whether the effects of judicial dialogue in this realm – for example, the obligation established by the CJEU which requires national courts to examine unfairness of contract terms *ex officio* – will transcend those areas of law directly affected by the preliminary reference (therefore leading to the expansion of the approach or interpretation identified to other areas of private law), or indeed, other areas made up of mandatory rules, remains to be seen. It seems that such steps are taking place, at least in the area of consumer law itself.[39]

Dialogue in European private law might be conceived as an empowerment tool[40] in three ways:

---

[38] Consider, for example, in Spain, where the judge is generally understood to have a passive role in relation to the parties to the (possibly) consumer protection-related case on the basis of the principle of disposition; on the basis of the CJEU's jurisprudence (largely but not exclusively), as discussed immediately below, relating to unfair contract terms, it is difficult for the judge to identify what his or her role should be, how far he or she should go in determining if the contract is a consumer one, the sufficiency of the evidence and legal arguments advanced and so forth. These considerations are also shaped by rules of national civil procedure, in which the European Commission has recently taken a significant interest. The Max Planck Institute in Luxembourg will submit a study (JUST/2014/RCON/PR/CIVI/0082) to the European Commission on the impact of national civil procedure on the enforcement of EU consumer rights (and on the operation of the principle of mutual trust) in December 2016.

[39] For example, the *ex officio* control requirements on the national courts no longer apply only in respect of the Unfair Contract Terms Directive 1993/13/EC but have been extended to consumer sales and consumer credit in Case C-497/13 *Faber* EU:C:2015:357 and Case C-377/14 *Radlinger* EU:C:2016:283, respectively. The spillover of these references into the national legal systems is not clear, however, as procedural rules still tend only to provide for an obligation for *ex officio* control in relation to unfair contract terms; even where a power might be developed along these lines in other areas of consumer law, it seems that judges remain reluctant to engage with it.

[40] The literature on the role of courts in European law making has been led by Joseph H.H. Weiler, 'The Transformation of Europe' (1991) 100 *Yale L.J.* 2403

(1) It might help national courts and the CJEU to manage commonalities and divergences – whether micro or macro – that emerge from the implementation of Union law in national private law systems and which shape its enforcement. On the face of it, the Union legislature or the CJEU is best placed to identify the existence of divergences or commonalities in national legal cultures, whether substantive (concerning the transposition of norms) or procedural (concerning rules and cultures of national civil procedure). Conflicts arise in a multilevel system where competences are divided and shared; they exist, for example, between interpretations rendered at the Union and national levels, and are generated inter alia within the national system or via spillovers from the descent of the preliminary ruling and the application of the CJEU's interpretations within the diverse national traditions of the Member States.[41] Dialogue might facilitate

---

and Karen J. Alter, *Establishing the Supremacy of European Law: The Making of an International Rule of Law in Europe* (OUP 2001).

[41] In this respect, it has been advanced that dialogue reflects neofunctionalist – and particularly, revised legal-orientated – understandings of integration, theories developed by Haas in the 1950s, and subsequently, by Alec Stone Sweet and others in the 1990s; Ernst Haas, *The Uniting of Europe* (Stanford University Press 1958) 16. It was considered that the construction of greater economic interdependence among states, as well as increased social and political interdependence (in respect of the free movement of goods, services, capital and labour) would generate further integration through 'spillover' effects, both political and functional in their nature (Leon Lindberg, *The Political Dynamics of European Economic Integration* (Stanford University Press 1963) 10). Reconceptualizations of neofunctionalism in the 1980s and 1990s highlighted the legal dimension of integration, with key European legal principles 'penetrating' or 'overlaying' national norms, shaping the interrelation between the national and EU legal orders; Anne-Marie Burley and Walter Mattli, 'Europe Before the Court: A Political Theory of Legal Integration' (1993) 47 *International Organizations* 41, 43 and Alec Stone Sweet and Wayne Sandholtz, 'European Integration and Supranational Governance' (1997) 4 *Journal of Public Policy* 297. Subsequently, the 'integration through law' school highlighted, in the context of the existing neofunctionalist, intergovernmentalist and supranationalist scholarship, the 'dual character of supranationalism', namely, the intertwinement of legal and political processes (Joseph H.H. Weiler, 'The Community System: The Dual Character of Supranationalism' (1981) Y. Eur. Law 267); law is understood as 'both the object and agent of integration' (that is, integration of law, and integration through law, respectively (Mauro Cappelletti, Monica Seccombe and Joseph H.H. Weiler (eds.), *Integration Through Law: Europe and the American Federal Experience* (de Gruyer 1985) 42). Further still, it has been suggested that the balance between cooperation and hierarchy inherent in the relationship between the national courts and the CJEU rather suggests that judicial dialogue reflects an understanding of cooperative supranationalism, and 'interaction, dialogue and compromise' (Anthony Arnull, 'Judicial

the scope for national courts (as well as the CJEU) to resolve, or at least manage, conflict. Based on the principle of effectiveness, judicial dialogue has provided national courts with new procedural instruments. Dialogue might therefore be conceived as a tool that empowers national courts against the national legislature; that is to say, it might facilitate the role of the national court, instead of, or at least complementary to, the legislature, in generating coherence and filling the gaps in a potentially fragmented – internally to a Member State and across the Member States – body of implementing legislation.[42]

(2) Dialogue might contribute to the better monitoring and enforcement of EU consumer law. It might consist of and include inter alia, the possible scope for national courts to police terms and practices beyond the specific indications given by the parties,[43] for example, in relation to the *ex officio* control of consumer contract terms.[44] It might also encompass the possibility for the national court to expand the effects of injunctions beyond the spheres of the litigants to the specific dispute, and furthermore, the extraction and application of general principles by various courts to areas which do not fall within the immediate scope of EU primary law or secondary law but which nevertheless come to form part of EU law. Such an impact is identifiable in the development of state liability, for example.[45]

(3) Dialogue might enable national courts and regulators to address social problems arising within national and European contexts. This might encompass, for example, issues that have become increasingly evident post-economic crisis; these concerns have included

---

Dialogue in the European Union' in Julie Dickson and Pavlos Eleftheriadis (eds.), *The Philosophical Foundations of European Union Law* (OUP 2012) 109, 119).

[42] See Cafaggi, n. 22, 289.

[43] While it might also empower private individuals in domestic and cross-border contexts, as in Case C-171/11 *Fra.Bo* EU:C:2012:453.

[44] Including inter alia Case C-240/98 *Océano* [2000] ECR I-4941, and the cases that followed, including, inter alia: Case C-227/08 *Martin Martin* EU:C:2009:792; Case C-137/08 *VB Pénzügyi Lízing* EU:C:2010:659; Case C-243/08 *Pannon GSM* EU:C:2009:350; Case C-453/10 *Pereničová and Perenič* EU:C:2012:144; Case C-618/10 *Banco Español de Crédito* EU:C:2012:349; Case C-470/12 *Pohotovosť* EU:C:2014:101; Cases C-482, 484, 485 and 487/13 *Unicaja Banco and Caixabank* EU:C:2015:21; Case C-497/13 *Faber* EU:C:2015:357; Case C-32/14 *ERTSE* EU:C:2015:637; and Case C-169/14 *Sánchez Morcillo* EU:C:2014:2099.

[45] C-6/90 *Francovich* [1991] ECR I-5357, C-46/93 *Brasserie du Pêcheur* [1996] ECR I-1029 and C-224/01 *Köbler* [2003] ECR I-10239, among others.

> many issues relating to consumer protection, such as consumer credit, housing (and the credit that accompanies it), and investor protection.[46]

Thus, institutional dialogue may be strategic; it may aim to change directly or indirectly, intentionally or unintentionally, national norms via legislation or case law. It may also operate as a vehicle of cross-referencing and cross-fertilization, as a means of exchange of knowledge, ideas and opinions, as a mechanism of compromise or as a tool of deliberation, in order to promote a specific outcome through collaboration. Indeed, in this light the book purports to facilitate learning and the exchange of knowledge and ideas between national and European judges and academics. National systems of private law diverge in respect of their engagement with particular implementation techniques, the determination of which will have further consequences in respect of the scope for spillover effects. Divergences in national systems will be relevant in terms of the determination of including EU legislation into civil codes or general statutes, or alternatively, the enacting of a single statute and thus the limitation of spillover effects.[47] In some Member States, consumer law exists as a separate and even insulated body of rules; in others it is integrated into civil codes. It might form part of private law with its own specificities concerning the number and intensity of mandatory provisions, the function of default rules, and the power of the judges to raise questions of their own motion.[48] It has been shown that the use of consumer codes in contrast to the transposition of Union legislation into individual statutes, or the integration of

---

[46] National courts have often complemented the tasks of regulators in monitoring renegotiations of loans and restructuring of personal debts and bankruptcy. See the contribution of Gomez and Lyczkowska herein.

[47] See Angus Johnston, 'Spillovers' from EU Law into National Law: (Un) intended Consequences for Private Law Relationships' in Leczykiewicz and Weatherill, n. 1, 357.

[48] This often also shapes the approach adopted by the national judge. For example, in terms of the role of the judge in Portugal, the judge will often apply general contract law as opposed to specific consumer law due to his or her lack of familiarity with the latter; see Catarina Frade and Mariana Pinheiro Almeida, 'Country Report Portugal' in Hans-W. Micklitz and Irina Domurath (eds), *Consumer Debt and Social Exclusion in Europe* (Ashgate 2015) 47, 60. The same situation also arises in Spain, where it is unclear whether the national judge should apply consumer legislation when the consumer's lawyer only invokes general provisions of the civil code or of contract law, and not specific consumer law legislation (see Max Planck Institute Study on National Civil Procedure, JUST/2014/RCON/PR/CIVI/0082, Fernando Gascón Inchausti, 'National Report of Spain'; forthcoming).

consumer law into a civil code, generates different consequences in terms of the relationship between private and consumer law. If each is conceived to be distinct, for example, the impact of judgments rendered by the CJEU via the preliminary reference procedure may be rather limited to the area of consumer law. That is to say, such a judgment is unlikely to have a broader impact across other areas of private law or across the systems of the Member States other than that of the referring court.

(iii) How do CJEU Judgments Promote or Reduce the Space for Institutional Interactions?

As this book aims to examine the role played by dialogue as a mechanism in adjudication in multilevel systems, the added value in looking beyond courts themselves towards the dialogue that exists between courts and legislatures, as well as regulatory and administrative authorities, will also be analysed. The choice and reach of the Union's legislative instrument constitutes only the initial step in EPL development; the effects of these determinations on the integration of EU law into national systems and of national legal systems into European law can only be evaluated by examining how it is applied and enforced at the national level (not only by courts but also by administrative and regulatory authorities). This necessitates an analysis of the dialogue that arises from the national courts and the CJEU, and the nature of the judgment given by the latter.[49] Much of the scholarship to date on the impact of EU primary and secondary legislation has not fully accounted for the role that the character of the judgment rendered by the CJEU might play in respect of the implementation, impact and evolution of Union law within the different national traditions and on the scope for dialogue between the Luxembourg Court and the national judge.[50] By making reference to the character of the CJEU's judgment, we can engage, for example, the distinction made by Tridimas between the specificity of the ruling rendered by the CJEU.[51] According to Tridimas'

---

[49] Previous attempts to uncover dialogue in the EU space have largely been confined to the sphere of constitutional dialogue; consequently, it has received relatively little explicit consideration in private law. Thus, while the text aims to build on the existing literature concerning judicial dialogue, it extends beyond this focus in order to engage substantive development areas directly concerning private law development in which key examples of judicial dialogue can be identified, thus allowing for the transcending of the boundaries between the public and private.

[50] See however Arthur S. Hartkamp, *European Law and National Private Law* (Intersentia 2nd edn., 2016). More broadly Weiler, n. 44.

[51] Tridimas, n. 23, 403, 409–10.

taxonomy, three types of rulings might be rendered by the CJEU: (1) one which is so specific that the national court has no discretion to exercise ('outcome cases'); (2) one which provides the national court with guidance as to the resolution of the dispute ('guidance cases'); and (3) one which is so general as to rather defer to the national court ('deference cases').[52] We can speculate as to how the nature of a ruling might not only impact the final decision of the referring court, in respect of which the preliminary ruling initially arose, but how it might also impact the nature of the subsequent decisions of the courts of the Member States and the nature of integration that emerges therefrom.[53] This impact might be reflective of a technique based on conform interpretation, might encompass disapplication of national rules,[54] might amount to the making of a (further or indeed separate) preliminary reference,[55] might result in the engagement of comparative analysis, or indeed, might generate a combination of these possible outcomes.[56] While these lines of enquiry rather extend beyond the scope of this text, we can posit that an approach to rendering a judgment based on conform or consistent interpretation might lead to a softer form of integration; an approach based on the disapplication of national rules suggests a stronger form, which might only be engaged if the national judge cannot identify a satisfactory solution via conform

---

52 This is explored, for example, in relation to the evolution of extra-contractual liability, and the scope for state liability, in Timmermans' contribution.

53 Further examples of these 'judicial techniques' can be found and are explained in greater detail in the 'JUDCOOP' Handbook: European University Institute, Centre for Judicial Cooperation, 'European Judicial Cooperation and Fundamental Rights: Some Practical Guidelines' (Available at: http://www.eui.eu/Projects/CentreForJudicialCooperation/Documents/JUDCOOPdeliverables/JUDCOOPdeliverables/JUDCOOP%20Guidelines%20-%20Multilingual%20version.pdf; Last Accessed: 16.05.2016).

54 Along the lines of the *Simmenthal* doctrine, Case C-106/77 *Amminstrazione delle Finanze dello Stato v Simmenthal* [1978] ECR I-0629. Case C-555/07 *Kücükdeveci*, n. 25, in relation to non-discrimination on the grounds of age.

55 The preliminary reference might be used for different purposes, depending on the court (for example, if a lower-court judge anticipated that his or her interpretation or disapplication of national law might generate a negative reaction from a higher-court judge), and depending on the basis of its engagement.

56 For example, in the case law on the rights of same-sex couples in Spain, the Spanish Constitutional Court adopted a combination of comparative reasoning and consistent interpretation techniques to open up a space for the recognition of same-sex relationships in the national legal systems; see, for example, Constitutional Court, STC 198/2012, 06.11.2012 (Available at: http://hj.tribunalconstitucional.es/HJ/es/Resolucion/Show/23106; Last Accessed: 21.06.2016), particularly significant in an area in which the existence of consensus across Europe is contentious.

interpretation.[57] Furthermore, the effect of the reference for a preliminary ruling might depend on the nature of the ruling rendered, which can be tied to the taxonomy advanced by Tridimas, namely, whether it is prescriptive (either detailed in advancing a particular solution or simply setting out a principle), promotional or deferential.

Judicial dialogue can also facilitate our understanding of how the level and degree of legal integration is shaped by the boundaries between consistent and inconsistent interpretations of EU law, defining the scope of spillover effects in respect of non-harmonized fields and the margin of discretion left to national institutions when implementing EU law and adapting those areas which have not been harmonized.[58] It is possible to elaborate upon how the interplay between the vertical and horizontal dialogue brings about new forms of development of European private law. The CJEU might be 'indirectly' pushed via the national courts to coordinate implementation processes that influence the role of the latter in monitoring and policing forms of market regulation through private law instruments. These would include mechanisms like fairness in contractual terms and deceptive and aggressive selling practices. More dramatic changes are likely to become evident as the interaction of the case law on freedoms and distinct areas of private law is examined in more depth;[59]

---

[57] Per, for example, the approach seemingly advocated by the CJEU in Case C-282/10 *Dominguez* EU:C:2012:33.

[58] This concerns, as noted above, the principle of procedural autonomy. National civil procedure has largely been deemed to be a matter that falls outwith the competence of the Union legislature, that is to say, which is not caught by the 'usual' internal market legal basis of Art.114 TFEU. Thus, with the exception of cross-border civil procedure, relating to issues of private international law, procedure is generally a matter for the Member States. The Union legislature has only made limited inroads into national procedure, with the Directives on Injunctions for the Protection of Consumers' Interest (Directive 2009/22/EC) and on Alternative Dispute Resolution for Consumer Disputes (Directive 2013/11/EU), the Regulation on Consumer Online Dispute Resolution (Regulation 524/2013/EU) and the Recommendations on Collective Redress (Commission Recommendation on Common Principles for Injunctive and Compensatory Collective Redress Mechanisms in the Member States Concerning Violations of Rights Granted Under Union Law of 11.06.2013).

[59] See Arthur S. Hartkamp, 'The Effect of the EC Treaty in Private Law: On Direct and Indirect Horizontal Effects of Primary Community Law' (2010) 18 *ERPL* 527; Paul Verbruggen, 'The Impact of Primary EU Law on Private Law Relationships: Horizontal Direct Effect under the Free Movement of Goods and Services' (2014) 22 *ERPL* 201; Emanuela Navarretta, 'Libertà fondamentali dell'U.E. e rapporti fra privati: il bilanciamento di interessi e i rimedi civilistici' in Francesco Mezzanotte (ed.), *Le 'libertà fondamentali' dell'Unione europea ed il diritto privato* (Rome Tre-Press 2016) 41.

for example, the expansion of the principle of the 'direct effect' of the four freedoms is likely to modify the systems of sources of law and the balance between 'private individual' and 'collective' autonomy.[60]

(iv) The Impact of Institutional Dialogue on the Development of European Private Law

The book adopts a particular methodology, to examine the entire 'cycle' of jurisprudence arising in the substantive areas of the contributions, from the reference of the national court, to the preliminary ruling of the CJEU, to the subsequent decision of the referring court. The chapters also examine the (potentially strategic) interaction that arises between the courts and with other institutions, including the national and European legislatures, regulatory agencies and alternative dispute resolution entities. Moreover, the contributions also begin to unpeel the notion of the 'impact' of the case on the other courts of the referring Member State (and beyond the area of law in which the reference arose, a cross-sectoral impact) and the impact of the case on the case law of other Member States (a cross-border impact).[61] Certain chapters do this by tracing the relevant cases, from the national court's decision to make a reference to the CJEU, to the reasoning and judgment rendered by the A-G and the Court, and the transfer of the case back to the referring national court.

This approach purports to facilitate the identification of pertinent conflicts between national and Union law, as they emerge in the national systems, and the putative tension that might arise as the case is referred back to the deciding court, for example, when the preliminary reference was motivated by conflicting interpretations of EU law. By use of this methodology, the scope for interaction (cooperative or conflicting), the use and mechanisms of dialogue and cooperation, and the subsequent impact, can be uncovered.

The component parts of this rough analytical framework of judicial dialogue are deepened in the contributions to the text, through substantive case studies cutting across areas of EPL. Relevant areas of substantive

---

[60] See Stephanie Law, 'The CJEU as a "Laboratory" of Comparative Analysis: A Theoretical and Case-Based Study of the Europeanisation of Private Law', EUI Ph.D. Thesis, 2014.

[61] This approach has been adopted in drafting the JUDCOOP handbook and is currently used in the ACTIONES and REJUS projects, led by Fabrizio Cafaggi and funded by the European Commission's Directorate-General for Justice and Consumers. This cycle can be identified in the cases stemming from *Aziz* to *Sanchez Morcillo*, for example.

law include: state liability, and the impact of CJEU jurisprudence and dialogue in the development of state liability at national level; consumer contract law, its contribution to the development of general contract law and market regulation via contract; and fundamental rights. These areas diverge in respect of the sources of their norms (consumer contract: legislation; fundamental rights: national constitutions/primary legislation/ general principles; state liability: CJEU case law), and the extent to which the nature of their development coincides with judicial dialogue. As noted above, where relevant, the chapters aim to track the relevant cases along different courses. Each chapter identifies: different types of conflict (i.e., between national and EU law and between EU law norms, including between fundamental freedoms and fundamental rights), the making of the preliminary reference by the national court and the factors shaping the decision to refer, the significance of judicial cooperation in the CJEU's rendering of its interpretation, the impact of the preliminary reference on the referring state, and the cross-border impact on other national legal orders. The chapters use this tracking mechanism as a means to identify the nature and the objectives of the dialogue arising therein. This might be vertical or horizontal; the chapters examine firstly the ascent of the case to the Luxembourg Court (and the rationales underpinning the reference; this might include empowerment, the scope for which diverges between sectors) and thereafter, its descent from the CJEU. The preliminary reference procedure establishes a direct vertical dialogue between the national courts and CJEU, and necessarily cuts across vertical and horizontal interactions at the national and European levels. With a contribution from Scirica, the book also offers a perspective that extends beyond the largely European focus that arises from the other chapters. This allows for a transatlantic analysis of the various techniques of judicial interaction,[62] to promote dialogue and resolve conflicts arising between the national courts and the CJEU, on the one hand, and the federal courts and the US Supreme Court, on the other. The EU and the US, two of the world's largest economies, are politically, economically and culturally intertwined at various levels.[63] There exists a considerable body of scholarship on

[62] Including, within the US system: (1) consistent interpretation; (2) preliminary reference; (3) proportionality; (4) comparative reasoning; (5) mutual recognition; (6) disapplication; and (7) deferential techniques; see the contribution of Scirica to this text.

[63] Following the Marshall Plan of 1948 (the Foreign Assistance Act 1948), the US first sent observers to the then-ECSC in 1953; diplomatic relations that evolved via the establishments of missions and delegations were formalised in 1990 with the adoption of the Transatlantic Declaration and advanced further by the New

diplomatic relations, security and defence, and of course, on trade between the EU and US as well as on those matters falling within the area of Justice and Home Affairs.[64] However, there has been little research undertaken on the scope for transatlantic judicial and institutional dialogue.[65] This book therefore facilitates a first step and aims to highlight the key paths of future research. The existence of cooperation and dialogue that are examined predominantly in the EU context – with a focus on the horizontal and vertical relationships between the national legal systems of the Member States and the EU, as well as the ECHR regime – could be extended in the abstract to EU-US cooperation, particularly in areas where it is necessary to develop mechanisms for managing the plurality of regulatory regimes.[66] From the perspective of EPL, the scope for cooperation and dialogue becomes increasingly pertinent to the issue of effective consumer enforcement and its related fields.[67]

The book also examines the significance of national traditions and cultures, and particularly, the manner in which national peculiarities influence the foundations of dialogue, that is, predominantly the determination

---

Transatlantic Agenda, adopted in 1995. The Transatlantic Economic Partnership was subsequently entered into, covering bilateral and multilateral trade and which has led to the development of mechanisms to avoid obstacles to trade and the liberalization of trade within the WTO context. The Transatlantic Economic Council was established in 2007 and six years later, US-EU High Level Working Group on Jobs and Growth advised that the EU and US begin to negotiate an agreement on trade and investment (what continues to be negotiated as the Transatlantic Trade and Investment Partnership).

[64] European Parliamentary Research Service, 'EU-US cooperation in Justice and Home Affairs – An Overview' PE 580.892 (Brussels 2016).

[65] Certain frameworks for dialogue have been advanced; these include, for example, the Trans-Atlantic Business Council, the Trans-Atlantic Consumer Dialogue and Trans-Atlantic Policy Network, all of which seem to be fundamentally pro-trade. Moreover, there have been studies – mostly political science, albeit with a key legal dimension – into the existence and character of transatlantic cooperation in various areas; see for example, Mark A. Pollack and Gregory C. Shaffer (eds), *Transatlantic Governance in the Global Economy* (Rowman & Littlefield 2001) and Mark A. Pollack, *The Political Economy of the Transatlantic Partnership* (RSCAS, European University Institute 2003).

[66] See Paul Schiff Berman, *Global Legal Pluralism* (CUP 2012) 152 *et seq.*

[67] Which includes, of course, the CJEU's finding of invalidity of the old Safe Harbour agreement in Case C-362/14 *Schrems* EU:C:2015:650 (which highlighted the need for clarifications from the US institutions in this context), the significance of the Safe Harbour Framework and the new EU-US Privacy Shield agreement, and which brings to the fore not only judicial cooperation but cooperation between regulatory and enforcement bodies (in the context of data protection between the European Data Protection Authorities and the Federal Trade Commission).

of the national court to make a preliminary reference to the CJEU, and consequences of dialogue, comparing the diverse, local institutional frameworks, which provide indications as to the openness or resilience of the Member States to the Europeanization of private law. The contributions aim to transcend the discussion of 'if dialogue takes place' and engage at a more fundamental level with its foundations, character and impact, looking to identify and evaluate the consequences of its different forms, that is, whether it might generate empowerment strategies with the purpose of providing the courts – national and European – with tools to facilitate and promote to compliance with Union legislation and CJEU jurisprudence, or to encourage directly or indirectly spillover effects in areas falling outside the Union's direct field of competence.[68]

(v) Actors and Dynamics of Institutional Dialogue in Private Law Enforcement in Light of the Charter of Fundamental Rights

As submitted above, institutional dialogue is stimulated by the application of the principles of equivalence and effectiveness in the context of the enforcement of EPL, and particularly consumer law rules; it is further advanced by the related notion of effective judicial protection, reflected in Art.47 CFR. The relationship between the actors engaged in the enforcement of EPL, whether courts or regulatory bodies, and Art.47 CFR, is a matter that continues to lack clarity.

An interesting issue concerning this relationship has recently been decided by the CJEU, in which the Polish Court of Appeal engaged the CJEU's decision in *Invitel* in its preliminary reference.[69] The case concerned whether a judicial ruling, in which contract terms are found to be unfair, can have subsequent binding force in respect of traders who are not party to the judicial proceedings in which the term is found to violate consumer law, but who use the same terms and conditions.[70] Polish law has recently been reformed;[71] while it is no longer the case,

---

[68] See Johnston, n. 51, 357.

[69] See *Biuro*, n. 30. The authors would like to extend particular thanks to Mateusz Grochowski for his assistance in better understanding the case and its background and who has also prepared the case note on the national judgment for the REJUS handbook

[70] See also Hans-Wolfgang Micklitz, 'A Common Approach to the Enforcement of Unfair Commercial Practices and Unfair Contract Terms' in Willem van Boom *et al* (eds), *The European Unfair Commercial Practices Directive: Impact, Enforcement Strategies and National Legal Systems* (Ashgate 2014) 173.

[71] Act Amending the Act on Competition and Consumer Protection, which came into force in April 2016. The previous situation was governed by Arts.

such judgments previously had *erga omnes* effect. That is to say, while individual control could be made on the basis of Art.385(1) of the Civil Code, abstract control could also be made by the judiciary. Moreover, the Court of Competition and Consumer Protection, a specialized court in Warsaw, also had jurisdiction to hear actions brought by all parties who had concluded a contract including such terms with a trader. If found to be unfair, the relevant terms were published in a register of unfair terms in line with Art.479(43) of the Code of Civil Procedure; this process of publication allowed for administrative control as the President of the Court of Competition and Consumer Protection was able to determine, by comparison, if contract terms challenged were the same or similar to those included in the register. It is worth noting that this body is an administrative one and is not specialized in the interpretation and application of contract law. The President could then impose an administrative fine on the trader for his violation of the unfair terms law. The practical result was that the judicial finding of unfairness affected not only the parties to the case but all traders using the same or similar terms. The reform repealed the provisions that regulated the 'in abstracto' review of contract terms, and shifted this procedure from the civil courts to the Office of the Protection of Competition and Consumers (represented by its President) with the aim of introducing a unified model of 'in abstracto' control; fines can still be imposed and the parties can appeal to the court itself to challenge the finding. Moreover, the courts can still undertake a review of contract terms 'in concreto', that is, in the context of the relevant contract challenged before it. The decision of the President of the Office will generally bind civil courts.

The reference to the CJEU – which is now largely historical in light of the Polish reform – was made by the Court of Appeal of Warsaw, hearing an appeal from a trader whose contract included unfair terms published in the register. The A-G's Opinion is particularly interesting as he reformulates part of the reference in order to attribute to it an Art.47 CFR dimension concerning the trader's right to be heard.[72] The A-G's

479[36]–479[45] of the Code of Civil Procedure of 17.11.1964. The new rules are introduced in Arts.23a–23d of the Act on Protection of Competition and Consumers of 16.02.2007.

[72] When the court holds a clause to be unfair, third parties cannot intervene either in the judicial or administrative proceedings; according to the A-G, this should preclude the *erga omnes* effect of the judgment because otherwise, the right to be heard, warranted to both consumers and traders by Art.47 CFR, would be violated.

Opinion challenged the system that previously operated in Poland[73] and called into question the legitimacy of the establishment of a "judicial" black list of unfair terms; rather, he considered this should be a matter for the legislature.[74] Moreover, he held that Art.3 UCTD provides the trader with the right to show that the standard term has been individually negotiated by the parties to the contract; in the absence of such a possibility, the A-G held that the trader's right to be heard in Art.47 CFR would also be undermined.[75] Furthermore, the A-G rejected the notion the Polish system could be said to be the same as that of concern in *Invitel*[76] because in the latter situation the effect of the judgment applied only in favour of and not to the disadvantage of third parties.[77] The judgment of the Court deviates fundamentally from the Opinion of the A-G. While acknowledging the Art.47 CFR dimension of the case, and highlighting that effective judicial remedies must be available to traders facing sanctions,[78] the Court found that the Polish (pre-reform) system was not precluded by the directive. As such, it held that the use of standard contract terms with content identical to that of terms previously declared unlawful by a court, and which have been listed in a national register of unfair standard terms, could be said to be unlawful also with regard to a trader who was not a party to the initial judicial proceedings. Essentially, the Court accepted the establishment of such registers by the courts. Contrary to the A-G, the Court, while it did not examine the *erga omnes* effects of those findings in detail, developed its own judgment in *Invitel* and provided that a court's identification of an unfair term may also bind other traders as to their future contracting.[79] The case shows the deep changes that a reference to Art.47 may generate in respect of the relationships between 'in abstracto'

---

[73] As noted above, the Polish system has been reformed between the time of the submission and the time of decision but the Court has nevertheless decided that it will issue a judgment.

[74] *Biuro*, n. 30, paras. 54–57.

[75] Ibid., paras. 64–70.

[76] Case C-472/10 *Invitel* EU:C:2012:242.

[77] That is, the same seller, supplier and trader but a different consumer; *Biuro*, n. 69, paras. 80–83.

[78] *Biuro*, n. *30*, paras. 26–27 and 43–45. Essentially, providing for review of the question of whether, in light of the relevant circumstances of the case, the terms are 'materially identical', especially in respect of the harmful effect caused to consumers and review of the proportionality of the amount of the fine established.

[79] The scope for the extension of the *erga omnes* effects of judicial decisions in which standard contract terms have been found to be unfair has been advanced by the authors in Fabrizio Cafaggi and Stephanie Law, 'Effect of Collective Proceedings' in Evelyn Terryn *et al* (eds), *Landmark Cases of EU Consumer Law: In Honour of Jules Stuyck* (Intersentia 2013) 653.

and 'in concreto' review of unfair terms and, more broadly, between individual and collective redress. Moreover, it illustrates the impact of dialogue between the national courts, administrative bodies and the CJEU in expanding the *erga omnes* effect of injunctive relief with regard to both consumers (as in the *Invitel* case) and traders (per the Court's judgment in *Biuro*).

From this perspective, numerous questions arise: what are the consequent influences of these trends on the choices made by the EU legislature and initially, of course, by the European Commission: Have the policy choices of the Commission shifted? Do we see a shift from legislation to adjudication? Moreover, do we see a shift from judicial to administrative enforcement, and therein from *ex post* to *ex ante*[80] regulation of consumer law, and EPL generally? From compensatory redress via individual private enforcement towards prevention and deterrence (whether individual or collective, private or public)?[81] How do the courts continue to shape EPL development? What is the impact on institutional actors

---

[80] *Ex ante* control is made in France for example by the *Commission des clauses abusives* and the *Commission d'examen des pratiques deloyales commerciales* and is established in Part 8 of the English Enterprise Act 2002 and the enforcement procedures of the Competition and Markets Authority.

[81] See Franziska Weber and Michael Faure, 'The Interplay between Public and Private Enforcement in European Private Law: Law and Economics Perspective' (2015) 23 *ERPL* 525, revisiting the conventional law and economics perspective defined by A. Mitchell Polinsky and Steven Shavell, 'An Economic Theory of Public Enforcement of Law (2000) 38 *J.Econ.Lit.* 45. A decision of significant importance, in which the Court deviates from the Opinion of the A-G, was rendered in December 2016 and will likely have a considerable policy impact and potentially, a deterrent one, across the Member States. In Joined Cases C-154/15, C-307/15 and C-308/15 *Gutiérrez Naranjo* EU:C:2016:980 paras. 61–62, the Court had to determine whether the temporal effect of a finding of unfairness – in this case with regard to *'cláusulas suelo'* or 'floor clauses', which set the 'floor' for minimum interest rates in Spanish mortgage contracts – should be limited. These clauses had been found to be unfair by the Spanish Supreme Court (Judgment No 241/2013 of 9 May 2013), and there was a dispute in the Spanish judiciary as to whether the consequences of the finding of unfairness (namely, the repayment of amounts undue) should be limited temporally and arise only in respect of payments made after the declaration of unfairness. The Court found that the consequences should not be so limited but should rather be retroactive. The result of the Court's judgment is that Spanish consumers can now claim from Spanish banks the repayment of amounts paid in excess on the basis of the unfair term, not only from the date of the finding of unfairness but from the beginning of their loan contract. While it is yet to be seen how it will be implemented in the Spanish system, the judgment is expected to generate considerable economic consequences on Spanish banks.

in EPL development, beyond the courts and the legislatures? Is EPL developing in such a way as to allow for the protection, of e.g., (EU and national) consumer rights in a networked framework?[82] Such issues arise for example in respect of regulators and administrative authorities who are increasingly engaged in a supervisory role across areas of fundamental significance for consumers, including financial regulation and investment protection, general services (energy, telecom and transport,[83] and so on) and competition law.[84] These bodies play a role in policing markets and market practices, one that is becoming increasingly significant at the EU level and across the Member States and which has yet unexplored constitutional dimensions reflected in Art.47 CFR.

OVERVIEW OF THE CONTRIBUTIONS

This book aims to contribute to the existing research agenda on judicial and institutional dialogue and cooperation by bringing together contributions from judges and legal scholars. The 'added value' of this scholarship is reflected in the engagement of the broad participant body, encompassing academics, practitioners, and national and European judges, as well as the scope, in light of the contributions taken together, for the cross-

---

[82] That is, in a framework of experimentalist governance; see Charles F. Sabel and Jonathan Zeitlin (eds), *Experimentalist Governance in the EU* (OUP 2010) and Charles F. Sabel and Jonathan Zeitlin, 'Experimentalist Governance' in David Levi-Faur (ed.), *The Oxford Handbook of Governance* (OUP 2012) 169. New forms of governance underpin the critical examinations undertaken throughout the book, concerning the enforcement of EPL norms against the background of the diversity of the Member States and dialogue between the EU and national institutions at play; it highlights the significance of the framework goals identified (particularly, the protection of consumer rights in light of the construction of the internal market), the communication between actors and institutions engaged in the identification of policy solutions (away from central actors like legislatures and courts to administrative agencies and civil society bodies including consumer protection associations), which are confronted with similar problems, learn from distinct, heterogeneous efforts through reporting endeavours, revise those solutions and begin to identify novel ones via these communication efforts.

[83] For example, in the area of energy provision amongst others, the EU's third package of energy market legislation aims to develop the role of consumers as market regulators by establishing rules that allow, for example, consumers to choose freely their own energy provider. For further information: <http://ec.europa.eu/energy/en/topics/markets-and-consumers/consumer-rights-and-protection>.

[84] See Hans-Wolfgang Micklitz, 'Regulatory Strategies on Services Contracts in EC Law' in Fabrizio Cafaggi and Horatia Muir Watt (eds), *The Regulatory Function of European Private Law* (Edward Elgar Publishing 2009) 16.

fertilization of ideas, opinions and information between national and European traditions and cultures. The chapters of the book attempt, in the different ways set out below, to examine the impact of judicial and institutional dialogue on the evolution of EPL, and the existence and consequences of a shift from a focus on the former to a focus on the latter. The notion of impact evaluation implies a metric but also a conceptual framework, which opens up as opposed to closes the debate on the processes by which European and domestic courts contribute to the creation, transformation and identity of EPL development.

The challenges in defining concretely what is meant by judicial (institutional) interaction, judicial (institutional) cooperation and judicial (institutional) dialogue are reflected in the contributions; indeed, each author tends to begin with a conceptualization of the term used for the purpose of their chapter, outlining the scope of the concept engaged, its limits and also the extent to which it extends beyond a focus on courts (see Cafaggi). The contributions deal with issues arising across substantive areas of EPL; these focuses range from state liability (Timmermans), fundamental rights protections for private parties (Colombi Ciacchi; Safjan; Timmermans) and consumer law (Cafaggi; Law; Gómez and Lyczkowska), and particularly, unfair contract terms regulation (Cafaggi; Józon). Moreover, certain contributions offer a comparative analysis, either between EU Member States (Józon on Hungary and Romania), as engaged by the CJEU (Timmermans) or between the EU and the US legal orders (Scirica on techniques of judicial interaction).

Timmermans' contribution 'looks behind' the 'judicial cooperation triggered by a preliminary reference' to the CJEU, particularly in matters concerning state liability and in cases where a conflict arises between the protection of an economic freedom and a fundamental right. He examines the determinations that give rise to the interaction encompassed in the preliminary reference procedure, that is, the motivation of the national courts in referring a question to the CJEU, at the understanding of this interaction on the part of the CJEU, at the nature of its reasoning and preliminary ruling, and on the way in which this affects the final decisions of the national courts. For this reason, he shifts his evaluation away from the usual lens of analysis, that is, the content of the reference, to focus on the way in which it is made and received, the nature and impact of the Court's judgment (particularly, whether it is concrete or less so) and the cooperation that exists – via the reference procedure – between judges sitting in national courts within one Member State and also that which might be characterized as cross-border. For Timmermans, dialogue is necessarily linked with cooperation, openness to which is necessary on the part of the national courts for the operation of the preliminary reference procedure.

His contribution therefore examines dialogue which might be more informal (for example, meetings of associations of judges or networks of lawyers and academics) or institutionalized (for example, the establishment of national or European networks or databases of case law allowing national judges quick and easy access to jurisprudence from other national courts and from the CJEU).

Gómez and Lyczkowska examine the existence of judicial interaction – that between the national courts and the CJEU – with the aim of identifying why the national courts, and particularly the Spanish courts, seek guidance from the CJEU. Fundamentally, this evaluation is made in light of the relatively large number of references made from the Spanish courts that have generated a line of cases leading to landmark rulings in European consumer law. At first glance, they consider that judicial interaction seems to be based on the notion of collaboration, whereby 'Spanish courts should be considered as very collaborative and committed participants in the development of European consumer law through the expansion and refinement of CJEU case law'. However, recognizing that the references made by the Spanish courts do not follow a consistent or coherent approach, and that the number of references has increased considerably in recent years (and generally only in relation to consumer law), Gómez and Lyczkowska turn to consider whether the examination of the engagement of the Spanish courts – and particularly those of first instance – might not be further picked apart. Thus, from a game-theoretical perspective, they offer an explanation for the behaviour of the Spanish courts and their interaction with the Spanish government on the one hand and the CJEU on the other. They reference two different 'channels' of interaction, building on previous scholarship – low-cost (where the national courts refer to CJEU case law) and high-cost (where the national court requests a preliminary reference from the CJEU for 'assistance' to solve social problems) channel, where the cost to the national court as to this interaction is shaped by the preferences of the national courts and the Spanish government in respect of the levels of unfair contract terms protection sought by each.

For Józon, 'judicial cooperation' is 'the dialogue that takes place between the CJEU and the domestic judiciaries on policy and which implicitly affects the methodology of judicial enforcement' (Józon, 1). It arises on the part of the national court when it searches for a solution to a problem of EU law that it cannot solve. Focusing on the jurisprudence before the Romanian and Hungarian courts and concerning the regulation of pre-formulated contract terms, Józon examines the extent to which these courts use or indeed refrain from using, the preliminary reference procedure (more so in Hungary, and less so in Romania), in light of, and as a tool of, their domestic judicial policy in the enforcement of consumer law. Moreover, she evaluates why these courts, operating in legal systems with similar legal cultures and traditions, that is, strongly positivistic, react so differently – in terms of their interaction with the CJEU – to the enforcement of the Unfair Contract Terms Directive. She identifies the different purposes for which the preliminary reference procedure might be used at national level, and the factors that frame its use. She concludes that the use of the preliminary reference procedure is reflective of the way in which EU legislation has been transposed at the domestic level by the legislature and the courts; thus, while the Romanian courts have been able to 'successfully integrate the policy-based and case-law-based reasoning of the CJEU into their domestic judicial discourse', the integration of this policy dimension is absent in the Hungarian system, with the result that the CJEU's interpretation 'remain a foreign body'. This approach in Romania has resulted in less of a need for preliminary references, in contrast to the situation in Hungary, with the result that the Hungarian courts have repeatedly requested preliminary rulings from the CJEU.

The chapter by Law aims to explore the significance of judicial cooperation to the Europeanization of private law through the lens of the evolution of a key concept of national and European private law, namely the concept of the consumer. The chapter first places the development of consumer law in a historical context, at the state and EU level. It recognizes at the outset the diversity of national legal traditions and the disparate character of the legislative consumer *acquis*, and the potential use, *prima facie*, of dialogue and its values as a mechanism for integration against this background, particularly via the preliminary reference procedure. In light of the potential problems that stem from the limitations of a formalistic and broad conceptualization of the consumer in Union and national legislation, and the aims and objectives underpinning, the chapter proceeds to examine how the notion of consumer has been legislated for by the EU legislature, key examples of its transposition in the Member States, and its interpretation in the national courts and before the CJEU. This perspective allows for an examination of the potentially lower or higher levels of protection afforded, than otherwise anticipated at the EU level, and for a re-examination of the scope for dialogue in light of the objectives of the Union legislature, and the CJEU, and against the background of an increasing focus on balancing the facilitation of the market with social and fundamental rights concerns.

Safjan argues that the nature of the dialogue that arises between courts is tied to the theoretical approach adopted to understand the relationships that exist between national constitutional standards of fundamental rights protection and those found in the Charter of Fundamental Rights

(Safjan); each potential theoretical conceptualization of this relationship, he asserts, generates 'a different degree of potential risk of collision and tensions between the different courts'. For Safjan, the potential risk for confrontation and scope for coexistence differ depending on how the application of fundamental rights protected in the CFR are applied in relation to national law; moreover, there exists differing potential for dialogue, which he examines in turn. This relationship might be restrictive, wherein it 'limits the application of the Charter to the national provisions which have been adopted specifically for the purposes of the implementation of EU law'; it might be abstract, which 'extends the application of the Charter to each part of the national law' or it might be functional, that is, 'located half way between the restrictive and the abstract approach, constitutes a kind of compromise between these two'. For Safjan, dialogue with the CJEU must be initiated by the national courts, with 'openness and sensitivity' on both sides, that is, so that this initiation does not become a unilateral, 'one-way message' from the domestic system. It provides a means to respond to the need of the courts to find a balance between the plurality of the Member States' constitutional identities and the integrated EU space, being a 'unique instrument in order to achieve consensus in this fragile matter', shaped by the values of the Union in Art.2 TEU.

The contribution of Colombi Ciacchi focuses on the dialogue that exists between the CJEU and the national courts in cases between private persons in which fundamental rights' protection is at issue, and in particular on the notion of judicial governance, understood as the examination and balancing of conflicting rights, interests and policies. Using two key pieces of jurisprudence as case studies, namely *Angonese*[85] and *Sturgeon*,[86] she identifies and evaluates the nature of the conflicts of rights, interests and policies arising in each case, from six types of conflicts set out in the introduction. She then proceeds to examine the dialogue – identifying a 'harmonious dialogue' from *Angonese*, that reflects the direct horizontal effect of the balancing of rights and freedoms on private relationships, and a 'hermeneutical dialogue' which 'runs along patterns of conflicts that are remarkably different from the ones in *Angonese*' in *Sturgeon* – that arises between the national courts and the CJEU in their assessment of those conflicts. Concluding by drawing comparative conclusions on how this dialogue contributes to judicial governance of European society, Colombi Ciacchi reflects on the two cases and their impact across national legal

[85] Case C-281/98 *Angonese* [2000] ECR I-4139.

[86] Joined Cases C-402/07 and C-432/07 *Sturgeon and Others* [2009] ECR I-10923.

systems, highlighting that while a barrage of criticism has been launched at *Sturgeon*, and while *Angonese* has been received much more smoothly, both cases reflect the CJEU's exercise of judicial governance and its protection of fundamental interests of private individuals in the face of their potentially being outweighed by the more powerful interests of private corporate actors.

From the perspective of a judge sitting in a US court, Scirica offers a contribution that allows for a comparative analysis of the mechanisms of judicial interaction in the EU and US systems. He identifies 'judicial interaction' as a set of techniques that could be used to construct a framework for the resolution of conflicts in the EU space, that is, 'to be used by European courts and judges to promote coherence and coordination in areas of fundamental rights protection'. He focuses on seven techniques, including: (1) consistent interpretation (Supremacy Clause doctrine); (2) preliminary reference (question certification); (3) proportionality (rational basis, intermediate scrutiny, strict scrutiny); (4) comparative reasoning (other federal circuit courts, supreme courts, treaties and American Law Institute); (5) mutual recognition (full faith and credit, recognition and enforcement of judgments, *stare decisis*); (6) disapplication (Supremacy Clause doctrine, pre-emption); and (7) deferential techniques (judicial restraint). Scirica thus first identifies the equivalent techniques existing in the EU legal order and in the US federal and state systems, proceeding to situate these techniques against the background of a succinct account of the US legal systems, and of judicial power sharing. The focus of the analysis then shifts to the operation of these techniques to solve conflicts in the US federal and state courts in respect of questions of fundamental rights, with a detailed discussion of three key pieces of Supreme Court jurisprudence.

The contribution of Cafaggi examines the existence, nature and impact of institutional dialogue on the enforcement of consumer law, and as a 'driver of innovation' of consumer law development. He identifies the scope for and character – whether horizontal or vertical – of both administrative and judicial dialogue, and the potential for dialogue to be transformed into trialogues or tetralogues when other institutional bodies, including for example the national legislature, also become engaged. He identifies, evaluates and compares the forms of institutional dialogue that shape judicial and administrative enforcement of consumer law, taking the jurisprudence that has contributed to the development of the *ex officio* powers of national courts to engage in the control of consumer law as a key example. Noting that the determinations to engage in dialogue are often strategic, these rationales are examined, as is the role played by the Charter of Fundamental Rights and by the principle of effective judicial protection, particularly in light of the limitations faced by administrative regulators, and the obstacles sometimes imposed by national procedural law. Concluding with an analysis of the impact of such dialogue – that is, spillovers – across the Member States, the chapter 'recombines' two types of dialogue in consumer protection: vertical judicial dialogue for civil law enforcement and administrative horizontal dialogue within European networks for administrative enforcement.

2. Looking behind the scenes of judicial cooperation in preliminary procedures

Christiaan Timmermans

INTRODUCTORY REMARKS

To look behind the scenes of the judicial dialogue between a national court and the European Court of Justice within the framework of the preliminary reference procedure: this is the invitation of the editors of this book. The idea is to have a closer look at the characteristics and context of the judicial cooperation triggered by a preliminary reference. What motivates a national court in using this procedure? Is its decision to refer or not to refer taken in isolation or might it also have been influenced by approaches followed by other courts, even from other Member States? What may we learn from the way, more particularly the more or less detailed and conclusive way, in which the CJEU conceives its answers, about how that Court envisages and effects this cooperation? What are the concrete and practical results of the preliminary ruling for the final outcome of the case itself and more generally for legal practice?

European legal scholarship has always been more interested in the contents of a preliminary ruling and its possible significance for the development of EU law than in its genesis, the question of the national court, and the final effects for the outcome of the case.[1] The approach advocated by the editors of this book is an inductive one. Case studies are to be made in a number of fields to see whether on that basis, more general conclusions could be drawn.

This contribution deals more particularly with cases of State liability for violations of Union law (the *Francovich*[2] and post-*Francovich* case

---

[1] See for an exception the 1985 Colloquium organized by the T.M.C.Asser Instituut; published as Henry G. Schermers *et al* (eds.), *Article 177 EEC: Experiences and Problems* (Elsevier Science Publishers 1987).

[2] Joined Cases C-6/90 and C-9/90 *Francovich and Bonifaci* [1991] ECR I-5357.

law, more particularly: *Brasserie du Pêcheur* and *Factortame*,[3] *Köbler*[4] and *Traghetti del Mediterraneo*[5]) and two prominent cases dealing with a conflict between an economic fundamental Treaty freedom and a fundamental social right (*Laval*[6] and *Viking Line*[7]). The issues to be looked into concern: the reasons for making the preliminary reference and the nature of the referring court; the nature and effect of the CJEU judgment; the application of the preliminary ruling by the referring national court; the interaction (if any) between courts within a Member State and courts from different Member States when using the preliminary procedure.

REASONS FOR THE PRELIMINARY REFERENCE AND NATURE OF THE REFERRING COURT

In all the above-mentioned cases we see a fairly usual scenario: the EU law argument pleaded by the litigant before the national court is the ultimate or only remaining argument allowing him to win the case. All these cases raise fundamental questions of EU law, mostly of a constitutional nature: can a Member State be held liable under EU law for failing to implement and apply EU law, also in case of legislative or judicial wrongdoing? Can a fundamental Treaty freedom (the right of establishment, the free movement of services) be successfully invoked to oppose the exercise of the fundamental social right of collective action? The answer to these questions will determine the outcome of the case. This explains at the same time why in most of these cases it has been a first instance or a lower court that has asked preliminary questions.[8] In a way, it is more noteworthy that in the *Brasserie du Pêcheur* case questions were only asked in the third instance, that is, by the *Bundesgerichtshof*. Obviously, where the lower courts referred the questions, they were willing to give the EU law argument a chance considering it not without merit. Indeed, this willingness of the national judge to apply EU law and turn to the CJEU for guidance, this

---

[3] Joined Cases C-46/93 and C-48/93 *Brasserie du Pêcheur and Factortame* [1996] ECR I-1029.

[4] Case C-224/01 *Köbler* [2003] ECR I-10239.

[5] Case C-173/03 *Traghetti del Mediterraneo* [2006] ECR I-5177.

[6] Case C-341/05 *Laval* [2007] ECR I-11767.

[7] Case C-438/05 *Viking Line* [2007] ECR I-10779.

[8] The three exceptions were *Brasserie du Pêcheur* (*Bundesgerichtshof*), *Laval* (Swedish Labour Court, but this is a first and last instance specialized court) and *Viking Line* where the UK Court of Appeal submitted the questions after the High Court in first instance had accepted the EU law argument.

openness for cooperation and dialogue, is the basis for the functioning of the preliminary reference procedure.

However, in none of these cases have I found an indication that the referring court, in making the preliminary reference, has been influenced by developments in the case law of other, possibly foreign, courts or informal contact with such courts.

NATURE AND EFFECT OF THE PRELIMINARY RULINGS

I want to address three aspects: the more or less conclusive nature of the answers of the CJEU, the role of comparative law in the State liability cases, and the way in which the CJEU has applied (or not applied) the principle of procedural autonomy in these cases.

i. The More or Less Conclusive Nature of the Preliminary Rulings

The above-mentioned judgments illustrate, with regard to the effect of the Court's rulings, a more general issue: that of their more or less conclusive nature, conclusive in the sense of in fact determining the outcome of the case before the national court. Applying the interpretation of Union law given by the Court to the facts of the case is the competence of the national court. To quote from *Brasserie du Pêcheur*: 'the national courts (. . .) have sole jurisdiction to (. . .) decide how to characterize the breaches of Community law at issue (. . .)'.[9] This concerns the question of whether the breach is sufficiently serious, one of the three conditions under Union law for establishing State liability. However, this statement should not be taken too literally. Indeed, the Court immediately adds that, with regard to the German rule allowing only *reines Bier*, that is beer produced in conformity with the *Reinheitsgebot*, to be marketed as beer, 'it would be difficult to regard the breach of Art.30 by that legislation as an excusable error, since the incompatibility of such rules with Art.30 was manifest in the light of earlier decisions of the Court (. . .)'.[10] *Factortame* uses still stronger language by qualifying the nationality condition for the registration of ships under the amended Merchant Shipping Act as 'direct discrimination manifestly contrary to Community law'.[11] In the same

9 *Brasserie du Pêcheur and Factortame*, n. 3, para. 58.
10 Ibid., para. 59.
11 Ibid., para. 61.

vein, the Court considered that not immediately applying the interim relief order of the President of the CJEU in *Factortame II* constituted in itself a sufficiently serious breach.[12] According to Lord Woolf, in his speech in the Court of Appeal decision applying the preliminary ruling, the CJEU provides a steer.[13] This might be deemed a euphemism. Other examples of a conclusive answer as to the existence or not of a serious breach are given by *Köbler* ('(. . .) the Court has available to it all the materials enabling it to establish whether the conditions necessary for the liability of the Member State to be incurred are fulfilled.');[14] *British Telecommunication* (no liability because of unclear drafting of a directive);[15] *Hedley Lomas* (yes, serious breach);[16] and *Dillenkofer* (no implementation of a directive within the delay prescribed: serious breach *per se)*.[17]

The *Laval* and *Viking Line* judgments contrast with regard to the conclusiveness of the answers. The *Laval* ruling is conclusive. The collective action of the trade unions in the *Laval* case – insofar as aiming at protecting workers' interests – could be considered as pursuing a legitimate interest capable of justifying restrictions of the right of *Laval* to benefit from the freedom to supply services under the Treaty. However, that justification failed insofar as the unions, by their collective action, aimed at obtaining a higher, more far-reaching protection of the workers of Laval going beyond the level of protection imposed by the Posted Workers Directive. As such, it clearly follows from the answer that the collective action in this case was contrary to EU law, and thus unlawful.[18]

The *Viking Line* decision is more cautious in this regard. Certainly, the Court gives a steer, to again quote Lord Woolf, but it leaves the final assessment of the suitability and proportionality of the unions' action to the Court of Appeal. To quote from the decision: '(. . .) even if it is ultimately for the national court, which has sole jurisdiction to assess the facts and interpret the national legislation, to determine whether and to what extent such collective action meets those requirements (of suitability and proportionality, CT) (. . .)'.[19] Is this to say, it is the sole jurisdiction of

---

[12] Ibid., para. 64. See, for the President's Order, Case 246/89R *Commission v United Kingdom* [1989] ECR I-3125.

[13] *Factortame Ltd and Others* [1998] EWCA Civ 1971 [20].

[14] *Köbler*, n. 4, para. 101.

[15] Case C-392/93 *British Telecommunications* [1996] ECR I-1631, para. 43.

[16] Case C-5/94 *Hedley Lomas* [1996] ECR I-2553.

[17] Joined Cases C-178/94, C-179/94, C-188/94, C-189/94 and C-190/94 *Dillenkofer* [1996] ECR I-4845, para. 26.

[18] *Laval* n. 6, para. 11.

[19] *Viking Line*, n. 7, para. 85.

the national court to assess the facts and interpret the national legislation? Yes, one can easily agree with this. However, is it ultimately also for that court to determine whether and to what extent such collective action is suitable and proportionate? Certainly, this is what happens in this case, as the final conclusion is left to the Court of Appeal. However, this statement cannot and should not be read as reflecting a general principle or a general rule. *Laval* and many other Court decisions clearly demonstrate the contrary. It might be sufficient to refer to the Sunday trading saga,[20] and more recent cases like *Schmidberger*,[21] *Omega Spielhallen*[22] and *Sayn Wittgenstein*.[23]

How can this difference in approach be explained? It might be that sometimes the Court wishes to give a clear signal to national courts and Member States more generally, as in *Köbler* and *British Telecommunication* that Union law does not oppose national law. Sometimes, the reason for a conclusive answer might be to avoid differences in application between national courts and ensure a uniform application of Union law, as in the Sunday trading cases.[24] In *Laval*, the Court was apparently keen to uphold the *effet utile* of the Posted Workers Directive and the balance struck by that Directive in respect of the principle of free movement and the necessity of a minimum level of protection for posted workers. It might also happen that the Court, as a matter of judicial policy, prefers to explicitly leave the final assessment in delicate cases of balancing conflicting rights to the national court; this can be identified, for instance, under a proportionality test, even when one might be able to read between the lines as to what the final conclusion should be.[25] In the end, the more or less conclusive nature of the preliminary rulings on interpretation – validity is of course a different matter – depends on the circumstances of the case and the Court's assessment of those circumstances.

It would be interesting to know how national courts react to this casuistry, and more particularly to the steering approach. One could imagine that having asked the question they would be generally satisfied with a

---

[20] After having left in *Torfaen* (Case C-145/88 *Torfaen* [1989] ECR I-3851) the final appreciation of the possible excessive nature of the effect on trade by a prohibition of trading on Sunday as a question of fact to the national court, the CJEU decided that question itself in Case C-312/89 *Conforama* [1991] ECR I-997, Case C-332/89 *Marchandise* [1991] ECR I-1027 and Case C-169/91 *Stoke-on-Trent* [1992] ECR I-6635.

[21] Case C-112/00 *Schmidberger* [2003) ECR I-5659.

[22] Case C-36/02 *Omega Spielhallen* [2004] ECR I-9641.

[23] Case C-208/09 *Sayn Wittgenstein* EU:C:2010:806.

[24] *Stoke-on-Trent*, n. 20, para. 14.

[25] See Case C-391/09 *Runevic-Vardyn* EU:C:2011:291.

clear and conclusive answer. This should normally allow for the case to be decided expeditiously, without having to reopen the procedure, hear the parties, proceed to further fact finding etc. The latter might be the more cumbersome for last instance courts, not allowed to proceed to fact finding and therefore obliged to refer the case back to a lower court. On the other hand, courts confronted with a conclusive answer might feel marginalized,[26] or even consider the CJEU to be trespassing on their domain. In that regard, it is interesting to note some lightly veiled critical remarks in the decision of the House of Lords in *Factortame*. Lord Slynn of Hadley stated:

> Although the question whether this was a sufficiently serious breach justifying the award of damages is a matter for the national courts, and therefore for your Lordships, to decide it is to be noted that in *Factortame III* [1996] Q.B. 404, 500, para.61 the European Court stated bluntly that the nationality condition constituted direct discrimination which was manifestly contrary to Community law.[27]

Lord Hope of Craighead, in that same judgment, observed:

> In various passages elsewhere in the judgment the court expressed its opinion about the nature of the breach for the consequences of which the respondents are claiming damages. But I would not be inclined to attach much importance to these expressions of opinion, because in para.58 of the judgment the court made it clear that it was for the national courts to assess the seriousness of the breach. The national courts have the sole jurisdiction to find the facts in the main proceedings. It is for them to decide how to characterize the breaches of Community law which are in issue.[28]

---

[26] See in that sense Gareth Davies, 'Abstractness and Concreteness in the Preliminary Reference Procedure: Implications for the Division of Powers and Effective Market Regulation' in Niamh Nic Shuibhne (ed.) *Regulating the Internal Market* (Edward Elgar Publishing 2006) 212.

[27] *R v Secretary of State for Transport, ex parte Factortame Ltd (No.5)* [2000] 1 AC 524 [542].

[28] Ibid., [550]. See also the decision of Mr Justice Laddie in the *Arsenal* case (*Arsenal Football Club plc v Matthew Reed* [2002] EWHC 2695 (CH)) refusing to apply the CJEU judgment, Case C-206/01 *Arsenal Football Club plc v Matthew Reed* [2002] ECR I-10273, because he considered the Court to have exceeded its competences by appreciating whether or not the use of the signs protected by the trade mark of Arsenal in the circumstances of the case could be qualified as trade mark use. This decision was overruled in appeal (*Arsenal Football Club plc v Matthew Reed* [2003] 2 CMLR 800); see also the case note of Anthony Arnull: 'Case Note: *Arsenal Football Club plc v Matthew Reed*' (2003) 40 CMLR 753.

After having served for ten years at the CJEU and attended numerous meetings with delegations of national courts, also discussing their experiences with the preliminary reference procedure, my personal impression is that the practice of the Court to give conclusive answers in cases where the facts and the relevant national law have been well established, generally does not meet with objections. It is interesting to note that the General Report about the preliminary reference procedure, submitted to the XVIII Colloquium of the Association of Councils of State and Supreme Administrative Courts (ACA Europe) in 2002 at Helsinki on the basis of the material produced by the national reports concludes that, apart from a few rare exceptions, in practice, national courts appear to have no difficulty in implementing a preliminary ruling.[29] In 2008, that same Association together with the Network of the Presidents of the Supreme Judicial Courts of the EU, produced another report on the preliminary procedure. One of the conclusions therein is to insist on the desirability for national courts, when referring questions, to submit full information both about the relevant national law and the facts and circumstances of the case in order to allow the CJEU to give 'a clear-cut and conclusive answer'.[30] At the same time, however, national courts are admonished not, 'as they sometimes are tempted to' to ask the Court, more or less, to solve their case, 'rather than to request an interpretation of EU law: an abstract question calling for an abstract answer, which is all the more useful for other courts in the EU'.[31] As such, this message is more nuanced.

In any event it is fairly obvious that the CJEU implicitly claims discretion, in cases where it considers itself sufficiently informed about the applicable national law and the facts of the case, to give a more or less conclusive answer. Does this approach remain within the limits of the

---

29 Heikki Kanninen, with d'Irma Telivuo (eds), *Rapport général sur le thème du colloque 'Le Renvoi Préjudiciel à la Cour de Justice des Communautés Européennes'* (Helsinki 2002) 36.

30 Association of the Councils of State and Supreme Administrative Jurisdictions of the European Union and Network of the Presidents of the Supreme Judicial Courts of the European Union, 'Report of the Working Group on the Preliminary Rulings Procedure', 13. The report is published on the website of ACA Europe at http://www.juradmin.eu/seminars/2007_DenHaag/Final_report.pdf. Cf. also the intervention of the President of the German Federal Labour Court, Ingrid Schmidt, insisting on the need for clear and unambiguous answers to preliminary questions, during a conference organized by the CJEU on this Report, published as *Réflexion autour de la procedure préjudicielle*: Actes du symposium réunissant les presidents des Cours Constitutionnelles et suprêmes des États Membres, 30–31 March 2009 (Luxembourg 2009) 69.

31 Report of the Working Group, ibid.

preliminary jurisdiction of the Court, which is to interpret Union law and not to apply it? Does a conclusive answer not encroach upon the competences of the national court because, by effectively deciding the case, the Court goes beyond the process of interpretation and applies the interpretation it has given to the facts of the case? It is of course also true that, in cases of a conclusive answer, it always remains for the national court to implement the preliminary ruling and on that basis decide the case. But is that answer not somewhat formalistic if in reality the substance of that decision has already been pre-established?

When discussing the Court's competence under the preliminary procedure, it is clear and undisputed that the Court may pronounce itself neither on the facts nor on the contents and interpretation of the applicable national rules. The question, which remains, and this is a classic issue in the analysis of the judicial decision-making process as well as in the literature about the preliminary procedure, is the following: where to draw the line between interpretation and application?[32] Obviously, an entirely abstract answer, detached from the facts of the case, would normally not be very helpful for the national court.[33] Abstract answers also would have the obvious risk of verging into rulemaking and establishing generally worded interpretations without the Court really being able to foresee all its practical consequences. *Dassonville* with its general and wide definition of what should be considered to be a measure of equivalent effect as a quantitative restriction on imports could be taken as an example.[34] So, it can only be welcomed that the Court has tended, when answering questions of interpretation, to tailor its answer to the factual and legal context of the case. As we know, the Court even refuses an answer if the questions submitted do not sufficiently explain that context, as well as the relevance of the interpretation requested, for deciding the case.[35]

What normally happens is that the Court, when interpreting the relevant rules of Union law, focuses on the facts and circumstances of the case in order to answer whether they fit the legal qualifications (*qualifications*

---

32 See André Donner, 'Les rapports entre la Compétence de la Cour de Justice des Communautés Européennes et les Tribunaux Internes', Académie de Droit International, Extrait du Recueil des Cours, Vol. II, 1965, 28. Cf. Also Koen Lenaerts, 'Form and Substance of the Preliminary Rulings Procedure', in Deirdre Curtin and Ton Heukels (eds), *Institutional Dynamics of European Integration: Essays in Honour of Henry G. Schermers* (Vol. II, Brill 1994), 355; Davies, n. 26, 214 *et seq*.

33 An example might be Joined Cases 16–20/79 *Danis* [1979] ECR 3327.

34 Case 8/74 *Dassonville* [1974] ECR 837.

35 Joined Cases C-320/90, C-321/90 and C-322/90 *Telemarsicabruzzo* [1993] ECR I-393, para. 5, Case C-153/00 *Der Weduwe* [2002] ECR I-11319, para. 33.

juridiques) embodied in the norm to be interpreted. Can the condition of a sufficiently serious breach, which forms part of the norm on State liability, be interpreted as also covering a situation such as the one in the case before the national court? Can the Treaty principle under Art.49 EC (as it then was), allowing restrictions to the free movement of services if justified to protect a legitimate public interest in connection with the Posted Workers Directive, be so interpreted as to consider a collective action – such as that undertaken by the trade unions in the *Laval* case – as not going beyond what is necessary to protect the workers of *Laval* when the protection envisaged (minimum rate of pay) falls outside the scope of the Posted Workers Directive or exceeding the minimum level of protection imposed by that directive? Can the provision of the Trademark Directive, prohibiting unauthorized trademark use for the same or similar products by a third party, be interpreted as also applying to a factual situation as that in the case before the national court?[36] Thijmen Koopmans has called this process of interpretation the factualization of the question of law.[37] The Court normally, when following this process, gives a generalizing twist to its answer by categorizing the situation of the case in hand. It clothes its answer in more abstract terms of interpretation: the relevant norm of EU law must be interpreted *in circumstances such as those* in the case before the referring court (. . .). A similar approach is followed when the question concerns the compatibility of a rule of national law: the relevant provision of Union law must be interpreted as opposing a rule *such as* (follows the reference to the national rule in question).

In taking this approach, the Court may interpret a rule of Union law in a more or less abstract manner, that is, more or less focused on the facts of the case. In doing so, it may move the line between interpretation and application, claim more or less space for interpretation and leave more or less space for application by the referring national court. To some extent this is also a question of formulation. In any event, I would argue that in following this approach the Court is fully respecting the limits of its preliminary jurisdiction and is, at the same time, able to give a useful answer to the national court.[38] However, it may be added that the Court would be better avoiding stressing the sole responsibility of the national court to legally qualify the circumstances of the case on the basis of the

---

[36] See *Arsenal*, n. 28.

[37] Thijmen Koopmans, 'Juridische Dialectiek' Mededelingen der Koninklijke Nederlandse Akademie van Wetenschappen, Afdeling Letterkunde, Nieuwe Reeks, deel 45-3 (Amsterdam 1982).

[38] See also in this regard, Case C-312/14 *Banif Plus Bank* EU:C:2015:794, paras 51 and 52.

interpretation it has given and, at the same time, wholly or partly proceed to that qualification itself, as it did in *Brasserie du Pêcheur* and *Factortame*, so as not to provoke unnecessary friction with the national courts.

ii. The Relative Use of the Comparative Law Method

The decisions in *Brasserie du Pêcheur* and *Köbler* are clear and important examples of cases in which the Court, in finding the law, pays considerable attention to comparative law materials. The Court has recourse to this material either as a source to discover the existence of a principle, in these cases that of State liability for legislative wrong doing,[39] or to confirm and strengthen the motivation for the existence of a principle it had already 'found' in the Union legal system itself.[40] The explicit use of the comparative law method of interpretation is fairly rare in the case law.[41] More particularly, it can be found in the important constitutional cases where written material is scarce or non-existing. Examples are identifiable in the early case law on fundamental rights and general principles of law.[42] All this has been extensively researched.[43] And there is of course the further example of the extra-contractual liability of the Union for which the comparative law method has been imposed by the Treaty itself, this liability having to be established 'in accordance with the general principles common to the laws of the Member States' (Art.340(2) TFEU). Recent examples, where the Court followed that Treaty injunction, are seen in its decisions in *FIAMM* (liability in case of lawful legislative acts)[44] and *Masdar* (unjust enrichment).[45]

However, it should not be concluded that comparative law remains only

---

[39] *Brasserie du Pêcheur and Factortame*, n. 3, paras 27, 41, 84 and 85.

[40] *Köbler*, n. 4, para. 48.

[41] For an early example see Joined Cases 7/56, 3/57 to 7/57 *Algera* [1957–1958] ECR (English Special Edition) 39.

[42] E.g., Case 11/70 *Internationale Handelsgesellschaft* [1970] ECR 1125, Joined Cases 46/87 and 227/88 *Hoechst* [1989] ECR 2859 paras 17 and 19. See also, of course, Art.6(3) TEU.

[43] See amongst many others Thijmen Koopmans, 'Comparative Law and the Courts' (1996) ICLQ 545; Walter van Gerven, 'Bridging the Gap between Community and National Laws: Towards a Principle of Homogeneity in the Field of Legal Remedies?' (1995) CMLRev. 701; Koen Lenaerts, 'Le droit comparé dans le travail du juge communautaire' (2001) *RTD eur.* 487, Takis Tridimas, *The General Principles of EU Law* (2nd Edn., OUP 2006) 23–5.

[44] Joined Cases C-120/06P and C-121/06P *FIAMM* [2008] ECR I-6513, para. 175.

[45] Case 47/07P *Masdar* [2008] ECR I-9761, para. 44.

of marginal importance for the interpretation of Union law. Indeed, much more frequent will be the cases in which the Court, when interpreting vague notions of Union law or filling gaps and without explicitly referring to it, finds inspiration in comparative law material. Such material might have been submitted in the Opinion of the Advocate General, as will be frequently the case, or occasionally also in the written pleadings of the parties, and those of the Commission more particularly. The Court itself regularly asks for a comparative law analysis to be prepared by its Research and Documentation Service. And finally, of course, the mere presence in the courtroom of representatives of various Member States' systems at least allows for the occasional comparative law input into the discussions. This will not necessarily all be reflected in the final judgment. But the absence of any reference does not at all exclude that the interpretative process in fact had a real comparative law dimension. The mostly hidden nature of this process might allow the Court, instead of looking for a solution, which is more generally accepted by the national law systems, to opt among those systems for a specific solution that appears most suitable for the characteristics of the Union legal system. Advocate General Poiares Maduro, in his Opinion in the *FIAMM* case, has well described this approach:

> Although the Court of Justice must certainly be guided by the most characteristic provisions of the systems of domestic law, it must above all ensure that it adopts a solution appropriate to the needs and specific features of the Community legal system. In other words, the Court has the task of drawing on the legal traditions of the Member States in order to find an answer to similar legal questions arising under Community law that both respects those traditions and is appropriate to the context of the Community legal order. From that point of view, even a solution adopted by a minority may be preferred if it best meets the requirements of the Community system.[46]

I may refer again to the abundant literature on this subject.[47] A well-known example is the reception in the case law of the proportionality principle as developed by German law or, perhaps less well known, the interpretation of the notion of *détournement de pouvoir* in the early case law of the Coal and Steel Court mixing elements of French administrative law, from which that notion originated of course, with elements of the German administrative law notion of *Ermessensmissbrauch*.[48]

---

[46] *FIAMM*, n. 44, para. 55.

[47] See the references at fn. 43.

[48] E.g. Case 8/55 *Fédération Charbonnière de la Belgique* [1956] ECR (English Special Edition) 292, and Case 2/57 *Hauts Fournaux de Chasse* [1958] ECR

Finally, it might well be that the comparative law method of interpretation will become less important, and has already done so. A specific interpretation or principle based partly or entirely on comparative law material, once accepted by the case law, will be further developed as an autonomous notion of Union law. The Court will normally refer to the precedents in its case law, not to the comparative law origins.[49] Moreover, general principles may, in the course of time, be codified by Treaty law.[50] This is what happened with the proportionality principle (Art.5(3) TEU) and of course also with fundamental rights by the Charter (albeit that, for their interpretation, due regard must be given to the constitutional traditions common to the Member States, Art.52(4) Charter). And of course that same reference remains with regard to fundamental rights in Art.6(3) TEU.

iii. Some of the Consequences of the State Liability Decisions for National Law and Practice

With regard to the effects of the State liability cases, I would like to add a comment about the question of how to articulate the EU law principles of State liability with the national regime on State liability and how to integrate the EU principles into the national regime. The well-known, three basic conditions for establishing State liability under Union law (sufficiently serious breach, the rule infringed must be intended to confer rights on individuals, causal link between the breach and the damage), are by themselves 'necessary and sufficient' (to quote from *Brasserie du Pêcheur*)[51] to establish such liability. The normative framework of the Union's State liability regime remains in principle limited to that. For the remainder, national tort law may be and, as far as procedures are concerned, has to be applied to fill the gaps. The Union's State liability regime must be implemented through national law. That is in full conformity with the decentralized structure of the Union. As a result, this liability regime

---

(English Special Edition) 199. See Christiaan W.A. Timmermans, *De administratieve rechter en beoordelingsvrijheden van bestuursorganen* (Thesis, Leuven 1973) 163.

49 See for an example *Traghetti del Mediterraneo*, n. 5.

50 See the decisions in *Laval*, n. 6, para. 90 and *Viking Line*, n. 7, para. 43 referring for the sources of the fundamental social right of collective action to the European Social Charter and the Community Charter of the Fundamental Social Rights of Workers, both mentioned in Art.151 TFEU, and finally also to Art.28 of the EU Charter of Fundamental Rights.

51 *Brasserie du Pêcheur and Factortame*, n. 3, para. 66.

is not really a uniform one and allows for differentiations according to Member States' law. In that respect there remains an important difference with regard to the regime of Union tort liability, which is, by its very nature, a uniform one.

As from the *Francovich* judgment, the Court has stressed that in the absence of Union legislation 'it is on the basis of the rules of national law on liability that the State must make reparation (. . .)'.[52] As far as procedural rules are concerned, this is not at all special and in full conformity with long-established case law regarding the so-called principle of procedural autonomy of Member States, which the Court also mentions in *Francovich*.[53] I shall refer to this principle as the *Rewe* test.[54] What I find striking, however, is that the Court explicitly extends the application of this principle of national autonomy, also to the substantive conditions for reparation of loss and damage. This has two important consequences. First, it confirms that the Union regime for State liability only establishes a minimum level of protection. Member States may go further. Second and more importantly, the freedom given to Member States and therefore their courts to apply substantive rules of national tort law is not unbridled. This freedom is subject to respect for the principles of equivalence and effectiveness.

This approach raises some questions on a dogmatic level. Applying the *Rewe* test to substantive rules is not so evident. The *Rewe* test explicitly requires, as a precondition for the application of national law, that there exists no Union legislation. How can this condition be applied to substantive instead of procedural rules? If a specific aspect of tort law is not regulated by Union law, and national law may therefore in principle be applied, how to apply in that case, the principle of effectiveness? Which Union rule should then be controlled as to whether its application is made impossible or excessively difficult? Applying the principle of effectiveness in this context might be either too little or too much. If the substantive rule of national law could be considered contrary to existing rules of Union law, this analysis of compatibility – which must also include the question of whether the national rule is in conformity with the functioning, that is the purport or the *effet utile* of the Union rules – must dictate that the national rule is considered to directly violate the Union rule. Applying then the principle of effectiveness does not go far enough; it is too limited.

---

[52] Joined Cases C-6/90 and C-9/90 *Francovich and Bonifaci* [1991] ECR I-5357, paras 42 and 43, referred to in *Brasserie du Pêcheur and Factortame*, n. 3, para. 67.

[53] *Francovich and Bonifaci*, ibid. para. 42.

[54] Case 33/76 *Rewe* [1976] ECR 1989.

However, if in the absence of any relevant rule of Union law such a violation cannot be established, the principle of effectiveness becomes of no avail.

The *Brasserie du Pêcheur* decision itself provides an illustration of this dilemma. The severe restrictions on liability for legislative acts imposed by German law (only compensation when an individual situation has been affected – *Einzelfallgesetzgebung*) or under UK law with regard to the high hurdle of proving a misfeasance in public office (which is not possible for acts of Parliament) were examined by the Court under the *Rewe* test and considered contrary to the principle of effectiveness.[55] In my view, these restrictions could as well have been considered directly contrary to the minimum conditions of Union law for State liability. That is exactly what the Court did with another strict requirement of German law, that of fault.[56] Likewise, in my view, the severe restriction of German tort law in case of legislative acts with regard to the kind of damage able to be compensated (e.g., *Enteignungsgleicher Eingriff*), could have been considered a direct violation of the Union conditions for liability instead of, as was the Court's approach, passing through the detour of the *Rewe* test.[57] Could it be that the Court has followed this approach as a gesture of courtesy towards the Member States?

A final remark. Applying the principle of equivalence in this context may have important and to some extent perhaps surprising consequences. According to this principle, Member States, when being allowed to apply national rules, must treat situations under Union law on an equal footing with situations under national law. So if under national tort law a violation of a rule of law is in itself sufficient to establish State liability, a State authority having no possibility for excuse (*l'illégalité fait la faute*, as in France and the Netherlands among others), the same should apply for a violation of Union law. Consequently, the condition of a sufficiently serious breach for cases of discretion would be considerably softened. One could say that, by virtue of the principle of equivalence, the Member State in question would be liable even where the minimum conditions for State liability under Union law are not satisfied. Another example would be the obligation to pay exemplary damages if that possibility would exist under national law. Paradoxically, in such cases, a Member State would be held liable to pay damages where the Union would not.

In a recent case note on *Francovich*, Baquero Cruz states: 'Union law

---

[55] *Brasserie du Pêcheur and Factortame*, n. 3 paras 71–73.
[56] Ibid., paras 79–80.
[57] Ibid., paras 86–87.

itself and its doctrinal elaboration is impressive on paper, but social reality does not always follow sufficiently.' 'To have the complete picture one needs to examine carefully its practical reception in the legal orders of the Member States. And there the picture is more blurred.'[58] With regard to its application in practice he qualifies *Francovich* as 'a monument kept in bad repair'.[59] Others have opined that the conditions upheld by the Court are much too strict to allow this case law to have a real impact on Member States' malpractice concerning the insufficient or incorrect implementation of Union law.[60]

I do not necessarily share the latter view, particularly not when comparing the result of *Brasserie du Pêcheur* and *Köbler* (liability for legislative and judicial tort) with the situation in that respect in many of our Member States. However, there exists a need for further analysis of the practical application of this case law. What the situation really is, I do not know, but it is certainly true that, in the now 20-plus years since *Francovich*, the number of cases on State liability brought before the Court has remained relatively small. But that does not necessarily have to imply that the impact of *Francovich* on State practice has been equally small.

It could well be that this case law has caused a real preventive effect in the sense of fostering a more Union law-abiding approach for fear of risking tort actions, both at the level of the central administration and the highest judiciaries in our Member States. From what I have occasionally heard in my own country, the Netherlands, a *Brasserie du Pêcheur* reference has sometimes been able to strengthen the argument of legal services of a ministry and focus the attention of the client. So does *Köbler*, I was told, sometimes echo in courtroom discussions strengthening the position of the Union law specialists on the national bench.

THE IMPLEMENTING DECISIONS OF THE REFERRING NATIONAL COURTS

With regard to these decisions, I shall limit myself to a few comments concerning only the decision of the House of Lords in the *Factortame* case and that of the Swedish Labour Court in the *Laval* case.

---

[58] Julio Baquero Cruz, 'Francovich and Imperfect Law' in Miguel Poiares Maduro and Loïc Azoulai (eds), *The Past and Future of EU Law* (Hart Publishing 2010) 418.

[59] Ibid., 420.

[60] Cf. also Damaso Ruiz and Jarabo Colomer, 'Once Upon a Time – Francovich: From Fairy Tale to Cruel Reality?' in ibid., 412.

The implementing decision in *Factortame* passed the three branches of the UK judiciary up to the House of Lords. In reading these judgments, one can only be impressed by the thoroughness and the quality of their reasoning.[61] The Law Lords sitting in the case confirmed unanimously the conclusions of the lower courts that there existed a sufficiently serious breach with regard to all three registration criteria for obtaining the British flag (nationality, residence, domicile), thus also the residence and domicile criteria for which the Court of Justice had accepted a certain amount of discretion on the part of the UK legislature.[62]

The final decision of the Swedish Labour Court in the *Laval* case also gives an excellent example of close and effective cooperation within the framework of the preliminary ruling procedure.[63] Not only does this decision, at least in my view, faithfully implement the ruling of the CJEU, but one is also struck by the thorough analysis by the Swedish Labour Court of the CJEU case law in considering Laval's claim for damages against the trade unions. The Labour Court in principle accepts the liability of the unions in qualifying their unlawful action as a sufficiently serious violation of EU law to establish such liability. It is interesting to note that the Court is applying the same three conditions as upheld by the CJEU for State liability. In the end, the damage claim is dismissed because Laval had not been able to sufficiently substantiate the economic losses it had stated having suffered. However, the Court condemned the unions to pay exemplary damages.

Indeed, after having read these implementing decisions, one is inclined to think that when researching the attitudes of national courts with regard to their cooperation with the CJEU through the preliminary procedure, it might be interesting to look more particularly also into cases where national courts did not refer where they could or should have done so.

---

61 Namely, the following: High Court 31 July 1997 [1997] EWHC Admin 756; Court of Appeal 8 April 1998 [1998] EWCA Civ 1971; House of Lords 13 July 1999 [2000] 1 AC 524.

62 *Brasserie du Pêcheur and Factortame*, n. 3, paras 61–63.

63 Case No. A268/04, the Labour Court, Sweden (Arbetsdomstolen), Judgment No. 89/09 of 2 December 2009, *Laval un Partneri Ltd* v *Svenska Bygggnadsarbetareförbundet et al.*

COOPERATION BETWEEN NATIONAL COURTS WITHIN AND BETWEEN MEMBER STATES FACILITATING THE FUNCTIONING OF THE PRELIMINARY PROCEDURE

I have found no traces in the preliminary references or the implementing decisions considered above of any interaction between national courts or references to the case law of other courts either of the same or a different Member State. It is obvious that in practice it might be useful for a national court, confronted with a specific question of Union law and considering to refer that question to the CJEU, to know whether other courts have been or are confronted with a similar question, whether there exists already any case law in the Member States on the subject, also whether there are already cases pending on the issue at the CJEU.

In the Netherlands, a specific infrastructure has been set up within the courts to improve access to and knowledge of Union law. First of all, a special database has been made available for the courts facilitating access to EU law, including the case law of the Luxembourg courts. Moreover, a special unit of the Ministry of Foreign Affairs regularly publishes on a website information about EU law developments including important new decisions of the CJEU. Finally, within each district court and court of appeal a member of the judiciary with expertise in the field of Union law is being designated to assist colleagues, where necessary and on request, with information and advice about issues of Union law. These judges are, together with representatives of the highest courts, members of a national network (the Eurogroup) meeting regularly to discuss new developments in the case law of the CJEU and exchange views on practical experiences. These informal exchanges might also allow some coordination in using the preliminary procedure in similar or connected cases.

Equally important will be to give members of the national judiciary easy access to relevant case law on matters of EU law in other Member States. Precisely for that purpose, a number of important initiatives setting up special databases have been taken both by the Association of Councils of State and Supreme Administrative Courts (ACA Europe)[64] and the Network of the Presidents of the Supreme Judicial Courts of the EU. The

---

64 ACA Europe has set up two databases: Dec.Nat. and Jurifast, the latter giving access to recent national judgments dealing with issues of EU law (see www.aca-europe.eu). The Network has opened a site (a common portal of case law, www.network-presidents.eu) with links to national databases.

Eur-Lex database also has introduced a special section on 'National Law' giving access to EU- relevant national case law.[65]

Both ACA Europe and the Network, more generally, play an important role in facilitating contacts between national courts and fostering informal judicial cooperation, also with the CJEU. Indeed, the CJEU is a founding member of ACA Europe and is represented on its governing board; at the same time, it is invited to the conferences organized by the Network, as member jurisdictions of ACA Europe and of the Network are invited to the conferences regularly organized by the CJEU. A good example of this cooperation is the report on the functioning of the preliminary procedure, already referred to, elaborated by ACA Europe in cooperation with the Network.[66] That report was extensively discussed during a conference organized by the CJEU in 2009.[67]

FINAL REMARKS

The decision of the Court of Appeal in *Factortame* gives an illustration of a possible, perhaps somewhat unexpected, consequence of the judicial cooperation through the preliminary procedure. It might happen that a particular solution developed by the CJEU in its case law is transplanted by national courts to purely national situations falling outside the scope of Union law. Interested parties might invoke to that effect constitutional principles of equal treatment and non-discrimination. Under English law, the State cannot be held liable for damage caused by legislative wrong-doing. That is why *Brasserie du Pêcheur* has been so innovative for the English legal system. Lord Woolf considered in his leading speech in the judgment of the Court of Appeal:

> So we leave for consideration on another occasion the circumstances, if any, in which, quite apart from any requirement of Community law, our law will give a remedy for damage caused by legislation enacted in breach of a superior legal rule. Traditionally this remedy has not been available in our law. Now that it is undoubtedly available in circumstances which contain a Community law element it may be right on some future occasion to re-examine that tradition.[68]

---

65 Available via eur-lex.europa.eu.

66 See the reports referred to in fn. 30.

67 Ibid.

68 *Factortame Ltd and Others* [1998] EWCA Civ 1971 [17].

3. Fields of application of the Charter of Fundamental Rights and constitutional dialogues in the European Union

Marek Safjan*

INTRODUCTION

Fundamental rights are a matter of privilege in the cooperation between the European Court of Justice (the 'ECJ') and the national courts, in particular the supreme and constitutional courts. It would at the same time be very difficult to find a more complex field of this cooperation, where the debate concentrates not only on the correct interpretation of law but also and first of all on the division of competences between European and national judges. The reason for potential disputes related to these questions is rather simple and almost self-evident: the ECJ, as well as the national constitutional courts, are the very guarantors of respect of fundamental rights and that function is enshrined in the ethos of each supreme jurisdiction. In this sense the competence with regard to the fundamental rights constitutes the necessary part of legitimization of the constitutional status of supreme national jurisdictions.

For the ECJ, fundamental rights are an extremely important part of the 'acquis communautaire' and also an essential component of the European identity. Human rights were introduced into the sphere of European law as a substantial element of general principles of law almost 50 years ago.[1] However, from today's perspective, there is no doubt that the entry into force of the Charter of Fundamental Rights (the 'Charter') as binding law on 1 December 2009[2] had a specific symbolic significance for the European

* The opinions expressed in this chapter are the author's alone.

[1] Cf. Judgment of 4 February 1959 in Case C-1/58 *Friedrich Stork et Cie v High Autority* [1959] ECR 43 and the judgment of 12 November 1969 in Case C-29/69 *Stauder v City of Ulm* [1969] ECR 419.

[2] [2012] OJ C362/02.

Union, being a clear confirmation of the trends consequently developed by the jurisprudence. What is more, it greatly helped stimulating further development of the legal order and the process of integration as a whole. It has been the starting point for a new stage of the human rights jurisprudence of the ECJ. Today, more than five years later, we may say that the quality, scope and frequency of the application of fundamental rights essentially changed the face of the Court's jurisprudence. The ECJ has become the Court of human rights for the European Union. How significant the impact of the formal act of including the Charter into the legal order of the EU would have on the whole EU legal system was difficult to foresee.

The interpretation and application of the European legal provisions which take fundamental rights into account is a crucial factor for the legal order because it opens new ways of legal reasoning and methodology. It also allows the Court to more easily recognize the purpose of certain legal mechanisms and their interdependency. For these reasons, supreme jurisdiction, neither at the national nor at the supranational level, may execute their functions without referring to fundamental rights and to the general principles of law. My personal experiences confirm this assumption.

As a former constitutional judge, I can firmly say that the openness towards fundamental rights protection and to the general principles of law were – at the first stage after the collapse of the communist system in my country – the very vehicle of transformation of the legal system. At the time they created substantive 'added values' to the concept of the rule of law. A similar impact of fundamental rights on the role of constitutional jurisprudence has also been observed in other national orders, where the totalitarian rule has paralyzed democratic development of society for many years (in Germany, Spain, Hungary, etc.). No doubt the application of fundamental rights standards was the most important aspect of the role played in the national systems.

As a European judge, I should assert that references to the fundamental rights guaranteed by the Charter have not only become current practice of the jurisprudence but also that they are a necessary element of the interpretation and the application of European provisions. Judgments such as, in recent years, *NS*,[3] *DEB*,[4] *Åkerberg Fransson*,[5] *Melloni*,[6]

[3] Judgment of 21 December 2011 in Joined Cases C-411/10 and C-493/10 *N.S. and Others* EU:C:2011:865.

[4] Judgment of 22 December 2010 in Case C-279/09 *DEB v Bundesrepublik Deutschland* EU:C:2010:811.

[5] Judgment of 26 February 2013 in Case C-617/10 *Åkerberg Fransson* EU:C:2013:280.

[6] Judgment of 26 February 2013 in Case C-399/11 *Melloni* EU:C:2013:107.

Jeremy F.,[7] *Trade Agency*[8] and many others, are good illustrations of the present trends in the jurisprudence. References made in the jurisprudence to the guarantees of fundamental rights are not simply ornamental. They influence the process of interpretation, of determination of the very content of particular norms, their extent and the legal consequences, and thus they provide for the enlargement of the field of application of the European rules in the national legal orders.

When fundamental rights protection is taken seriously, both at European and at national level, we are confronted with competing jurisdictions, each of them embodying their own ethos of fundamental rights scrutiny.[9] Being founded on the same axiological background, the constitutional values and those expressed by the Charter are very similar. However, this common source does not ensure uniformity of the Member States' constitutional standards. The differences reside not only in the content of a particular guarantee but also in a diverse hierarchy established between particular rights and freedoms. The approach to the relations between the right to privacy on the one hand, and to the freedom of expression on the other hand, constitutes a perfect example. The limitations of these rights determined by the principle of proportionality are not the same in all national legal orders and the scope of the admissible interferences with these rights depends on the axiological concepts accepted in a given national legal system.[10]

The European legal space is based on a pluralism of national legal systems, including a diversity of fundamental rights standards guaranteed by the constitutional provisions of each Member State. The idea of diversity is beautiful and at the same time very appealing because it allows – at least theoretically – for the combination of completely different components: on the one hand, the concept of a more and more

---

[7] Judgment of 30 May 2013 in Case C-168/13 *Jeremy F.* EU:C:2013:358.

[8] Judgment of 6 September 2012 in Case C-619/10 *Trade Agency* EU:C:2010:531.

[9] The specific issues related to the application of the standards enshrined in the European Convention of Human Rights ('ECHR') and the relations between CJEU and ECtHR after envisaged ratification of the European Convention by the European Union are not the subject of my analysis in this chapter. The topic merits a separate presentation.

[10] It explains, to some degree, why the recent judgment of the CJEU in Case C-131/12 *Google Spain and Google Inc.*EU:C:2014:317, judgment of 18 May 2014, provoked such different reactions and commentaries in the Anglo-Saxon and continental newspapers. The former represent a culture more focused on the freedom of expression, while the latter – on the right to privacy.

integrated European space of law and on the other hand, the national and constitutional identity of each Member State.

Nevertheless, diversity is not only extremely difficult to achieve in practice but also poses a risk to the coherence and effectiveness of EU law. A greater margin of autonomy allowing for the shaping of the standards of basic rights protection seems more risky for the coherence and the effectiveness of the European rules and vice versa. An indication of just how fragile the equilibrium between the two above-mentioned components (coherence and pluralism) is the recent jurisprudence of the constitutional courts. It is not necessary to describe in detail the well-known and largely discussed decisions of the German Federal Constitutional Court in issuing a 'warning' aimed at preventing interference with the German constitutional identity, that the ECJ's *ultra vires* jurisprudence going beyond the competencies attributed to that jurisdiction could constitute.[11] Less known but very strong and clear in their messages are the relatively recent decisions of the Czech[12] and the Polish[13] Constitutional Courts in which the priority of the constitutional standards of fundamental rights protection over the European standards was expressly underlined. In the former case, which concerned *Slovak Pensions*, the Czech Constitutional Court expressly recognized that the interpretation of the standard of protection stemming from the ECJ jurisprudence was erroneous and for this reason should not be applied. In the latter case, the Polish Constitutional Court accepted its own competence to perform the constitutional review of EU Regulations on the basis of the constitutional guarantees related to the right to fair trial and consequently admitted theoretically its own prerogative to suspend the binding force of a European Regulation – in this case the Brussels I Regulation[14] – on the Polish territory, if its non-conformity with the Polish Constitution has been established.

It is not my intention to present in these short remarks the complexity of the relations between the two legal orders. I would rather like to focus my observations on the issue of coexistence of the constitutional and the Charter standards of fundamental rights, when the latter is applicable

---

11 Cf. Judgments of German Federal Constitutional Court of 6 July 2010, *Honeywell*, 2 BvR 2661/06, and of 24 April 2013, *Counter-Terrorisme Database*, 1 BvR1215/07.

12 Cf. Judgment of Czech Constitutional Court of 31 January 2012, Pl. ÚS 5/12: *Slovak Pensions*.

13 Cf. Judgment of Polish Constitutional Court of 16 November 2011, SK 45/09, *Brussels I*.

14 Council Regulation (EC) No. 44/2001 of 22 December 2000 on jurisdiction and the recognition and enforcement of judgments in civil and commercial matters.

to the national legal provisions which implement EU law. In this field, a potential confrontation between these standards is clearly visible and the question of coexistence and its necessary premises becomes particularly important.

POSSIBLE SCENARIOS

Theoretically, three different scenarios which describe the diverse approaches to the question of relations between the constitutional and the Charter standards of fundamental rights may be described. The 'sense or non-sense' of the dialogue between the national and European jurisdictions has to be examined, because in each of these scenarios there appears to be a different degree of potential risk of collision and tensions between the different courts. The distinguishing criterion is the scope of application of the Charter in the field covered by national legal acts[15] which are in principle the subject of the national constitutional review. A *restrictive approach* limits the application of the Charter to the national provisions which have been adopted specifically for the purposes of the implementation of EU law.

An *abstract approach*, completely opposite to the above-mentioned one, extends the application of the Charter to each part of the national law which generally belongs to the legal field covered by the European provisions however, no concrete connection can be identified.[16] As an example one could refer to the bulk of environmental law, agriculture or public health. A *functional approach*, located halfway between the restrictive and the abstract approach, constitutes a kind of compromise between these two. From the restrictive approach, this concept differs insofar as it concerns not only the specific provisions adopted specifically

---

[15] Cf. Art.51(1) of the Charter reads as follows: 'The provisions of this Charter are addressed (. . .) to the Member States only when they are implementing Union law. (. . .).' Cf. regarding Art.51 of the Charter, Koen Lenaerts, 'Exploring the Limits of the EU Charter of Fundamental Rights' (2010) *European Constitutional Law Review* 375; and Daniel Sarmiento, 'Who's Afraid Of The Charter? The Court of Justice, National Courts and the New Framework of Fundamental Rights Protection in Europe' (2013) *CMLR* 1267; and also Marek Safjan, 'Areas of Application of the Charter of Fundamental Rights of the European Union: Fields of Conflict?', (2011) *EUI Working Paper* no. 22.

[16] Cf. Judgments in cases: Case C-144/95 *Maurin* [1996] ECR I-2909 paras 11–12; Case C-40/11 *Iida* EU:C:2012:691 para.79; C-87/12 *Ymeraga and Others* EU:C:2013:291 para.41; C-206/13 *Siragusa* EU:C:2014:126 paras 26–27, which can to some extent illustrate this approach.

for implementation purposes but also other national provisions, which are necessary to ensure an effective application of the European provisions. From the abstract approach, this concept differs because it does not content itself with a general and abstract connection between EU and national provisions but, quite to the contrary, requires the indication of a concrete, precisely identified rule of EU law applicable within the scope of national law, so that the Charter could be applied.[17]

It is clear that each of these theoretical approaches represents a different potential for the constitutional dialogue between the national and EU jurisdictions. The scope of application of the Charter, on the one hand, and the scope of application of the constitutional standards on the other, constitute 'communicating vessels' in the sense that, in principle, the larger the application of the Charter, the narrower the field of operation left for the constitutional standards of fundamental rights, and vice versa. The two extreme approaches capture the interdependence perfectly: the *restrictive approach* to the Charter leaves a large space for the constitutional standards and the *abstract approach* in fact strongly limits the potential field of application of these standards. The *functional approach* makes the coexistence of the two systems of fundamental rights standards possible.

In recent ECJ case law, the trend towards a larger application of the Charter guarantees is rather evident. Nevertheless, the pure *abstract approach* was rejected. It is manifested by a series of judgments adopting a *functional approach* to the concept of implementation of European law into national legal orders.[18] The radiation of the EU law on the national legal systems allows for the application of the Charter to national provisions which were not established to implement EU law but are necessary to ensure an effective application of the European provisions. In that sense, the *Åkerberg Fransson* judgment[19] is the result, and the confirmation by the Grand Chamber of the ECJ, of a consequent adherence to the functional approach in the case law established in the former ECJ jurisprudence.[20]

---

[17] Cf. Judgment of 5 October 2010 in Case C-400/10 *McB.* EU:C:2010:582, and in *DEB v Bundesrepublik Deutschland*, n.4.

[18] Cf. *McB.* ibid., and in *DEB v Bundesrepublik Deutschland*, ibid.

[19] Cf. Judgment in *Åkerberg Fransson*, n.5.

[20] Cf. the case-law cited in *Åkerberg Fransson*, ibid. At the same time it would not be right to see some essential, revolutionary change in the scope of application of the fundamental rights guaranteed by the Charter in relation to the national regulations. The CJEU maintains a stance that, in accordance with its Art.51, the application of the Charter always requires to establish which EU legal provision is applied and interpreted in the national legal order. Such requirements have not been met in *Siragusa*, n.16, judgment of 6 March 2014, in which the CJEU

It must be recalled that this judgment has been adopted with regard to Swedish law, which was the legal basis for two procedures: criminal and administrative, initiated against Mr Åkerberg Fransson, who infringed the duty to pay VAT and in this context also committed a fraud. With regard to the two procedures related to the same facts, the ECJ interpreted the *ne bis in idem* principle, despite the fact that the national legal acts had not been adopted for the purpose of the implementation of EU law.[21] The judgment expressly stresses that even national provisions adopted without any connection (direct or indirect) with EU law have to observe the Charter standards if they are to serve as national instruments in implementing European law,[22] and in that sense it is a clear example of the functional approach to the application of the Charter in the case law. The consequence of this approach is that a high number of national laws could be covered by a potential application of the Charter. In such a landscape, is there still space for a dialogue between the European and national jurisdictions?

It would be very hard to deny that the national legal acts which are potentially the subject of evaluation from the Charter perspective could also be the subject of the constitutional review from the point of view of

---

declared its incompetence due to a lack of a sufficient linking point between EU law and Italian law concerning the landscape protection. This judgment is not a withdrawal from *Åkerberg Fransson* line but a confirmation of the criteria of the application of the Charter adopted therein. Similarly, Case C-390/12 *Pfleger e.a.* EU:C:2014:281, judgment of 30 April 2014, in which the CJEU concluded it was unnecessary to carry out an analysis in the scope of the Charter in view of a possible infringement of Art.56 TFEU by a national regulation (para.60) – cannot be considered as a 'retreat' from the *Åkerberg Fransson* line. As for the requirement of a link between the Charter and European law, see also Allan Rosas, 'When is the EU Charter of Fundamental Rights Applicable at the National Level' (2012) 4 *Jurisprudence* 1269 and 'Implementing' EU law in the Member States: Some Observations on the Applicability of the Charter of Fundamental Rights' in Luc Weitzel (ed.), *L'Europe des droits fondamentaux, Hommage à Albert Weitzel* (Pedone 2013); and also Allan Rosas and Heidi Kaila, 'L'application de la Charte des droits fondamentaux de l'Union européenne par la Cour de Justice: un premier bilan' (2011) 1 *Il Dritto dell'Unione Europea* 8 and Thomas von Danwitz, 'L'autonomie du droit de l'Union et la mise en œuvre de la Charte des droits fondamentaux de l'Union européenne', in Brunessen Bertrand, Fabrice Picod, Sébastien Roland (eds), *Mélanges en l'honneur de C. Blumann* (Bruylant 2015).

[21] Cf. Opinion of the Advocate General J. Kokott delivered on 15 December 2011 in the case C-489/10 *Bonda* EU:C:2012:319, who stressed that the notion of 'implementation' relates not only to the national acts which were adopted explicitly when the Member State implements EU law but also to the acts which already existed, para.20.

[22] Cf. Judgment in *Åkerberg Fransson*, n.5, para.29.

application of fundamental rights. Is it not a kind of a specific 'dictate' of the Charter standards imposed by the principle of primacy of EU law which can marginalize the role of the Constitutional Courts in their sphere of activity thus depriving them of the most important part of their prerogatives, that is, the interpretation of the fundamental rights standards that are to be applied in the course of the constitutional review? The approach stressing the exclusive application of the Charter standards of fundamental rights in such a situation seemed, before the *Åkerberg Fransson* judgment, to be the only possible scenario.

From this perspective the importance of the *Åkerberg Fransson* judgment is significant because the space for the application of the national constitutional standards to the national provisions implementing EU law was expressly stated.[23] However, it does not concern all the potential situations (hypothesis) in which this specific overlap of the fundamental rights standards may appear.

First, it may concern situations in which the European lawmaker has left a large margin of appreciation to the national legislators to shape adequate national instruments which are necessary for the effective application of EU law. Exactly such a situation occurred in the context of Swedish law in the *Åkerberg Fransson* case. EU law did not determine exhaustively the scope and the sanctions related to the responsibility for non-payment of VAT, imposing on the national lawmakers the duty to establish, in the framework of their own competence, the necessary legal acts including administrative or criminal procedures.[24]

Secondly, the application of the national constitutional standards becomes possible when the threefold condition that primacy, unity and

---

23 Cf. ibid., paras. 29–30, reads as follows:

29. That said, where a court of a Member State is called upon to review whether fundamental rights are complied with by a national provision or measure which, in a situation where action of the Member States is not entirely determined by European Union law, implements the latter for the purposes of Art.51(1) of the Charter, national authorities and courts remain free to apply national standards of protection of fundamental rights, provided that the level of protection provided for by the Charter, as interpreted by the Court, and the primacy, unity and effectiveness of European Union law are not thereby compromised (. . .).
30. For this purpose, where national courts find it necessary to interpret the Charter they may, and in some cases must, make a reference to the Court of Justice for a preliminary ruling under Art.267 TFEU.

24 *A contrario*, are not at issue national legal acts which constitute only a technical, necessary component of the legal rules contained in a EU legal act which decided upon all important elements of a given solution.

effectiveness of EU law are observed, is met. This solution seems to allow for the achievement of two different goals at once, a wide application of the Charter on the one hand, and room for the Constitutional standards, on the other hand. This opens a potential dialogue between the national and European courts in this field. While this approach is very appealing, we cannot avoid addressing complex questions which arise in this matter and which show not only the positive effects of this concept but also some negative ones or, at least, complicated dilemmas.

These questions relate, as indicated above, to the area where the national and the Charter standards of fundamental rights may potentially overlap. We should recall that the mere existence in the national order of a standard of protection of a fundamental right which would be higher than that under EU law, does not in itself determine the choice in favour of the national guarantees.[25] The concept adopted in EU law in this regard[26] differs from the European Convention of Human Rights,[27] which automatically imposes the application of the higher standard of protection whenever there is competition between two standards, i.e., conventional and constitutional (national). The conditions mentioned in the *Åkerberg Fransson* judgment, necessary for the application of constitutional standards of fundamental rights, directly refer to the hypothesis in which a national standard was higher than the one adopted in EU law.[28]

---

[25] Cf. Judgment in *Melloni*, n.6, para.63, in which this option was definitively rejected.

[26] Cf. Art.53 of the Charter, which reads as follows:

> Nothing in this Charter, shall be interpreted as restricting or adversely affecting human rights and fundamental freedoms as recognised, in their respective fields of application, by Union law and international law and by international agreements to which the Union or all the Member States are party, including the European Convention for the Protection of Human Rights and Fundamental Freedoms, and by the Member States 'constitutions'.

[27] According to Art.53 ECHR the use of a higher standard of fundamental rights protection is a justification against the use of the ECHR standard. Cf. with reference: Clemens Ladenburger, 'European Institutional Report', in Julia Laffranque (ed.), *The Protection of Fundamental Rights Post-Lisbon*: *FIDE XXV Congress* (Tartu University Press, 2012) 175 and S. Iglesias Sánchez, 'The Court and the Charter: The Impact of the Entry into Force of the Lisbon Treaty on the ECJ's Approach to Fundamental Rights' (2012) 49 *Common Market Law Review* 1565, 1605.

[28] The situation evaluated in the *Åkerberg Fransson* case was that the *ne bis in idem* protection of an individual by the Swedish law was stronger than the one required by the Charter. The guarantees stemming from the ECHR jurisprudence on Art.4 of Protocol 7 ECHR (Cf. ECtHR, case *Sergey Zolotoukhine v Russia*,

For this reason it must be asked whether not only the higher standards of protection of the human rights but also these which ensure the same or similar levels of protection may be applied, when the conditions established by the *Åkerberg Fransson* case are met? Should the answer be positive, another question arises, namely, what are the criteria to qualify the standards as representing the same level of protection?

The answer is only apparently simple and evident. These questions do not cause complications only in the 'ideal legal space'. Different constellations have to be considered, for instance that the national constitution ensures the same content of the guarantees, but sets up its own unique hierarchy in relation to other fundamental rights; that the scope of protection is the same but the proportionality principle applied in the national context allows deeper interference into fundamental rights than would be admissible on the basis of the EU provisions; finally, that the normative content of the rights is similar although some components of a particular right are applied differently in the constitutional and European jurisprudence. A good example is the *ne bis in idem* principle itself, because – being expressed in some legal systems in the identical formula – it is frequently interpreted differently in respect of substantive elements such as the notions of 'penalty' or 'criminal procedure'. These few examples show that perfect similarity, or even comparability, between the national and European level of protection is a hypothesis which is not easily attainable.

One thing seems to be uncontroversial: the level of protection in the national systems cannot be lower than the one guaranteed by the Charter. In this sense, even with the application of the national constitutional standards, the Charter constitutes a very minimal level of protection which should be observed in all cases. But in reality, even this thesis can face some of the above-mentioned problems.

The approach adopted in recent ECJ jurisprudence has opened up a new perspective of coexistence between the national and European legal orders but it is not free from risk for the coherence and uniformity of the interpretation of fundamental rights in relation to EU provisions. However,

judgment of 10 February 2009, no. 14939/03, ECHR 2009), were enshrined in the Swedish constitutional system, that excluded the possibility of criminal and administrative proceedings in the same case. The standard elaborated on Art.50 of the Charter is not so protective, allowing – conformingly to the test established in the *Engel* judgment (Cf. ECtHR, case *Engel and others v The Netherlands*, judgment of 8 June 1976, no. 5370/72, Series A, No. 22) – parallel administrative and criminal proceedings. However, in the Swedish legal system the higher standard of protection of fundamental rights, based on a constitutional standard stemming from the *Zolotoukhine* jurisprudence, might be applied.

it should be asked what its practical implications for the national judges could be.

First, it is recommended focusing the analysis on the results of the application of fundamental rights and not on their normative and formal content. In fact, only the final effect of the application (meaning the degree of protection of a concrete fundamental right, taking into account its place in the entire legal system, established jurisprudence and admissible limitations according to the proportionality principle) should be relevant for the finding of similarity between the national and Charter standards of fundamental rights.

Secondly, the existence of a long and well-established line of jurisprudence in EU law regarding a particular fundamental right constitutes a strong argument or even a kind of presumption in favour of the application of the Charter rather than of the constitutional standards of fundamental rights. The risk of a potential conflict between the requirements of the uniform application of fundamental rights would then be smaller.

A firm position of the ECJ, shaped during the long development of the jurisprudence, may constitute an important component of the common constitutional traditions of the Member States. However, when there is no legislative consensus at the EU level on the scale and the content of the protected values contained in the particular fundamental right, the field of diversification of the fundamental rights standards becomes wide open because constitutional standards of protection of fundamental rights come into play. For this reason the following observation made by Koen Lenaerts can be accepted:

> (. . .) pluralism is not an absolute value, the level of protection granted to a fundamental right by a national legal order must comply with any constitutional consensus that exists at EU level (. . .) It is the existence or absence of an EU legislative consensus that indicates whether the Member States are developing at the same pace and in the same manner or whether national societies are evolving in accordance with their own scale of values. That being said, national diversity and EU legislative consensus must both comply with values which are regarded as pan-European, i.e. those that are the object of a constitutional consensus at EU level.[29]

In conclusion on this point, I would say that, in the current landscape, the dialogue between Constitutional and European Courts has become more useful and more necessary than before. The existence of a grey zone

---

[29] Cf. also Koen Lenaerts, 'EU Values and Constitutional Pluralism', a lecture delivered at Warsaw University on 11 April 2014.

of potential competition between two separate orders now is not only a hypothesis but actually part of the reality. One has to accept this 'grey zone' as an inevitable secondary effect of the recent jurisprudence of the ECJ, if the approach of extending the scope of constitutional dialogue between the European and national jurisdictions is maintained. This dialogue is not easy because – as mentioned above – even the comparability of the guarantees present a great challenge for the judges who must decide on the national procedures.

It is worth noting that the effectiveness of the EU provisions is not a unique determinant for the choice between the Charter and constitutional standards.[30] In fact, some recent decisions of the ECJ confirm that the efficiency of the EU provisions must give way to the protection of substantive elements of the guarantees provided by the Charter.[31] This is why the primary criterion to gauge a standard of fundamental rights is the preservation of the essence of fundamental rights. One cannot preclude *a priori* that the national constitutional standard can provide better guarantees for the preservation of the substance of a particular fundamental right than the Charter standard.[32]

I believe that the recent jurisprudence of the ECJ has left a relatively large discretion to the constitutional courts, in which they may effectively operate and exert influence on the ECJ jurisprudence. The dialogue can guarantee the participation of the national supreme courts' jurisdictions in the shaping of the standards of protection required by the Charter,

---

[30] Cf. Marek Safjan and Dominik Düsterhaus, 'A Union of Effective Judicial Protection' (2014) 33 *Yearbook of European Law* 3.

[31] Cf. in particular judgments in cases: Case C-7/98 *Krombach* [2000] ECR I-1935; Case C-619/10 *Trade Agency* EU:C:2010:531; Case C-472/11 *Banif Plus Bank* EU:C:2013:88. In these judgments the CJEU concluded that the fundamental elements constituting protection of the right to fair trial must be respected even at the cost of lower efficiency of a European regulation in a given case.

[32] The recent judgment in Joined Cases C-293/12-594/12 *Digital Rights* EU:C:2014:238 on data retention by telecom companies, seems to illustrate that the analysis included in a judgment of a national constitutional court applying a fundamental right may precede a CJEU judgment. In the judgment on data retention the CJEU declared the EU directive invalid because it infringes the right to privacy. It was preceded by a judgment of the German Federal Constitutional Court, which reviewed national regulations implementing EU law, which were found incompliant with the German Constitution (BVerfG, 1 BvR 256/08 from 2.3.2010). It could also be noted that judgments of national courts referring to the protection of the right to privacy in the context of data processing by the Internet search engines (as for example the judgment by LG Hamburg in Mosley case; 24.1.2014 – 324 O 264/11) preceded the CJEU judgment in Case C-131/12 *Google Spain and Google Inc.* EU:C:2014:317.

which are to be interpreted with respect to the constitutional traditions of the Members States. In fact, Art.52(4) of the Charter imposes the respect for the constitutional traditions of the Member States when the Charter is applied.

However, so that the dialogue is efficient, at least two conditions are to be met. First, according to para.29 of the *Åkerberg Fransson* judgment,[33] the exchange between the ECJ and national judges has to be initiated – this initiative belongs to the national courts. Secondly, openness and sensitivity to the arguments provided by the other party of the dialogue is needed, the exchange between the European and national jurisdictions is not to be transformed into a 'one-way message' – this requirement should be addressed first of all to the European courts.

MIXED BEAUTY OF THE CONSTITUTIONAL IDENTITY

The disputes related to the possible coexistence of the national and the Charter standards of fundamental rights concentrate rather on the interpretation of Art.51(1) of the Charter and not on the question of constitutional identity. However, in this context it seems to be especially important to answer the question of what possibilities the Member States would have if they wanted to replace the application of the Charter standards with their own constitutional standards, when their 'constitutional identity' is at stake. Ever since the *Melloni* judgment,[34] the mere existence of a higher standard of a fundamental right in the national system is not a sufficient argument to refuse the application of an established interpretation of a fundamental right standard, as interpreted by the ECJ and ECtHR, if this solution does not comply with the requirements of primacy, unity and effectiveness of EU law. Would the preservation of the constitutional identity then be a good and sufficient argument?

It is worth recalling that the identification of 'constitutional traditions' as representing the 'constitutional identity' is an erroneous approach. Constitutional traditions of the Member States belong to the common heritage of European law and they are an essential component – as mentioned above – of the correct interpretation of the fundamental rights guaranteed by the Charter. In this sense the 'constitutional identity'

---

33 Cf. *Åkerberg Fransson*, n.5, para.29.

34 Cf. *Melloni*, n.6. Regarding the conditions for the applicability of constitutional standards, see also *Åkerberg Fransson*, ibid., para.29.

is a specific sublimation of the common constitutional axiology of the Member States, which is one of the criteria used by the ECJ in its interpretation of the content of the constitutional standards which should be respected in EU law.

For these reasons constitutional traditions do not equal constitutional identity. The former is a general and abstract concept being the synthesis of the trends in the legal systems of the Member States, whereas the latter is attributed to a specific legal system. The sources of the 'constitutional identity' are located in a normative idea of 'national identity'.[35] The national identity constitutes an 'added value' to the idea of constitutional traditions and only jointly they constitute the constitutional identity.[36]

There are certain crucial arguments in favour of respecting the specific constitutional values enshrined in the national legal systems. The European Union is created as a pluralistic organization and – as mentioned above – diversity is one of its strongest features.[37]

Paradoxically, diversity in the EU is also the source of both strengths and weaknesses. As a matter of fact, on the one hand it ensures the coexistence of different nations and cultures, but on the other hand it illustrates the fact that the process of the creation of a new and completely integrated

[35] Therefore, in this sense, 'national identity' is directly related to the fundamental structure of the state, also regarding its regional and local governmental structure.

[36] Art.4(2) TEU states as follows: 'The Union shall respect the equality of Member States before the Treaties as well as their national identities, inherent in their fundamental structures, political and constitutional, inclusive of regional and local self-government.(. . .).' Cf. literature on constitutional identity, e.g., Dominique Ritleng, 'Propos introductifs: Le droit constitutionnel national aux prises avec le droit européen: l'exemple de la Hongrie' (2013) 2013/3 *Revue des Affaires Européennes* 441; Stéphanie L. Shaelou, 'Nous les peuples'. L'identité constitutionnelle dans la jurisprudence tchèque, polonaise et lettone' in Laurence Burgorgue-Larse, *L'identité constitutionnelle saisie par les juges en Europe*, *Cahiers Européens (1)* (Pedone 2011); Vlad Constantinesco, 'La confrontation entre identité constitutionnelle européenne et identité constitutionnelles nationales. Convergence ou contradiction ? Contrepoint ou hiérarchie ?' in Jean-Claude Masclet, Hélène Ruiz Fabri, Chahira Boutayeb and Stéphane Rodrigues (eds), *L'Union européenne: Mélanges en l'honneur du professeur P. Manin*, (Pedone 2010); Barbara Guastaferro, 'Beyond the 'Exceptionalism' of Constitutional Conflicts: The 'Ordinary' Functions of the Identity Clause' (2012) 31 *Yearbook of European Law* 263.

[37] Cf. Lenaerts, lecture, n.29; and also 'Human Rights Protection Through Judicial Dialogue Between National Courts and the European Court of Justice', in André Alen *et al* (eds), *Liberae Cogitationes, Liber amicorum Marc Bossuyt* (Intersentia 2013). In this matter cf. also Neil Walker, 'The Idea of Constitutional Pluralism' (2002) 3 *Modern Law Review* 317.

European nation is complex and slow. The idea of constitutional identity expresses both of these faces of the pluralism of the EU. On the one hand, it potentially enhances flexibility in the application of EU rules and ensures better adaptation to the needs and specific culture of each Member State, but – on the other hand – it jeopardizes the coherent application of the Charter standards of fundamental rights.

No doubt, an unlimited and overly broad use of the idea of constitutional identity would become damaging for the very concept of EU law and it could even cause the collapse of the entire system. In particular, the risk would appear in two hypothetical situations.

First, if a constitutional court wished to act only as the ultimate jurisdictional arbitrator in establishing the borders imposed by the concept of the constitutional identity, it would *de facto* decide about admissibility of the implementation of European law into the national order.

Secondly, the notion of constitutional identity would cover a very large spectrum of constitutional rules[38] (in particular in the matter of the fundamental rights) including their interpretation in the constitutional jurisprudence.[39] A broad concept could for instance legitimize refusal to implement EU provisions or become a definitive defence argument, a specific '*ultima ratio*' in the proceeding for failure of a Member State to fulfil obligations under the Treaty. In some sense, it would be a return to the situation existing before the cases of *Internationale*

[38] According to this approach, each constitutional regulation carries the idea of national identity. It is worth noting that such an approach towards constitutional identity was criticized by the Advocate General P. Maduro in the opinion delivered on 8 April 2008 in Case C-213/07 *Michaniki* [2008] ECR I-9999, para.33 and also by the Advocate General N. Wahl in the opinion delivered on 10 April 2014 in Joined Cases C-58/13 and C-59/13 *Torresi* EU:C:2014:2088. For example, in the latter, the Italian court referred to the Italian national identity resulting from the Italian Constitution, which requires that a special state exam should be passed by the candidates who wish to be registered as Members of the Italian Bar. According to the Advocate General no rule enshrined in a national constitution can limit the uniform application of EU provisions, let alone constitute a parameter for the legality of those rules (para.100).

[39] Cf. the judgment of the Constitutional Tribunal on the Treaty of Lisbon (Polish Constitutional Court; judgment of 24 November 2010, K 32/09, *Treaty of Lisbon*) and the position of the German Federal Constitutional Court (Judgment of 30 June 2009, 2 BvE 2/08, *Treaty of Lisbon*). Such a wide approach poses an obvious risk of confrontation, especially because it leaves out the fact that EU law has a constitutional consensus (e.g., the standard of individual fundamental rights as interpreted by the CJEU), which should be treated as a relevant point of reference when assessing the compliance of national solutions with EU law. Cf. also Lenaerts, n.29.

Handelsgesellschaft[40] or *Costa v E.N.E.L.*[41] In fact, the principle of primacy of EU law would be evacuated.

Nevertheless, I could not accept that the reference to the idea of constitutional identity would be subordinated to the same conditions which are generally required for the application of the national constitutional fundamental rights standards (meaning primacy, effectiveness and unity of EU law) as it has been stressed in the recent jurisprudence of the ECJ. We have to recall that these conditions have been settled on the basis of Art.53 of the Charter, which concerns, inter alia, the relations between the fundamental rights standards guaranteed by the national constitutions and EU law, but does not include a reference to the idea of constitutional identity. Finally, those judgments do not establish whether primacy, effectiveness and unity have 'absolute significance' and – consequently – whether they are applied also to the standards which are determined by the concept of the constitutional identity. In this sense the question could be treated as still being open.

The solution has to be found between two 'extremes', i.e., absolute respect for the constitutional pluralism of the EU Member States and the fully integrated European legal space. It is not the first time that the EU legal order, or rather the idea of integration itself, has been confronted with challenges which require a combination of the components which seem to be, by their own nature, in opposition. However, it is an inherent feature of the EU legal space and the result of experience collected for over 60 years that an apparently non-existent solution may be found through dialogue because of the will and determination of all parties to find a consensus. The same mechanism shall be applied to the dispute between the 'constitutional identity' and the principle of primacy of EU law. The dialogue between national and European jurisdictions is a unique instrument in order to achieve consensus in this fragile matter.

The Court's jurisprudence has sent some signs which confirm that the idea of constitutional identity may be used as a ground for justification in the framework of the so-called derogation clauses. Even in the absence of any direct reference to constitutional identity, the *Omega* case[42] (human dignity *vs* freedom to provide services) is one of the best examples. However, other cases, such as *Sayn-Wittgenstein*[43] (republicanism *vs* free

[40] Cf. Case C-11/70 *Internationale Handelsgesellschaft* [1970] ECR-1125.

[41] Case C-6/64 *Flaminio Costa v. E.N.E.L* [1964] ECR-1141.

[42] Judgment of 14 October 2004 in Case C-36/02 *Omega* [2004] ECR I-9609.

[43] Judgment of 22 December 2010 in Case C-208/09 *Sayn-Wittgenstein* EU:C:2010:806.

movement) or *Runevič-Vardyn and Wardyn*[44] (national language *vs* free movement) confirm the trend. The solutions in these cases are rather well received by the doctrine.[45] Generally, the concept of application of the substantive values of the constitutional system through the use of the derogation clauses is largely accepted.[46] Nevertheless, the crucial point of the debate is who – and according to what criterion – the selection of the substantive components of the constitutional system should be decided. This is particularly so when only a very general definition of the constitutional identity of a Member State is provided by its constitutional doctrine or jurisprudence.

I believe that an approach which makes a clear division between the European and national levels of jurisdiction and attributes competence in this matter to one or the other jurisdiction would be an unjustified simplification. Of course, national courts are in the best position to identify the elements of constitutional identity of a given Member State. No doubt, the characteristics of constitutional identity of a given Member State may not be set out discretionally in the ECJ jurisprudence. Reference to these characteristics must be made by the national judges. However, this 'national concept of the constitutional identity' must be confronted with the goals and values of the European legal order. The search for the equilibrium between two legal orders belongs to the European judges.

It has to be underlined that the values expressed in Art.2 TEU may constitute – from an EU law perspective – the 'ultimate line' behind which

---

[44] Judgment of 12 May 2011 in Case C-391/09 *Runevič-Vardyn and Wardyn* EU:C:2011:291.

[45] Cf. Koen Lenaerts, 'The EU Charter of Fundamental Rights: Scope of Application and Methods of Interpretation' in Maria Teresa D'Alessio, Vincent Kronenberger, Valerio Placco (eds.), *De Rome à Lisbonne: les juridictions de l'Union à la croisée des chemins: Mélanges en l'honneur de Paolo Mengozzi* (Bruylant 2013), and also Koen Lenaerts and José A. Gutiérrez-Fons, 'The Place of the Charter in the EU Constitutional Edifice' in Steve Peers *et al*, The EU Charter of Fundamental Rights – A Commentary (Hart 2014) 1559–93; Armin von Bogdandy and Stephan Schill, 'Overcoming Absolute Primacy: Respect for National Identity Under the Lisbon Treaty' (2011) 48 *Common Market Law Review* 1417; Vojtech Belling, 'Supranational Fundamental Rights or Primacy of Sovereignty? Legal Effects of the So-called Opt-out from the EU Charter' (2012) 2 *European Law Journal* 254.

[46] One has to bear in mind that the derogation allowing for the application of different solutions in the national legal system cannot infringe the general principles of the EU law; Cf. the judgment in Case C-260/89 *ERT* [1991] ECR I-2925), see also the Explanation relating to Art.51 of the Charter [2007] OJ C303/17. However, this judgment did not concern the constitutional identity.

the observance of the constitutional identity would become impossible[47] because it should not reach the point where the axiological construction on which the EU has been built, would be undermined. In other words, it is the constitutional identity of the European Union that should create the framework for the potential dialogue between the judges. The European identity is not an abstract concept because it stems from the constitutional traditions of the Member States or the European Convention of Human Rights.[48] The space to look for common points is therefore quite large and it is this aspect which provides for the strength and the sense of the judicial dialogue.

This ideal of a rational equilibrium will never be reached without a dialogue and a necessary degree of openness manifested by the parties of the debate. I strongly believe that the framework for this dialogue has been well determined by the values and axiology which are expressed by the formula of Art.2 TEU and which has been shared by all the courts participating in the debate. Instead of continuing a never-ending debate about 'which court is the court of the last word', rationality requires the debate is focused on the real issues and, above all, on the question of what kind of European Union is needed in the future.

---

[47] In this sense, it is sometimes debated whether the concept of constitutional identity of the European Union could provide a basis for the application of a 'reverse *Solange*-like' reasoning, which would delineate – with reference to national legal orders – the borders outside which national solutions would be an *ultra vires* form in respect to EU law. It would allow for an adequate reaction to the risk of authoritarian trends that might occur in some Member States. Cf. Mathias Kumm in a panel discussion: 'In the era of legal pluralism. The relationship between the EU, national and international courts, and the interplay of the multiple sources of law', at FIDE Congress in Copenhagen, May 2014. Apart from the constitutional identity context, the supposition based on the assumption that each national legal system observes the fundamental rights, may be overturned. For example in the Joined Cases C-411/10 and C-493/10 *N.S. and Others* EU:C:2011:865, the CJEU evaluated the practice of national authorities in the procedures applied to refugees.

[48] Cf. also Bruno de Witte, 'Article 53: Level of Protection' in Steve Peers *et al* (eds), *The EU Charter of Fundamental Rights – A Commentary* (Hart 2014), who says: 'In interpreting the relevant provisions of the Charter, the Court of Justice and the courts of the Member States must have due regard to the level of protection offered by similar rights contained in international human rights conventions such as the ECHR and in the common constitutional traditions of the Member States.'

4. The structure of US federal and state courts and mechanisms for formal and informal resolution of conflicts

Anthony J. Scirica*

INTRODUCTION

This chapter on judicial cooperation in the United States and the protection of fundamental rights was initially presented at a conference organized by the Center for Judicial Cooperation at the European University Institute. The Center has undertaken an important project. The goal is to craft a set of "judicial interaction" principles to guide jurists in resolving conflicts between legal systems within the EU. These principles include: (1) consistent interpretation, (2) preliminary reference, (3) proportionality, (4) comparative reasoning, (5) mutual recognition, (6) disapplication, and (7) deferential techniques. Collectively, these concepts seek to promote coherence and coordination in the protection of fundamental rights.

Each of these principles has a parallel in the US legal system. This chapter will address some of these parallel US concepts and focus on answering the question: How do US federal courts resolve conflicts within our various legal systems involving questions of fundamental rights? I will answer this question by discussing the central elements of judicial power sharing in the US and by illustrating how our analogous "judicial interaction" principles operate through three landmark Supreme Court cases.

But first, some background. In the United States, the US Constitution,

* Presentation originally given by the Honorable Anthony J. Scirica at the Centre for Judicial Cooperation at the European University Institute, Conference on Judicial Cooperation Techniques for the Protection of European Fundamental Rights: Past and Future Perspectives, May 2014. Some changes have been made to reflect legal developments since the presentation was originally delivered.

the laws of the United States and treaties made under its authority, are the supreme law. The Constitution creates a federal system of power sharing between the national government and state governments. The federal government and all of the state governments have their own court systems. The Supreme Court is the highest court for all questions of federal law, whether they arise in federal-court or state-court cases. Under the Supreme Court are the federal appellate courts, called courts of appeals, and the federal trial courts, called district courts. There are 94 federal judicial districts, which are divided into 12 regional circuits. Each regional circuit has a US court of appeals that hears appeals from the district courts in its circuit and appeals from federal administrative agencies. Having lost in federal trial court, a party is normally entitled to appeal to a federal court of appeals. Because the Supreme Court is usually under no obligation to hear an appeal and hears fewer than 100 cases each year, a decision by a court of appeals is generally final.[1] But the federal court system is not the only forum available to litigants. Indeed, federal courts are courts of limited subject-matter jurisdiction, and the majority of litigation in the US occurs in the trial and appellate courts of the 50 states. We have, then, a system of judicial federalism in which much jurisdiction and interpretive authority is shared by federal and state courts.

Judicial interaction is a set of principles used by courts and judges in Europe to promote coherence and coordination in areas of fundamental rights protection. A list of principles, and their US analogues, can be identified:

(1) Consistent interpretation—roughly analogous to a principle embodied in the US Constitution's Supremacy Clause.
(2) Preliminary reference—question certification.
(3) Proportionality—a type of scrutiny to be applied when analyzing a fundamental rights issue:
    - *Rational basis*—the enactment in question must be *rationally related* to a *legitimate* government interest.
    - *Intermediate scrutiny*—the enactment in question must be *substantially related* to an *important* government interest.
    - *Strict scrutiny*—the enactment in question must be *narrowly tailored* to advance a *compelling* government interest, and must be the *least restrictive means* of advancing that interest.
(4) Comparative reasoning—looking to the law of other federal circuit courts, state supreme courts, and occasionally other nations, as well

---

1 In 2013, there were 56,475 appeals filed in the US courts of appeals.

as treaties and American Law Institute (ALI) publications to inform a court's analysis of an issue[2] (see Example 2 below).

(5) Mutual recognition—full faith and credit; recognition and enforcement of judgments; *stare decisis* (see Example 1 below).

(6) Disapplication—roughly analogous to principles embodied in the US Supremacy Clause (see Examples 1 and 2 below).

(7) Deferential techniques—e.g., judicial restraint, narrow holdings; constitutional avoidance; abstention doctrines (see Example 3 below).

BACKGROUND: CENTRAL ELEMENTS OF JUDICIAL POWER SHARING

i. Vertical Power Sharing (i.e., Federal/State, Pan-EU/National)

a. Federal law vs. state law

The United States has a dual system; that is to say, in the US, the federal government and each state government has its own court system. The Tenth Amendment to the US Constitution states: "The powers not delegated to the United States by the Constitution, nor prohibited by it to the States, are reserved to the States respectively, or to the people." This amendment restates the principle of federalism that federal law is delegated and interstitial. Any power not expressly or impliedly given to the federal government is reserved to the states.

Examples of areas of law traditionally, although not exclusively, within the province of the states are the following: probate law; family law; property law; tort law; contract law; land use law; much of the criminal law and state administrative law. On the other hand, examples of areas of law traditionally within the province of the federal government include: federal constitutional law; interstate commerce; immigration law; admiralty law; securities law; antitrust law (anti-monopoly law); some criminal law and federal administrative law. Both the states and the federal government have strong traditions of consumer and environmental protection.

b. Federalism

Federal courts are courts of limited jurisdiction while state courts are courts of general jurisdiction. The jurisdiction of federal courts is defined

---

[2] The Restatements or Principles of the American Law Institute are not binding, but provide persuasive authority or guidance. (The European Law Institute is patterned on the ALI.)

in the US Constitution (Art. III, Section 2, Clause 1) and extends to: all cases (1) arising under the Constitution, laws of the US, and treaties, (2) affecting ambassadors, other public ministers, and consuls, and (3) of admiralty and maritime jurisdiction, and controversies (4) to which the US shall be a party, (5) between two or more states, (6) between a state and citizens of another state, (7) between citizens of different states, (8) between citizens of the same state claiming lands under grants of different states, and (9) between a state, or the citizens thereof, and foreign states, citizens, or subjects.

The relationship between state and federal courts may be described in two ways. Some describe it as a federalist model, that is to say, a system of dual sovereignty, wherein decentralization promotes experimentation and decentralizes power, and where state courts are competent to vindicate federal rights as well as state rights.[3] In the alternative, the relationship between state and federal courts might be described as a nationalist model. The Civil War/Reconstruction amendments (the Thirteenth, Fourteenth, and Fifteenth Amendments) reshuffled the deck, making the federal government more "supreme" than before (to the extent that there was no longer a presumption of parity between state and federal courts).

c. Constitutional supremacy

The Supremacy Clause of the US Constitution (Art. VI, Clause 2) provides:

> The Constitution, and the Laws of the United States which shall be made in Pursuance thereof; and all Treaties made, or which shall be made, under the Authority of the United States, shall be the supreme Law of the Land; and the Judges in every state shall be bound thereby, any Thing in the Constitution or Laws of any State to the Contrary notwithstanding.

Under the Supremacy Clause, state courts must follow and enforce federal law and federal rights. Federal courts are the supreme authority in the interpretation of the federal Constitution and federal laws.

State courts have obligations to hear federal claims. That is to say, state courts must give effect to federal laws that provide jurisdiction in state courts, even where federal law does not command states to hear claims

---

3 The so-called Madisonian Compromise—the decision at the Constitutional Convention to let Congress decide whether to create lower federal courts in addition to the Supreme Court—was premised on the assumption that state courts are adequate and available protectors of individual liberties. Federal courts had no "federal question" jurisdiction until 1869.

under the law (i.e., state courts cannot refuse to enforce a federal law just because it is a federal law). The Supremacy Clause makes federal law the law of the states too, and state judges may be bound by federal laws, even when they are contrary to state policies. State courts have the competence to decide federal claims (including claims regarding fundamental rights such as rights to equal protection, free speech, and due process). Accordingly, there are many cases where federal and state courts have concurrent jurisdiction.

d. Preemption

The federal preemption doctrine, which derives from the Supremacy Clause, preempts a state law that conflicts with federal law. A federal law that conflicts with a state law will trump—preempt—that state law: "[W]e have long recognized that state laws that conflict with federal law are 'without effect.'"[4]

An example can be identified in *Cooper v. Aaron* (*see* Example 1 below).[5] Preemption can be either express or implied. When the US Constitution or Congress expressly preempts state law, courts determine whether the challenged state law is one that the federal law is *intended* to preempt. In cases of implied preemption, courts look beyond the express language of the federal law to determine whether it "occupies the field" that the state is attempting to regulate, or whether enforcement of the state law might frustrate a federal purpose. Federal law is said to occupy the field when there is no room left for state regulation. Courts look to the pervasiveness of the federal scheme, the federal interest at stake, and the danger of frustration of federal goals in making their determination about whether a challenged state law can stand.

e. Writs and injunctions

The All Writs Act, the Anti-Injunction Act and abstention doctrines are also tools to manage vertical power sharing. The All Writs Act allows federal courts to issue "all writs necessary or appropriate in aid of their respective jurisdictions."[6] It gives federal courts discretion to enjoin state judicial proceedings. At the same time, the Anti-Injunction Act bars federal court interference with state court proceedings except in limited circumstances. Federal courts may enjoin a state proceeding when

---

4 *Altria Grp., Inc. v. Good*, 555 US 70 (2008) [76] (quoting *Maryland v. Louisiana*, 451 US 725 (1981) [746]).

5 *Cooper v. Aaron*, 358 US 1 (1958).

6 28 USC. § 1651(a).

necessary: (1) to give full effect to a federal right or remedy; (2) to protect or preserve the federal court's exercise of its jurisdiction or a prior federal judgment; or (3) if expressly authorized by Congress.

Federal courts may abstain when cases involving the same issues are brought in both federal and state court. Federal courts rely on abstention doctrines when refusing to hear a case within their jurisdiction if hearing the case would offend principles of comity, equitable discretion, or sound judicial administration. Nevertheless, abstention is not common and federal courts have a general obligation to hear cases where they have jurisdiction. Examples of abstention doctrines include the following:

(1) *Pullman* abstention[7]—federal courts should not adjudicate the constitutionality of state enactments fairly open to interpretation until state courts have been afforded a reasonable opportunity to pass on them.
(2) *Younger* abstention[8]—federal courts should not hear certain civil claims brought by a person who is currently being prosecuted in state court for a matter related to that claim.
(3) *Colorado River* abstention[9]—federal courts, in exceptional circumstances, may abstain out of deference to state court proceedings to avoid duplicative or piecemeal litigation.
(4) *Burford* abstention[10]—federal courts, sitting in diversity jurisdiction,[11] may abstain where the state courts likely have greater expertise in a particularly complex area of state law.
(5) *Thibodaux* abstention[12]—federal courts, sitting in diversity jurisdiction, may abstain to allow a state to decide issues of state law that are of great public importance to that state, to the extent that a federal determination would infringe on state sovereignty.

Abstention doctrines serve, in part, to protect the principle of comity in the US legal system. Comity is the legal principle that legal entities—such as courts from different jurisdictions—will mutually recognize each other's legal authority and acts. The underlying notion is that different

---

7 *R.R. Comm'n v. Pullman Co.*, 312 US 496 (1941).

8 *Younger v. Harris*, 401 US 37 (1971).

9 *Colo. River Water Conservation Dist. v. United States*, 424 US 800 (1976).

10 *Burford v. Sun Oil Co.*, 319 US 315 (1943).

11 In diversity jurisdiction, federal courts can hear cases between citizens of different states, even if they do not involve a question of federal law.

12 *Louisiana Power & Light Co. v. City of Thibodaux*, 360 US 25 (1959).

jurisdictions will reciprocate with each other out of deference, mutuality, and respect.

f. Rules of Decision Act (28 USC. § 1652)

Diversity jurisdiction allows federal courts to hear cases between citizens of different states. The Rules of Decision Act requires federal courts exercising diversity jurisdiction to apply *state substantive law* unless there is federal statutory law on point. The Rules of Decision Act states: "The laws of the several states, except where the Constitution or treaties of the United States or Acts of Congress otherwise require or provide, shall be regarded as rules of decision in civil actions in the courts of the United States, in cases where they apply."[13]

Although the Rules of Decision Act was adopted in the Judiciary Act of 1789, federal courts did not always follow it in practice. In *Swift v. Tyson*,[14] the Supreme Court held that federal courts exercising diversity jurisdiction need not apply state judge-made common law. Following *Swift*, federal courts sitting in diversity applied state statutory law, if there was a state statute on point. If there was no state statute on point, federal courts could apply federal common law and ignore the state's judge-made common law.

Almost a century later, in *Erie Railroad Company v. Tompkins*,[15] the Supreme Court overruled *Swift* and held that federal courts exercising diversity jurisdiction lacked the power to create general federal common law when hearing state law claims. As a result, federal courts exercising diversity jurisdiction now apply both state statutory and state judge-made common law when hearing state law claims. In so doing, federal courts apply the law as espoused by state supreme courts; if a state supreme court has not ruled directly on the particular issue, federal courts must *predict* how the state supreme court would rule, and do so primarily by looking to decisions of the state's appellate courts. But federal courts still apply federal procedural law. State and federal courts also commonly look to the American Law Institute for persuasive authority or guidance.[16]

g. Question certification

A certified question is a formal request by one court to another court for an opinion on a question of law. It is an alternative to abstention and is

---

13 28 USC. § 1652.

14 41 US 1 (1842).

15 304 US 64 (1938).

16 The European Union now has a European Law Institute modeled on the ALI.

considered a more efficient way to obtain answers to questions of state law. Consider the following scenario: A federal court, exercising diversity jurisdiction, is asked to resolve a matter that turns on state law. The federal court must apply the choice-of-law rules (and accordingly, frequently the substantive law) of the state in which it sits under *Erie*. If the state law is unclear or uncertain, the federal court may, instead of trying to predict how the state's highest court would rule, decide to certify a question regarding the interpretation of the state law to that state's highest court. The Supreme Court urged the use of certified questions in its 1960 decision in *Clay v. Sun Insurance Office*.[17] Since then, all US courts of appeals have employed question certification.

For example, the Third Circuit Court of Appeals, on which I sit, has a rule that when the procedures of the highest court of a state provide for certification to that court by a federal court of questions arising under the laws of that state which will control the outcome of a case pending in the federal court, our court, *sua sponte* or on motion of a party, may certify such a question to the state court in accordance with the procedures of that court, and will stay the case in our court to await the state court's decision about whether to accept the question certified. A state court has discretion to decline to answer the question.

Many states allow certified questions addressed from a federal court, either by virtue of legislation or the ruling of a state supreme court that the supreme court possesses inherent judicial power to decide state law questions submitted by another jurisdiction. Many states have adopted a uniform act called the Uniform Certification of Questions of Law Act,[18] providing that a state's highest court may answer questions of law certified to it by the US Supreme Court, a federal court of appeals, or a federal district court, if the question is determinative of the federal proceeding or there is no controlling state supreme court precedent addressing the question.

States that permit certified questions do not consider the practice to be rendering an advisory opinion—which is generally forbidden in our system since it does not constitute a requisite "case or controversy"—because the certified question relates to an actual dispute. But some states interpret their constitutions in accord with the federal Constitution and have found that a certified question does not present a case or controversy on which it may rule.

---

[17] 363 US 207 (1960) [212].

[18] Unif. Certification of Questions of Law Act (1995).

h. Recognition and enforcement of judgments

Recognition occurs when a court recognizes the validity of a judicial ruling on a claim that was previously litigated. Enforcement occurs when a US court uses its coercive powers to compel a defendant to satisfy a judgment rendered in a different court, domestic or foreign.

First, in terms of the recognition and enforcement of domestic judgments, the Full Faith and Credit Clause of the US Constitution requires state and federal courts, as a matter of federal law, to recognize and enforce valid final judgments of other courts. Art. IV, Section 1 of the US Constitution provides: "Full Faith and Credit shall be given in each State to the public Acts, Records, and judicial Proceedings of every other State. And the Congress may by general Laws prescribe the Manner in which such Acts, Records and Proceedings shall be proved, and the Effect thereof."

The purpose of the Full Faith and Credit Clause was to unify the country. If one state's court rules on an issue, the losing party cannot simply go to another state and try to win there. The issue has already been decided and preclusion doctrines, a form of recognition, apply to bar the claim.[19]

The enforceability of state court judgments under the Full Faith and Credit Clause is subject to limited exceptions, which arise where: (1) there is a lack of personal jurisdiction; (2) there is a lack of subject-matter jurisdiction; (3) the defendant did not receive notice or opportunity to be heard; or (4) the judgment was obtained by fraud.

Federal courts are required to recognize and enforce state court judgments under the Full Faith and Credit Statute.[20] The statute provides that records and judicial proceedings of any US state court have the same full faith and credit in every court within the US as they have by law or usage in the state court from which they are taken. Even when a federal court is determining a federal cause of action, it must give the same preclusive effect to a state court judgment that the judgment would have received under the law of the state in which it was rendered per *Allen v. McCurry*.[21]

The same exceptions available to state courts in declining to enforce out of state judgments (lack of personal and subject-matter jurisdiction, no notice and opportunity to be heard, fraud) apply to federal courts. Federal courts must apply the preclusion rules of the state from which the judgment was taken in determining the effect of the state-court judgment. The

[19] See the discussion of preclusion doctrines below.
[20] 28 USC. § 1738.
[21] 449 US 90 (1980).

Rooker-Feldman Doctrine provides that only the US Supreme Court has jurisdiction to review a state court decision, so lower federal courts lack jurisdiction to review final determinations of state courts.[22] But federal courts can conduct collateral review of state-court criminal convictions.

State courts are required to recognize and enforce federal-court judgments. Neither the Full Faith and Credit Clause nor the Full Faith and Credit Statute apply to state-court recognition of federal judgments. Authority for this principle stems from Art. III of the US Constitution, which recognizes a "judicial power" to decide "cases" and "controversies," and the Supremacy Clause. Congress can also bind state courts to federal preclusionary rules through (1) statutes enacted pursuant to a substantive power (e.g., the Federal Tort Claims Act) and (2) as a necessary and proper means of implementing Art. III.

In terms of the recognition and enforcement of foreign judgments, there is no federal standard that governs the recognition or enforcement by US courts of foreign-court judgments, and the US is not a party to any international agreement on the recognition of judgments (except the New York Convention on the recognition of foreign arbitral awards).

The US has sought some bilateral agreements with other countries (e.g., the United Kingdom) on the mutual recognition of judgments, but those attempts have failed. Negotiations on a Hague Jurisdiction and Judgments Convention were initiated in 1992 but suspended in 2001 because of disagreements over the scope of judicial jurisdiction. The US State Department has sought federal legislation concerning the recognition of foreign judgments. The ALI has also proposed draft legislation. Regardless, today the recognition of foreign judgments is generally a matter of state law.[23]

Certain foreign judgments are presumptively entitled to recognition if they are "final and conclusive and enforceable where rendered" even if subject to appeal. If judgment meets this standard, it is conclusive "to the extent it grants or denies recovery of a sum of money."

Mandatory grounds for the non-recognition of a foreign judgment include: (1) biased or unfair foreign courts; (2) a lack of personal jurisdiction; and (3) a lack of subject-matter jurisdiction. Discretionary grounds for the non-recognition of a foreign judgment include: (1) a lack of notice; (2) fraud; (3) public policy; (4) the existence of an inconsist-

---

[22] *See Rooker v. Fidelity Trust Co.*, 263 US 413 (1923); *D.C. Court of Appeals v. Feldman*, 460 US 462 (1983).

[23] It is worth noting that a majority of states have adopted a Uniform Foreign Money Judgments Recognition Act.

ent judgment; (5) a violation of a forum-selection clause; and (6) an inconvenient forum.

In a minority of states, state common law applies to the recognition of foreign judgments. That is to say, a minority of states adhere to state common law derived from the Supreme Court's 1895 decision in *Hilton v. Guyot*, which recognized international comity as a source of authority for US courts to recognize foreign judgments.[24]

In that case, a French citizen sought to enforce in the US a French court judgment against two New York residents arising out of business in France. The Court held that US courts may recognize foreign judgments but should give "due regard" to international law and the rights of US citizens or others under their jurisdiction. It adopted a rule of general common law permitting the enforcement of foreign judgments except where: (1) there has been no "due citation or voluntary appearance of the defendant"; (2) there exists no personal jurisdiction over the defendant; (3) there exists no subject-matter jurisdiction over the dispute; (4) there has been a showing of fraud or irregularity in the foreign proceeding; (5) the foreign cause of action violates US public policy; or (6) the foreign proceeding has been biased or unfair. Moreover, a court could decline to enforce a foreign judgment because of lack of reciprocity; that is to say, on the basis that foreign courts would not reciprocally enforce a US judgment in the reverse circumstances.

ii. Horizontal Power Sharing (i.e., Federal/Federal, EU/EU)

a. *Stare decisis*

Stare decisis is the common-law principle that provides that judges should respect the legal rules and interpretations found in prior decisions. Who creates binding precedent? In the United States, it is the US Supreme Court, US courts of appeals, state supreme courts, and state courts of appeals. Judges must follow the precedent of higher courts within their own system (vertical *stare decisis*). In most appellate courts, appellate judges also follow the precedent of their own court (horizontal *stare decisis*). It is, of course, possible to reconsider prior decisions.

b. Levels of scrutiny

US courts employ a hierarchy of standards to weigh the government's interest against a constitutional right or principle.[25] The US courts apply

---

24 159 US 113 (1895).

25 This parallels the EU's principle of proportionality.

one of three levels of scrutiny, based on the particular fundamental right at issue. Under strict scrutiny, the enactment in question must be narrowly tailored to advance a compelling government interest, and must be the least restrictive means of advancing that interest (e.g., discrimination based on race or religion; content-based speech restrictions). Under intermediate scrutiny—the enactment in question must be substantially related to an important government interest (e.g., discrimination based on gender; content-neutral speech restrictions—time, place, manner). Under rational basis scrutiny, the enactment in question must be rationally related to a legitimate government interest (e.g., most economic legislation). As with *stare decisis*, consistently using these tiers of scrutiny helps to ensure that like cases are treated alike by judges within the same system.

c. Preclusion doctrines

The doctrines of claim preclusion and issue preclusion aim to prevent re-litigation of cases or issues that have already been judged on the merits. They have the following purposes: (1) to enhance respect for the final judgments of other courts; (2) to prevent forum shopping and legal harassment; and (3) to promote judicial economy.

Claim preclusion (*res judicata*) provides that a final judgment on the merits of an action precludes the parties from re-litigating claims that were or could have been raised in that action. To apply, claim preclusion requires a final judgment on the merits in a prior suit involving the same parties and a subsequent suit based on the same cause of action. If claim preclusion applies, the court will dismiss as precluded the claim that was or could have been raised previously.

Issue preclusion (collateral estoppel) proscribes the re-litigation of issues of fact or law that have already been fully litigated in an earlier case. When an issue of fact or law is actually litigated and determined by a valid and final judgment, and the determination is essential to the judgment, the determination is conclusive in a subsequent action between the parties, whether on the same or a different claim. If issue preclusion applies, the court will bar a party from re-litigating the issue of fact or law that was determined in the prior proceeding.

d. Constitutional avoidance

Ashwander v. Tennessee Valley Authority[26] was the Supreme Court's first decision elaborating the doctrine of constitutional avoidance—the principle of avoiding a ruling on a constitutional question if the matter can be

---

[26] 297 US 288 (1936).

resolved on some other ground (often statutory).[27] In a concurring opinion in that case, Justice Brandeis argued that he would have affirmed the judgment below without reaching the constitutional issues presented. He stated: "Considerations of propriety as well as long-established practice, demand that we refrain from passing upon the constitutionality of an act of Congress unless obliged to do so. . . ." This principle of constitutional avoidance is important, Justice Brandeis reasoned, because judges are fallible, and passing upon the validity of an act of Congress is a grave and delicate power.

In his *Ashwander* concurrence, Justice Brandeis outlined seven rules under which the Court should avoid a constitutional question even though it falls within its jurisdiction:

(1) the Court will not pass upon the constitutionality of legislation in a "friendly, non-adversary" proceeding—to address a constitutional question requires a "real, earnest, and vital controversy between individuals";
(2) the Court will not anticipate a question of constitutional law in advance of the necessity of deciding it;
(3) the Court will not formulate a rule of constitutional law broader than is required by the precise facts to which it is to be applied;
(4) the Court will not pass upon a constitutional question presented by the record if there is some other ground on which the case may be disposed;
(5) the Court will not pass upon the validity of a statute upon the complaint of one who fails to show he is injured by the statute's operation;
(6) (of less relevance today) the Court will not pass upon the constitutionality of a statute at the insistence of one who has availed him of its benefits;[28] and
(7) when the validity of an act of Congress is called into question, it is a cardinal principle that the Court will firstly ascertain whether a construction of the statute is fairly possible by which the question may be avoided.

---

27 The underlying dispute concerned the Tennessee Valley Authority's construction of the Wilson Dam, and whether the Authority, a New Deal-era federal government program, was constitutional. The Supreme Court upheld Congress's authority to construct the dam.

28 Federal Rule of Civil Procedure 8(a) now allows alternative or inconsistent allegations.

Pullman abstention is also relevant to constitutional avoidance. In *Pullman*, the Supreme Court held that where a case presents a federal constitutional question, but determining a pending state-law question would obviate the need to reach the constitutional question, a federal court should abstain from hearing the case and allow the state court to decide the issue.[29] *Pullman* abstention is appropriate if (1) the case presents state and federal constitutional grounds for relief, (2) the proper resolution of the state ground is unclear, and (3) the disposition of the state ground could eliminate the need to reach the constitutional issue.

e. *Forum non conveniens*

Forum non conveniens is the discretionary power to decline jurisdiction and dismiss a case where a court in a different judicial system—often another country's court—is better suited to hear it. This sort of dismissal does not prevent re-filing in another forum.[30] Either the defendant or the court itself may invoke *forum non conveniens* to dismiss a case. *Forum non conveniens* requires a strong showing. Dismissal is proper only when (1) an adequate alternative forum is available, and (2) a balance of the parties' relative interests weighs heavily in favor of dismissal.

A court must afford some deference to the plaintiff's choice of forum. The Supreme Court has said "there is ordinarily a strong presumption in favor of the plaintiff's choice of forum, which may be overcome only when the private and public interest factors clearly point towards dismissal and trial in the alternative forum."[31] The private interest factors include: (1) the location of evidence and witnesses; (2) the residence of the parties; and (3) how a change in forum would affect each party's case—for example, whether the alternative forum would provide an adequate remedy. The public interest factors include: (1) the relative administrative burdens of the two court systems (e.g., the congestion of each court, the burdens on jurors required to examine translated testimony); and (2) the relative interests of the two forums, or their "public policy" regarding the issues presented.

A court may condition its *forum non conveniens* dismissal on, for example, the defendant's agreement that it will waive certain defenses that would prevent the plaintiff from re-filing, or the alternative forum's agreement to use American-style discovery. *Forum non conveniens* dis-

---

[29] That is to say, *Pullman* is *Ashwander* and federalism combined.

[30] Because we have federal statutes authorizing the transfer of venue within the federal system, 28 USC. §§ 1404, 1406, *forum non conveniens* applies only when the superior forum is in a foreign country or is a state court or territorial court.

[31] *Piper Aircraft Co. v. Reyno*, 454 US 235 (1981) [255].

missals were relatively rare in the past, but with the increase in federal court cases involving overseas events (e.g., airplane crashes, international trade disputes), the mechanism has been employed to limit federal courts' disposition of cases with only tangential connections to the US.

f. Multidistrict litigation (MDL)

Multidistrict litigation arises when multiple cases are filed against the same or multiple defendant(s) in federal and state courts[32] (overlapping and competing cases). MDL permits the centralization of mass civil claims or complex civil claims, such as securities fraud claims, antitrust claims, toxic tort claims, products liability claims (against, e.g., cigarette manufacturers or pharmaceutical companies), and personal-injury actions.

The federal statute creating the MDL procedure (28 USC. § 1407) was enacted in 1968 and permits civil actions filed or removed to federal court to be transferred to one district for coordinated or consolidated pretrial proceedings if the actions "involve one or more common questions of fact." The Judicial Panel on Multidistrict Litigation—composed of seven federal judges appointed by the Chief Justice of the United States—may, upon its own initiative, transfer an action if it determines that such transfer "will be for the convenience of parties and witnesses and will promote the just and efficient conduct of such actions." A party to a civil action may also move the panel to transfer its case.

The MDL statute does not grant the transferee court discretion to retain the cases for trial, rather than remand it back to the original court (even when both courts would prefer to keep the case in the transferee court for trial). But in practice, most cases are settled either by class actions or an aggregated non-class settlement. The largest and longest-lasting MDL is in the Eastern District of Pennsylvania.[33] This MDL was created in 1991 by the Judicial Panel on Multidistrict Litigation to manage all asbestos personal injury and wrongful death cases in the federal courts. As of March 24, 2014, nearly 187,000 cases have been transferred to MDL No. 875. Of that total, 183,713 of those cases have been terminated and 2,876 cases remain pending.

g. Federal/state

This kind of litigation arises when multiple claims are filed with state and federal courts. There is cooperation between the courts, sometimes by

---

[32] Unless claims filed in state courts are lawfully removed (removal jurisdiction) to federal court, they are not subject to the MDL process.

[33] MDL No. 875, *In Re: Asbestos Prods. Liab. Litig.*

telephone—sharing pretrial proceedings, creating a joint document repository for use in federal and state cases, and other coordination. Otherwise, there would be a race to judgment.

h. Bankruptcy

Federal courts have exclusive jurisdiction over bankruptcy under the US Constitution (Art. I, Section 8, Clause 4)—bankruptcy cases cannot be filed in state court. The Bankruptcy Code, codified as title 11 of the United States Code, has been amended several times since its enactment. It is the uniform federal law that governs all bankruptcy cases in the US. The procedural aspects of the bankruptcy process are governed by the Federal Rules of Bankruptcy Procedure and the local rules of each bankruptcy court. The Bankruptcy Rules incorporate many of the ordinary rules of federal civil procedure, and also contain a set of official forms for use in bankruptcy cases. The Bankruptcy Code and Bankruptcy Rules (and local rules) set forth the formal legal procedures for dealing with the debt problems of individuals and businesses.

There is usually a separate bankruptcy court for each judicial district in the country. Each state has one or more districts. There are 90 bankruptcy districts across the country. The overwhelming majority of all proceedings in bankruptcy are held before a US bankruptcy judge, whose decisions are subject to appeal—first to the district court, then the court of appeals—and may be reviewed by the US Supreme Court.

Having sketched out the general framework of power sharing among courts in the US, I will turn to four landmark Supreme Court cases embodying the principles of judicial interaction I have described.

EXAMPLES OF LANDMARK SUPREME COURT CASES

i. Example 1: *Brown v. Board of Education*, 347 US 483 (1954) (*Brown I*), *Brown v. Board of Education*, 349 US 294 (1955) (*Brown II*) *and Cooper v. Aaron*, 358 US 1 (1958)

The Equal Protection Clause of the US Constitution (Fourteenth Amendment, Clause 1) provides: "No state shall . . . deny to any person within its jurisdiction the equal protection of the laws." The Equal Protection Clause also applies against the federal government, as it has been read into the Fifth Amendment through the doctrine of reverse incorporation. In *Brown*, the Supreme Court (Warren, C.J.) held that the state-ordered segregation of public schools violated the Equal Protection Clause.

a. Facts

The plaintiffs were African American elementary and high school students who were denied access to public schools in their communities that only white children could attend. In 17 states, public education was segregated—schools were designated either for white students or for African American students. Four more states permitted but did not require segregation in public education. At the time, constitutional law permitted segregation of public schools so long as the schools designated for African American students were equal in tangible respects, for example, if segregated schools were of equal quality in teachers, buildings, and curricula. This doctrine of "separate but equal" was established in the Supreme Court's 1896 decision *Plessy v. Ferguson*,[34] which had upheld state laws requiring racial segregation in public facilities. In practice, the separate facilities were of vastly inferior quality.

b. Principles illustrated by the cases

The cases illustrate two of the proposed principles. First, they illustrate disapplication through the US Constitution's Supremacy Clause, which provides that federal law is supreme and that state courts must follow federal law when a conflict arises between federal law and state law. Second, they illustrate mutual recognition through *stare decisis*, under which the courts follow prior precedent; where the relevant precedent is a Supreme Court holding, the Supreme Court follows it unless it finds good reason to depart (which the cases also illustrate).

Principle 1: disapplication (US supremacy clause) Supreme Court precedent interpreting the Constitution is the binding law of the land. In *Brown I* the Supreme Court consolidated four cases challenging segregation laws in Kansas, Virginia, South Carolina, and Delaware. In three of the four cases (all but the Delaware case), the federal district courts upheld the state segregation laws under the "separate but equal" doctrine established in *Plessy v. Ferguson*.

The Delaware state court found the segregated black schools in the city of Wilmington vastly inferior to nearby white schools. Exercising its equity powers, it ordered the immediate admission of the plaintiffs to white schools in their communities. But the court also recognized that "a lower court [cannot] reject a principle of United States Constitutional law which has been adopted by fair implication by the highest court of the

---

34 163 US 537 (1896).

land."[35] Moreover, the judge reasoned, "I believe the 'separate but equal' doctrine in education should be rejected . . . but I also believe its rejection must come from [the Supreme] Court."

In *Brown I*, the Supreme Court finally rejected the "separate but equal" doctrine. At least in the context of education, the Supreme Court in *Brown I* held that *Plessy*'s declaration of "separate but equal" no longer had force. The principle behind the Supremacy Clause meant that the holding of *Brown I* bound state and federal courts alike.

Once the Supreme Court determined that "separate educational facilities are inherently unequal" and denied equal protection to African American students, the states were required to eliminate segregation.[36] But the Supreme Court's decision in *Brown I* was not harmoniously received by all the states. In the wake of the decision, some states resisted desegregation.

The Court postponed deciding how it would effectuate its holding in *Brown I* until the next term. In a case often referred to as *Brown II*, the Court delegated to the courts that had heard the four cases consolidated in *Brown I* the task of deciding whether state school authorities were implementing the Constitution in good faith. Noting that "[a]ll provisions of federal, state, or local law" must yield to the principle that "discrimination in public education is unconstitutional," the Court instructed the lower courts to enter any orders and decrees necessary to eliminate racial segregation in the public schools "with all deliberate speed".[37] These pronouncements reflected the Supremacy Clause in action.

Principle 2: mutual recognition (stare decisis) *Stare decisis* is the principle that once a constitutional case is decided, its holding generally remains the law (unless or until the Constitution is amended to provide otherwise), even if the personnel on a court changes. *Brown I* and *Brown II* reflect both this rule and an exception to it.

As noted, in *Plessy*, the Supreme Court had upheld state laws requiring racial segregation in public facilities. By 1954, it had become apparent that separate educational facilities were inherently unequal, and that the principle articulated in *Plessy* was so fundamentally inconsistent with the US Constitution that it could not be permitted to remain the law. Accordingly, the Court broke with *stare decisis* and overruled its own precedent. The Court could do so because *stare decisis* is, as the Court has

---

35 *Belton v. Gebhart*, 87 A.2d 862 (Del. Ch. Ct. 1952) [865].

36 *Brown v. Bd. of Educ.*, 347 US 483 (1954) [495].

37 *Brown v. Bd. of Educ.* (*Brown II*), 349 US 294 (1955) [300].

noted, not an "inexorable command" or a "mechanical formula," but "a principle of policy."[38]

In contrast, the Court relied heavily on *stare decisis* to bolster its *Brown I* decision in *Brown II*. In *Brown II*,[39] the Court gestured toward the principle of *stare decisis* when it said that "the vitality of the [] constitutional principles [set forth in *Brown I*] cannot be allowed to yield simply because of disagreement with them."[40] Accordingly, it determined that the defendants—local boards of education, acting as agents of the states—would have to "make a prompt and reasonable start toward full compliance" with its previous ruling.[41]

* * *

A follow-on case further demonstrates these two principles in action. The Supreme Court held in *Cooper v. Aaron*, 358 US 1 (1958) (Warren, C.J.), that states are bound by the Supreme Court's decisions interpreting federal constitutional law. Even where a school board's desegregation plan is met with resistance, the board, acting as a state agent, must comply with the holdings in *Brown I* and *Brown II* and bring about the end of racial segregation in the public schools "with all deliberate speed."

After *Brown*, the Little Rock, Arkansas School Board began formulating a plan to desegregate its schools. But the Arkansas legislature amended the state's constitution to oppose the *Brown I* and *Brown II* decisions and enacted a law relieving children from compulsory attendance at desegregated schools. Nonetheless, the Little Rock School Board continued with preparations to carry out its desegregation plan, and set a date—September 2, 1957—on which nine African American students would be admitted to the previously all-white Central High School.

The day before desegregation was to go into effect in Little Rock, the Arkansas Governor dispatched the Arkansas National Guard to Central High School. Every morning for three weeks, the students attempted to enter the school but were blocked by the National Guard. After the district court granted an injunction against the Governor enjoining him from preventing the students from entering the high school, the National Guard withdrew from the school. Eventually, the US Government dispatched federal troops to Central High School so that the students could

38 *Payne v. Tennessee*, 501 US 808 (1991) [828].
39 *Brown II*, 349 US 294 (1955) [301].
40 Ibid., [300].
41 Ibid., [300].

be admitted. Federal troops remained at Central High School for the rest of the school year.

The US Constitution is the supreme law of the land, and the US Supreme Court is the ultimate authority in expounding its meaning. The decisions in *Brown* interpreted the Fourteenth Amendment and are therefore the supreme law of the land. They must be followed by the states. As the Court in *Cooper v. Aaron* explained eloquently, "It is, of course, quite true that the responsibility for public education is primarily the concern of the States, but it is equally true that such responsibilities, like all other state activity, must be exercised consistently with federal constitutional requirements as they apply to state action." Under our federal system of government, the equal protection principles announced in *Brown*, and the states' obedience to those principles, "are indispensable for the protection of the freedoms guaranteed by our fundamental charter for all of us. Our constitutional ideal of equal justice under law is thus made a living truth."[42]

ii. Example 2: *New York Times Co. v. Sullivan*, 376 US 254 (1964)

In the post-*Brown* era in the American South, segregationists used libel suits against media outlets and civil rights activists to try to impede the granting of civil rights and bankrupt the leaders of the Civil Rights Movement. This case is an example of federal constitutional principles of free speech overriding state defamation law. Normally, defamation law, and tort law generally, are matters of state law, subject to state supreme court interpretation. But in this case, the federal Constitution trumped state law. The Court (Brennan, J.) held that the First Amendment limits a state's power to award damages for libel in actions brought by public officials against critics of their official conduct, in effect bringing state law in accordance with the Constitution.

a. Facts

Sullivan, an elected City Commissioner in Montgomery, Alabama, brought a state civil libel action against the *New York Times* and four civil rights activists, alleging that statements in an advertisement calling attention to civil rights violations in the American South and defending the Rev. Dr. Martin Luther King, Jr. defamed Sullivan. It was uncontroverted that many statements in the advertisement were either false or inaccurate

---

42 *Cooper v. Aaron*, 358 US 1 (1958) [19–20].

descriptions of the events they described. A jury awarded Sullivan $500,000, and the Supreme Court of Alabama affirmed this decision.

b. Principles illustrated by the case

This case illustrates two of the proposed principles: the principle of the Supremacy Clause and the principle of persuasive authority. In respect of the first, the First Amendment protections for speech and the press limit a state's ability to award damages in a libel action under state law. The Court departed from the traditional common law standard, which required a defendant to prove the statement's truth, by placing the burden on the plaintiff to prove the statement's untruth. In respect of the second, the Court articulated an "actual malice" standard governing recovery by a public official in a libel action, derived from state court opinions.

Principle 1: disapplication (US supremacy clause) State libel law is subject to the First Amendment. The adoption of the Fourteenth Amendment incorporated the First Amendment against the states.[43] State judges must interpret state libel law consistent with the First Amendment. In *N.Y. Times Co.*, Alabama's libel law was held to be constitutionally deficient because it placed the burden on the speaker to prove truth, and that stifled speech. The Court departed from the traditional common law of defamation because it determined that the First Amendment's guarantees of freedom of speech and of the press compelled a different rule of law. The Court's holding promotes the consistency of the law throughout the US by requiring state defamation laws to respect First Amendment safeguards.

Principle 2: comparative reasoning The Court adopted the rule that a public official is able to recover damages for libel relating to his official conduct only if he proves that the statement was made with "actual malice"—with knowledge that it was false or with reckless disregard of its falsity. The "actual malice" standard had been adopted by numerous state courts. This reflects the principle of persuasive authority. The Court elevated a rule that many states had adopted into one of federal constitutional law.

The Court also looked to its own prior precedent. It had previously held that a public official enjoyed an absolute privilege from a private libel suit for statements made "within the outer perimeter" of his official duties.[44]

---

[43] Incorporation is the process by which a provision of the federal Constitution is read to apply to state governments.

[44] *Barr v. Matteo*, 360 US 564 (1959).

The Court believed that a similar privilege should be extended to private citizens for criticism of the official conduct of government officials.

iii. Example 3: *Younger v. Harris*, 401 US 37 (1971)

Federal courts rely on abstention doctrines when refusing to hear a case within their jurisdiction if hearing the case would offend comity, equitable discretion, or judicial administration. Federal courts may abstain when multiple cases involving the same issues are brought in both federal and state court. *Younger v. Harris* is a landmark case in abstention doctrine and reflects the historic common-law maxim that equity will not enjoin a criminal prosecution.

Younger serves, in part, to protect the principle of comity in the US legal system. Comity is the legal principle that legal entities—such as courts from different jurisdictions—will mutually recognize each other's legal authority and acts. The underlying notion is that different jurisdictions will reciprocate with each other out of deference, mutuality, and respect. In *Younger*, the Court (Black, J.) held a federal court should not interfere with a state prosecution, even if the prosecution sought to enforce a law that likely violated the federal Constitution.

a. Facts

Harris was charged in state court with violating a California criminal law proscribing the teaching of any doctrine that advocates the commission of a crime, sabotage, or act of terrorism as a means of effecting political change. After the state prosecution began, he filed a complaint in federal court asking the federal court to issue an injunction to stop a California District Attorney (Younger) from prosecuting him, because the act of prosecution itself violated his First Amendment rights. The federal court refused to intervene because to do so would violate US notions of comity and "Our Federalism."

b. Principles illustrated by the case

The case illustrates the proposed principle of using deferential techniques. Two US statutes are particularly relevant in this regard: the All Writs Act, which allows federal courts to issue "all writs necessary or appropriate in aid of their respective jurisdictions" and gives federal courts broad discretion to interfere with state judicial proceedings, and the Anti-Injunction Act, which bars federal court interference with state court proceedings except in extremely rare circumstances. But the case is significant for creating a new abstention doctrine. Abstention is the process by which a federal court will occasionally refuse to hear a case, even if it has the power to do so, when it appears a state court is in a better position to hear it.

Principle: deferential techniques The All Writs Act gives federal courts broad discretion to interfere with state judicial proceedings. Under the Act, the federal court in *Younger* could have issued an injunction to stop the state court proceeding in order to ensure that the First Amendment was properly interpreted and respected. This power to interfere with state courts, however, is tempered by the Anti-Injunction Act and US courts' policies of abstention.

We have long had laws that prevent the federal government from interfering too much with state courts. A statute first passed in 1793 unconditionally provided, "[N]or shall a writ of injunction be granted to stay proceedings in any court of a state." The current version of that statute—the Anti-Injunction Act—is almost identical, but creates only three exceptions to the rule: (1) if Congress explicitly authorizes the federal courts to do so; (2) if it is "necessary in aid of [the federal courts'] jurisdiction;" or (3) to protect or effectuate the federal courts' judgments. Federal judges also created an exception to allow a federal court to interfere when a failure to enjoin the state prosecution would result in irreparable harm (*Ex Parte Young*). But the Court in *Younger* did not address this statute. *Younger*, rather, illustrates that even when a court *can* interfere, it often *chooses* not to.

In *Younger*, the Supreme Court discussed the larger question of how the federal government should interact with state governments. It stressed notions of "comity" and "Our Federalism." The notions together capture the "proper respect for state functions, a recognition of the fact that the entire country is made up of a Union of separate state governments, and a continuance of the belief that the National Government will fare best if the States and their institutions are left free to perform their separate functions in their separate ways."[45]

It also described the US federal system as "a system in which there is sensitivity to the legitimate interests of both State and National Governments, and in which the National Government, anxious though it may be to vindicate and protect federal rights and federal interests, always endeavors to do so in ways that will not unduly interfere with the legitimate activities of the states."[46] With these principles in mind, the Court in *Younger* decided that it was improper to interfere with an ongoing state

---

45 *Younger v. Harris*, 401 US 37 (1971) [44].
46 Ibid.

prosecution, even if it could have done so under the All Writs Act. This is true even if the state law appears, on its face, to be inconsistent with federal constitutional law, and even if the federal right that needs to be protected is a core constitutional right (in *Younger* it was free speech).

But this does not mean that a federal court will never interfere with an ongoing state prosecution. The Court has said it would be proper to interfere if: (1) the state prosecution has been brought in bad faith to harass the defendant; and (2) the individual does not have a chance to raise his federal constitutional claims in the state process. The federal courts respect state courts and trust them to interpret the federal constitution and to protect the rights found therein. This trust and respect means that even if federal courts have the power to interfere with state court proceedings under the All Writs Act, they will choose to stay their hand and allow the state court system to operate.[47]

CONCLUSION

US federal courts employ several principles analogous to those of "judicial interaction" to resolve conflicts within our legal systems on questions of fundamental rights. This chapter has aimed at illustrating how these principles operate within the US legal systems, and at complementing the perspectives of European institutions on judicial interaction.

---

[47] Contrast *Brown* and *New York Times Co.*, discussed above.

5. Spanish courts, the European Court and consumer law: some thoughts on their interaction

Fernando Gómez Pomar and Karolina Lyczkowska*

I. INTRODUCTION

European consumer law has grown and evolved by means of legislative measures (harmonization Directives) initiated by the European Commission and agreed – more or less reluctantly, depending on the case – by the Member States. However, it has taken its current shape and content, and increasingly so, through judicial lawmaking. The Court of Justice of the European Union (CJEU) has been at the helm of such endeavours of courts' production of consumer law. This prominent role of the CJEU in crafting European consumer law has been made possible, to a large extent, by the cooperation and complicity of national courts seeking guidance from the CJEU in the interpretation of the EU consumer *acquis* (or, as we hypothesize, perhaps in pursuit of their own policy goals in the field with the instrumental assistance of the CJEU).

To those familiar with European consumer law, it is not significant news to state that some of the landmark consumer decisions of the CJEU have been prompted by preliminary references of Spanish courts: *Océano*,[1]

* We would like to thank Marco Celentani for very helpful comments. Fernando Gómez would like to thank the research funding from ICREA, an agency of the Government of Catalonia.

[1] Joined Cases C-240/98, C-244/98 *Océano Grupo Editorial SA v Rocio Murciano Quintero and Salvat Editores SA* EU:C:2000:346.

Mostaza Claro,[2] *El Corte Inglés*,[3] *Banesto*,[4] *Aziz*,[5] to cite just a few. At first blush, thus, it would appear as if Spanish courts should be considered as very collaborative and committed participants in the development of European consumer law through the expansion and refinement of CJEU case law.

The truth is, however, that the inclination of Spanish courts to ask the CJEU how to deal with the conformity with EU law of legal solutions on various issues of consumer contracting has not followed a uniform or predictable path. Until a few years ago, while not insignificant, Spanish courts had not been particularly prominent or energetic in respect of their preliminary reference activity in the consumer context or, for that matter, in other areas of law.

In more recent years, the scenario changed abruptly. Spanish judges, especially those of first instance,[6] have been very active in referring questions for preliminary rulings to the CJEU in connection with the consumer *acquis*, and particularly on the compatibility with European law of different Spanish rules governing mortgage foreclosure. These referrals concern both the mortgage rules pre-existing the financial crisis, and the rules that the successive Spanish governments and legislatures have passed in response to the social unrest generated by the sharp increase in mortgage loan foreclosures, and as a reaction to some decisions by the CJEU dealing precisely with this set of rules.

Social and economic conditions have played a large role in this observable trend in Spanish courts. The severe economic crisis experienced by Spain and other economies after 2008 hit the housing market in several countries – very prominently, Spain – particularly hard. It hit more

---

[2] Case C-168/05 *Mostaza Claro v Centro Movil Milenium SL* EU:C:2006:675.

[3] Case C-192/94 *El Corte Inglés* EU:C:1996:88. In this decision, the European Court ruled that Directive 87/102 on consumer credit could not by itself have direct horizontal effect. Specifically, the provision whose applicability was discussed was the right of action of a consumer against a lender, based on lack of conformity or defects in the supply of goods or services, which was contemplated in the mentioned Directive, but not in the national law, due to delays in transposition. Therefore, without prejudice as to the binding nature of Directives as regards Member States, a consumer would not be entitled to a right to claim grounded on a provision in a Directive that has not been yet transposed.

[4] Case C-618/10 *Banesto* EU:C:2012:349.

[5] Case C-415/11 *Aziz* EU:C:2013:164.

[6] Appeal Courts and the Supreme Court appear to have been more reluctant to raise preliminary references before the CJEU. See Juan Mayoral Díaz-Asensio *et al*, 'El juez español como juez de la Unión Europea,' (2013) 48 *Revista Española de Derecho Europeo* 136.

severely mortgage debtors who, in large numbers, had acquired homes in the years preceding the crisis (2002–07). This period had experienced a housing boom in various places (including Ireland, Spain, UK, and the US). In the case of Spain, the combination of heavy household indebtedness levels secured by home mortgages,[7] on the one hand, and rising unemployment and decreasing household revenues ensuing from the economic recession, on the other, resulted in an explosion of mortgage defaults and foreclosures. This, in turn, negatively affected economic activity generally, and aggravated the recession.[8]

The official quarterly data from the Spanish Council on the Judiciary (*Consejo General del Poder Judicial*) on mortgage foreclosure proceedings (addressed against both households and firms: there exists no disaggregated data until well into the financial crisis) in Spanish courts clearly illustrate the phenomenon. The number of proceedings jumps from around 5,500 per quarter in 2007, to over 27,000 per quarter in 2010, an almost fivefold increase in three years. Figure 5.1 shows this devastating evolution.

Those households who acquired homes in the peak of the housing boom (2004–07) were those most hard hit. According to data on home foreclosures in the second quarter of 2014 just published by the Spanish Statistical Office (*Instituto Nacional de Estadística*), almost 53 per cent of foreclosures affect mortgages agreed in the span of just three years: 2005, 2006 and 2007.[9]

The scenario we have just sketched has surely led Spanish courts to be confronted – unexpectedly, and we would add, reluctantly – with the pressing need to cope on their own with a social emergency affecting large numbers of families. Furthermore it was a situation widely publicized

---

[7] The levels of indebtedness reached peak levels with the housing boom, in large part due to a relaxation in the risk assessment standards observed by Spanish banks (especially savings banks) leading to unjustifiably high loan-to-value transactions, and to interest rate spreads that were too low given the economic conditions of borrowers: See, Ozlem Akin *et al*, 'The Real Estate and Credit Bubble: Evidence from Spain', (2014) *SERIEs-Journal of the Spanish Economic Association* 223.

[8] On the role of over-indebtedness, and particularly on that of home mortgage debt burdening lower-income families in precipitating and deepening the financial crisis, see, Atif Mian and Amir Sufi, *House of Debt: How They (and You) Caused the Great Recession, and How We Can Prevent It from Happening Again* (University of Chicago Press 2014).

[9] See Instituto Nacional de Estadística, 'Estadística sobre Ejecuciones Hipotecarias (EH); Segundo trimestre de 2014', Datos provisionales available at: http://www.ine.es/daco/daco42/eh/eh0214.pdf.

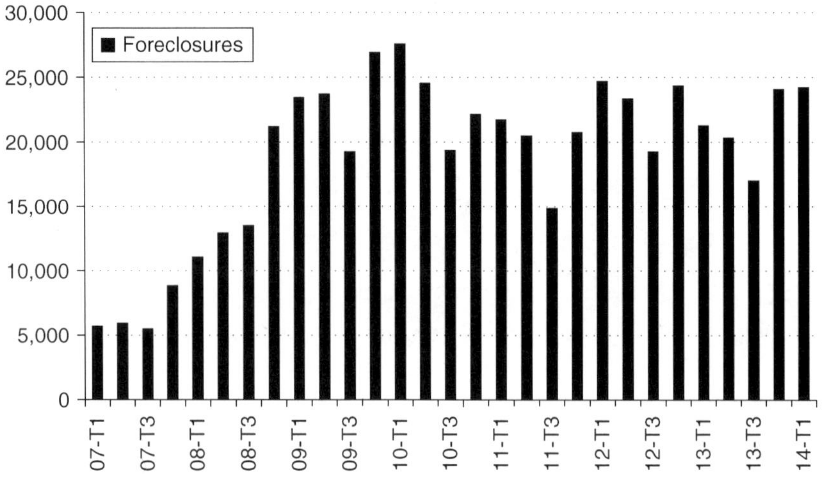

Figure 5.1 Mortgage foreclosures in Spain 2007–14

by the media. Why, in the face of this dilemma, they have resorted to the CJEU for assistance in trying to find (some) legal tools to respond to mounting questions about their role in protecting citizens' rights in times of distress, is not entirely obvious. It is true that several (though not by any means the majority of) Spanish legal scholars started to criticize the Spanish mortgage system, the foreclosure regime in particular, and denounced the timid mortgage reforms sponsored by the Spanish legislature as chaotic and insufficient for the purpose of protecting mortgage debtors.[10]

From this perspective, European law (whatever this may exactly mean in the complex scenario of mortgage loan contracts between firms and consumers, where consumer protection rules, the procedural autonomy of the Member States, and fundamental rights in the Charter may be intertwined) was perceived by some courts and commentators as a source – perhaps even the only safe one – of legal solutions to a perceived scenario of social urgency, at least in the short term. And mistakenly or not, most courts and observers consider that 'time is of the essence' in relation to this problem.

Spanish courts, then, turned to the protective rules against unfair

[10] See, amongst others, María Angeles Alcalá Díaz, *La protección del deudor hipotecario* (Aranzadi 2013) 211 *et seq.*; José María Fernández Seijo, *La defensa de los consumidores en las ejecuciones hipotecarias* (Bosch 2013) 238.

contract terms enshrined in European law, and more particularly, to the CJEU as the authoritative interpreter of their meaning, scope, and application, for a tool to cope with the social pressure to provide legal responses to the unrest caused by the foreclosure crisis in Spain. In this chapter, we try to offer some (rationality-based) explanations of the phenomenon, and advance a tentative theory of the interaction between Spanish courts (specially, lower courts), the Spanish government or political establishment, and the CJEU in times of economic depression.

The last chapter in the saga involving the lower Spanish courts and preliminary references on consumer law issues has been written by a very recent decision of the CJEU.[11] This decision holds that the previous case law of the Spanish Supreme Court (Decisions of 9 May 2013 and 25 March 2015) placing temporal limitations on the restitution of amounts paid by consumers to financial institutions on the basis of certain terms in a mortgage loan contract that were later declared unfair, is incompatible with European law.[12] The Commercial Court No. 1 of Granada and the Alicante Provincial Appeals Court had asked whether the rulings and the case law of the Spanish Supreme Court were compatible with Directive 93/13. The CJEU held in its response that EU law precludes national case law in accordance with which the restitutionary effects connected with the invalidity of an unfair term are restricted to the amounts overpaid after the delivery of the decision holding that the term is unfair. The Bank of Spain estimates that this CJEU ruling will have an impact of around 4 billion euros on the balance sheet of the Spanish banking industry. The story, however, may not be over yet, and new developments are likely to arrive in the coming months.

This chapter will be organized as follows: in Section II we will show how preliminary references by Spanish courts have evolved over time, and we refer to the literature that has dealt with the drivers of preliminary reference activity in Spain and in other Member States. Section III will present a summary of the main issues raised by preliminary

---

[11] Judgment of 21 December 2016 (Joined Cases C-154/15, *Francisco Gutiérrez Naranjo v Cajasur Banco SAU*, C-307/15 *Ana María Palacios Martínez v Banco Bilbao Vizcaya Argentaria*, and C-308/15 *Banco Popular Español SA v Emilio Irles López and Teresa Torres Andreu* EU:C:2016:980).

[12] Notwithstanding the importance of this decision and the magnitude of its effects, we will not analyze it here, since it was rendered a considerable time after the chapter was prepared for publication, and just before the final proofs were reviewed. Nevertheless, we believe that this last episode fits very well into the tentative theory we present in this chapter.

references from Spanish courts to the CJEU in the consumer context. Section IV will present a sketch of a stylized game-theoretic explanation for the behaviour of Spanish courts in this matter as a strategy in their interaction with a Spanish government with divergent policy views on how to deal with mortgage loan defaults. Section V briefly concludes the chapter.

II. DYNAMICS AND RATIONALES OF PRELIMINARY REFERENCES

Our first task is to verify whether data support our intuition that Spanish courts have increased preliminary reference filings as a response to the challenges posed by the mortgage foreclosure crisis in Spain and the societal perception of the gravity of the situation. The salience of the issues involved, and our academic proximity to the matter at hand, may have biased our estimates of the effects – and their dimension – of the economic recession on the willingness of Spanish courts to resort to the CJEU for solutions in the consumer context.

Data on preliminary references filed by Spanish courts as contained in Table 5.1 below seem to broadly confirm our intuitions. Although consumer law and consumer protection had figured – albeit not prominently – among the subject matters over which Spanish courts had sought guidance from the CJEU in the past, both in absolute terms, and relative to the total number of references from Spanish courts, the numbers have increased very significantly since the crisis, and especially after the consequences of the crisis started to be felt by large portions of the Spanish population in terms of rising unemployment, salary adjustments, and perhaps specifically from the perspective of lower civil and commercial courts, of mortgage foreclosures and evictions.

By simply looking at the raw numbers, one gets the impression that the number of preliminary references from Spanish courts dealing with consumer law was not at all remarkable prior to the 2008 meltdown of the Spanish economy. An even more pronounced increase is observable since 2012; by the middle of the year 2014, the Spanish courts had initiated a surprisingly large – given the prior record – number of 12 preliminary reference proceedings on a consumer-related legal issue. Obviously, this has had a significant effect on the total number of referrals originating in Spanish courts.

Graphically (see Figure 5.2), the evolution of the total number of references and those concerning consumer matters shows the new post-crisis scenario.

Table 5.1 Preliminary references (including consumer-related referrals) filed by Spanish courts to the CJEU 1994–2014

Year	Number of requests regarding consumer protection	Total number of requests
1994	1	13
1995	0	10
1996	0	6
1997	1	9
1998*	1	55
1999	0	4
2000	1	5
2001	0	4
2002	0	3
2003	0	8
2004	1	8
2005	1	10
2006	0	17
2007	0	14
2008	3	17
2009	0	11
2010	2	22
2011	2	27
2012	5	16
2013	9	26
2014	12	28

Note: * It should be noted that the peak of total number of requests in 1998, showing 55 referrals, in reality corresponds to only 16 different matters, since there were joined cases (cases C-240/98 to C-244/98, and C-110/98 to C-147/98) dealing with exactly the same issue and provision.

Figure 5.3 below shows the percentage of the total number of Spanish referrals represented by consumer-related referrals. The pattern after 2008 appears to be distinct from that observable in the second half of the 1990s and the first years of the new millennium. The percentages (with the outlier year of 2009) are consistently larger, particularly in 2012–14. This is an important detail, given the self-reinforcing nature of the strategic incentives to refer matters to the CJEU in order to advance policy preferences divergent from those of the government and legislature.

Moreover, the correlation between the numbers of consumer-oriented preliminary references from Spanish courts to mortgage foreclosure levels in Spain appears to be present. We do not imply however that these figures alone indicate that the economic conditions for large number of families in

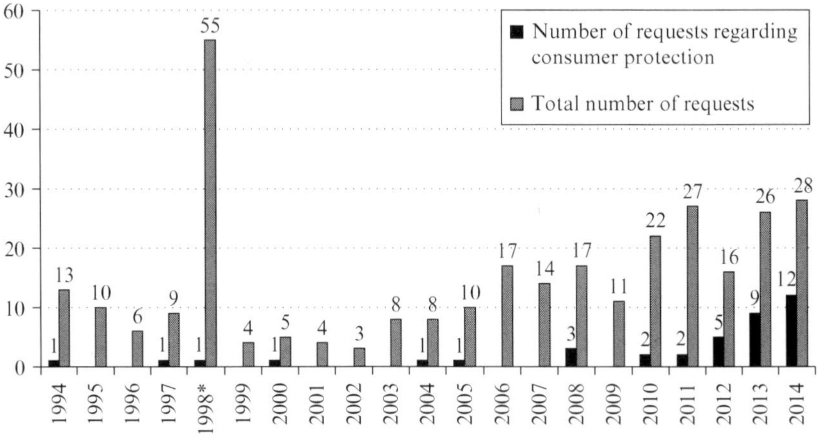

Note: See note to Table 5.1.

Figure 5.2 Evolution of questions referred for a preliminary ruling requested by Spanish courts to the CJEU

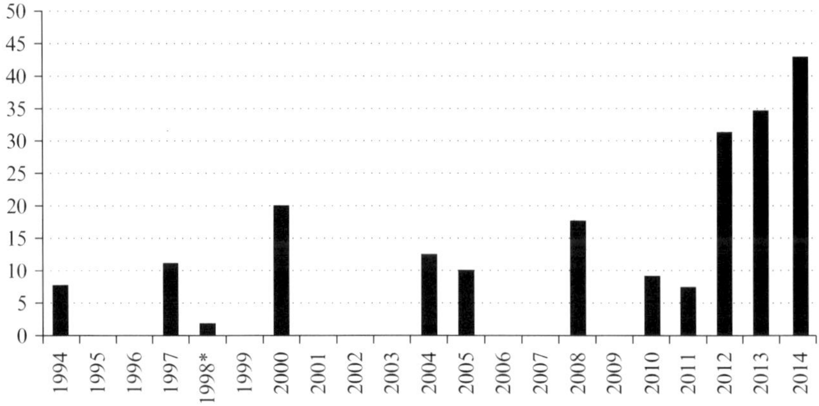

Figure 5.3 Percentage of the total number of Spanish referrals to the CJEU represented by consumer-related referrals

the aftermath of the financial crisis has 'caused' an increase in the number of consumer-related preliminary references.

It seems consistent with the above data, however, particularly if the numbers are complemented with the more detailed analysis of the content of the referrals by Spanish courts in recent years presented in Section III below, to argue, as we do, that an important driver of the willingness of Spanish courts (on their own motion, or prompted by the lawyers to the parties facing foreclosure and eviction) to initiate preliminary references on consumer law matters, has been the mortgage foreclosure crisis in Spain after 2012. The foreclosure crisis does not appear to recede (at least for now), even while the overall Spanish economic situation appears to return to positive growth levels (at least at the time of writing this contribution). Data from the Spanish statistical office (INE) reveal that the number of home foreclosures in the second quarter of the year 2014 was up by more than 8 per cent over the same quarter of 2013.

Some previous contributions have looked into the behaviour of the Spanish courts *vis-à-vis* European law, and more particularly, at the interaction between the courts in Spain and the CJEU, essentially through two channels: a 'low-cost' one, represented by citations to CJEU case law, and a 'high-cost' one by means of asking the CJEU for a preliminary ruling. Ramos Romeu (2006)[13] has looked empirically at the attitude of Spanish courts towards the precedents set by the CJEU. With a large database of Spanish decisions that either apply or cite European law, the study finds that Spanish courts tend to 'shield' themselves more often behind citations of the CJEU case law when enforcing the supremacy of European law over domestic Spanish law, and also when they are ruling against the Spanish government. Despite this, the author claims that Spanish courts do not seem to be very politically strategic, since he finds that the – favourable or unfavourable – position of the Spanish government in office *vis-à-vis* a given policy enshrined in a piece of European law, as proxied by the presence of the government in the underlying litigation, does not seem to have great explanatory power in respect of the behaviour of Spanish courts dealing with European law issues.

Mayoral[14] uses a database of adjudicatory practices of the Spanish Supreme Court concerning European law (and comprising, inter alia, preliminary references and citations to CJEU case law) to conclude that the 'threat' of retaliation by political authorities is an important explanatory variable for citing precedents of the CJEU, a 'shielding' strategy to protect their own judgments that may run against the preferences of governmental authorities. The study also claims that there is some 'substitution' effect

---

[13] Francisco Ramos Romeu, 'Law and Politics in the Application of EC Law: Spanish Courts and the ECJ 1986-2000' (2006) 43 *Common Market Law Review* 395.

[14] Juan Mayoral Díaz-Asensio, 'Government Contained? Explaining Spanish Supreme Court's decisions on EU law', European University Institute Working Paper (EUI 2012).

between preliminary references and citations to prior case law of the CJEU, and that the Spanish Supreme Court could prefer to select previous CJEU rulings that fit the legal or policy preferences of the Spanish Supreme Court, rather than risking a new ruling from the CJEU that may not correspond to those preferences.

Even if the latter contention were true generally (and we remain agnostic towards it), the use of citations of older CJEU cases instead of 'prompting' a new – and obviously uncertain in its outcome, content and wording – decision by the CJEU, the appeal of the citation route as an alternative to the preliminary reference one would tend to decrease when: (i) the issue is salient in public opinion, and thus the stakes are higher; (ii) the available CJEU case law does not seem specific enough on the point giving rise to public attention; and (iii) the national legislation or policy that may be put into question by European law is recent, and even posterior in time to the available CJEU case law (a factor that, additionally, would show a commitment by the government to preserve and defend its own policy view as it is passing legislation that does not fully conform with some readings of CJEU precedents). In sum, the 'substitution' effect of the 'low-cost' alternative may be significantly weaker under certain circumstances. Moreover, arguably, this might have been the case of the Spanish scenario in the mortgage foreclosure crisis post-2008.

The pattern of preliminary references across countries and over time has been the subject of an important body of literature. Stone Sweet and Brunell[15] try to offer an explanation of the large differences across Member States in preliminary reference activity, essentially based on a demand theory by firms with transnational operations who put pressure on their national courts in order to facilitate the filing of preliminary references on points of European law that could affect their transnational activities. Tridimas[16] suggests several mutually interacting factors to explain the reluctance of English courts to use the preliminary reference procedure. Tridimas and Tridimas[17] offer a public choice theory of the use of the preliminary reference system, as the outcome of optimizing behaviour by

---

15 Alex Stone Sweet and Thomas Brunell, 'The European Court and the National Courts: A Statistical Analysis of Preliminary References 1961–1995' (1008) 51 *Journal of European Public Policy* 66.

16 Takis Tridimas, 'Knocking on Heaven's Door: Fragmentation, Efficiency and Defiance in the Preliminary Reference Procedure' (2003) 1 *Common Market Law Review* 9.

17 George Tridimas and Takis Tridimas, 'National Courts and the European Court of Justice: A Public Choice Analysis of the Preliminary Reference Procedure' (2004) 24 *International Review of Law and Economics* 125.

private litigants, national courts and the CJEU, where national courts are essentially seeking to expand their opportunities to influence policy by shifting the battleground from the domestic to the European one, when their position is less vulnerable to political bodies. Carrubba and Murrah[18] empirically examine the determinants of preliminary reference filings and find that public support for European integration, and political salience and information, have a positive influence on the number of procedures initiated. Vink, Claes and Arnold[19] empirically reject the hypothesis that cross-border trade explains the variation in preliminary reference activity. Hornuf and Voigt[20] find several factors – of a multifarious nature – empirically affecting the level of use of preliminary references: the size of the economy, the structure of the national economy – smaller primary sector – the number of law students at the *College d'Europe*, certain characteristics of constitutional judicial review in the national legal system, Protestantism as a religion in society, being the most significant in this varied group of explanatory factors. Mayoral[21] explores differences in the use of the preliminary reference procedure by courts in old Member States and by those of the more recent Central and Eastern European Members, and finds that the number of supreme courts in a country (some countries just have one, as is the case in Spain, while others possess a relevant number, such as Germany) and the structure of judicial review powers in a national legal system, appear to be relevant explanatory factors.

We do not intend to generalize our theory on the recent trend of references by Spanish courts in the consumer area. It is true that consumer law is one of the most significant legal fields in terms of preliminary references (after taxation),[22] but there are many other features of our setting that may not be sufficiently representative in order to make this a basis for a broader

---

[18] Clifford Carrubba and Lacey Murrah, 'Legal Integration and the Use of the Preliminary Ruling Process in the European Union' (2005) 59 *International Organization* 399.

[19] Maarten Vink, Monica Claes and Christine Arnold, 'Explaining the Use of Preliminary References by Domestic Courts in EU Member States: A Mixed-Method Comparative Analysis' (Mimeo 2009).

[20] Lars Hornuf and Stefan Voigt, 'Analyzing Preliminary References as the Powerbase of the European Court of Justice' (2014) 39 *European Journal of Law and Economics* 287.

[21] Juan Mayoral Díaz-Asensio, 'Overcoming the Legal Iron Curtain: Similarities and Differences in the Use of Preliminary References Between New and Old Member States' (2012) 4 *Perspectives on Federalism*.

[22] Lars Hornuf and Stefan Voigt, 'Analyzing Preliminary References as the Powerbase of the European Court of Justice' (2014) 39 *European Journal of Law and Economics* 287.

theory. However, we think our stylized explanation of the Spanish case in consumer matters sheds some light on the interplay between national lawmakers, national courts and the CJEU.

III. THE ISSUES COVERED IN THE SPANISH-ORIGINATED CASES

In this section we will summarize the substantive issues that have been decided by the CJEU when responding to references raised by Spanish courts in the consumer context. The discussion looks back historically at the case law, at least from the perspective of the recent wave of references, since we think it is illustrative to show the similarities – and the differences, which are clear – in the types of cases and issues raised over time by Spanish courts in their preliminary reference activity.

The Spanish courts turned to the CJEU for the interpretation of the scope of applicability of Directive 85/577 in respect of contracts negotiated away from business premises[23] and the possibility of the court acting on its own motion for the benefit of the consumer (*Océano* case). Actually, this last motive has appeared in several requests for preliminary rulings. In some of these cases, the CJEU has provided the Spanish courts with the tools necessary to strengthen the consumer's position in the referred case, while in others it has decided to set the limits of the available protection, as in the *Corte Inglés* case or *Asturcom*[24] cases.

i. Courts Acting *Pro Consumatore* of Their Own Motion: The Limits of the Doctrine

The *Océano* judgment[25] is known for opening the discussion on the judge acting of his own motion, which has been followed subsequently in the CJEU resolutions of other Spanish requests for preliminary rulings. In

---

23 The Directive excludes contracts concerning rights *in rem* over immovable property. However, as other services included in the contract for use of immovable property on a time-share basis were of higher value than the right to use a time-share apartment, the mentioned exception shall not apply according to the judgment in Case C-423/97 *Travel Vac* EU:C:1999:197. Therefore, the consumer enjoyed a right of withdrawal, which is not subject to any form or condition, meaning that it cannot imply payment of any kind of damages for the sole reason of having exercised the right to withdraw.

24 Case C-40/08 *Asturcom* EU:C:2009:615, see below.

25 *Océano Grupo Editorial*, n.1.

that case, a contract for sale of encyclopedias was signed; it included a clause by virtue of which all disputes arising from it were to be discussed in the court of territorial jurisdiction of the seller's seat (Barcelona). When the seller filed a lawsuit claiming that the price of the books had not been paid, the relevant Spanish court looked into the contract and considered that the aforementioned clause was legally unfair. Therefore, it refrained from granting the firm's claim, referring to the CJEU for a preliminary ruling on whether it was possible for it, on its own, to consider the unfair term as a motive for not admitting the lawsuit. The CJEU finally stated that there is a great risk, due to lack of knowledge and awareness about the content of the law and the rights and remedies granted by it, that consumers would not challenge unfair contract terms. This suggests that in order to ensure the effective protection of consumers' interests, it must be possible for the court to exercise the power to evaluate these kinds of terms of its own motion. However, in the case at hand, there was another obstacle to overcome: Directive 93/13 on unfair terms had not yet been transposed into Spanish law, although the facts post-dated the expiry of the period allowed in the Directive for the transposition. The CJEU ruled that, taking this into account, national provisions applicable for the reason of time should be interpreted, to the extent possible, in accordance with the Directive and in such a way that would allow for the court's examination and determination of unfairness of its own motion.

In the *Mostaza Claro* case,[26] the discussion focused on the validity of the arbitration clause in a contract for mobile telephone services. As the consumer did not comply with the minimum subscription period set out in the agreement, the service provider initiated arbitration proceedings and obtained a favourable arbitration award. During the enforcement proceedings (seeking the content of the arbitration award to be enforced by the court), the consumer contested the arbitral decision on the basis (raising the issue for the first time) of the unfair nature of the arbitration clause, after having failed to do so in any way in the course of the prior arbitration proceedings. The Spanish court referred the case to the CJEU, asking if it was possible to avoid an arbitration award on the grounds of the arbitration clause being unfair, even though the consumer did not challenge it properly during the arbitration proceedings. The CJEU answered in the affirmative, justifying its response on the basis of the imbalance of power between the consumer and the professional. In the circumstances of the case, such a power vested upon the court was considered the only feasible way to ensure that the consumer would not be bound by an unfair

[26] *Mostaza Claro*, n.2.

term. Therefore, the *Océano* case doctrine was extended to include the case of the passive consumer, at least one who is passive during the arbitration process predating the court proceedings.

However, this doctrine was slightly modified in the judgment of 6 October 2009 (Case C-40/08 *Asturcom*), where the existence of an unfair arbitration clause was also observed by the Spanish court, after a lawsuit was brought by a telephone service provider in order to enforce an arbitration award. Nevertheless, unlike in *Mostaza Claro*, the consumer neither participated in the arbitration proceedings, nor brought a claim or counter-claim for annulment of the award before the court. The CJEU stated that a two-month period – that during which the consumer could have challenged the arbitration award – is a reasonable one, and therefore the award had lawfully acquired the force of *res iudicata*. This time limit was declared consistent with the principle of effectiveness. Therefore, the *Asturcom* case seems to set a limit on the *Océano* and *Mostaza Claro* doctrine in respect of the powers granted to courts to overcome the passivity of the consumer.

Nonetheless, in the judgment of 3 October 2013 (Case C-32/12 *Duarte Hueros*[27]), the CJEU, somewhat surprisingly, extended its doctrine once more in a Spanish case, when it decided that the national judge may, of its own motion, grant the reduction of price due to the lack of conformity, even though the consumer requested only the rescission of the contract. In this case, the car bought by a consumer presented some defects in its sliding roof and leaked when it rained. After several unsuccessful attempts to repair it, the consumer requested that the vehicle be replaced. However, the court found the lack of conformity to be minor, and therefore the remedy of rescission of the contract claimed by the consumer could not be granted. The consumer had not requested a reduction in the sale price, as a remedy to the non-conformity of the good, in her lawsuit. The CJEU ruled that even though Spanish civil procedure imposes that the judicial decision should be commensurate with the request made by the parties (i.e., that it cannot go beyond, or grant something different from the plaintiff's request for judicial relief), these rules are not compatible with European legislation, as they undermine the effectiveness of consumer protection intended by European consumer law. Therefore, according to the CJEU, Directive 1999/44 on certain aspects of the sale of consumer goods and associated guarantees, should be interpreted as precluding national legislation on this point, to the effect that a reduction of the price of the consumer good may be decided unilaterally by the court, even though it has not been requested

[27] Case C-32/12 *Duarte Hueros* EU:C:2013:637.

by the consumer and it is not clear – at least explicitly – that it better satisfies the consumer's interests.[28]

In the judgment of 17 December 2009 (Case C-227/08 *Martin Martin*[29]), the CJEU confirmed the possibility for the national judge to act *ex officio*. In the case brought before the European Court, a consumer had bought some books and CDs at home, signing a contract with the publisher's representative. When she failed to pay some instalments, the professional resorted to the court to initiate an order for payment. However, the court noticed that the contract did not include a provision allowing the consumer to withdraw her consent within a period of seven days, a provision which is required to form part of those contracts negotiated away from business premises according to the national legislation transposing Directive 85/577. Once again, the consumer did not advance the claim and the court was in doubt as to whether it could raise this infringement *ex officio*. According to the judgment of the CJEU, the public interest underlying the protection of the consumer's rights justifies that national courts may act of their own motion in this regard.

ii. Financial Contracts: Unfair Terms and Mortgage Foreclosure

The second main area of questions referred to the CJEU for preliminary ruling in matters of consumer law are those related to financial contracts, especially linked to mortgage loan foreclosure and the unfair terms that the loan contracts may contain. The problem of courts acting on their own motion also appears here repeatedly.

The *Banesto* case[30] is an example of a question regarding the unfair

---

[28] On the analysis of the Directive's solutions on the lack of conformity from an economic perspective, see among others, Fernando Gómez Pomar, 'Directiva 1999/44/CE sobre determinados aspectos de la venta y las garantías de los bienes de consumo: una perspectiva económica' (2001) 4/2001 *Indret* 20. For a critical assessment of the judgment of 3 October 2013, see Ángel Carrasco Perera, 'Consumidor que reclama judicialmente únicamente la resolución del contrato de compraventa de un bien y posibilidad judicial de conceder una reducción adecuada del precio' (2013) *Revista CESCO* (available at: http://blog.uclm.es/cesco/files/2013/10/Consumidor-que-reclama-judicialmente-%C3%BAnicamente-la-resoluci%C3%B3n-del-contrato-de-compraventa-de-un-bien.pdf); Faustino Cordón Moreno, 'La posibilidad de que el juez otorgue de oficio una tutela jurisdiccional no pedida por el consumidor (STJUE de 3 de octubre de 2013)' (2013) 8/2013 *Revista CESCO* (available at: http://blog.uclm.es/cesco/files/2013/11/La-posibilidad-de-que-el-juez-otorgue-de-oficio-una-tutela-jurisdiccional-no-pedida-por-el-consumidor.pdf).

[29] Case C-227/08 *Martin Martin* EU:C:2009:792.

[30] *Banesto*, n.4.

interest rate for late payments in a loan contract with a consumer. In the case, the default interest was set at a rate of 29 per cent (not terribly unusual at the time in respect of a non-secured personal loan to a consumer, it must be said). The bank filed a suit for payment of the seven monthly payments missed by the consumer before the court, including the applicable default interest. Nevertheless, the court found the default interest excessive and, therefore, unfair. However, given the failure of the consumer to raise an objection on this matter, the Spanish court decided to refer the question to the CJEU in order to clarify whether it could declare the clause void *ex officio*, even though national legislation did not allow it. The CJEU stated that the principle of effectiveness implies that national rules must be interpreted in a way that does not make impossible or excessively difficult the exercise of consumers' rights. Therefore, national courts must be able to raise this infringement on their own initiative. However, Directive 93/13 does not provide for a modification of the contract in respect of the unfair clause, permitting only the elimination of the unfair term.

This judgment has had an important impact on the prevalent view in the Spanish legal system as to the effects of unfair clauses. Until a recent reform following the CJEU ruling, Spanish legislation on consumers' rights envisaged the possibility of the court 'moderating' or modifying equitably the rights and obligations of the parties in the case that it found an unfair term to exist.[31] This was especially true in respect of those cases in which the interest rates for late payments were found to be excessive, where a great deal of case law had been decided in favour of the reduction of the interest rate to an 'acceptable' amount (normally, 2.5 times legal interest[32]). However, as the moderation option seemed to be an alternative to the total elimination of the clause, some of the courts preferred the option of an absolute elimination, therefore factually reducing the interest rate for late payments to 0 per cent, with an eye to giving the right incentives to credit institutions to avoid using unfair terms in this area. Nevertheless, there were also decisions which ruled that, after the elimination of the unfair default interest clause, Art.1108 of the Spanish Civil Code should be applied as a default legal rule, which states that, in the absence of a contract term indicating the interest rate for late payments, the 'legal' interest – set by default by said provision of the Spanish

---

[31] Art.83 of the Royal Legislative Decree 1/2007, of 1st November, on consumers and user's rights. Modified by Law 3/2014, of 27 March.

[32] By analogy with Art.20 of the Law 16/2011, of 24 June, on Consumer Credit Contracts which sets this limit for credit overdraft facilities.

Civil Code – applies.[33] After the *Banesto* case and, especially, following the reform affected by Law 3/2014, of 27 March, which implemented the doctrine of that judgment into Spanish consumer law, it seems clear that the only possible way to proceed in the case of finding a given term to be unfair (interest rate or otherwise) is to eliminate it entirely, and use the default legal regime that is applicable in order to fill the gap in the contract.

With respect to unfair terms, the judgment of 16 January 2014 (Case C-226/12, *Constructora Principado SA v José Ignacio Menéndez Álvarez*[34]) addressing the notion of 'significant imbalance' for the purposes of a finding of unfairness in a contract term, must also be taken into account. In a contract for the purchase of a dwelling, the duty to pay the local tax on the increase in value of the urban land (approx. 1,000 euros in that case) had been allocated to the purchaser by a given contract clause. After paying the tax, the consumer brought a claim against the construction company requesting reimbursement on the grounds that the clause imposing the payment of the tax on the purchaser was not negotiated, and it caused a significant imbalance in the rights and obligations of the parties to the contract. The company insisted that the whole contract should be taken into consideration and that from this point of view the alleged imbalance was not significant in economic terms. The Spanish court referred the case to the CJEU for a preliminary ruling on the meaning of this expression, and the latter stated that the existence of significant imbalance does not require the cost charged to the consumer to have a significant economic or monetary impact. There is a significant imbalance when there is serious impairment of the legal situation in which the consumer is placed.

The *Aziz* case probably constitutes the landmark case, and the most notorious tribute to the relevance of the interactions of Spanish courts with the CJEU. It must be noted, however, that similar questions on the compatibility of Spanish enforcement proceedings with EU law had been answered by the CJEU in its decision of 14 November 2013 (Cases C-537/12 and C-116/13[35]), which derive from proceedings prior to *Aziz*.

The judgment of 14 March 2013 (Case C-415/11 *Aziz*)[36] has been very

---

[33] A summary of the case law and applicable solutions in Spanish law before the *Banesto* case can be found in Karolina Lyczkowska, 'Los intereses en los contratos de préstamo y las normas que rigen su licitud' (2013) 5/2013 *Revista CESCO* (available at: http://cesco.revista.uclm.es/index.php/cesco/issue/view/52/showToc).

[34] EU:C:2014:10.

[35] Joined Cases C-537/12 and 116/13 *Banco Popular* EU:C:2013:759.

[36] With a commentary by Francisco Javier Gómez Gálligo, 'La doctrina del Tribunal de Justicia de la Unión Europea sobre calificación de las cláusulas

influential in Spanish law. It has given rise to various legal reforms following the CJEU's ruling that the Spanish Civil Procedure Code was not compatible with the level of protection that European law grants to consumers. Mr. Aziz had concluded a loan contract secured by a mortgage on his family home. One of the contract's clauses – made in full compliance with Spanish law at the time – stated that in the event of default the bank could bring enforcement proceedings and, for this purpose, the bank may immediately quantify the outstanding amount of the debt by submitting an appropriate certificate with the filing of the lawsuit. When Mr. Aziz stopped paying the loan, the bank instituted enforcement proceedings which led to a judicial auction of the mortgaged property. However, shortly before the court declared that the bank could take possession of the mortgaged property, Mr. Aziz applied to the court for a declaration seeking the annulment of the aforementioned clause, on the ground that it was unfair; he also sought the dismissal of the entire enforcement proceeding.

According to Spanish law at the time, such a declaratory proceeding (the one to decide whether the clause was unfair and thus, whether the foreclosure based on the enforcement of that clause should be cancelled) could not itself suspend the mortgage enforcement proceedings; as such, the court decided to refer a question for preliminary ruling to the CJEU. The latter finally decided that the relevant Spanish procedural rules impaired the protection intended by Directive 93/13, as the objection to enforcement proceedings on the grounds of existence of unfair terms in the contract was not accepted, and thus, the declaratory proceedings had no suspending effect; the consequence was that the vesting of mortgaged property in a third party was irreversible (only monetary compensation would have been available to the consumer prevailing in the declaratory proceedings). As a result, several reforms (implemented by virtue of Law 1/2013, of 14 May) had to be rushed through by the Spanish government in order to strengthen the consumer's protection in Spanish law in compliance with the requirements set out in the *Aziz* decision; this affected both the Spanish Mortgage Act and the Civil Procedure Code.

Even though the *Aziz* case resulted in several reforms of the Spanish enforcement procedures, the recent ruling of the CJEU in the *Sánchez Morcillo* case[37] clearly shows the insufficiency of the efforts by the Spanish government to update the procedural framework of mortgage enforce-

abusivas en los préstamos hipotecarios' (2014) 741 *Revista Crítica de Derecho Inmobiliario* 153.

[37] Case C-169/14 *Sánchez Morcillo and Abril García* EU:C:2014:2099.

ment proceedings to the standards of effective consumer protection sought by the CJEU. The ruling provides an answer to the preliminary reference raised by the Provincial Appeals Court of Castellón, regarding the impossibility of challenging the judicial decision that dismisses the debtor's opposition in mortgage enforcement proceedings.

In the aftermath of the *Aziz* case, the Civil Procedure Code was amended to the effect that the unfairness of a contractual clause was added to the list of possible causes that a consumer could allege in order to suspend mortgage enforcement proceedings, if the first instance court deciding such proceedings ruled against the consumer and rejected the plea of unfairness, and thus decided to continue with the foreclosure proceedings, and its decision could not be appealed by the consumer. However, if the court ruled in favour of the consumer and the foreclosure proceedings were stopped, the enforcing creditor was entitled to challenge the decision by filing a full appeal against it.

In the *Sánchez Morcillo* case, the CJEU decided that this situation violates the principle of equality of defence resources available to the parties of a case and, therefore, it is not in accordance with Directive 93/13 on unfair terms in consumer contracts. The ruling does not seem to fully grasp the scope and properly understand the principles of the Spanish Enforcement Proceedings, when it suggests *obiter dicta* that the whole foreclosure system may be non-compliant with the European Union's principles.[38] Nevertheless, a swift reform of the Spanish Civil Procedure Code has been carried out in order to comply with the judgment; it focuses solely on the availability of an appeal against the court of first instance's ruling in these circumstances also for those decisions in which the court rules against the consumer, upholding the continuation of the foreclosure proceedings.[39]

iii. Other Questions on Mortgage Enforcement

After *Aziz*, the wave of referrals did not slow down. On the contrary, it was perceived by courts throughout the country as clear evidence of a clever way to implement relevant changes in the Spanish legal system

---

[38] For more details on the ruling, and a critical commentary, see Angel Carrasco Perera and Karolina Lyczkowska, 'Un nuevo (y esta vez defectuoso) pronunciamiento del TJUE sobre el procedimiento hipotecario español' (2014) 10/2014 *Revista CESCO* (available at: http://www.uclm.es/centro/cesco/pdf/trabajos/33/27.pdf).

[39] See Art.695 of Spanish Civil Proceedings Act, as modified by the Royal Decree 11/2014, of September 5.

in the midst of the foreclosure crisis that had been initiated some years before; this did not appear to recede after 2013. Moreover, there were genuine problems with the interpretation of the reformed Spanish rules following the *Aziz* case, and in respect of the implications of the *Banesto* case doctrine concerning unfair interest rates and the effects of a finding of unfairness. Some of the preliminary references raised by Spanish courts are the ones submitted by the first instance judges of the courts of Marchena,[40] Santander,[41] and Miranda de Ebro.[42]

The Marchena court asked how the judge or the notary should act after observing an unfair contractual term related to a default payment interest rate. According to the reform enacted by Law 1/2013 in the Mortgage Act, the late payment interest rate in a mortgage loan shall never exceed three times the legal interest rate applicable at the moment. However, for mortgages agreed before it entered into force, Law 1/2013 envisages the possibility for the enforcing party to recalculate the interest rate in order to meet the new legal limit. On the other hand, in the case of especially vulnerable debtors, Royal Decree-Law 6/2012 establishes that the interest for late payments shall never exceed the sum of the ordinary interest rate plus 2 percentage points. Royal Decree-Law 6/2012 does not contain a transition rule, but it is possible that some courts could take it into account at the moment of recalculation, based on analogical reasoning. In the view of the Marchena judge, these possibilities may be inconsistent with the doctrine of the CJEU in the *Banesto* case, which states that the unfair terms in contracts with consumers shall be eliminated, without modifications being allowed either by the court or by the party having imposed the unfair term. The Avila judge raised a very similar concern.[43]

In its judgment of 21 January 2015, the CJEU states that while no modification of the unfair term by the judge is allowed, the obligation to respect the cap – imposed generally by a national provision in Spanish law to mortgage loan contracts for the acquisition of the consumer's home – on the default interest rate of three times the statutory interest rate, has to be understood without prejudice to the assessment by the court of the fairness or unfairness of the term setting the default interest, below the cap, naturally. Therefore insofar as Law 1/2013 does not prevent the national

---

[40] Order of the First Instance Court of Marchena, 16 August 2013.

[41] Order of the First Instance Court of Santander, 19 November 2013.

[42] Order of the First Instance Court of Miranda de Ebro, 15 February 2014.

[43] Reference for a preliminary ruling presented by the First Instance Court of Ávila on February 11, 2014 (Case C-75/14 *Banco de Caja España de Inversiones, Salamanca y Soria* ECLI:EU:C:2015:198). After CJUE Judgment of 21 January 2015, the Ávila Court decided to withdraw its reference for a preliminary ruling.

court from analysing and declaring the unfairness of a contract term, and subsequently removing that clause if it is found to be unfair, Directive 93/13 does not preclude the application of such a national provision.

The Santander court also referred to the CJEU its doubts about the motives that may lead a judge to consider a clause of acceleration of a mortgage loan contract to be unfair. Since the latest reform enacted in Spanish law by Law 1/2013, at least three consecutive monthly quotas must remain unpaid before the bank is able to trigger the acceleration clause. However, there are cases (involving contracts agreed prior to Law 1/2013) in which, even though the contractual clause stipulates that the missed payment of just one monthly quota is sufficient to give the bank the option of accelerating, credit institutions typically prefer to wait until at least three quotas are left unpaid before initiating the enforcement. The Santander court asked whether it should declare the unfair term to be void in these cases, taking into account that *de facto* the mortgage had not been accelerated by the bank before the legal minimum of three monthly quotas had been met. The CJEU Judgment of 11 June 2015 concludes that the mere fact that the suspicious contractual clause has not been applied in the case at hand does not preclude the national judge from analysing it and declaring its unfairness, applying all the consequences established in Directive 93/13.

Finally, the Miranda de Ebro court asked whether the number of monthly unpaid quotas should be the only factor to be taken into consideration in the determination of whether an acceleration clause is fair or unfair, that is, without taking into account the duration of the loan, or the percentage of the loan amount that remains unpaid in relation to the amounts already reimbursed by the consumer. It refers to the same doubts in relation to the default interest rate, that is, whether a clause that meets the cap fixed by Law 1/2013 (three times the statutory interest rate) could be considered unfair in light of the other circumstances of the case. The CJEU judgment of 8 July 2015 confirms that Directive 93/13 does not preclude the application of Law 1/2013 in so far as it does not prevent the national court from analysing and declaring the unfairness of a contract term. As to the first question, the judgment indicates that the unfairness analysis must always take into account the nature of goods and services which are the object of the contract and consider all the circumstances at the conclusion of the contract.

IV. STRATEGIC INTERPRETATION OF THE RECENT SURGE IN REFERENCES

As is clear from sections II and III above, the number of references from Spanish courts on matters of consumer law has skyrocketed in recent years. In this section, we explore a game-theoretical explanation of why Spanish courts have engaged in this intense exercise of raising preliminary references in the aftermath of the financial crisis and its ensuing mortgage foreclosure surge.

In the following analysis we make several simplifying assumptions in order to sharpen the focus upon the main drivers of the strategic interaction between the Spanish courts and the Spanish government, and how the possibility of using a reference for a preliminary ruling by the CJEU alters the payoffs and likely outcome of the interaction.

Let us first consider a setting in which there is no effective possibility of making a preliminary reference to the CJEU (for whatever reason: imagine the issues involved do not present a relevant connection with EU law, or where the reputational costs of raising the preliminary reference are too high to be worthy of the filing). We have two players, the government (representing the political majority in the lawmaking bodies[44] in Spain) and the courts (that we assume may be characterized by a median judge or a representative judge set of preferences).[45]

We assume further that there is a relevant difference in preferences concerning the level of protection for consumers in the area of mortgage loans and mortgage foreclosure, between the government and the courts. We believe this is a reasonable assumption in face of the observable facts in the recent Spanish experience: in the midst of a major outbreak of mortgage defaults, given the surge in unemployment and decreasing household revenues, the extremely high levels of homeowners' indebtedness, and the fall in house prices, the government did not promote or set in motion, on its own initiative, any important changes to the legal framework of mortgage loans

[44] Just as a side note, the political majority changed in the middle of the relevant period (2008–14) but no significant difference was observable between the two in terms of consumer protection in financial matters.

[45] This does not mean that all courts have the same preferences over the issues at stake. For instance, in the matter solved by the CJEU judgment of 21 December 2016, it is clear that a substantial number of lower courts disagreed with the 'Salomonic' solution found by the Spanish Supreme Court (that is, to consider certain terms as unfair but to limit in temporal terms the restitutionary consequences so as to soften the impact on the financial sector and reduce the incentive to present thousands of restitutionary claims); this profound disagreement led to the preliminary references and, in the end, to the CJEU decision.

and mortgage enforcement. The measures introduced by Royal Decree-Law 6/2012 for vulnerable debtors, including a Code of Good Practice for financial institutions dealing with the restructuring of mortgage debt affecting the place of residence of the debtor, had very little bite in reality: the analysis of the conditions for benefitting consumers, of the most important relief measure, offered an estimate of no more than 0.77 per cent of total households, or 7.6 per cent of those households of which all members were unemployed, being eligible to benefit.[46] The more significant (but reluctant) changes brought about by Law 1/2013 substantially followed the case law of the CJEU and, especially, the *Aziz* case. Moreover, no major improvements towards alleviating mortgage debt in personal bankruptcy have been introduced, despite numerous amendments to the Spanish Bankruptcy Act in recent years, and despite the clear pressure from international bodies, such as the IMF,[47] to lighten the debt burden on consumers through some type of bankruptcy debt discharge or 'fresh start'.

We are agnostic as to the reasons for such a governmental position (intact, as we already noticed, throughout two political cycles) *vis-à-vis* the level of consumer protection in mortgage loans, and towards the overall desirability of that attitude. It may well simply reflect a phenomenon of the 'capture' of the lawmakers and regulators by the financial industry, as the trend has been characterized by the public choice literature. Capture, in itself, is also something that may have very different root causes: a higher level of expertise in the industry compared to that held by lawmakers and regulators; the effectiveness of interest group pressure by the financial sector; revolving-doors between industry and regulators, outright corruption, and so forth.

The reluctance to significantly expand the legal protection of mortgaged households, however, may have much more benign underlying reasons. It may simply correspond to a – fuller and more informed – assessment of the ultimate economic and social consequences of enhanced consumer protection in this area: it may be that increasing the level of consumer protection for mortgage debtors would irreparably endanger the financial standing of the Spanish banking system, and thus, the national and European financial stability overall. Whatever the (more or less laudable, depending on one's own views) reasons underlying the reluctance of the Spanish government to alter the *status quo* in favour of heightened levels of legal

---

[46] Marco Celentani and Fernando Gómez Pomar, 'La dación en pago en el Código de Buenas Prácticas: ¿cuántos se benefician?' (2012) *Nada es Gratis*; available at: http://nadaesgratis.es/celentani/la-dacion-en-pago-en-el-codigo-de-buenas-practicas-cuantos-se-benefician.

[47] IMF, Country Report N° 13/245, and Country Report N° 14/193.

relief for mortgage-indebted consumers, the observation drawn about the position of the government is hardly contestable, and it is this observation that matters for our explanation of the preliminary reference activity of the Spanish courts.

As to the courts, while it is obviously difficult to advance a general statement about their preferences, there are indications consistent with a perceptible feeling of uneasiness among courts, and especially lower courts, about the adequacy of the legal framework in the Spanish legal system towards mortgage debt and mortgage enforcement. Spanish courts have taken over (probably unwillingly) the largest portion of the burdensome task of dealing with unfair terms (in financial contracts but also in other areas of consumer contracting) and with other potential infringements of consumer protection legislation. Public authorities and agencies, both those in charge of consumer protection generally, at the national and regional levels, and the sectorial regulators and supervisors (the Bank of Spain for the financial sector; the *Comisión Nacional del Mercado de Valores* for capital markets) have been mostly passive or at least timid in addressing potential violations of consumer protection law.

Perhaps this has been particularly visible in the financial contracting context. Thus, courts, willingly or unwillingly, have had to step in and assume a major role in this regard. The phenomenon has led to a very significant amount of litigation and an increase in the caseload of Spanish civil courts.[48]

Moreover, it is also safe to assume that, due to a combination of factors, Spanish law was not in fact very protective or supportive (compared to other major European legal systems) of over-indebted consumers in mortgage-secured loan contracts. There are manifold reasons for this characterization. Some are factual or economic: the levels of home ownership in Spain have been in recent decades – and remain – extraordinarily high for European standards (mostly due to the historic unattractiveness of being a residential landlord in Spain[49]); moreover, the level of mortgage debt

[48] Federico della Negra, 'The private enforcement of the MiFID conduct of business rules. An overview of the Italian and Spanish experiences', (2014) 10 (4) *European Review of Contract Law* 571. Even ADR has not been widely used in Spain with the exception of the scheme introduced to address the case of preferential participations (PPR) that were sold to retail investors by financial institutions, most of them now in public hands following the banking crisis that ensued following the economic meltdown in Spain.

[49] Juan Mora-Sanguinetti, 'The Regulation of Residential Tenancy Markets in Post-War Western Europe: An Economic Analysis' (2011) 8 *European Journal of Comparative Economics* 47.

taken by households has been very high, especially in the housing boom years, where the risk assessment standards of Spanish banks and, particularly savings banks, relaxed with the consequence that extremely high loan-to-value ratios were financed, including to low-income consumers.[50]

Other reasons are of a legal nature: the privileged status of the mortgage as a security[51] has given rise to a very efficient property registry; moreover, a set of particularly speedy[52] court – and out of court, though these have not been widely used in practice – proceedings, have been deployed by the Spanish legal system at the service of mortgage loans. In addition to this, the absence of almost any – in fact, any at all, before Law 1/2013 – avenue or possibility for debt discharge in personal bankruptcy[53] adds to the picture of consumers defaulting on a large scale in respect of their piles of mortgage debt, leading to foreclosures that imply losing the home to the lender and remaining personally liable for the unpaid amount of the loan. The inadequate performance of consumer protection agencies or financial regulators has also left ample room for suspicions of unfairness in a number of loan contract clauses (including, for instance, the high default interest rates in the *Banesto* case discussed above).

---

[50] Ozlem Akin *et al*, 'The Real Estate and Credit Bubble: Evidence from Spain' (2014) *SERIEs-Journal of the Spanish Economic Association* 223. For a comparison of these variables across most Eurozone countries, see Olympia Bover *et al*, 'The Distribution of Debt across Euro-Area Countries: The Role of Individual Characteristics, Institutions, and Credit Conditions' (2016) 12 (2) *International Journal of Central Banking* 71.

[51] The legal effects of mortgages, and the favourable comparison between mortgage enforcement outcomes versus bankruptcy outcomes, seem to be the most important factors explaining why Spanish firms use mortgage security for their debt much more often and to a larger extent than their counterparts in other European economies: Marco Celentani, Miguel García Posada and Fernando Gómez Pomar, 'The Spanish Business Bankruptcy and the Crisis', Working Paper 2010–11, FEDEA (2010); Miguel García Posada and Juan Mora-Sanguinetti, 'Why do Spanish Firms Rarely Use the Bankruptcy System? The Role of the Mortgage Institution' Working Paper 1234, Banco de España (2012); Miguel García Posada and Juan Mora-Sanguinetti, 'Are There Alternatives to Bankruptcy? A Study of Small Business Distress in Spain' (2014) 5 *SERIEs-Journal of the Spanish Economic Association* 287.

[52] Not just with respect to other types of court proceedings in Spain, but also compared to mortgage enforcement proceedings in other European countries. According to the mortgage industry views, Spain had one of the most (if not 'the' most) effective and timely court enforcement mechanism for mortgages.

[53] This leads to extremely low levels of consumer bankruptcy in Spain, since the benefit to the debtor of filing for bankruptcy is virtually zero, while transaction costs are not trivial: See, Fernando Gómez Pomar and Marco Celentani, 'Tarea urgente: el concurso personal' (2012) 1/2012 *InDret*.

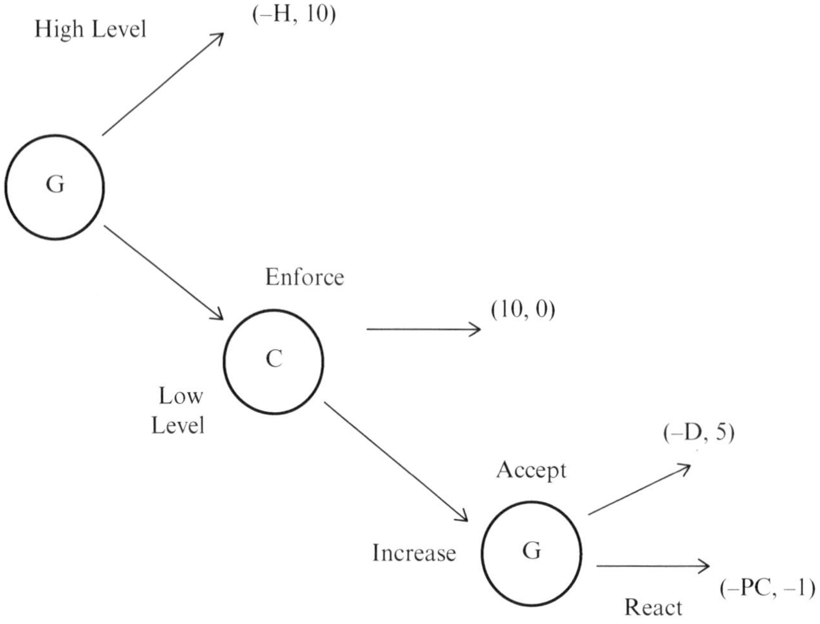

Figure 5.4 Interaction without the CJEU

In Figure 5.4, we present a very stylized version of the interaction between government and courts.

If the government opts to change the legal *status quo* and to implement a high level (through rules and/or agency activity on unfair terms, changes in the rules governing mortgage loans, or changes in the procedural rules through which mortgage defaults lead to foreclosure), the courts would be satisfied with the outcome of a high protective level that they find desirable. This results in an attractive payoff for the courts (10),[54] who would observe their preferred policies implemented in reality. It is not very attractive for the government, who would incur a negative payoff of −H, reflecting the overall negative effects – or perception of effects – arising from the high level of protection afforded to mortgage debtors: active opposition by banking sector, negative systemic effects on the financial system and the economy, for instance, could add to this negative payoff.

If the government decides to keep the existing 'low' (at least, relatively

[54] Obviously this figure is arbitrary. We provide a numerical value just for simplicity in the most complex interaction with the CJEU.

or comparatively low) level of mortgage debtor protection, the courts face two potential courses of action in this situation: (i) they may choose to abide by the low level that does not correspond to their preferences, thus providing satisfaction to the government, but sacrificing their preferred view (hence the payoffs of 10 for the government, and 0 for the courts); or (ii) they may opt to find (existing or created) avenues to increase the level of legal protection afforded to mortgage debtors in reality.[55]

In the latter case, the government, in turn, may accommodate the substantive increase in the level of protection granted by the courts, by failing to react against it. However, the government may also counteract the departure from existing law brought about by the courts, for instance by blocking explicitly the legal avenue opened up by the courts, or by clarifying any potential loopholes in the low protection regime so as to make it extremely hard or virtually impossible for courts – even when they are willing to do so – to depart from it in the future.[56]

In the first case, the government will experience a cost (−D), and the courts will obtain a positive payoff, since their preferred policy outcome will prevail; this outcome will, however, be a lower one than if such an outcome would have been reached by the simple enforcement of the level of protection awarded by existing written law (it seems reasonable to assume that courts, especially those operating within the civil law

---

[55] For instance, in two notorious decisions by Spanish courts in 2010, despite the clear outcome to the contrary according to the applicable legal rules, mortgage debtors were discharged of the outstanding debt after the bank had taken possession of the mortgaged property: Order of the Appeals Court of Navarra of 17 October 2010 (in mortgage foreclosure proceedings); Order of the Commercial Court No. 3 of Barcelona of 26 October 2010 (in bankruptcy proceedings). In our stylized account, we do not consider individual departures from enforcement by isolated courts, but a response upheld by a reasonably large number of courts so that the prevailing legal outcome in the circumstances is deemed to have changed. Very recently, using Directive 93/13, the Commercial Court No. 10 of Barcelona of 7 December 2016 has considered a mortgage loan clause that did not limit the debtor's liability to the value of the mortgaged property to be unfair. Again, this is an outcome that is hardly consistent with a plain interpretation of the relevant provisions of Spanish law.

[56] This is not an unimaginable or remote scenario. In recent years, the Spanish legal regime on financial guarantees (contained in Royal Decree-Law 5/2005, of March 11) was amended several times in order to enhance the legal status of banks in derivatives contracts to counteract interpretation by courts that shed doubt on the privileged status of creditors in derivatives contracts, especially in interest rate swaps. See on this interplay between lawmaker and courts, Isabel Sáez Lacave, 'Los derivados en el concurso. La racionalidad del régimen especial y las peculiaridades españolas' (2013) 4/2013 *InDret*.

tradition, will incur costs if, in order to obtain their preferred policy end result, they are placed in the position of 'bending' or 'circumventing' the legal provisions in force).

In the second case, the government, in order to overcome the move by the courts to increase mortgage debtors' protections, would need to incur political costs (−PC), in the form of criticism arising from public opinion, media, courts, legal commentators, and so on, concerning the new piece of legislation opposing the courts' interpretation and preferred policy choice. Of course, it is difficult to predict how large these costs are, or are likely to be, in the abstract. Courts, in turn, following the reaction by the government, would not only see their preferred policy outcome – a high level of protection – discarded, but would have fruitlessly incurred the costs of circumventing the law in the first place, and perhaps also 'confronting', to some extent, the legal change ensuing their previous increase in the level of protection afforded to mortgage debtors.

The equilibrium strategies for the government and the courts will depend on the relative value of the relevant costs involved (H, D, PC) as well as on the information available to the players when deciding upon their strategies. If we assume that there is perfect information on the level of costs involved, one would characterize the resulting equilibria in the following way:[57]

(i) if PC<D, then (Low level) is a sub-game perfect Nash equilibrium. The reason is as follows: given the relatively low political cost for the government of 'correcting' the courts' deviation from the legally-imposed, low level of protection, the threat of retaliation by the government in case the courts fail to enforce the government's preferred policy option is sufficient to guarantee faithful enforcement by courts. Anticipating this reaction, the government prefers to stick to the low level of protection instead of giving up beforehand and shifting to the high level of mortgage debtors' protection.
(ii) if PC>D, the equilibrium strategies depend on the relationship between H and D. There are two cases: If D>H, then (High level) is a sub-game perfect Nash equilibrium. Here, government retaliation following the courts' departure is not credible for the government (the political costs of pursuing this action are too high), and thus, courts will always impose their preferred view of the high protection

[57] We only present strategies on the equilibrium path, and do not fully explore all possible equilibria nor formally characterize the ones we present, as it is unnecessary for the purposes of the present contribution.

Table 5.2 Summary of strategies on the equilibrium path without CJEU

	PC < D	PC > D
H > D	(Low level; Enforce)	(Low level, Accept; Increase)
H < D	(Low level; Enforce)	(High level)

level. Anticipating this, and knowing that accommodating this attitude by the courts is more costly than giving up its preferred policy in advance, and thus directly moving to adopt an increase in the level of debtors' protection, the government simply and rationally acts upon this. If H>D, then (Low level, Accept; Increase) is a Nash equilibrium. Again, the government's reaction against the courts' attitude is too costly, but the government – which always enjoys a first mover advantage since it can change or amend the law at any moment that it wishes to do so – prefers to stick to low protection levels, obviously well aware that the courts will depart from such a level, and that after, the government is not willing to incur the (high) costs of reacting against the court-imposed enhanced protection level.

In terms of the resulting legal regime, in case (i) the low level of protection would prevail (and courts would not risk altering it due to their anticipated fear of governmental retaliation). In case (ii), on the contrary, courts will see that their preferred policy option is achieved, although perhaps at the cost (for them) of 'bending' written law to expand the level of protection of mortgage debtors. As we clarified before, we do not make any claims as to the desirability of one or the other outcome. We simply try to illustrate how the interaction between the courts and the government will be shaped by the structure of the costs of different actions for the latter. This interaction will be altered when courts are able to resort, instead of squarely increasing the level of protection for mortgage debtors, to making a preliminary reference to the CJEU, who may – but is not certain to – find that the low level of protection maintained by the Spanish government is inconsistent with European law.

In Table 5.2 we summarize the equilibrium strategies of the game when courts cannot effectively refer the matter to the CJEU.

In our second interaction we introduce the CJEU, not as a player with its own payoffs, but as an external instrument that, through the use of preliminary references, courts may use in their interaction with the government on consumer protection issues. Figure 5.5 below shows the interaction with the important addition of the preliminary reference option for the courts. The rest of the interaction remains as in Figure 5.4 above.

Essentially what we have now is a situation in which, if the government sticks to the low protection level, courts, before deciding to enforce it, or to depart from it, have the choice of asking the CJEU for a preliminary ruling on whether a certain feature of the low level of protection package is or is not consistent with European consumer law. Going down the preliminary reference route implies some direct costs for the Spanish referring court (i.e., delay in deciding the matter and effort in drafting the preliminary reference). Additionally, it also implies, with some positive probability, given that the CJEU ruling is not under the control of the referring Spanish court, foregone benefits for the referring courts: once a preliminary reference has been raised before the CJEU, if the latter upholds the compatibility of the Spanish low level of protection with European law, it becomes harder (perhaps even virtually impossible, as we have assumed in our stylized description summarized in Figure 5.5 below) for the Spanish courts then not to abide by the written Spanish rules and increase the level of protection on their own. Thus, there are both – certain – direct costs and – uncertain – opportunity costs of making preliminary references.

After receiving the request for a preliminary ruling, the CJEU opts (with an exogenous probability, p, that may depend on a number of factors, such as the content of European law, or the policy views of the CJEU on consumer matters or on the procedural autonomy of Member States, among others[58]) to revise the level of mortgage debtor protection in Spain on the basis of the requirements of the consumer *acquis*, or decides with probability (1−p) that no revision is necessary to satisfy the conditions arising from European law.

In the first case, we assume that it becomes too costly for the government to react, or even to ignore, the decision of the CJEU (political embarrassment, international obligations, pressure from other Member States, reciprocity-based motivations to comply with the decisions of the CJEU). Obviously, if the CJEU finds against the compatibility of the low level of protection regime with EU law, the government incurs a cost (−Dcj, to indicate that the cost is imposed by accommodating an adverse ruling, i.e., not by the Spanish courts, but by the CJEU), since the preferred outcome (at least in respect of the dimensions covered by the CJEU ruling) is no longer sustainable. Whether Dcj is larger or smaller than D is a matter of

[58] For the purposes of our analysis – since we are interested in the incentives and behavior of national actors – we do not need to elaborate a theory about why the CJEU may decide one way or the other in cases such as those we are considering here. Rather, we can simply assume that there is a certain probability of ruling one way or the other.

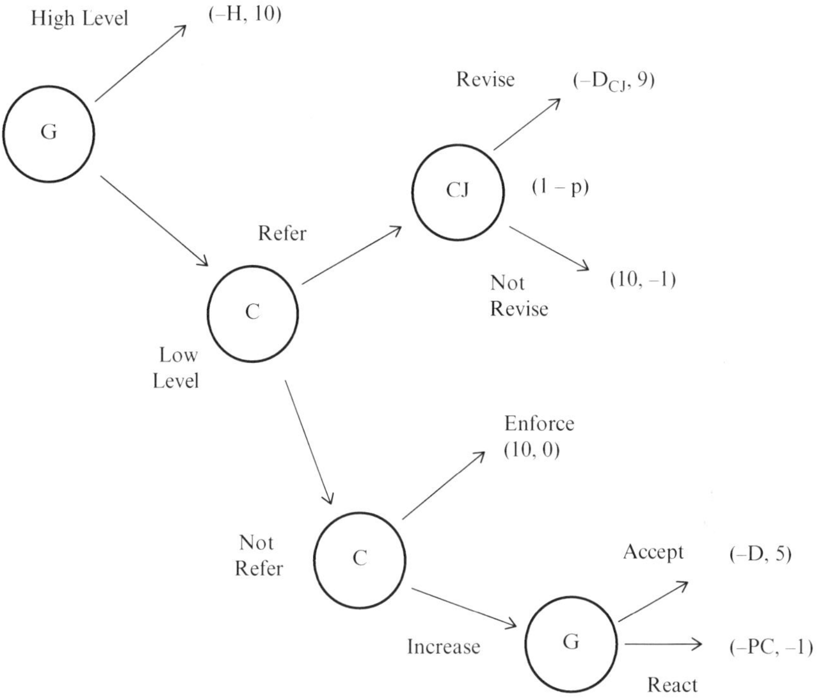

Figure 5.5 Interaction with the CJEU

debate, as will be expanded below; as a result, the comparison is probably not amenable to a generalizable answer.

The costs for the government of an adverse CJEU decision on the level of protection may be higher than those of a domestic ruling, for a variety of reasons: salience of the ruling (given the position and resonance of CJEU compared to purely Spanish decisions, especially if not originating in the Spanish Supreme Court or the Spanish Constitutional Court), political embarrassment at European level, and the larger impact of the ruling. But they may also be lower: the CJEU tends not to be too precise on the scope of its preliminary rulings, and leaves ample space for implementation to the Member States; moreover, the pressure from interest groups in the financial industry would be lower, since the possibility of a reaction against the ruling is virtually non-existent, which is not the case with a domestic decision increasing the level of the debtor's protection.

According to the above, we may either have Dcj ≤ D or Dcj ≥ D, depending on the specificities of the circumstances and the issues involved. In fact, this adds considerable uncertainty to the calculations by the courts

Table 5.3 Summary of strategies on the equilibrium path with CJEU

	p	p < 1/10	1/10 < p <3/5	p > 3/5
D > PC	H < p.Dcj	As in	(High level)	(High level)
	H > p.Dcj	Table 2	(Low level; Refer)	(Low level; Refer)
D < PC	H < D		(High level)	
	H > D		(Low level, Accept; Not Refer, Increase)	
	H < p.Dcj			(High level)
	H > p.Dcj			(Low level, Refer)

considering the convenience of filing a preliminary reference to the CJEU; it would be hard to make general predictions on many of the possible scenarios.

We can, however, draw some useful implications from this stylized representation of the more complex interactions between national courts and the government in the presence of preliminary references to the CJEU. In Table 5.3 we present a summary of the equilibrium strategies in this game of the government and the courts in the presence of the CJEU. It is obvious that the latter significantly alters the interplay between the government and Spanish courts. The effects are complex, as a cursory view at Table 5.3 will confirm.

First, we know from our discussion of Figure 5.4 above, that when PC<D, the courts correctly anticipate that, in the absence of some other pressure, the government will stick to low protection levels, and they are aware that the cost structure makes them vulnerable to retaliation by the government, which will force them into obediently implementing the policy option that it prefers (and not that preferred by the courts). In this scenario, the preliminary reference option entails no opportunity costs for courts, since the probability of prevailing in terms of the preferred policy option is zero without the intervention of the CJEU. Only the direct costs of presenting the request for a preliminary ruling matter. If the estimated probability of obtaining a favourable decision (in respect of their preferences; in this case, against the compatibility of the Spanish low protection level regime with European consumer law) is not too low, so as to overcome, in terms of the expected achievement of desired policy outcomes, the direct costs of the preliminary reference filing, the courts will refer to the CJEU.

This implies that the use of preliminary references is likely (although not only, as Figure 5.4 clearly shows) to be observed in reality when the government faces relatively low costs of overcoming a purely domestic 'rebellion' by courts against low levels of mortgage debtors' protection, and when the chances of a revision forced by the CJEU on the Spanish level of protection are deemed by the courts to be not too low. This low level of costs may be inferred from credible signals sent by the government concerning the level of costs in case of retaliation against local courts departure from written law.

Additionally, an increase in the *ex ante* estimates by courts of the chances of a favourable (as to their preferred policy option) decision by the CJEU, unsurprisingly enhances the incentives of national courts to call the European Court to intervene. Such an estimate may have been raised by the CJEU itself in deciding previous related cases. By showing in a first case its willingness – and the relevant legal basis – to strike down low protection national rules, it encourages more filings in the same area by raising, to a greater or lesser extent, the assessment made by potentially referring courts as to the likelihood of reaching their preferred policy outcome through the preliminary reference route.

In fact, a larger p (that is, the probability of the CJEU forcing a revision of the level of protection set by the government) makes the relationship between PC and D (crucial, in the interaction without the CJEU) less important, and raises the relevance of the relationship between H and Dcj. Thus, in the interaction that involves the CJEU, preliminary references may also be used as a 'threat' by courts to convince the government to raise the level of protection in the first place (and at the same time, with the added benefit for the courts of avoiding the costs for them associated with departing from the written rules in domestic law). This will be the case when $D<PC$, and $p\ Dcj>H$. In this scenario, the government will rationally prefer to concede in advance and shift to the high-level protection regime.

An additional motivation to use the preliminary reference option may be the potential of this procedure to reduce the costs for the courts to achieve their desired policy goals. A direct departure from existing legal rules may be too costly for courts to undertake, in absolute terms or relative to the costs of abiding with their less preferred policy outcome. If a preliminary reference filing reduces the costs of such a departure – in respect of the issue specifically covered by that reference, or for other sufficiently close issues – this cost-reducing (for courts to increase the level of protection) property of preliminary references will also help the courts in two scenarios: when $D>H$, and the courts' cost of departing from existing law are high, because the reduction in costs may shift the equilibrium outcome towards (High level); and when $D<PC$, because departing from the existing law equilibrium is less costly for courts.

In sum, there are several avenues through which the availability of preliminary references in the area of mortgage debtors' protection will be helpful to courts in order to enhance the likelihood of obtaining their desired policy option, or to reduce the costs necessary for them to achieve that result.

We believe that the strategic advantages that the use (whether actual or threatened) of the preliminary reference procedure give to Spanish courts has been at work in recent years in the consumer context. A few observations as to the way in which events unfolded seem to correspond to at least one of the advantageous effects for courts. In the area of mortgage debtors' protection, even in the midst of a very serious foreclosure crisis, the Spanish government (in the two political cycles affected) had sent various signals showing that it was committed to the low protection regime and that it would use legislation to avoid any deleterious consequences of consumer protection developments on the mortgage loans portion of the banks' balance sheets.

Among these signals, we could refer to: the very narrow reach of moratoria in foreclosures and similar relief measures, even for severely distressed households; a lack of change to substantive mortgage laws, and merely cosmetic ones in enforcement procedure; and the refusal to introduce, in the various amendments to the Bankruptcy Act implemented during the crisis years, any form of debt discharge and fresh start for consumers. All these signals could be interpreted as indicating not only an unwillingness to alter the existing legal framework, but also to resist, or counteract, case law developments producing all but minor fractures in that structure.

On the other hand, the CJEU also appeared to send signals (in the *Banesto*, and very obviously, in the *Aziz* case) that it was prepared and willing to review the entire substantive and procedural legal ensemble of Spanish rules governing mortgage loans under quite exacting standards of effectiveness of consumer protection in respect of unfair terms (of which perhaps there was no shortage in loan contracts now in default and leading to foreclosures). This led to a window of opportunity for Spanish courts willing to incur some costs to provide relief to consumers defaulting on mortgage loans. With a closer or looser (sometimes very loose indeed) link to the provisions of European law relating to unfair contract terms, they sought new rulings by the CJEU on different issues affecting mortgage loan contracts and their enforcement. They tried to maximize the chances of 'prevailing' on different dimensions of the Spanish legal framework governing mortgage loans. Evidence of this is that the referrals have been closely attached, in their formulation, to previous rulings of the CJEU concerning Spanish law on mortgage loans and their enforcement. It seems that the referrals generate (favourable to the courts' preferred policy options in general) rulings that, in turn, generate more new referrals.

It does not seem unfair to think that we are currently in the middle of this type of process. Our stylized depiction of the interaction, we believe, sheds light on the forces and the factors bearing on the observed trend in preliminary references in the consumer setting by Spanish courts, and on the consequences they may entail for Spanish law on mortgage loans and mortgage foreclosure, and perhaps for Spanish consumer law more generally.

A very legitimate issue to be raised would be that of timing, concerning the discrepancy in policy preferences between the government and the courts. The Spanish regime governing mortgage foreclosures was by no means new. It had been in force for a long time, and apparently, the courts had not revealed themselves as unhappy with the set of solutions in place, and had routinely enforced them without hesitation. Why has the dramatic change in the macroeconomic situation had such a profound effect on the preferred policy views of courts compared to those of the government?

One may conjecture that courts are aware that mortgage loan foreclosure, with a higher or lower level of protection to consumers, is necessary to alleviate the debtor's moral hazard, otherwise pervasive without legal means to impose negative consequences on loan default. In good economic times, however, defaults on mortgage loans are more likely to be ascribed to undesirable behaviour by debtors than in rough economic times for all households. Thus the advantages of a high protection regime would be perceived to be low, or at least lower than in a harsher economic climate. When economic conditions change, courts may rationally change their perception about the root causes of default, thus making the high protection alternative more appealing to them as a preferred policy option. The government may, despite the new macroeconomic scenario, still prefer the low protection regime for the variety of factors and reasons mentioned above, ranging from capture to prudent anticipation of systemic consequences.

V. CONCLUSIONS

The pattern of preliminary references by Spanish courts dealing with consumer matters offers a very interesting setting to explore the reasons and factors behind – uncoordinated and disaggregated, at least on the face of it – decisions by courts to refer issues to the CJEU. Undoubtedly, the fact that Spanish civil and commercial courts have been confronted with the pressing need to cope on their own with a social emergency affecting large numbers of families who face serious risk of eviction and foreclosures on their homes, in situations of severe economic distress, and with very high levels of indebtedness, has played a large part in the recent upward trend of preliminary references.

In the chapter we have explored the economic environment that has given rise to a challenge for courts to provide answers through the law to social needs affecting wide portions of the population. We have essentially tried to offer an explanation for the observed pattern of preliminary references. In our explanation, we have emphasized the strategic underpinnings of the interactions giving rise to the wave of preliminary references.

It is not because we think that the purely legal dimensions concerning the interpretation of different provisions of the Spanish legal regime and the principles of consumer protection underlying European consumer law, and particularly Directive 93/13, are not important in explaining how and why Spanish courts and the CJEU act as they did and continue to do. Moreover the influence of legal factors is not, we conjecture, idiosyncratic to the courts in Spain in their dealings with the CJEU. We think, however, that our stylized explanation of the Spanish case law in consumer matters allows us to understand in a somewhat more precise form, several relevant features of the interplay between national lawmakers, national courts and the CJEU. This is not only relevant in the special circumstances of the mortgage loan foreclosure crisis afflicting Spain in recent years but, we hope, also in a broader context.

6. The methodology of judicial cooperation in unfair contract terms law

Mónika Józon

> Methodology is not a neutral science. Indeed methodological choices in practice are among the most political ones and the most relevant ones, because they determine knowledge production by setting the rules of the game. (. . .) Who wins the battle over methodology lays the foundation of the whole paradigm, which will be elaborated in all its details. [1] (*Martijn Hesselink*)

INTRODUCTION

Unfair contract terms law is certainly the most challenging testing ground of European private law, in respect of the impact of the global financial crisis. This chapter explores the judicial cooperation between Member State courts and the CJEU in search of solutions in response to the fast-changing *'judicial needs'* of the law of unfair contract terms. Judicial cooperation is understood for the purposes of this chapter as the dialogue that takes place between the CJEU and the domestic judiciaries on policy and which implicitly affects the methodology of judicial enforcement. The focus of the comparative study is Hungary and Romania, two jurisdictions that share many commonalities and particularities, specific to the Central-Eastern European Member States. Hungary, belonging to the German legal family, joined the EU in 2004 and is today the leading country along with Spain in respect of the number of preliminary references sent to the CJEU; as such, it significantly contributes to the *'judicial unification'* of unfair contract terms law in Europe. The identification and analysis of why similar problems are found in jurisdictions as diverse as Hungary and Spain would necessitate a separate chapter that goes beyond the aims of this book.

---

[1] Martijn Hesselink, 'A European Legal Method? On European Private Law and Scientific Method' (2009) 15 *European Law Journal* 34.

However, this chapter explores a more challenging question: the reasons why two countries with similar legal-cultural, economic and judicial inheritance (i.e., Hungary and Romania) cope so differently in their task of enforcing the Unfair Contract Terms Directive (hereinafter, UCTD). Romania, having a strong French legal tradition, joined the EU in 2007 and its judiciary has successfully handled the interpretation problems arising out of the interplay of domestic private law with the requirements of the UCTD. The policy-type reasoning of the CJEU constitutes an integral part of the private law thinking and judicial methodology. For this reason, only a few questions have been referred to the CJEU by the Romanian courts. However, the preliminary references reflect only the tip of the iceberg of the interpretation problems arising at the Member State level. They do not necessarily fully reveal the private law realities of the specific country, because this procedure may be used for very different purposes within the domestic legal and political environment. Thus this chapter also aims to explore the specific domestic function(s) underpinning the preliminary reference procedure in order to identify what types of *'judicial externalities'* are created at the European level by the referring courts acting as driving forces of two interrelated processes: that of *bottom-up unification* via the Europeanization of specific domestic private law problems, and the *subsequent internalization* arising from the transposition of European judicial solutions in line with domestic judicial policy. The risks and costs of such judicial externalities are discussed both domestically and in a European dimension.

THE IMPACT OF THE CJEU RULINGS ON DOMESTIC CASE LAW AND THE POLICY ON PRELIMINARY REFERENCES

For the purposes of this research, around 100 judgments and court decisions were assessed in Hungary and Romania. This case review focused on both the highest and lower courts. In Romania, there is a rich and settled case law (including judgments of the highest courts) on unfair contract terms law, which has allowed for an assessment of the evolution of the specific cases from the lowest to the highest courts, the focus of the analysis being on the latter. In Hungary, the target of analysis was different because there did not yet exist a settled body of case law on unfair contract terms law and the highest court had issued only a few judgments. This is why in Hungary the impact of the European case law on the judiciary can be assessed in a different way, by analysing above all the appeal court judgments and the *hard* and *soft 'judicial instruments'* (law unification decisions[2] and civil chamber opinions[3]) by which the Kúria (the highest Hungarian court) guides the judiciary in the process of the judicial enforcement of European-rooted private law. Thus, in Hungary, the appeal court judgments predominantly reflect the realities of justice provision, in the real meaning of the word, in the field of unfair contract terms law.

The preliminary references that have reached the CJEU from the two countries have been analysed in order to reveal the domestic function of the procedure of making a reference and the contribution of the preliminary rulings of the CJEU to the development of domestic consumer policy and judicial methodology. In Romania, as the development of unfair contract terms law has taken place outside the domain of preliminary references, the interpretation problems were not imported to the level of European judicial discourse; on the contrary, in Hungary, the preliminary references constituted the necessary way towards development. This has to do with the significant differences in the judicial policy on unfair contract terms law in each country, an issue that will be developed in more detail in this chapter.

The majority of court cases in both countries concern consumer credit; in this field, both in Hungary and Romania, unfair contracting was practised on a large scale by credit institutions before the global financial crisis manifested itself in 2008, resulting in several thousand instances of litigation. In other fields, such as telecommunications,[4] insurance, immovable agency,[5] the sale and purchase of goods,[6] and local public services,[7] the case law is less significant in number and has experienced a different evolution in some aspects in comparison to consumer credit. Thus, to a certain extent one can talk in both countries, even if to different degrees, of a two-tier case law depending on the subject matter of the consumer contract and the policy of the courts towards the social impact and economic sensitivity of the relevant area.

---

[2] Law Unification decisions are issued by the Kúria when the need for futher development of the case law requires this or where it aims to unify diverging case law. These are compulsory for the judiciary.

[3] Chamber Opinions are non-mandatory guidance of the Kúria, which however had a far-reaching impact on the judiciary, as the Civil Chamber Opinion no. 2/2012 demonstrates.

[4] Fővárosi Ítélőtábla, 14. GF.40.605/2013/7 (decision of May 8, 2014).

[5] Győri Ítélőtábla, Pf. IV. 20. 335/2009/4 (decision of September 22, 2010), Pécsi Ítélőtábla, Pf. III.20. 099/2012/12 (decision of November 13, 2012).

[6] Szegedi Ítélőtábla, Pf. 20. 751/2011/4 (decision of March 22, 2012), Fővárosi Bíróság, V.G. 40. 389/2011/9 (decision of October 28, 2011).

[7] Győri Ítélőtábla, Gf. II. 20. 148/2012/4 (decision of September 5, 2012).

The first judgments concerning unfair contract terms were delivered in non-consumer credit cases well before consumer loan agreements started being challenged on a large-scale basis under the UCTD. The research revealed that the courts did not have significant difficulties in employing the unfairness test in the case of traditional contracts, such as agency and the sale and purchase of goods and insurance. The judge could easily apply the unfairness test of the UCTD on the basis of well-established case law and doctrine on the specific contract type, usually establishing, on the basis of the *scope and aim* of the contract, whether the business entity acted in good faith and whether the contract caused significant disadvantage to the detriment of the consumer. These judgments in Hungary established unfairness under Art.209A of the Civil Code (the implementing rules of the UCTD) without entering into a consumer policy discourse and without quoting European case law, since the domestic contract law provided sufficient tools for the national judge to establish unfairness. However, when highly technical and sophisticated consumer contracts reached the court, such as those concerning telecommunication services (mobile telephony services[8]), the national judge encountered difficulties in assessing the contract on the basis of the same method and referred the case to the CJEU in the hope of obtaining detailed normative criteria that could be engaged to balance the interests of the parties. In fact, as Hungarian judges have recounted, within the framework of interviews conducted for the purposes of this project in early 2013, in such cases, it was indeed the high level of the technicality of the contract that made the assessment difficult. It would far exceed the limits of this chapter to discuss in length the two-tier approach, however examples from two fields, namely of telecommunications and immovable agency, are sufficiently illustrative.

In Hungary, the clause on the use of personal data and those on the transactions costs applied for payment of the bills by post or payment of bills at the customer offices of the service provider, constituted the focus of the unfairness test of service contracts in telecommunications. Indeed, in a recent case, the court considered the practice of Telekom in charging clients of fixed-line telephone service transaction costs on the payment of bills by post or through customer services to be unfair, for the reason that the consumer does receive a service in respect of this charge.[9] The court established unfairness referring to highest court decisions (law unification decisions 3/2011 and the chamber opinion no. 2/2012 of the Kúria),

[8] Case C-243/08 *Pannon* EU:C:2009:350; Case C-472/10 *Invitel* EU:C:2012:242.

[9] Fővárosi Ítélőtábla, 14. GF.40.605/2013/7 (decision of May 8, 2014).

without any detailed reasoning and without reference to the case law of the CJEU (notwithstanding the *Invitel* ruling on similar facts).

In Romania, the courts encountered fewer difficulties in respect of telecommunication cases (even in the field of mobile telephony services) because the judges were not looking to the general provisions of the contract law, but assessing the rights and obligations of the parties and re-establishing a contractual equilibrium by reasoning with the policy of UCTD. In the field of mobile telephony, the court has declared the clauses on payment delay that established a penalty exceeding the amount due to be paid, to be unfair.[10] The Romanian tribunals referred to the *Océano* ruling (C-240/98[11]) in support of acting on their own motion, emphasizing that the implementing law transposes the UCTD and thus that the consumer policy argument of the European unfair contract terms law applies. The Tribunal of Buzău highlighted the public order nature of the UCTD, from which it deduced the absolute nullity of the unfair clause.[12] These judgments established that the payment delay penalty was in obvious disproportion to the damage that may be caused by the consumer's late payment. In cases concerning mobile telephony services, the whole range of decisions starting with those of the first instance courts, and continuing to those of the second and also including the decisions of the highest court, presents similar developments, following the same pattern. First instance judgments are the same as those elaborated by the highest court decisions, at a level comparable to the judgments on consumer credit. This means that in Romania, unlike in Hungary, there is no significant difference in judicial methodology between consumer credit and other cases.

In the field of immovable intermediation (agency agreements), the use of the traditional contract law reasoning and of the domestic case law on the specific contract type had led to different outcomes in the two countries. The Hungarian courts came to the conclusion that the clause entitling the

---

[10] ÎCCJ Sentința comercială nr.2815/2010, 18 august 2010, ÎCCJ (Secția Comercială) Decizia nr. 192/2011, 19 ianuarie 2011, Tribunalul Buzău, Decizia nr. 539 din 03.10.2012, Tribunalul Buzău, Decizia nr. 53 din 30.04.2012, Tribunalul Brașov, Decizia nr. 53 din 4. 01. 2012, Tribunalul Călărasi, Sentința civilă nr. 539 din 03.10.2012, Judecătoria Văleni de Munte, Sentința civilă nr. 39 din 28.02.2013, Judecătoria Hîrșova, Sentința civilă nr. 716 din 17.11.2011, Judecătoria Turnu Măgurele, Sentința comercială nr. 493 din 16.08.2011, Judecătoria Tulcea, Sentință civilă nr. 574 din 23.02.2009, Judecătoria Constanța Sentința civilă nr. 2907 din 18.02.2009, Judecătoria Agnita, Sentința civilă nr. 322 din 14.09.2010, Judecătoria Sectorului IV București, Sentința civilă nr.1618 din 23.02.2011.

[11] Joined Cases C-240/98-244/98 *Océano Grupo Editorial SA v Rocio Murciano Quintero and Dalvat Editores SA* [2000] ECR I-4941.

[12] Tribunalul Buzău, Decizia nr. 539 din 03.10. 2012.

agent to commission, even when the immovable property was sold by the seller himself, to be unfair since the agent did not perform a service on the basis of which he could charge such commission.[13] The Hungarian Kúria established in 2005, on the basis of the provisions of the Civil Code, that the agency agreement is a 'result obligation' and not a 'diligence obligation', such that a clause that entitles the agent to commission even when the agent did not intermediate for the principal lacks good faith.[14] In Romania, the attempts to apply unfair contract terms law to litigation concerning immovable agency, have mostly failed for the reason that these contracts were considered to be negotiated agreements.[15] In these cases, the parties initiating the litigation have usually been consumer protection authorities, the public prosecutor (in Hungary) or consumer associations; and their success rate is relatively high. This was not the case in consumer credit cases before 2013, which were usually initiated by the consumers themselves; and, at least in Hungary, their success rate was very low. It may seem strange why there was no effective involvement of the consumer protection authorities in Hungary and Romania in the case of long-term, high-value service contracts, as opposed to low-value consumer goods or consumer service contracts.[16] However, the assessment of the pending cases and the pending investigation of the consumer protection authorities has shown that in both countries there has been a revival of non-consumer credit cases (with a focus on telecommunications); this comes following the spending of significant judicial resources in recent years in the field of consumer credit, by virtue of which the problems relating to the interpretation of unfair contract terms law have been set out.

In the field of consumer credit, the different evolution of the judicial methodology and policy is more obvious. In Hungary, between 2010 and 2014, one can distinguish three stages of development. The period before 2013 was characterized mostly by the use of general contract law as legal basis for challenging the validity of consumer loan contracts, mostly ignoring the existence of the Hungarian law implementing the UCTD. The second stage of development can be identified as beginning in 2013

---

13 Szegedi Ítélőtábla, Gf. I. 30, 552/2011/3 (decision of March 22, 2012), Pécsi Ítélőtábla, Pf. III. 20. 099/2012/12 (decision of November 22, 2012).

14 Kúria 1333/2005.számú elvi gazdasági határozat (authoritative decision of the economic chamber of the highest court).

15 ÎCCJ Secția comercială, Decizia nr. 1646 din 18 aprilie 2011, Judecătoria Ploiești, Sentința civilă din 14. 01.2013.

16 The reasons are discussed in length in Mónika Józon, 'Hungary Report' in Hans-Wolfgang Micklitz and Irina Domurath (eds.) *Consumer Debt and Social Exclusion in Europe* (Ashgate 2015) 85–98.

when appeal courts in particular and also some courts of first instance, started referring to the case law of the CJEU; notwithstanding, reasoning in respect of the policy discourse on consumer protection is still missing in these courts. The Hungarian case law seems to have experienced, since mid-2014, a new era of development, stemming from the *Kásler*[17] ruling of the CJEU, followed by the legislative codification of the highest court case law and the enactment of specific procedural rules on the enforcement of unfair contract terms law in the field of consumer credit.

The determination of why the Hungarian courts for a long time hesitated to apply the mandatory unfair contract terms law of their own motion in consumer credit cases, while doing so in other fields, remains an open question; as such, only assumptions can be made here. The answer might be found in the policy of the Kúria, which did not sufficiently encourage the lower courts to effectively assume the law-framing role granted to the courts in the assessment of unfairness via the UCTD and did not clearly articulate the policy of European unfair contract terms law. Both the Kúria,[18] by the end of 2013, and the Constitutional Court,[19] by March 2014, have made clear in their decisions that they are in favour of the legislative reestablishment of contractual equilibrium in consumer credit cases as opposed to the identification of judicial solutions. In Hungary, almost all first-generation consumer credit cases failed for the reason that the consumers could not successfully prove the invalidity of the contract under the general rules of contract law since consumers were treated by judges as equal parties to the credit institution and the behaviour of the credit institutions was assessed by application of the general standards of contract law. The case law assessment commissioned by the Kúria at the end of 2012 identified a significant number of cases that were adjudicated outside the framework of unfair contract terms law.[20] In these cases, the courts often experimented with a breadth of legal bases on which they might establish contract nullity in general contract law (including bad faith, immorality, usury, sham, impossibility, infringement of customary contracting practice).

Only at end of 2013 did the Kúria react to this situation with a clear message in the law unification decision no. 6/2013; it provided that general

---

17 Case C-26/13 *Kásler* EU:C:2014:282.

18 6/2013 számú PJE határozat (http://www.lb.hu/hu/joghat/62013-szamu-pje-hatarozat).

19 8/2014 (II.2) AB határozat http://public.mkab.hu/dev/dontesek.nsf/0/EE3A84E45401B26EC1257C32006000E6?Open Document.

20 http://www.lb.hu/sites/default/files/joggyak/joggyakorlat_osszefoglalo_velemeny.pdf.

contract law is not suitable for assessing the unfairness of consumer credit agreements. However, even in this case, the Kúria did not make it sufficiently clear to the judiciary that the implementing provisions of the UCTD constitute mandatory law in consumer contracts; it only mentions the unfair contract terms law as 'another ground of invalidity'. Therefore, one can find among the cases ruled upon by first instance and appeal courts at the end of 2013 and even at the beginning of 2014 *hybrid reasoning*, where the judge considers it necessary to argue also on the basis of the general rules of the Civil Code in respect of why it has established unfairness. This was the case, for example, in the Appeal Court of Pécs, with reference to the *Banco Espaañol*[21] decision, or the Appeal Court of Budapest, with reference to *Jörös*.[22]

The case law, evolving since 2013 and based on unfair contract terms law, can be classified into two categories: (a) those decisions making no reference to the case law of the CJEU, in which the courts establish unfairness on the basis of the UCTD and the Hungarian implementing law, by the use of the test established in the Civil Chamber Opinion no. 2/2012 of the Kúria[23] or Law Unification Decision no. 6/2013;[24] and (b) those decisions which refer to the rulings of the CJEU.[25] By 2013, it had developed almost into a custom that the majority of Hungarian courts did not quote directly the ruling of the CJEU, but only the interpretation (reception) of the CJEU case law by the Kúria. In these sets of reasoning, the solutions are derived from the domestic higher court decisions, that is, from Hungarian law itself. The approach of the courts is rather positivistic and is not analytical; they do not comment or further elaborate on the Kúria's

[21] Pécsi Ítélőtábla, Pf. VI. 20. 238/2013/9 (decision of September 19, 2013).

[22] Fővárosi Ítélőtábla 6. Pf. 20. 353/2013 (decision of December 12, 2013).

[23] Szegedi Ítélőtábla, Pf.II.20.758/2013/5 (decision of April 8, 2014) Szegedi Ítélőtábla Pf.II. 20.716/2013/8 (decision of April 2, 2014), Pécsi Ítélőtábla Pf. VI.20.235/2013/3 (decision of January 30, 2014). Debreceni Ítélőtábla Pf. II.20.279/2013/5 (decision of June 27, 2013), Szegedi Ítélőtábla Pf.20.892/2013/6 (decision of March 5, 2013) Szegedi Ítélőtábla, Pf. 20.831/2013/3 (decision of March 14, 2013).

[24] Szegedi Ítélőtábla, Pf. 20.831/2013/3 (decision of March 14, 2014), Fővárosi Törvényszék, 45. Pf. 641. 234/2013/7 (decision of April 11, 2014), Szegedi Ítélőtábla, Pf. II 20. 851/2013/3 (decision of April 30, 2014).

[25] Fővárosi Ítélőtábla, 5. Pf. 21.122/2013/10 (decision of February 14, 2012), Pécsi Ítélőtábla a Pf.VI.20.238/2013/9 (decision of September 19, 2013) Fővárosi Ítélőtábla, 5. Pf. 21. 122/2013/10 (decision of February 7, 2014), Fővárosi Ítélőtábla, 5 Pf. 21. 882/2013/4 (decision of March 6, 2014), Fővárosi Ítélőtábla, Pf. V. tanácsa (decision of December 10, 2013), Fővárosi Ítélőtábla 5. Pf. 21. 122/2013/10 (decision of February 7, 2014), Fővárosi Ítélőtábla 5. Pf. 21. 882/2013/4 (decision of March 6, 2014).

approach. This judicial technique employed by the Hungarian courts did not bring with it the greater internalization of unfair contract terms law into domestic private law. However, the low impact felt by the domestic judiciary in respect of CJEU rulings is not only a result of the policy and approach of the Kúria as to the judicial transposition of the CJEU rulings, but also reflects the general attitude of the Hungarian courts towards European law and its methodology, that is, as one which differs from the traditional domestic style of reasoning. While, beginning in 2013, an increasing number of appeal court judgments were delivered with reference to the interpretations issued by the CJEU, national judges do not usually invoke the reasoning of the CJEU. The most-cited CJEU rulings are *Banco Español*[26] (on the lack of entitlement of the judge to replace the unfair term);[27] *Jörös*[28] (on the obligation of the domestic court to act of its own motion);[29] and *Aziz*[30] (on the notion that a significant imbalance can be established when the clause puts the consumer in a more disadvantaged position than he would have been under domestic law; the clause is unfair because if there was real negotiation, it is unlikely that the consumer would accept such a clause).[31] Since mid-2014, there has arisen a third generation of case law concerning the impact of the *Kásler*[32] ruling on the policy of the highest Hungarian court and on the Hungarian legislature. Notwithstanding, there does not yet exist a body of uniform case law in Hungary on unfair contract terms law in the field of consumer credit. While the Appeal Court of Budapest has, since the end of 2013, become something of a leader in reasoning based on CJEU rulings, other courts, such as the Appeal Court of Győr, the Appeal Court of Szeged[33] and the Appeal Court of Pécs,[34] remain bound to the reasoning style based on

---

[26] Case C-618/10 *Banco Español* EU:C:2012:349.

[27] Pécsi Ítélőtábla, Pf.VI.20.238/2013/9 (decision of September 19, 2013), Fővárosi Ítélőtábla, 5. Pf. 21. 122/2013/10 (decision of February 7, 2014); Fővárosi Ítélőtábla, 5 Pf. 21. 882/2013/4 (decision of March 6, 2014).

[28] Case C-397/11 *Erika Jőrös* EU:C:2013:340.

[29] Fővárosi Ítélőtábla, Pf. V. tanácsa (decision of December 10, 2013), Fővárosi Ítélőtábla 5. Pf. 21. 122/2013/10 (decision of February 7, 2014), Fővárosi Ítélőtábla, 6 Pf.20.353/2013/4 (decision of December 12, 2013), Fővárosi Ítélőtábla, 6 Pf 2013/4 (decision of December 12, 2013).

[30] Case C-415/11 *Mohamed Aziz* EU:C:2013:164.

[31] Fővárosi Ítélőtábla, Pf. V. tanácsa (decision of December 10, 2013), Fővárosi Ítélőtábla 5. Pf. 21. 122/2013/10 (decision of February 7, 2014), Fővárosi Ítélőtábla 5. Pf. 21. 882/2013/4 (decision of March 6, 2014).

[32] Case C-26/13 *Kásler*, n. 17

[33] Szegedi Ítélőtábla, Pf.II. 20.758/2013/5 (decision of April 8, 2013), Szegedi Ítélőtábla Pf. II. 20. 892/2013/6 (decision of March 5, 2014).

[34] Pécsi Ítélőtábla, Pf. VI. 20. 235/2013/3 (decision of January 30, 2014).

the decisions of the Kúria (and mostly on the Civil Chamber Opinion no. 2/2012 of the Kúria). Examples can even be found in the judgments of the Appeal Court of Budapest issued in mid-2014 where no reference is made to CJEU case law.[35]

The weaknesses in networking between the courts are also revealed by the high number of preliminary references stemming from the Hungarian courts on similar issues. No cases can be reported from Hungary in which the referring court would have withdrawn the reference because a new ruling had been issued in the meantime, or because the defendant would have reacted positively upon a ruling, with the result that it was not necessary to deal with the case. It seems that in Hungary the judicial development of unfair contract terms law takes place on the basis of a *bottom-up* approach, led by appeal courts, despite the centralized guidance of the Kúria via the transposition into its own decisions of the case law of the CJEU in the form of law unification decisions and civil chamber opinions. Since the impact of the CJEU case law is low in Hungary and the majority of the Hungarian courts do not refer directly to the CJEU ruling but to Kúria decisions, it is worth analysing closely the approach of the Kúria on the judicial transposition of the European rulings. Certainly, it has to do with the low impact of the CJEU case law that the Kúria has, in some instances, reinterpreted the ruling via its own reading of policy. For example, on the issue of the unfairness of arbitration clauses in consumer agreements, the Kúria went further than the CJEU and considered the use of arbitration clauses in consumer contracts *per se unfair* where their inclusion had not been individually negotiated with the consumer.[36] The Kúria's own interpretation of CJEU case law is also identifiable in the civil chamber opinion no. 2/2011,[37] in which it was explained that:

> the Civil Code establishes two ways for finding unfairness: on one hand on the basis of judicial assessment, and on the other hand upon Art.209(4) and Government decision no 18/1999 that mentions the unfair clauses. In case of adjudication, the court must consider the dispositive rules as well, while these give expression to the equilibrium of the parties, contractual risks, and division of obligations. It is a sign of unfairness the significant derogation from the dispositive rules of the Civil Code or such obligations that endanger the realization of the contractual purpose.

---

[35] Fővárosi Ítélőtábla, 14. Gf. 40. 605/2013/7 (decision of May 8, 2014).

[36] 3/2013. számú PJE határozat (law unification decision no. 3/2013) http://kuria-birosag.hu/hu/joghat/32013-szamu-pje-hatarozat.

[37] 2011. (XII. 12.) PK vélemény a fogyasztói szerződés érvényességével kapcsolatos egyes kérdésekről http://www.lb.hu/hu/kollvel/22011-xii-12-pk-velemeny-fogyasztoi-szerzodes-ervenyessegevel-kapcsolatos-egyes-kerdesekrol.

The judicial transposition of the rulings of the CJEU by the highest court runs the risk that the lower courts skip or underestimate the relevance of the European law dimension of the rule and of the policy underpinning it. It may also significantly weaken the methodological impact of the CJEU case law on the Hungarian judiciary, because the ruling loses its Union law dimension once it is transposed into the mandatory decision of the Kúria, and where no reference is made to the policy reasoning of the CJEU.

In Hungary, the lack of consumer policy reasoning had driven the courts to use the preliminary reference procedure as a tool of domestic judicial policy. The courts employed the preliminary reference mainly for two purposes. First, it has almost turned into common practice to seek justification from Luxembourg in support of the interpretation of domestic law in light of EU law. References on the interpretation of Art.6(1), with a focus on the obligation of the domestic courts to act of their own motion,[38] can be categorized in such a way. The referring courts sometimes consider themselves to be prevented from acting of their own motion in enforcing the UCTD by domestic civil procedural rules and by mandatory national case law (including Constitutional Court decisions and Kúria decisions), including when the party to the litigation (namely, the consumer) did not request the unfairness control.[39] Such references usually do not encompass an analysis of the relevant case law of the CJEU, as it is the problem of interpretation that is the subject matter of the request made; the aim of the court is to obtain reinforcement from Luxembourg on the interpretation of domestic law in light of European law. The relevant European case law, which usually consists of rulings issued in response to Hungarian references,[40] is generally only enlisted without commentary as to the application of the rulings within the context of domestic law. In a few instances, the difference in the state of facts and the state of law between the litigation before the referring court and that which has constituted the basis of the CJEU ruling, is invoked in support of the request for a preliminary ruling.[41] In such cases the referring courts have difficulties in establishing the applicability of the earlier rulings of the CJEU issued in respect of similar problems of interpretation, while no attention is paid to the potential of the policy foundation of the rulings that would guide the court.

38 *Pannon*, n. 8; *Invitel*, n. 8; Case C-397/11 *Erika Jőrös*, n. 28; Case C-472/11 *Banif Plus Bank* EU:C:2013:88; Case C-32/14 *ERSTE Bank* EU:C:2015:637; Case C-567/13 *Baczó and Vizsnyiczai* ECLI:EU:C:2015:88; *Kásler*. n. 17.

39 *Erika Jőrös*, n. 28; *Banif Plus Bank*, ibid.

40 As was the case with the referring courts in *Erika Jőrös*, ibid., and *Banif Plus Bank*, ibid.

41 Case C-137/08 *Pénzügyi Lízing* EU:C:2010:659 and *Invitel*, n. 8.

This approach is well exemplified by the reasoning of the referring court in *Invitel*;[42] while the court had mentioned *Océano* as relevant CJEU case law, it justified the reference on the basis that the case reached the court under an *actio popularis*, whereby the interest of the consumers as a group had been affected, and that as such, further interpretation of the Directive and the case law of the CJEU was necessary.

In respect of the second category of questions referred, the national courts aimed to obtain additional criteria from the CJEU on the assessment of unfairness. In these references, the domestic decision also usually lacks both an analysis of relevant EU case law within the context of the domestic law and an analysis of the making of the reference for a preliminary ruling. These cases concern the interpretation of Art.3(1)[43] and Art.4(2).[44] Unfortunately, there is no central data in Hungary upon which it would be possible to assess the outcome of the cases referred to the Luxembourg Court.

However, since the enactment of Law XXXVIII in August 2014, one can notice a change in the attitude of both the lower courts and the Kúria in using the preliminary reference procedure. Such requests have been consequently rejected, while we see significant steps – at least at the level of the highest courts – to integrate the court's reasoning into the text and analysis of the aims of the UCTD (the most referred to cases since August 2014, have *Kásler*[45] and C-92/11 *RWE Vertrieb AG*[46]).[47] Since mid-2014, a third generation of case law has been evolving, concerning the impact of the legislative developments in Hungary following the *Kásler*[48] ruling of the CJEU.

In reality, the *Kásler* ruling did not bring with it more efficient individual justice; on the contrary, the ruling was perceived by the judiciary as a green light to further legislative intervention into consumer contract law, instead of assuming a greater role for the judiciary in respect of European unfair contract terms law, in light of the CJEU's rulings. As a result, August 2014 saw the beginning of a wave of legislative interventions into consumer credit agreements concluded in the past. Law

---

42 *Invitel*, n. 8.

43 *Pénzügyi Lízing*, n. 43; *Invitel*, n. 8 and Case C-342/13 *Katalin Sebestyén* EU:C:2014:1857.

44 *Kásler*, n. 17.

45 Pfv. V.21.785/2014/5; Pfv. VI. 20. 597/2015/4; Pfv. VI. 20.596/2015/5.

46 Pfv. VI. 20. 597/2015/4; Pfv. VI. 20.596/2015/5.

47 Pfv. V. 20. 627/2015/5; Pfv. VI. 20. 596/2015/5; PfV. VI. 20. 453/2015/4; Pfv. V. 21. 785/2014/5; Pfv. V. 20. 597/2015/4.

48 *Kásler*, n. 17.

XXXVIII of 2014,[49] issued on August 8, 2014, made it mandatory for credit institutions to submit their standard contracts to a fairness control at the Budapest-Capital Regional Court, which issued declaratory judgments on the fairness of the clauses. This new law institutionalized and significantly sped up the unfairness control of consumer credit agreements; it set very short deadlines within which the banks should submit the agreements for assessment – under the sanction of a presumption of unfairness – and introduced a simplified court procedure with time limitations for the court.

In addition the law empowered the state to act on behalf of consumers which means that the consumer does not have to initiate individual litigation under Law XXXVIII of 2014.

The assessment of the court judgments issued under the framework of Law XXXVIII of 2014 reveals that most of the agreements of the banks failed the fairness test. However, it is important to signal that although the law was enacted in reaction to the weak judicial enforcement of the European unfair contract terms law, surprisingly, not only have the credit institutions,[50] as they are obliged to do, initiated constitutional control of the new laws, but some judges of the Budapest-Capital Regional Court[51] and the Appeal Court of Budapest[52] have also done so; moreover, a significant number of private persons are among the applicants.[53] More precisely, 380 complaints were submitted by debtors/consumers at the beginning of 2016.

This type of legislative intervention into contracts shifted the judicial discourse from the field of private law into the field of constitutional law.

---

[49] 2014. évi XXXVIII. törvény a Kúriának a pénzügyi intézmények fogyazstói kölcsönszerződéseire vonatkozó jogegységi határozatával kapcsolatos egyes kérdések rendezéséről (Law 38 of August 18, 2014)

[50] 7/2015. (III. 19.) AB határozat (decision no. 7 of 2015 of the Constitutional Court); 3121/2015. (VII. 9.) AB határozat; 3143/2015. (VII. 24.) AB határozat.

[51] 34/2014. (XI. 14.) AB határozat (decision no. 34 of 2014 of the Constitutional Court); 11/2015. (V. 14.) AB határozat.

[52] 2/2015. (II. 2.) AB határozat (decision no. 2 of 2015 of the Constitutional Court).

[53] 3048/2015. (III. 2.) AB végzés (decision no. 3048 of 2015 of the Constitutional Court); 3057/2015. (III. 31.) AB határozat (decision no. 3057 of 2015 of the Constitutional Court); 3083/2015. (V. 8.) AB végzés (decision no. 3083 of 2015 of the Consititional Court); 3084/2015. (V. 8.) AB végzés (decision no. 3084 of 2015 of the Constituional Court); 3087/2015. (V. 19.) AB végzés; 3147/2015. (VII. 24.) AB határozat; 3168/2015. (VII. 24.) AB végzés; A IV/962/2015. számú ügyben hozott AB végzés; A IV/996/2015. számú ügyben hozott AB végzés; A IV/990/2015. számú ügyben hozott AB végzés; A IV/1194/2015. számú ügyben hozott AB végzés.

It seems that in Hungary, constitutional control is considered to constitute the ultimate justice in private law development, this time against legislative intervention into private contracts. It is also worthwhile mentioning that in March 2014 the Hungarian government asked the Constitutional Court to exercise constitutional control of the provisions of Hungarian law implementing the UCTD, of private law judgments in consumer credit cases, of private loan agreements;[54] in this judgment, the Constitutional Court in fact reinforced the legitimacy of legislative intervention into consumer credit agreements on the basis that the shifting contractual circumstances affected a large number of people and that such intervention was necessary to re-establish the balance between the parties on the same principle as that of *rebus sic stantibus*.

In addition to the use of constitutional control, the credit institutions have also made use of the review procedure available at the highest court to challenge the decisions issued by lower courts under Law XXXVIII of 2014. It would far exceed the limits of this chapter to analyse these cases; as such, the key developments that reflect changes in court policy will be discussed. Above all, under Art.4 of the UCTD, the credit institutions challenged the legislative intervention into contracts concluded in the past, by considering this to be a retroactive application of the new law and the limitation by law of the power of the judiciary to adjudicate in respect of unfair terms. They also asserted an infringement of the Charter of Fundamental Rights arising from the short procedural deadlines imposed on the banks to submit their contract to the fairness control; moreover, they argued that the reimbursement obligation under the new law of the payments charged under the unfair contract terms to constitute deprivation of property. These highest court judgments, which confirmed the findings of the Tribunal of Budapest and of the Appeal Court of Budapest, seem to open up a new decade in the judicial methodology of dealing with unfair contract terms law in respect of the impact of the case law of the CJEU.

First, the Kúria[55] justifies Law XXXVIII in light of the UCTD and the case law of the CJEU on the procedural autonomy of the Member States, which pertains where issues are not dealt with by the EU directives (including issues of private enforcement and remedies). However, the reasoning of the Kúria is in all cases built predominantly on the findings of the Constitutional Court, which rejected in its earlier decisions the notion

---

54 Decision no. 8 of 2014 of the Constitutional Court.
55 Pfv. V. 20 627/2015/5; Pfv. VI. 20. 597/2015/4.

that Law XXXVIII would have retroactive effect;[56] it provided that 'it follows from the aim of Directive 93/13 such an interpretation according to which in case of mass use of unfair contract terms the Member State may intervene also by legislation and may amend the procedural rules in such way to be able to act instead of the consumers in their interest and to pursue their interest in court'.[57] The Kúria then adds to its reasoning the notion that where there is a lack of EU intervention in procedural rules, i.e., on the enforcement of claims, Arts. 6 and 7 of the UCTD confer procedural autonomy on Member States, subject to respect for the principles of effectiveness and equivalence as established by the CJEU (C-121/04 *Adeneler*, para.95; C- 364/07 *Spyridon*, paras.126–149).[58] Thus, the Kúria found that procedural autonomy also implies that the Member States may consider certain contract clauses to be unfair by law or may assume that such clauses are unfair, unless proven otherwise,[59] in response to the allegations concerning the legislative obligation on banks to submit their standard contract to the fairness control and the presumption of unfairness in case of non-compliance with this obligation. It is also worthwhile mentioning in this context that the Kúria had, in an earlier judgment, established that it is lawful to assess unfairness in a uniform way, and retroactively, in respect of contracts concluded before the issuance of Law XXXVIIII of 2014. This was found to be the case for contracts concluded after May 1, 2004, since the criteria of unfairness established in the Hungarian rules implementing the UCTD, and those of the case law of the Kúria and the CJEU, were in place even before the enactment of Law XXXVIII of 2014.[60] In support of this, the Kúria invoked the CJEU case, C-92/11 *RWE Vertrieb AG*. The *Rewe* ruling (para.58) seems to constitute the standard defence against the challenge to the presumption of unfairness and the special procedures on the control of unfairness; it was engaged to support the Kúria's pleading that the new law in fact codifies principles previously established by the Kúria and the CJEU, and which have been binding on the parties since May 1, 2004.[61] As to the policy underpinning of the presumption of unfairness, the Kúria refers to legal certainty and the efficient administration of justice to justify the introduction of a 'concentrated procedural scheme'.[62] In this

56 A 34/2014 (XI.14) AB határozat, (71-114).
57 A 34/2014 (XI.14) AB határozat, (131).
58 Pfv. V. 20 627/2015/5.
59 Ibid.
60 Pfv. V. 21. 785/2014/5.
61 Pvf. VI. 20. 597/2015/4.
62 Pfv. VI. 20. 596/2015/5.

issue as well, it also referred to the decision of the Constitutional Court[63] in which it was established that the aims of the Directive provide that, in the case of the mass use of unfair terms, legislative intervention may be made in the Member State.[64] Concerning the compatibility of the new law with Art.4(1) of the UCTD, in relation to which the credit institutions argued that Art.4(1) requires a case-by-case analysis of the goods and services and of all circumstances that exist at the moment of the contract conclusion, the Kúria established that according to the new law, unfairness should be viewed *as a question of law*, taking into account all clauses of the contract. It invoked C-26/13 *Kásler* in support of this finding.[65] Furthermore, the Kúria also had to assess the new law on enforcement procedures against Art.17 (the right to property) of the Charter of Fundamental Rights.[66] In this respect it established, again on basis of the Constitutional Court decision referred to above, that the contested law does not have a retroactive effect on the issue of unfairness or on the consequences of unfairness, because the unfairness control follows from EU law and the Hungarian rules implementing the UCTD, in force since May 1, 2004 (when Hungary joined the EU); thus, there could be no deprivation of property, as the credit institutions were not entitled to make earnings based on unfair terms.[67] The Kúria also invoked the case law of the Strasbourg Court[68] and established that as unfair terms are void under both EU and Hungarian law, according to the Charter of Fundamental Rights and the ECHR, their use does not generate rights that can be exercised by banks.[69] It seems that the Kúria has found a public policy justification for the relationship between EU law and the national control of unfair contract terms from the case law of the Constitutional Court that has significantly contributed over the past two years to the interpretation of national law with the aim of ensuring a more effective enforcement of unfair contract terms law. However, Law XXXVIII of August 8, 2014, was only the beginning of the legislative wave aimed at re-establishing fairness in consumer credit agreements concluded in the past. It was followed by a series of other laws that give rise to the consequences of unfairness in the relationship between the consumer and the

---

63 AB 34/2014 (XI.14) Constituional Court decision no. 34 of 2014.

64 Pfv. VI. 20. 596/2015/5.

65 Pvf. VI. 20. 453/2015/4.

66 Pvf. VI. 20. 596/2015/5.

67 Pfv. V.758/2014/5 (judgment no. 758 of December 1, 2014); Pvf. VI. 20. 597/2015/4 (judgment no. 597 of May 8, 2015).

68 *Marckx v. Belgium*, A31 (1979); *X. v. Federal Republic of Germany*, App. No. 8410/78 (1979) *S. v. United Kingdom*, App. No. 11716/85 (1986).

69 Pvf. 20.597/2015; Pfv. VI. 20.453/2015/4.

credit institutions, that is, the reimbursement of payments charged under the unfair terms.[70] Pending cases were suspended by law for the period of the mandatory reimbursement procedure and were reopened in 2016.

Not all credit institutions voluntarily complied with this legal obligation to reimburse consumers; in these cases, the National Bank of Hungary was empowered legally to act in the name and interests of consumers against the non-complying credit institutions and in April 2015, brought 16 banks to court for their lack of compliance. The high success rate of these suits (five were won at first instance, one on appeal and five at the highest court), reveal the efficiency of justice provision based on mandatory laws versus EU jurisprudence. In November 2015, suits were initiated against another eight large banks. One can therefore identify in Hungary a firm paternalism in the recent development of procedural rules aimed at achieving effectiveness in the procedural enforcement of unfair contract terms law versus the long-standing judicial ignorance of consumer policy considerations in the individual provision of justice by civil law courts. However, there is not yet social consensus on the issue of legislative intervention in consumer contracts. While the impact of the global financial crisis on Hungarian households was largely a result of the unfair contracting practices of these credit institutions and the long-standing lack of judicial enforcement of unfair terms, it seems that consumers are still not fully satisfied with the legislative solutions. In November 2015, 11 cases were pending before the Constitutional Court, in which consumers had requested constitutional control over Law LXXVII of 2014,[71] to the

---

[70] 2014. évi XL. tv. a Kúriának a pénzügyi intézmények fogyasztói kölcsönszerződéseire vonatkozó jogegységi határozatával kapcsolatos egyes kérdések rendezéséről szóló 2014. évi XXXVIII. törvényben rögzített elszámolás szabályairól és egyes egyéb rendelkezésekről; 53/2014. (XII.10.) MNB rend. a pénzügyi intézmények fogyasztói kölcsönszerződéseinek érvénytelen szerződéses kikötéseire tekintettel szükséges elszámolás módszertanának általános szabályairól szóló 42/2014. (XI.7.) MNB rendelet módosításáról (MK 2014/171. szám); 54/2014. (XII.10.) MNB rend. a pénzügyi intézmények fogyasztói kölcsönszerződéseinek érvénytelen szerződéses kikötéseire tekintettel szükséges elszámolás módszertanának különös szabályairól (MK 2014/171. szám); 55/2014. (XII.10.) MNB rend. a pénzügyi intézmények fogyasztói kölcsönszerződéseinek érvénytelen szerződéses kikötéseire tekintettel szükséges elszámolás során alkalmazott becslési eljárásról és az elszámolás pénzügyi teljesítésének időpontjáról (MK 2014/171. szám); 58/2014. (XII. 17.) MNB rendelet a fogyasztói kölcsönszerződések érvénytelen szerződéses kikötéseire tekintettel szükséges elszámoláshoz, valamint a fogyasztói kölcsönszerződések módosulásához kapcsolódó fogyasztóvédelmi rendelkezésekről.

[71] Az egyes fogyasztói kölcsönszerződések devizanemének módosulásával és a kamatszabályokkal kapcsolatos kérdések rendezéséről szóló 2014. évi LXXVII. törvény.

extent that it aimed to protect consumers and also introduced a mandatory conversion of the loan denominated in foreign currency into HUF at the exchange rate fixed by law, as well as mandatory rules on interest rates in contracts concluded in the past.[72] A new wave of case law is expected to emerge as the several hundred cases suspended by the law are re-opened over the course of 2016.

The evolution of the Romanian unfair contract terms case law in the field of consumer credit shows a different and more successful evolution from the point of view of the consumers. A temporal analysis of the Romanian approach (both at the level of the highest and lower courts) reveals that the courts have come to the same conclusions at almost the same time; as a result, there has been no significant divergence within the case law, neither in terms of regional spread nor within the hierarchy of the court system. This is testimony to the well-functioning institutional network, both formal and informal, in Romania. The ÎCCJ (the highest court of Romania) confirms the findings of the appeal courts and the lower courts in the vast majority of cases. Both the ÎCCJ and the appeal courts use the policy-based reasoning of the CJEU without difficulty for the elucidation of problems of interpretation, thus binding and tying the implementing law with the 'living' Union law, as framed by the CJEU. This is an extraordinary achievement in a strongly positivistic legal culture, such as that which exists in Romania. However, the central merit of the ÎCCJ consists in the legal theoretical clarification of the function and the place of the new private law institution within the system of domestic contract law, particularly in respect of the interplay of the policy on unfair contract terms law with the general principles of contract law. This achievement of the Romanian judiciary was not an overnight success. Indeed, the judgments issued by the ÎCCJ during 2010–12 did not usually refer to the case law of the CJEU (this being the rule), although they were built on the basis of the UCTD. In the very few instances in which the case law of the CJEU was quoted, this was done in a rather formalistic, as opposed to analytical, way; moreover, the analysis of EU rules within the context of domestic private law was missing.

These earlier cases present similarities in style when compared to the recently issued Hungarian judgments, in which references to the case law of the CJEU have begun to be made. This means that one can identify a delay in judicial developments of about two years between the two countries, in favour of the Romanian courts. In Romania, the pattern of argumentation within the ÎCCJ is the construction of reasoning based

---

[72] On earlier debtor rescue schemes in Hungary, see Józon, n. 16.

mainly on the text and interpretation of the UCTD as interpreted by the CJEU and less on the domestic rules implementing the UCTD. The solutions advanced by the Romanian courts are 'openly' deemed to originate in EU law, as a natural consequence of Romania's EU membership. The judicial reception of the policy of EU unfair terms law was successful in Romania because the ÎCCJ steadily sent the message to lower courts that the domestic law on unfair contract terms stems from EU law and that, as such, the courts are obliged to apply the case law of the CJEU by virtue of the obligation arising from the Accession Treaty of Romania to the EU and from the Constitution of Romania.[73] One can identify cases at both the levels of the highest and lower courts in which the judge overtly refers to the obligations stemming from the Accession Treaty to the EU and the Constitution.[74] The principle of supremacy of EU law was also reinforced in the new Civil Code (Art.5), which entered into force in November 2012.[75] It must be mentioned in this context that consumer law (including unfair contract terms law) is regulated outside the Civil Code of Romania by special laws; thus this commitment concerns the interpretation of the private law *lex generalis* in line with EU law.[76] In May 2013, the ÎCCJ went even further, stating that the obligation to interpret domestic law in light of EU law *also involves the methods of interpretation of the CJEU.*[77] Thus, the Romanian judiciary provides both a public and a private law basis for its effective enforcement of EU law. Due to this solid legal foundation of the courts' obligation to interpret domestic law according to EU law, in the

[73] Art.148 of the Romanian Constitution states in para. 2 that: 'As consequence of accession, the Founding Treaties of the EU and the rest of community laws prevail over conflicting domestic provisions, according to the conditions set in the Accession Treaties', to which para. 3 adds: 'The Romanian Parliament, the President, the Government and judiciary are guardians of the obligations resulting from accession and those provided under paragraph (2)'.

[74] ÎCCJ Decizia 992/2014 din 13 martie 2014 (case submitted at the Tribunal of Constanța), ÎCCJ Decizia 302/2014 din 30 ianuarie 2014 (case submitted at the Tribunal of Bucharest), ÎCCJ Decizia 2214/2013 din 4 iunie 2013 (case submitted at the Court of First Instance of Bucharest), ÎCCJ Decizia 949/2013 din 7 martie 2013 (case submitted at the Tribunal of Brașov), ÎCCJ Decizia 4821/2012 din 5 decembrie 2012 (case submitted at the Tribunal of Vîlcea), ÎCCJ Decizia nr. 1646 din 18 aprilie 2011 (case submitted at the Tribunal of Bucharest), ÎCCJ Decizia nr. 1222 din 7 martie 2012 (case submitted at the Tribunal of Bucharest).

[75] Civil Code, Art.5 on the supremacy of community law: 'In areas governed by the present code the provisions of the European law prevail regardless of the legal quality and status of the parties.'

[76] More details in: Mónika Józon,'The Influence of European Private Law on the New Romanian Civil Code' (2012) 2012/3 *ZEUP* 568.

[77] ÎCCJ Decizia 1936/2013.

field of unfair contract terms, the latter is deemed to be an integral part of the judicial reasoning, in the same way as any other interpretative method of domestic law; indeed, I would say even on equal footing. It is obvious for the Romanian courts that EU law operates with autonomous concepts and principles strongly tied to the policy of the Directives. The analysis of the reach of domestic case law confirms that in Romania, European private law has had a *significant methodological impact on private law in the field of unfair contract terms*. The following methodological pattern can be identified, in more or less complete form, in the decisions issued during the period of 2010–14. The ÎCCJ first opens its reasoning by recalling that Law 193/2000 implements the UCTD and therefore must be interpreted in line with the Directive and the case law of the CJEU[78] as a consequence of Romania's EU membership,[79] and then turns to explain that the Directive does not only protect individual interests, but is targeted at the consumers as a collective. Thus, it protects public order under a special protection regime. It is on this basis that the obligation of the national judge to act of its own motion and the absolute nullity of the contract as a consequence of a finding of unfairness is derived.[80] On the issue of the court acting of its own motion, the ÎCCJ[81] refers to C-240/98 *Océano*;[82] the lower courts make a similar reference;[83] a number of cases, including C-168/05 *Mostaza ClaroI*,[84] C-241/98 *Salvat Editores*[85] and C-76/10 *Pohotovost'*[86] are usually invoked in support of the public interest argument. For this reason, in Romania, the interplay of the public law provisions of the domestic consumer credit law with those of the UCTD did not cause major problems of interpretation. In cases where the defence raised the principles of general contract law against the consumer policy arguments of the court, the ÎCCJ did not hesitate to establish that the Directive attenuates the principle of *pacta sunt servanda*, conferring on the court the right to declare void the

---

78 ÎCCJ Decizia 686/2013 din 21 februarie 2013, ÎCCJ Decizia 1719/2014 din 15 mai 2014.

79 ÎCCJ 686/2013.

80 ÎCCJ Decizia 3885/2013 din 12 noiembrie 2013, ÎCCJ Decizia 586/2013, ÎCCJ Decizia 950/2013, ÎCCJ Decizia 288/2012.

81 ÎCCJ Decizia 2815/2010, ÎCCJ Decizia 1719/2014.

82 Joined Cases C-240/98-244/98 *Océano*, n. 11.

83 Trib. Brasov Decizia 53/2012.

84 Case C-168/05 *Mostaza Claro* [2006] ECR I-10421; ÎCCJ Decizia 3885/2013, ÎCCJ Decizia 950/2013, ÎCCJ Decizia 288/2012.

85 Case C-241/98 *Salvat Editores* EU:C:2000:346; ÎCCJ Decizia 3885/2013, ÎCCJ Decizia 586/2013, ÎCCJ Decizia 950/2013.

86 Case C-76/10 *Pohotovost'* EU:2010:685; ÎCCJ Decizia 3885/2013, ÎCCJ Decizia 2875/2013, ÎCCJ Decizia 686/2013, ÎCCJ Decizia 950/2013.

unfair clauses, since contractual freedom is not deemed to constitute an absolute and discretionary freedom of contract.[87] As a consequence of the consumer policy-led enforcement practice and the well-functioning institutional cooperation within the judiciary, only a few preliminary references on unfair terms law have reached the CJEU from Romania; moreover, half of these were subsequently withdrawn. In Romania, the courts often refuse to refer the case to the CJEU; this was the case, for example, with the Appeal Court of Brașov,[88] which found sufficient tools in the existing case law of the CJEU to provide a response to the litigating party demanding the reference to the CJEU.

Unlike their Hungarian counterparts, neither the ÎCCJ nor the lower courts used the preliminary reference procedure as a tool of domestic judicial policy. They considered that they could solve the problems of interpretation arising from the interplay of the unfair contract terms law with domestic private law, with reference to the CJEU's existing policy reasoning. Thus, Romanian requests for preliminary rulings did not reach a critical number that would allow for conclusions to be drawn on the impact of the case law of the CJEU on the national framing of judicial questions via own preliminary references. Until the end of 2015, of the right requests submitted by the Romanian courts,[89] three had been subsequently withdrawn[90] and in one case the request was rejected by the CJEU.[91] The withdrawn requests concerned the interpretation of Art.4(2) of the UCTD and Article3(g) and (j) of Directive 48/2008. Concerning Art.4(2), the referring courts raised the question whether the national court may proceed with the unfairness test of the main subject and price of

---

[87] ÎCCJ Decizia 2875/2013.

[88] ÎCCJ Decizia 950/2013.

[89] Case C-123/12 *SC Volksbank* EU:C:2013:460 (submitted on 15.12.2011 by the Tribunal of Giurgiu); Case C-108/12 *SC Volkbank Romania* EU:C:2013:658 (submitted by the court of first instance Craiova); Case C-571/11 *SC Volksbank Romania* EU:C:2012:726 (submitted on 14.11.2011 by the Tribunal of Cluj); Case C-143/13 *Matei* EU:C:2015:127 (reference submitted on 28.11.2013 by the Tribunalul of Argeș); Case C-92/14 *Tudoran* EU:C:2014:2051; Case C-110/14 *Costea* EU:C:2015:538 (submitted on 25.02.2014 by the Court of First Instance of Oradea); Case C-348/14 *Bucura* EU:C:2015:447; Case C-534/15 *Dumitras* ((submitted on 12.10.2015 by the court of first instance of Satu Mare).

[90] Case C-571/11 *SC Volksbank Romania* EU:C:2012:726 (submitted on 14.11.2011 by the Tribunal of Cluj); Case C-108/12 *SC Volkbank Romania* EU:C:2013:658 (submitted by the court of first instance Craiova); Case C-123/12 *SC Volksbank* EU:C:2013:460 (submitted on 15.12.2011 by the Tribunal of Giurgiu).

[91] Case C-92/14 *Tudoran* EU:C:2014:2051 (submitted on 25. 02. 2024 by the Court of First Instance Câmpulung).

the contract where the Member State had transposed Art.4(2) into domestic law. There is no information available as to why the referring courts have withdrawn the reference.

Before 2014, the few Romanian references were rather isolated instances, made by lower courts calling for *European aid* since there is a settled body of case law in Romania on the major interpretation issues of the UCTD, in line with the letter and policy of the case law of the CJEU. However, the newest references raise new questions concerning the concept of 'consumer' with the aim of enlarging the domain of protection that may shape further Union policy on unfair contract terms. In 2014, one referring court asked whether a loan agreement, concluded for private purposes but secured with a mortgage, constituted on a building which serves a professional purpose, would fall under the UCTD.[92] In another reference, the court wanted to know whether a co-debtor to a loan agreement concluded between the bank and a business entity qualifies as consumer in the situation where the person contracting for the loan acts outside the purposes of his business.[93] The judicial debate on the consumer concept continued in 2015, when the CJEU was asked whether a contract concerning a mortgage granted by private persons would fall under the scope of unfairness control, when the contract is accessory to a loan agreement concluded between a bank and a business entity.[94]

The recent ruling in *Bucura* where the CJEU provides a broad interpretation for the concept of consumer, meaning that a natural person who becomes a co-debtor under a contract concluded with a seller or supplier comes within the concept of 'consumer' since that person is acting for purposes which can be regarded as outside his trade or profession, confirms this new tendency of the Romanian courts to test the limits of EU unfair contract terms law.[95]

The comparative assessment of the two jurisdictions offers important lessons for the CJEU on the cross-jurisdictional impact and function of its rulings. First, a central finding of the research is that the case law of the CJEU is used as a *toolbox* from which the courts pick up rules, interpretations, issues identified and strands of reasoning in line with their domestic judicial policy and not necessarily the questions clarified or refined in the

[92] Case C-110/14 *Costea* EU:C:2015:538 (submitted on 25.02.2014 by the court of first instance of Oradea).

[93] Case C-348/14 *Bucura* EU:C:2015:447 (submitted on 21.07.2014 by the court of first instance of Câmpulung).

[94] Case C-534/15 *Dumitras* (submitted on 12.10.2015 by the court of first instance of Satu Mare).

[95] Case C-348/14 *Maria Bucura v. SC Bankpost SA*, EU:C:2015:447 para. 67.

specific ruling. Some rulings are ignored and others engaged, depending on the policy discourse in the Member State. Sometimes the court uses the actual ruling to clarify a question different from that which constitutes the subject matter of that ruling, in search of answers to an issue that is only referenced by the CJEU, e.g., from its earlier case law. For this reason, it is difficult to measure the impact of the specific ruling, because the reference to a specific case is not conclusive in itself. Secondly, within the two jurisdictions, the courts quote different rulings for the purposes of clarifying the same or similar issues, depending again on the policy preference of the referring court. The most obvious example is the issue of the court's *'own motion'*, in respect of which the Romanian ÎCCJ has quoted the joined ruling in *Océano and Salvatores*;[96] very few Hungarian judgments refer to the *Jörös* case,[97] notwithstanding that the obligation of the court to act of its own motion was clarified within the context of earlier rulings delivered in response to Hungarian references, such as *Pannon*[98], *Invitel*[99] and *Pénzügyi Lízing*.[100] The Romanian ÎCCJ constantly refers to the *Caja*[101] ruling to justify its policy preference for a stricter standard (the application of the unfairness test to the main subject of the contract and the price of the contract)[102] whereas the Hungarian courts do not refer to *Caja*. Moreover, *Salvat Editores*[103] and *Pohotovost'* [104] are used by the ÎCCJ[105] as central strands of reasoning underpinning the public interest protected by UCTD, while no Hungarian cases building on the reasoning of public policy protected by the UCTD or on the argument that the consumer is the weaker party compared to the business entity and therefore needs special protection, have been identified.

---

96 ÎCCJ Decizia 3885, 2013 din 12. 11.2012, ÎCCJ Decizia 950/2013 din 7 martie 2013, ÎCCJ Decizia 586/2013, ICCJ 990/2014, Trib. Brașov, Decizia 53/2012 din 30.4.2012, ÎCCJ Decizia 2815/2010 din 18 august 2010.

97 Fővárosi Ítélőtábla, 6. Pf. 20.353/2013/4 (decision of December 12, 2013), Fővárosi Ítélőtábla, 5. Pf.21.882/2013/.4 (decision of March 6, 2014).

98 Case C-243/08 *Pannon* EU:C:2009:350.

99 Case C- 472/10 *Invitel* EU:C:2012:242.

100 Case C-137/08 *Pénzügyi Lízing* EU:C:2010:659.

101 Case C-484/08 *Caja de Ahorros* EU:C:2010:309.

102 ÎCCJ Decizia 453/2014 din 10 aprilie 2014, ÎCCJ Decizia 990/2014, ÎCCJ Decizia 1768/2014 din 23 aprilie 2014, ÎCCJ Decizia 2875/2013 din 26 septembrie 2013, ÎCCJ Decizia 686/2013 din 21 februarie 2013, ÎCCJ Decizia 749/2013 din 28 februarie 2013, ÎCCJ Decizia 950/2013 din martie 2013.

103 Case C-241/98 *Salvat Editores* EU:C:2000:346.

104 Case C-76/10 *Pohotovost'* EU:2010:685.

105 ÎCCJ Decizia 3885/2013 din 12 noiembrie 2013, ÎCCJ Decizia 686/2013 din 2013, ICCJ Decizia 950/2013 din 7 martie 2013, ÎCCJ Decizia 686/2013 din 21 februarie 2013.

Hungarian courts identified in *Aziz*[106] a good ground of justification for the use of the dispositive rules of the domestic civil law as reference criteria applicable to the unfairness test.[107] The Kúria also issued in the summer of 2013 a decision in line with the central message of *Aziz*, providing that the finding of unfairness suspends the enforcement procedure. However, it did not refer to the ruling of the CJEU. In Romania, *Aziz* seems not to have been engaged because the Romanian courts tend to use the consumer policy argument to balance the interests of the contracting parties and not the dispositive provisions of the *lex generalis*, the Civil Code. As such, no case can be reported from Romania that refers to *Aziz*. The *Pannon*[108] ruling is engaged by the Romanian tribunal[109] in support of the special protection of the consumer as the weaker party, whereas the main message from this ruling for the Hungarian courts was that unfairness can be invoked only when the consumer does not opt in favour of maintaining the unfair terms,. It is striking that on the basis of the same provision of the UCTD – Art.6(1) – the two jurisdictions came to different conclusions on the issue of nullity. Romanian courts see in Art.6(1) a case for *absolute nullity*, whereas the Hungarians plead for *relative nullity*.

FACTORS DRIVING THE DIFFERENT EVOLUTION OF THE CASE LAW: THE ROLE OF HARMONIZATION STRATEGIES, DOMESTIC LEGAL DOCTRINE AND JUDICIAL POLICY

i. The Transposition Strategy of the UCTD and National Policy on Unfair Contract Terms

The approach of the two countries differs in many respects in relation to the transposition of the UCTD. However, there is no linearity between the transposition/codification strategy and effectiveness in enforcement. One would think that the transposition of the UCTD into the body of the Civil Code would grant a higher degree of internalization in terms of 'new' institution in private law thinking, whether doctrinal or judicial. Hungary transposed the main provisions of the Directive into the old Civil Code in

[106] Case C-415/11 *Mohamed Aziz* EU:C:2013:164.

[107] Fővárosi Ítélőtábla 5. Pf.21.882/2013/4 (decision of March 6, 2014), Fővárosi Ítélőtábla 5. Pf. 21.122/2013/10 (decision of February 7, 2014), Fővárosi Ítélőtábla 5. Pf. 21. 882/2013/4.

[108] Case C-243/08 *Pannon*, n. 8.

[109] Tribunalul Calaraşi, Sentinţă civilă nr.15801 din 12. 12. 2012.

Art.209A and continues with this tradition in the new Civil Code (Articles 102–105), which entered into force on March 15, 2014. Notwithstanding, as will be seen below, unfair contract terms law is not functionally integrated into private law when it comes to enforcement. On the contrary, in Romania, where not only the unfair contract terms law, but also consumer law in general, is traditionally codified outside the Civil Code in the form of special laws, the process of judicial internalization has been more successful. In Romania, Law No.193/2000 provides in Art.1(3) for a mandatory obligation on the part of the business entities to avoid applying unfair clauses in consumer contracts. Thus, in Romania, a company that practises unfair contract terms infringes a mandatory provision of the law on unfair contract terms and thus acts in bad faith. This provides a clear message, both for business and courts, resulting from the implementing rules.

In Hungary, unfair contract terms law is integrated into the Civil Code as 'another ground' of invalidity within the relevant part; for a long time, neither the courts, nor the legal society considered it to constitute a mandatory *lex specialis* that overrides the general grounds of invalidity, because the 'policy' could not be codified into the Civil Code. Therefore, unfairness was treated as any other legal basis for challenging the validity of a contract.[110] One can say that the transposition (via codification) of the unfair contract terms law into the highest instrument of domestic private law had trapped this new private law institution for several years in a kind of deadlock of private law conservatism in Hungary. However, the transposition of the Directive, whether into a higher or lower level instrument, i.e., the Civil Code or special law, of domestic private law, would not have affected the subsequent enforcement of EU law, if the judicial culture of the Member State was sufficiently receptive towards the policy and methodology of the case law of the CJEU.

Another important difference between the two jurisdictions that has made an imprint on subsequent case law is the approach based on the minimalistic nature of harmonization and the possibility for the institution of a stricter consumer protection regime at the domestic level within the scope and aims of the Directive. There is a series of judgments of the highest court in Romania which refer to the *Caja*[111] ruling of the CJEU, in which the ÎCCJ makes clear that the UCTD is minimalistic in consumer protection, which renders it possible for the Member States to extend the

[110] 6/2013 számú PJE határozat (http://www.lb.hu/hu/joghat/62013-szamu-pje-hatarozat).

[111] Case C-484/08 *Caja de Ahorros* EU:C:2010:309.

unfairness test to the subject matter of the contract or adequacy of the price or remuneration.[112] The Hungarian courts have not yet made use of *Caja* in their reasoning. In February 2013, the Kúria considered it necessary to address this question before the CJEU in its *Kásler* reference;[113] in March 2013, the Romanian ÎCCJ rejected[114] a similar request considering that the *Caja* and the *Pohotovosť*[115] rulings of the CJEU render this issue of interpretation sufficiently clear. In Hungary, thousands of instances of consumer credit litigation raise this issue, but the possibility to implement a stricter level of consumer protection does not seem to have been fully explored and employed under the Directive, notwithstanding that the general policy discourse on consumer credit strongly goes in this direction.

ii. General Contract Law and the UCTD: The Role of Legal Doctrine

Legal literature and legal doctrine failed to keep up with the speedy evolution of case law both in Romania and Hungary. Only isolated attempts can be reported within the domestic scholarship on legal-theoretical and doctrinal clarifications concerning unfair contract terms law within the context of domestic private law, and these have not had a significant impact on the developments of judicial policy (luckily). Thus, such attempts do not qualify as factors framing the domestic case law or having a significant influence on the impact of the European case law in respect of the domestic regulation of unfair contract terms. First, in Romania, it is not possible to report on a significant number of cases, as in Hungary, which was built on general contract law. The ÎCCJ continuously sent concise and clear legal-doctrinal, as well as policy, messages to the lower courts when these lines of defence were raised in litigation, clarifying that the weaker position of the consumer justifies the application of consumer protection law as opposed to general contract law.[116] The starting point of this clarification was a 2011 judgment in which the ÎCCJ stated that the principle of *pacta sunt servanda*, set out in Art.969 of the old Civil Code, implies that the contract should not be deemed to be contrary to the mandatory rules of law or to public order and good morals; as such, the judicial removal of the unfair clause does not infringe the principle

[112] ÎCCJ Decizia 749/2013 din 28 februarie 2013.
[113] Case C-26/13 *Kásler* EU:C:2014:282.
[114] ÎCCJ Decizia 950/2013 din 7 martie 2013.
[115] Case C-76/10 *Pohotovosť'* EU:2010:685.
[116] ÎCCJ Decizia 1453/2014 din 10 aprilie 2014, ÎCCJ Decizia 1519/2014 din 5 mai 2014, ÎCCJ Decizia 990/2014 din 13 martie 2014, ÎCCJ Decizia 298/2014 din 30 ianuarie, 2014.

of *pacta sunt servanda*.[117] In subsequent decisions, the ÎCCJ has further elaborated on the delimitation of unfairness control from the principle of contractual autonomy and *pacta sunt servanda*. In 2013, the ÎCCJ provided the following in respect of Law 193/2000:

> (. . .) it was conferred to the national judge the power to intervene and to correct the excessive contractual imbalances, but not to fully destroy the concept of contractual freedom and the obligatory force of contracts assumed by the parties. This is why the judge can only intervene in exceptional cases when the contract would be unfair. Directive 93/13 only attenuates the principle of pacta sunt servanda by conferring the right to the judge to annul the contract, thus it does not infringe the freedom to contract provided in Art.989 of the old Civil Code.

However, the ÎCCJ concluded its reasoning by making clear that Art.989(1) on contractual freedom does not provide for an absolute or discretionary freedom to contract.[118]

For the moment, it is a well-settled formula of the ÎCCJ that the UCTD attenuates contractual freedom that is not absolute and discretionary; this has been reinforced in recent judgments.[119] In line with this reasoning, it should also be mentioned that there is another way to relate this new, private law institution taking the form of the unfairness test to general contract law. This is the 'cause of contract' theory[120] that the court adduces from Art.966 of the old Civil Code, which states that the cause must be legal and moral, and from Art.968 old Civil Code, which defines illegal cause as that prohibited by the law, good morals or public order; an unfair clause that infringes Law 193/2000 (more specifically, the obligation not to apply unfair terms) deprives the contract fully or partially of its cause, seriously compromising the contractual equilibrium. The comparison of unfair contract terms law to *leisure, cause and loyalty* has been advanced in the Romanian literature[121] with reference to a similar debate occurring in respect of the French civil law doctrine; thus far, however, the theoretical elucidation of such a comparison has not taken place within the context of Romanian law. Although the Romanian civil law tradition has been strongly bound to French doctrine, today's case law does not follow

117 ÎCCJ Decizia 688/2011 of February 16, 2011.

118 ÎCCJ Decizia 1768/2013 din 23 aprilie 2013, ÎCCJ Decizia 2875/2013 din septembrie 2013.

119 ÎCCJ Decizia 298/2014.

120 ÎCCJ Decizia 686/2013 din 21 feburarie 2013.

121 Emilia Mihai, 'General Law Notions Involved in the Regulation of Unfair Terms' (2010) *Curentul Juridic* 94.

French doctrinal debates. The Romanian courts build their arguments on the basis of typical EU consumer policy reasoning found in the rulings of the CJEU. It seems that the missing impact of the doctrinal debate in respect of the case law (that in general characterizes the Romanian judicial style, since the courts do not challenge doctrinal explanations) had led to the more speedy internalization of consumer policy arguments into the Romanian judicial culture than has been the case in Hungary. Even when the courts have entered into doctrinal elaborations, it was ultimately the policy reasoning that justified the finding of unfairness. In the Romanian case law, the reference to traditional principles is only used as a tool to clarify differences or to locate the new rules within the system of contract law; it has not really been used to draw artificial analogies. This case law has had an important role in the systemic integration of unfair contract terms law into domestic private law; the ÎCCJ has recalled, in support of the obligation of the judges to act of their own motion, the central policy message from the *Salvat Editores* case; it deduces as a justification of judicial intervention, the public interest dimension that is part of the economic public order. This differs from the traditional justification for judicial intervention arising from principles of general contract law. It has concluded its reasoning by bringing the discourse back to the grounds of traditional contract law, recalling that the aim of the UCTD is to re-establish the contractual equilibrium between the business entity and the weaker party in order to grant consumers a freedom to contract that is real and effective.[122] One can conclude that not only the ÎCCJ, but also the lower courts, have perceived correctly the *hybrid nature* (public order protected by private law) of the UCTD. In this context, it is perhaps worth mentioning that the Romanian legal culture has become very open towards foreign solutions during the past years and handles well the dynamism of private law under European and global influences, including the proceduralization of the positive law. The new Civil Code fully reflects this attitude since it was significantly inspired by foreign law, including mixed legal systems, such as Quebec.[123]

On the contrary, in Hungary, one can find judicial efforts to build analogies or to justify the finding of unfairness, under the old theories, on the basis of the rules implementing the UCTD. For example, in search of an explanation as to why the unilateral amendment of the contract by the

[122] ÎCCJ Decizia 1936/2014, ÎCCJ Decizia 3885/2013, ÎCCJ Decizia 2875/2013.

[123] Mónika Józon, 'Unification of Private Law and 'Mixed Jurisdictions': A Model for Civil Codes in Europe' (2014) 1 *European Journal of Comparative Law and Governance*.

credit institution under Art.209A of the old Civil Code (the implementing norms of the UCTD) is not acceptable, the courts went back to an old doctrine of *unilateral authority*, developed at the beginning of the nineteenth century. The Appeal Court of Budapest in its law unification decision issued on December 6, 2013,[124] argued that, in such cases, the unilateral authority would harm the equality of the parties and would hamper the existence of the civil law relationship. Such decisions show that in Hungary it is still difficult for the courts to locate the new body of contract law within the system of domestic private law and that there is an inner voluntary constraint (since it is not imposed by an authority) *to clothe the finding* of unfairness in, or at least to relate it to an existing theory or doctrine. This is true notwithstanding that it would be much simpler to acknowledge the existence of the new institution based on principles that differ from traditional contract law. The Appeal Court of Budapest also makes only a brief statement in its judgment, providing that 'the bank is not entitled for unilateral authority also on the basis of the national law interpreted in the light of the UCTD and the case law of the CJEU'. Here again, the national unfair contract terms law appears to have a 'residual role', while the national court tries to defend, under the old theory, something which is entirely different.

In a more recent judgment issued on February 7, 2014, the same court, after considering the case law of the CJEU in *Invitel*, *Banco Español*, *Aziz* and *Jörös* in a number of pages, found it necessary to again refer to the notion that the contested clause provided the bank with *unilateral authority* in amending the loan agreement in an arbitrary way, without justification. For this reason, the clause was found to be unfair.[125] The same doctrine appears in the decision of the Szeged Court of Appeal (April 8, 2014) in a softer formulation: the judge emphasized that the credit institution is not above the debtor (in the meaning of being subordinated to the bank) and as such, is not entitled to establish obligations to the detriment of the debtor.[126] One can see that the emphasis is on the business entity even if the court has established unfairness; it is also interesting that while the court uses the concept of consumer, it is not part of the judicial reasoning (i.e., in the sense that the consumer is deemed to be a weaker party vis-à-vis the bank).

By establishing the relevance of the harmonization strategy and of legal doctrine in respect of the subsequent evolution of the enforcement practice

124 Fővárosi Ítélőtábla 5. Pf. tanácsa, 2013 december 6.-i döntése.
125 Fővárosi Ítélőtábla 5. Pf. 21.122/2013/10.
126 Szegedi i Ítélőtábla Pf. II. 20. 758/2013/5.

of European unfair contract terms law, the case law assessment demonstrates that the implementation strategy is to a large extent neutral if the judiciary properly acknowledges the policy of the EU Directive and has the freedom and the willingness under domestic law to adapt the judicial methodology accordingly. In these countries, the effective enforcement of unfair contract terms law seems to depend mainly on three factors: (a) the legal scope provided to courts under domestic law for judicial law-framing; (b) the willingness of the courts to actually assume such a role; and (c) the treatment of the CJEU case law as a source of law and thus as an integral part of the domestic judicial methodology. The interplay of these factors has manifested itself most explicitly in the approach of the courts in respect of the general definition of the UCTD on unfairness, the judicial requirement of the court to act of its own motion and the consequences of a finding of unfairness.

However, in these issues as well the situation in the two countries again differs. Finding unfairness within the process of individual justice provision and engaging the tools elaborated by the CJEU does not seem to be a problem for the Romanian courts. This is why we do not find Romanian references for preliminary rulings, i.e., those that seek normative criteria from the CJEU on how to establish unfairness, similar to those made by Hungarians. In Romania, the ÎCCJ made clear in 2012[127] that in unfair contract terms law, the general notion of fairness in the Civil Code does not apply. It rather delimited the unfair contract terms law from the general requirement of the Civil Code on fairness by establishing that Art.970 of the old Civil Code is a rule of general applicability, whereas Law 193/2009 introduces the notion of contractual equilibrium, which supposes a fair sharing of rights and obligations between the parties. In the interpretation of the ÎCCJ, the notion of contractual imbalance encompasses a discrepancy of the elements of the contracts and alters the global contractual harmony, considerations that affect either the creation of the contract or its execution. The ÎCCJ made clear to the judiciary that the contractual imbalance, which is the subject of Law 193/2000, manifests itself specifically in each case concerning each type of abusive clause; usually, the imbalance results *ex re* from the use of such a clause. However, the significance of the imbalance can be assessed upon the service to be provided under the contract, reciprocity or lack of reciprocity in obligations and rights within the context of the entire contract. In addition, the Romanian courts are certainly better assisted than the

---

127 ÎCCJ Decizia 12/2012 din 17 ianuarie 2012.

Hungarians, as Law 193/2000 explicitly states in Art.1(3) that the business entities are bound not to apply unfair clauses.

In Hungary, the difficulty for the courts in proceeding with the unfairness assessment on the basis of the general criteria may also have to do with the initial transposition approach in respect of Art.3 of the UCTD. In 2009, following an infringement procedure of the European Commission against Hungary, Art.3 was amended, making clear to the courts that the unfairness test differs from the general principle of the Civil Code on good faith, because it is aimed at providing special protection to a weaker party, i.e., the consumer; the new text of Art.209 followed the general concept of the Civil Code in Art.4(1) on fairness.[128] This is why the definition of unfairness refers both to the terms of good faith and to fairness. Since neither the Civil Code nor the case law contains a definition of good faith within the specific context of unfair contract terms law, the judiciary, and more specifically the Kúria, has elaborated sector-specific tests, as in the field of consumer credit in respect of the unilateral amendment of contract clauses by the banks.

The '*fairness test*' elaborated in the Civil Chamber Opinion 2/2012 (customarily applied by the courts) consists of the following cumulative conditions: the clause must be clear and intelligible to the consumer (the principle of clarity and intelligibility); there must be adherence to the conditions of unilateral amendment of the contract (the principle of effective determination); the conditions of unilateral amendment must be objective (the principle of objectiveness); the circumstances described in the contract must actually and proportionally influence the interest rate, the costs and charges (the principle of effectiveness and proportionality); the consumer must be able to foresee under which circumstances and to what extent new burdens might be attributed to him in the future (the principle of transparency); the clause on unilateral amendment of the contract must allow the consumer to terminate the contract under the changed circumstances (the principle of revocability); and must also include the right of the consumer to make use of the changes in circumstances that benefit him (the principle of symmetry).

The approach of the courts in respect of the consequences of unfairness is more than suggestive with regard to how they have perceived and employed their law-framing role in the field of unfair contract terms. In this regard, the approaches of the two jurisdictions in *Banco Español*[129]

---

[128] Civil Code, Art.4(1): 'In civil law relationships the parties should be guided by the requirements of good faith and fairness.'

[129] Case C-618/10 *Banco Español* EU:C:2012:349.

and on the issue of nullity were compared. In Hungary, the courts may have found themselves confused as to their role in providing individual justice based on unfair terms law since the Kúria was sending conflicting messages in respect of the scope for judicial law-framing. While lower courts submitted several requests to the CJEU for preliminary references in the hope of obtaining more detailed normative criteria for assessing unfairness in consumer credit cases, the Kúria and the Constitutional Court were more in favour of legislative intervention in order to clarify the criteria. Finally, the Szeged Court of Appeal replaced an unfair clause in 2012, and at the beginning of 2013, the Kúria referred a question to the CJEU on whether the national court may replace the unfair terms with a dispositive provision of national civil law (i.e., general contract law), pleading in favour of judicial replacement of the unfair terms. However, in December 2013, while the reference was still pending at the CJEU, the Kúria made clear in a Law Unification Decision (no. 6/2013) that it is the task of the legislature and not of the individual justice to render a finding of unfairness. Moreover, in December 2013, the Kúria instructed the courts that contracts should remain in force in cases where, in the absence of the unfair term, the contract could not be performed. During this period, in which a new generation of cases was evolving based on unfair contract terms law, the rest of the courts were quoting the *Banco Español* case and refraining from replacing the unfair terms.[130] Upon the CJEU's rendering of the *Kásler* ruling, the Kúria provided its own judgment in respect of the *Kásler* case by substituting the unfair term with the dispositive provisions of the Civil Code.[131] Shortly afterwards, the Kúria issued a law unification decision (no. 2/2014) in June, which provided that the dispositive rule would be applied only until such a time as special provisions were enacted. In August 2014, the envisaged special law was enacted, which provides that both the judicial rule on the replacement of the unfair term, as established in the Law Unification Decision no. 2/2014, and the unfairness test elaborated by the Kúria in its civil chamber opinion no. 2/2012,[132] should be considered mandatory. In light of this post-*Kásler* development in Hungary, one can establish that the *Kásler* ruling of the

[130] Fővárosi Ítélőtábla 5. Pf.21.122/2013/10 (decision of February 7, 2014), Fővárosi Ítélőtábla 5. Pf. 21. 882/2013.4 (decision of March 6, 2014), Pécsi Ítélőtábla Pf.VI.20.238/2013/9 (decision of September 19, 2013).

[131] Judgment of June 3, 2014 in which the Kúria applied Art.231 (2) of the Civil Code.

[132] 2014. évi XXXVIII. törvény a Kúriának a pénzügyi intézmények fogyazstói kölcsönszerződéseire vonatkozó jogegységi határozatával kapcsolatos egyes kérdések rendezéséről (Law 38 of August 18, 2014).

CJEU has not yet had any significant impact on the judicial methodology of the unfairness assessment of clauses in respect of the unilateral amendment of contract clauses in consumer credit agreements, since the Kúria codified the earlier test that it had elaborated in 2012. The role of the courts in judicial law-making has seemed to stagnate in Hungary, while the legislature seems to have gained more ground. In Romania, while battling similar social and economic consequences to Hungary concerning consumer over-indebtedness, the courts have followed the CJEU ruling in *Banco Español*[133] throughout.

On the issue of nullity, the difference in approach in the two countries is rooted in the *policy approach of the judiciary on the interests protected* by EU unfair contract terms law. Where consumer policy is an integral part of the judicial discourse, as in Romania, the courts have come easily to the conclusion, under the rule established by the CJEU in *Salvat Editores*[134] (para. 50), that by virtue of the UCTD,[135] absolute nullity arises. This finding has had a further impact on how seriously the courts have taken the obligation to act of their own motion, on the lapse of time under national law and also in respect of the consequences of unfairness in the relationship between the contracting parties (i.e., restoration of the situation before the contract conclusion). The ÎCCJ, led by the policy of the UCTD, has rejected the doctrine of relative nullity, which has a rich case law and a solid theoretical foundation within Romanian civil law.

However, even in Hungary, the argument of relative nullity has often been invoked in defence in lower courts. In Hungary, where the consumer policy discourse was missing until recently, the Kúria established in the Law Unification Decision no. 3/2013 (October 15, 2013) that it follows from Art.6(1) of the Directive that the sanction of unfairness is relative nullity: 'taking into consideration that upon Art.6(1) of the directive the consequence of unfairness is relative nullity, the court can only then establish this, when this is invoked in the interest of the consumer'. It did this after recalling that 'it is the task of the Member States courts' to assess of their own motion the (un)fairness of clauses not individually negotiated with consumers. In support of this instruction, the Kúria referred to C-168/05 *Claro*, para.38, C-243/08 *Pannon*, paras.31–32 and C-137/08 *VB*

---

133 Tribunalul Oradea, decizia din 1 iulie 2013, Curtea de Apel București în ÎCCJ Decizia 3885 din 12 noiembrie 2013, Judecătoria Ploiești, Sentința civilă din 14. 01. 2014, Judecătoria Tg, Jiu Sentința civilă din 14.01.2013.

134 Case C-241/98 *Salvat Editores* EU:C:2000:346.

135 ÎCCJ Decizia 3885/2013 din 12 noiembrie 2013, ÎCCJ Decizia 2875/2013 din 26 septembrie 2013, ÎCCJ Decizia 686/2013 din 21 februarie 2013, ÎCCJ Decizia 950/2013 din 7 martie 2013, ÎCCJ Decizia 288/2012 din 27 ianuarie 2012.

Pénzügyi Lízing. The legal literature did not develop further reasons as to why relative nullity derives from the UCTD. A leading commentary on the New Civil Code advances the argument 'because it can be invoked only in the interest of the consumer' as an explanation for the finding of relative nullity.[136]

CONCLUSION

The research conducted for the purposes of this book has mapped and assessed the factors framing judicial cooperation within the EU in two Central-Eastern European countries with no tradition in consumer protection law before 1990: Hungary and Romania. Since these countries inherited a strongly positivistic legal culture from the communist period, even in the field of private law, where traditionally the courts do not debate and frame policy, the research has also aimed at establishing the extent to which such an inheritance had influenced the judicial methodology on unfair contract terms law and the impact of CJEU case law on domestic judicial policy. Surprisingly, the assessment of the interplay of case law, policy and doctrine, calls into question some of the classical assumptions made in relation to the judicial culture of the Central-Eastern European Member States of the EU, namely: (a) the legal positivism as a main source of the different developments in case law compared to Western Europe; (b) that legal positivism supposes a less active role of the courts in framing new law; (c) that the policy-based reasoning of the CJEU poses a major source of difficulty in the process of the internalization of European law; and (d) the doctrinal transposition of new European private law institutions as a major factor of the internalization of European private law in these countries.

The comparative study has thus revealed that legal positivism is no longer a central factor for the judicial developments of the twenty-first century in former communist countries, at least in the field of unfair contract terms law. In a country with a strong legal positivistic background, such as Romania, the courts have been able to successfully integrate the policy-based and case law-based reasoning of the CJEU into their domestic judicial discourse. Moreover, Romanian courts have for the moment, a well-functioning methodology of judicial transposition of the UCTD and the case law of the CJEU into the '*tool system*' of the Romanian private law, without stripping the newly arrived private law institution of

136 Polgári Jog. VI. HVG Orac, 2012, p. 160.

its policy aims. The Romanian courts have made a successful use of the law-framing role attributed by the CJEU to the domestic courts, in terms of the enforcement of the UCTD, because the courts have not searched for the legitimacy of the unfair contract terms law under existing patterns of the domestic private law, but have rather acknowledged the different and independent functions of the unfair contract terms law within the private law system. They have recognized that unfair contract term law implies a different judicial methodology than that of traditional domestic contract law, which stems from its European law origin.

The comparative case law study confirms that the *central ingredient of effective judicial enforcement* and successful internalization of the unfair contract terms law into the domestic private law is the *integration of the policy of the UCTD and the policy-based reasoning of the CJEU into the domestic judicial methodology*. Without this policy ingredient, the rules developed by the CJEU would remain a foreign body within the private law system, as the case of Hungary well illustrates. The simple rendering of a decision, without the policy reasoning of the CJEU, could not be properly employed in Hungary as a tool to establish unfairness, because the balancing of the interests of the parties engages the consumer as a weaker party and requires acknowledgement of the *public policy* aim of the UCTD. The case of Hungary illustrates that top-down judicial guidance of the domestic judiciary, using existing private law concepts, rules and principles under the traditional judicial methodology at any price, does not necessarily lead to effective judicial enforcement; the same is true of the clotting of the European rulings into domestic judicial instruments (i.e., the unification and chamber opinions of the highest courts and of the codification of the CJEU rulings into mandatory law), as long as none of these instruments properly reflect the policy-reasoning of the CJEU. It is too early to make value judgements on the evolving trend in Hungary to transpose the domestic and European case law into mandatory laws in order to strengthen judicial enforcement. However, such experiments may hamper the dynamism of unfair terms law at both the level of the EU and the Member States.

On the other hand, as the case of Romania demonstrates, a policy-led functional transposition of the new piece of private law enacted at the European level does not necessarily affect the unity of the Member State civil law thinking and judicial culture. The conservatism of legal scholarship and the low scope for internalization of consumer policy has led to artificial domestic solutions in Hungary that have more significantly affected its system of private law and civil justice than the European policy-led enforcement in Romania. The strong conservatism of the judiciary may lead to radical legislative steps, and even to regulatory measures that may have a more significant effect on contractual freedom than an EU Directive that leaves considerable leeway to the judiciary, as is the case with the UCTD. The influence of unfair contract terms law on the unity of domestic private law is in fact in the hands of the domestic judiciary.

The effectiveness of domestic enforcement and the degree to which the judiciary has exploited the preliminary rulings of the CJEU was determined only to a very limited extent by the legal-theoretical elaborations of legal scholarship on the new private law institution. In both countries, the courts in particular have taken the lead in the theoretical clarification of the interplay of unfair contract terms law with the traditional principles of contract law, which is a positive development in terms of the traditionally positivistic judicial cultures of these countries. It is a common feature of both jurisdictions that the courts remain independent from attempts in the legal doctrine to draw analogies between unfair contract terms law and the traditional private law institutions. This is mostly due to the judicial culture that traditionally does not functionally integrate doctrine within the judicial discourse. Such judicial efforts have followed different routes in the two countries, with different success rates. In Romania, they resulted in a Europeanization of the domestic theories in light of European policy, the theories (including that of *pacta sunt servanda*) being reframed for cases of contract unfairness, whereas in Hungary, the judicial transposition used the old theories without adapting or reframing these according to consumer policy considerations (for example, relative nullity). It seems that policy could well substitute for the weak or missing legal-theoretical foundation of unfair terms law in Romania.

The comparative study confirms that understanding and employing the policy beyond the law is the tool and road towards methodological developments in the case law. The number and style of the preliminary references that reach the CJEU from a specific jurisdiction is not conclusive in itself to determining the impact of EU law in the specific jurisdiction. The low number of references can be a sign, as in the case of Romania, of effective judicial enforcement, whereas a lack of effective enforcement may exist beyond the high number of references. The level of development of the judicial methodology has resulted in different '*domestic functions*' of the procedure of preliminary references. In Romania, the courts have succeeded in employing the policy of unfair contract terms as a tool to balance and adjudicate, successfully solving the interpretation problems resulting from the interplay of the Directive with domestic contract law and civil procedural law with reference to policy reasoning, whereas in Hungary, where there is a lack of policy reasoning, the courts have repeatedly asked the CJEU for more detailed criteria to assess unfairness, since they do not see in the rulings of the CJEU the '*tool*' to solve the interpretation problems they face within the context of the domestic law. As is typical for the Hungarian references, the requests ask for normative criteria that would allow for scrutiny in handling the cases, instead of identifying the scope for more freedom in judicial law-framing. The notion of '*proceduralization*' of the unfair consumer contract law has not yet been properly understood and exploited by the Hungarian courts. In a reaction to this situation, the Hungarian legislature has issued mandatory laws in the second half of 2014, having no other option than to do so, since by the end of 2013 and mid-2014, the Kúria and the Constitutional Court had openly encouraged the legislature to intervene in order to re-establish the contractual equilibrium between consumers and credit institutions. Therefore value judgements on legislative interventions in Hungary to re-establish fairness should necessarily consider its own judicial culture.

The case of Hungary illustrates that the judiciary acts as an independent actor in respect of the landscape of the evolving European private law, where the 'dialogue' nowadays takes place between the different levels of the judiciary (national and European), rather than in the arena of politics. Unfair contract terms law has experienced a fast-evolving, *bottom-up unification* via preliminary references, pursued mainly by Hungarian and Spanish courts. '*Judicial policy*' may turn into a powerful force within society, competing with the legislative or the executive in framing economic and social policy, especially in those fields where different societal interests clash, such as consumer credit. The judiciaries of the two countries have acted in different ways and with different aims, however they both acted as '*autonomous policy makers*', over which neither the executive nor the legislature can exercise direct control in democratic societies, since this is forbidden under the principle of the separation of powers.

The dialogue between the referring courts and the CJEU is more or less effective depending on how the concerned jurisdiction perceives the function of the procedure of preliminary reference and the function of the rulings. The two may perform different functions, which may not always converge with those stemming from EU law. The national question-framing may be transposed into the EU problem-setting context, giving rise not only to sensitive issues of national judicial policy, but may even exceed the domain of private law or even that of the law, trying to handle the relevant social and economic consequences of regulatory failures or of market failures. Thus, the referring courts may generate '*judicial externalities*' that drive the unfair terms law in unexpected directions outside a common European platform. It remains an open question how, with what tools and at what levels (domestic or European) such externalities might be managed. Undoubtedly, these externalities are feeding back into systemic problems that arise in the process of the interplay of new European private law institutions with domestic private law and civil procedural law, especially where considerable scope is left to the Member States. Such systemic problems are inherent to the enforcement process and should be solved by judicial tools from within the domestic system; this necessarily implies a certain degree of '*proceduralization*' of domestic private law. Otherwise it will continue to give rise to methodological incompatibilities in respect of the interplay of domestic law and EU law on unfair contract terms. This presupposes the acknowledgement by the domestic judiciaries that less substantive rules and more judicial tools are and will be provided by the CJEU via the preliminary reference procedure in response to their interpretation problems; this ultimately implies that the judiciary will adopt a more active law-framing role. As long as this is not properly perceived and implemented by the referring jurisdictions, they will not fully explore the potential of the rulings of the CJEU in elaborating solutions workable within their own judicial systems. Paradoxically, at present the CJEU turns to be the guardian of judicial autonomy of the Member States, consequently reinforcing the scope for judicial law-framing by Member States' courts.

7. The CJEU's interpretation of the consumer: what significance of judicial cooperation?

Stephanie Law*

INTRODUCTION

This chapter examines a key concept of national and European private law, from the perspective of the existence and significance of judicial cooperation. Having emerged initially in the nation states – tied to national markets and national cultures and traditions – the consumer has come to constitute one of the key actors in the European integration project; the final consumer is a member of European society,[1] entitled to the protections and opportunities afforded to European citizens and plays a key role in the operation of the internal market, transacting for goods and services both within his or her own, and in other Member States.

Indeed, consumer law has traditionally been used as a means of facilitating the internal market. This has been necessary due to the limits of the European Union's competences to legislate for consumer law. In line with Art.5 TEU, Union action and policy must generally be advanced in a manner compliant with the principles of conferral,[2] proportionality[3]

* Much of this chapter was written while the author was a Postdoctoral Research Fellow in the Faculty of Law at McGill University, Montréal; she would like to thank The Leverhulme Trust for funding. The author would also like to thank the participants of the initial workshop held in April 2013 at the European University Institute, Florence while she was a Ph.D. researcher there, and in particular, Fabrizio Cafaggi.

[1] Of course, members of European society, or European citizens, cannot be understood only as consumers.

[2] Art.5(2) TEU.

[3] Art.5(4) TEU. In terms of the principle of proportionality, the CJEU has identified a relatively broad discretion to the Union such that only if the Union action is 'manifestly inappropriate' will it be conceived as disproportionate (C-344/04 *IATA and ELFAA* EU:C:2006:10, para. 83).

and subsidiarity.[4] Receiving no mention in the Rome Treaty, consumer interest was acknowledged in the Single European Act of 1987[5] and found explicit recognition as a legislative competence only in the Treaty of Maastricht in 1993;[6] this basis for legislating was cemented in the Treaty of Amsterdam, in its Art.153 (previously, Article 129(a), now Art.169 TFEU), which provided that the Union should ensure a high level of protection via the protection of distinct and identifiable consumer rights. In practice, however, Art.169 has been of limited use;[7] consumer law has rather been based on Art.114 TFEU,[8] which requires the existence of a barrier to trade that affects the functioning of the internal market.[9] Thus, the determination of the Union legislature to legislate for consumer law came also with a political and policy choice to harmonise national laws deemed to constitute barriers to trade. The Union's harmonisation policy brought together its negative integration competences[10] – much broader

---

4 Art.5(3) TEU.

5 In Art.100A, Single European Act 1987 which explicitly referred to the need to ensure a high level of consumer protection in the drafting of internal market legislation.

6 Treaty of Maastricht, Art.3(s) and Art.129(a). Previously, the Commission had adopted measures at the end of the 1970s and into the 1980s that provided for the protection of consumers engaged in the market. It recognised in the 1970s five basic rights of consumers – protection of health and safety, protection of economic interests, right to information and education, right to redress and a right to representation and participation – and adopted in 1975, its first action plan: European Council, Resolution on a Preliminary Programme of the European Economic Community for a Consumer Protection and Information Policy, OJ 1975 C92/1, 14/04/1975. For example, the Directive on consumer protection as regards food price labelling, based on Art.235 EEC Treaty (then Art.308 EC Treaty; now Art.352 TFEU), the Directive on Misleading and Comparative Advertising 84/450/EEC (which has been amended considerably and since the implementation of the Directive on Unfair Commercial Practices applies now only to B2B transactions in Directive2006/114/EC), and the Directive on Contracts Negotiated Away from Business Premises 85/577/EEC, both of which were based on Art.100 EEC, now Art.114 TFEU.

7 Art.169 TFEU has only been used as a legal basis for one directive, namely, Directive 98/6/EC. However, Reich has suggested that it can and indeed should be used more: Norbert Reich, 'A European Contract Law, or an EU Contract Law Regulation for Consumers?' (2005) 28 *Journal of Consumer Policy* 383, 400.

8 There is a reference in Art.169(2)(a) TFEU to Art.114 TFEU as the basis upon which consumer protection regulation might be based, 'in the context of the completion of the internal market'.

9 Reference must now also be made to Art.38 CFR, which provides that: 'Union policies shall ensure a high level of consumer protection', and which post-Lisbon, per Art.6(1) TEU is binding on the Union as primary law.

10 That is, free movement and competition law, which respectively, aim to remove national measures that constitute barriers to trade and which cannot be

in terms of the promotion of the market and exercised already via the CJEU[11] – and its legislative competences; as such, it identified national rules that restricted trade with the aim of protecting consumers but could nevertheless be deemed to be compliant with Treaty rules. This determination eventually led to the discussion of the character of the consumer identity and the scope of consumer legislation, that is to say, in terms of what – if any – discretion should be left to the Member States to determine whether they might provide for or indeed maintain a higher level of consumer protection than that envisaged by the Union. The Union legislature's resolution as to the degree of discretion to be left to the Member States came to be reflected in the distinction between minimum, maximum and targeted maximum harmonisation. These determinations have had a number of consequences. The choice to harmonise led, initially, to an institutional move away from the courts to the legislature, that is, from negative to positive harmonisation. As a result, EU consumer law – like EU private law, more generally[12] – is famously piecemeal and fragmented, both in character and substance. The body of consumer law-related instruments currently stands at over 15; two further proposals were introduced at the end of 2015[13] and a revision of the consumer *acquis* is expected to take place over the next two to three years.[14] Across these instruments, there exists no overarching concept of the consumer. Moreover, both on its face (that is, given the choice of Art.114 TFEU as a legal basis) and indeed also substantively, the consumer concept has been seen to be more tightly linked to the facilitation of the internal market at the Union level than to the protection of other values and interests that might be held by the consumer.[15] This has been characterised as reflecting

justified, and to remove practices that undermine competition and thus constitute a barrier to trade. The integration is negative in the sense that such measures and practices are removed but not replaced by positive norms.

[11] Initially, and perhaps still most famously, C-120/78 *Rewe v Bundesmonopolverwaltung für Branntwein* EU:C:1979:42.

[12] The same limitations as to legislative competence apply in respect of efforts at European private law development.

[13] Proposal for a Directive Concerning Certain Aspects of Contracts for the Supply of Digital Content (COM(2015)634 final) and Proposal for a Directive Concerning Contracts for the Online and Other Distance Sales of Goods (COM (2015)635 final).

[14] European Commission, 'REFIT Fitness Check of Consumer Law' proposed initially in European Commission Staff Working Document, 'REFIT – Mapping of Acquis' SWD(2013) 401 final.

[15] See Hans-Wolfgang Micklitz, 'The Consumer: Marketised, Fragmentised, Constitutionalised' in Dorota Leczykiewickz and Stephen Weatherill (eds), *The Images of the Consumer in EU Law: Legislation, Free Movement and Competition*

a shift from the protection offered within the nation states in line with notions of social justice to one which focuses on the promotion of the consumer's economic efficiency in order to stimulate his participation in, and thus the functioning of, the market. While the Union legislature has – in the absence of a solid competency basis – set out a framework of the consumer concept (one which will be set out below), it has left a considerable interpretative task to the CJEU, one which it has engaged via the preliminary reference procedure, and necessarily with the participation of the national courts.

Prima facie, the concept of the consumer is unproblematic: one can find a definition in almost every consumer protection-orientated EU instrument, and in others. Thus, one should simply identify the relevant applicable law (the national law transposing the directive), take the definition found in that piece of legislation, identify the existence of the consumer in the factual situation and apply the relevant consumer protection rules to those facts. However, at the outset of this example, various problems arise. The consumer is an important concept that delineates the scope and shapes the character of consumer protection, as well as other areas of law. How does one know to look to consumer protection rules, if one cannot first identify the existence of the consumer? Can a European concept of consumer be identified, given that the EU directives, as well as the national substantive and procedural rules, shaped by their own diversities, provide for different understandings? Is it necessary? Does the shift from minimum to maximum to targeted maximum harmonisation affect the interpretation rendered by the CJEU, and the discretion, if any, afforded to the Member States with regard to the understanding for which their legislature and courts provide?

This chapter aims to examine the consumer concept from the perspective of judicial cooperation; beginning by identifying a working understanding of judicial cooperation, the chapter provides a brief outline of the character of European private law development, and the relationship between the national courts and the CJEU via the preliminary reference procedure; it then proceeds to identify the skeleton definition of the consumer concept that can be found in Union legislation. Thereafter, the CJEU's interpretation of the consumer concept, a jurisdiction that has opened up as the national courts increasingly refer cases concerning both substantive and

---

Law (Hart 2016) 21, who argues that it is necessary to look beyond this instrumentalism which has led to a predominant focus on certain values, namely economic efficiency and social justice.

procedural protection[16] to Luxembourg,[17] is analysed. The chapter concludes by drawing some short conclusions about the future development of consumer law in line with a framework of cooperation.

JUDICIAL COOPERATION, UNITAS IN DIVERSITATE AND THE PRELIMINARY REFERENCE PROCEDURE

Judicial cooperation is difficult to define adequately; it is complex and multifaceted. For the purposes of this chapter, it is conceived as a mechanism of communication between courts,[18] which has not only a legal but also a cultural, social and political character.[19] Cooperation might of course extend beyond courts,[20] or be conceived in a narrower way,

---

[16] The CJEU's foray into procedural consumer protection is reflected predominantly – but not exclusively – in its development of a power and subsequently of an obligation on the part of the national courts to examine consumer protection law of its own motion (*ex officio*) in order to ensure the effective and equivalent protection of consumer rights derived from EU law.

[17] Some of the factors shaping the determination of the national court to refer are examined in the chapter of Gómez Pomar and Lyczkowska, and that of Józon, herein. According to Judge Lenaerts' introduction to the 2015 Annual Report of the CJEU, 2015 saw the highest number of cases brought before the CJEU (Available at: http://curia.europa.eu/jcms/jcms/Jo2_7000/fr/; Last Accessed: 04.06.2016). In 2015, 39 new references having consumer protection as their subject matter were made. As of June 2016, according to the website of the CJEU, there are pending 65 cases having consumer protection as their subject matter, 59 of which are references for preliminary rulings. This necessarily includes references initiated in 2015.

[18] This broad understanding ties dialogue to the systems-theory notion of legal texts as 'legal acts are those communicative events that change legal structures' (Günther Teubner, 'Introduction to Autopoietic Law' in Günther Teubner (ed.), *Autopoietic Law: A New Approach to Law and Society* (de Gruyter 1988) 4.

[19] Neil Walker, 'Flexibility within a Metaconstitutional Frame: Reflections on the Future of Legal Authority in Europe' in Grainne de Búrca and Joanne Scott, *Constitutional Change in the EU: From Uniformity to Flexibility?* (Hart 2000) 21.

[20] In which not only national, European and international courts, but also national and Union legislative institutions, as well as civil society bodies and individuals, are engaged. While this discussion falls outwith the scope of this chapter, it is worth setting out the four ways in which, per Dehousse, the CJEU can interact with the Union legislative institutions: 1) setting the agenda of the Union; 2) as a policy innovator (for example, recognising the principle of mutual recognition in *Cassis de Dijon* (Case C-120/78 *Cassis de Dijon* [1979] ECR 649), which came to constitute a policy determination underpinning the Union's legislative and judicial approach); 3) legitimising and providing a basis for EU legislation; and 4)

for example, as judicial dialogue. Judicial cooperation might be vertical or horizontal, direct or indirect[21] and one type might trigger another; that is to say, vertical cooperation, arising via the preliminary reference procedure between the national courts and the CJEU, might translate into horizontal cooperation, either between courts operating beyond the national legal systems – the CJEU and the ECtHR, for example – or between national courts. Cooperation might be unilateral, i.e., with one active and another passive party or parties, or active, which generates a mutual interaction and exchange that is on-going, with the propensity to intensify over time. Cooperation by its very name connotes certain values, which points rather to the latter understanding; it has been said that for 'constructive dialogue', each participant must show 'an openness to outside influence and a focus on the persuasive force of law rather than its pedigree or its binding nature'.[22] This openness itself should promote the recognition and acceptance of the 'other', of commonalities and diversities, of cooperation and compromise, and of consistency, reciprocity and respect.[23]

Are these values particularly important in light of the character of

highlighting the obstacles to market development or advocating the amendment of existing legislation: Renaud Dehousse, *The European Court of Justice: The Politics of Judicial Integration* (Macmillan 1998) 82–96.

[21] Rosas distinguishes between 'dialogue' and 'relationships between courts', and further, between vertical relationships, those arising from the preliminary reference procedure, 'semi-vertical' relations between the CJEU and other international courts, relations arising from overlapping or competing jurisdictions and horizontal relations between courts at the same level; this taxonomy, while not followed strictly here, explains well the possible understandings of horizontal and vertical dialogue: Allan Rosas, 'The European Court of Justice in Context: Forms and Patterns of Judicial Dialogue' (2007) 1 *EJLS*; (<http://www.ejls.eu/2/24UK.pdf>; Last Accessed: 03.03.2015).

[22] Anthony Arnull, 'Judicial Dialogue in the EU' in Julie Dickson and Pavlos Eleftheriadis (eds.), *Philosophical Foundations of European Union Law* (OUP 2012), 114, citing Kent Roach, 'Constitutional and Common Law Dialogues Between the Supreme Court and Canadian Legislatures' (2001) 80 *Canadian Bar Rev* 481, 539 and Jeremy Waldron, 'Some Models of Dialogue Between Judges and Legislators' (2004) 23 *Supreme Court L Rev* (2d) 7.

[23] Further, reference can also be made to the purposes for which dialogue might be used, as set out by Markesinis *et al.* These include: the identification of Union legal principles; gap filling; the identification of a harmonised response to a problem found across legal orders; the reference to a 'foreign' response as experience to allay fears about the adoption of that particular approach or to illustrate that the solution 'works'; to provide support where the norm being applied has international origins; and where the matter is rather technical as opposed to 'value-laden': Basil Markesinis *et al*, *Judicial Recourse to Foreign Law: A New Source of Inspiration?* (Routledge 2006), 109–38.

European private law development and the nature of the European space? They inherently seem to be. It is characterised from a macro perspective by a plurality of national, international and transnational legal orders and traditions (as well as cultures and identities),[24] sources of law, dispute resolution bodies and legal actors, and from a micro perspective by a plurality of norms, including rules, principles and concepts. The national legal orders, along with their legal, political, cultural and socio-economic commonalities and divergences, are brought together in the Union as an institution, that is, by the EU membership of the Member States; the character of the result is reflected in the Union's unofficial motto of *unitas in diversitate*,[25] one of two dimensions of culture formalised in the Treaty structure.[26] In terms of legislating for EU law, unity in diversity gives rise to a paradox.[27] On the one hand, by acknowledging the embeddedness of norms and legal development in the cultures and traditions of the nation states,[28] it provides the basis for the respect, protection and maintenance of the traditions, customs, cultures and languages of Member States in the

---

[24] The Treaties refer to the recognition and respect of the national cultures and traditions, including in Art.4(2) TEU, which requires that the Union 'respect the equality of Member States before the Treaties as well as their national identities, inherent in their fundamental structures, political and constitutional, inclusive of regional and local self-government'. This provision has been engaged explicitly by the CJEU in, for example, the case of Case C-208/09 *Sayn-Wittgenstein* EU:C:2010:806, which concerned the law on the abolition of the nobility; this law, which has constitutional status, was deemed to be reflective of national identity, aiming to implement the principle of equal treatment and the removal by the Austrian state of the 'nobility' part of a name (where it had previously been registered in another Member State). The Court highlighted that Union measures must 'respect the national identities of its Member States' (Judgment, para. 92) and not only reflects the CJEU's acknowledgement of the diversities potentially affecting the application of its interpretation across the Union space but also shapes the relationship between the national and Union courts, particularly in light of a 'division of labour'.

[25] The catchphrase of the ill-fated European constitution, Art.I-8, Draft European Constitutional Treaty, OJ C 310/1, 16.12.2004.

[26] On the other hand, the Treaties provide for the construction of a European cultural policy: Rachel Crauford-Smith, 'Cultural Policy' in Paul P. Craig and Grainne de Búrca, (eds), *The Evolution of EU Law* (2nd edn., OUP 2011), 869–94.

[27] See Jennifer Hendry, '"Unity in Diversity": Questions of (Legal) Culture in the European Union' (2008) 3 *Journal of Comparative Law* 289 and Jennifer Hendry, *Unitas in Diversitate? On Legal Cultures and the Europeanisation of Law*, PhD Thesis (EUI 2009) 18.

[28] The TEU's Preamble establishes that the Treaties aim, 'drawing inspiration from the cultural, religious and humanist inheritance of Europe, from which have developed the universal values of the inviolable and inalienable rights of the human person, freedom, democracy equality and the rule of law'. . .'to deepen the

formation, interpretation and application of Union law.[29] On the other, however, by promoting the 'common heritage' of the Member States,[30] it advances, via legislative and judicial law-making, the negation of this diversity.

Can judicial cooperation facilitate the identification of a balance between commonality and diversity, that is, particularly to ensure that commonality is not starkly promoted in the name of the internal market at the expense of the other values that underpin both the national and the European orders, including diversity, and of course, the protection of certain groups, including consumers?[31] Broadly speaking, the weight attached to the preservation of the plurality of distinct national (and other) legal orders embedded in their own cultures and traditions on the one hand[32] and the lessening of such a discretion via the promotion of

---

solidarity between their peoples while respecting their history, their culture and their traditions'.

[29] The TEU not only provides the basis for the respect and protection of diversities across the Member States but also the scope for overt, positive action on the part of the Union institutions, including the legislature and CJEU. Indeed, Art.3 TEU establishes that they should advance the 'promotion of peace, its values and the well-being of its peoples', the construction of an internal market and the establishment of an area of freedom, security and justice, the promotion of social justice and protection, solidarity and 'economic, social and territorial cohesion', within the context of the respect of cultural and linguistic diversity; this should 'ensure that Europe's cultural heritage is safeguarded and enhanced'. The Treaties therefore provide for recognition not only of the cultural but also of the economic, in terms of the construction of the internal market and the promotion of social cohesion, the political, with reference to the promotion of peace and territorial cohesion, the social, in respect of the promotion of social justice, and protection, solidarity, and social cohesion, and the legal dimensions of Europeanisation, with reference to the area of freedom, security and justice.

[30] Declaration on European Identity, 1973 (12 Bull. EC 118); Art.67(1) TFEU refers to the significance of the 'different legal systems and traditions of the Member States' with regard to the Union as an area of freedom, security and justice. Art.6 of the same Treaty not only requires respect for Member States' national identities, per Art.6(3), but also highlights the need for commonality, per Art.6(1), in respect of the principles upon which the Union is based. Furthermore, the national identities of Member States are recognised as being worthy of protection under Art.167 TFEU, which following Art.151 EC, obliges the EU to 'contribute to the flowering of the cultures of the Member States, while respecting their national and regional diversity and at the same time bringing the common cultural heritage to the fore'.

[31] Explored further in the section that follows.

[32] Following Schiff Berman (Paul Schiff Berman, 'Global Legal Pluralism' (2007) 80 S.Cal.L.Rev. 1237), Tuori engages with legal pluralism as both a descriptive and normative understanding, 'purportedly able to tack between the shoals

harmonisation (to varying degrees[33]) and uniform norms on the other,[34] is shaped by and reflected in the descriptive and ideological framing of European integration and the Europeanisation of law. The scope for such a balancing task arises where these legal orders meet; one such meeting point arises at the CJEU's interpretative jurisdiction, founded primarily although not exclusively, through the preliminary reference procedure.

The preliminary reference procedure is a mechanism that allows the national courts to refer a question to the CJEU where a preliminary ruling or interpretation on EU law[35] is necessary for the resolution of the dispute before it,[36] linking both sets of courts through an institutionalised process governed by Art.267 TFEU and the guidance offered by the CJEU.[37] The

---

of old-time state sovereigntism and potentially difference-levelling universalism'; Kaarlo Tuori, 'Towards a Theory of Transnational Law: A Very First Draft' (2010) (on file with the author), 17.

[33] These processes of legal development are reflected in the efforts at private law legislation and, indeed, the shift from minimum to maximum to targeted maximum harmonisation in the Union legislature.

[34] The shifts in the Commission from minimum to maximum to targeted maximum harmonisation should be considered: European Commission, 'Green Paper on the Review of the Consumer Acquis' COM(2006) 744 and European Commission, 'Proposal for a Directive on Consumer Rights', COM(2008) 614 final.

[35] Following the abandonment of the pillar structure, post-Lisbon, the CJEU's jurisdiction arising from the preliminary reference procedure has been enlarged; it can now hear cases concerning all matters relating to freedom, security and justice. This shift to an obligation to refer, per Art.267(3) TFEU – and the scope for state liability if a referral is not made, per Case C-224/01 *Köbler* [2003] ECR I-10239 – perhaps reflects the increase in recent years of the number of cases being heard before the CJEU.

[36] Or where EU legislation has not been implemented satisfactorily in the Member State; DG for Internal Policies, Citizens' Rights and Constitutional Affairs, 'Note: Extent of Harmonisation in Consumer Contract Law' (2010), PE 432.728, 14.

[37] Including Case C-283/81 *CILFIT* [1982] ECR I-3415 and more recently, Case C-160/14 *Ferreira da Silva e Brito and Others* EU:C:2015:565, in which the CJEU held at paras. 43 and 44 that particularly where there is diversity across the national systems as to how a concept of EU legislation should be interpreted, giving:

> rise to a great deal of uncertainty on the part of many national courts and tribunals which, as a consequence, have found it necessary to make a reference to the Court of Justice. That uncertainty shows not only that there are difficulties of interpretation, but also that there is a risk of divergences in judicial decisions within the European Union.

In such a case, 'a national court or tribunal against whose decisions there is no judicial remedy under national law must comply with its obligation to make a determination of whether to refer, when to make a reference[38] and the content of the question referred[39] is one for the national court; in certain cases, the national courts are obliged to refer per Art.267 TFEU.[40]

The following section engages the preliminary reference procedure as an analytical lens through which the interpretation of the concept of consumer is examined. The analysis begins by briefly identifying the embeddedness of the consumer in the cultural, social and political contexts of the nation states and proceeds to examine the emergence of the consumer concept at the Union level in various legislative efforts, and its putative clarification in the Consumer Rights Directive.[41] It is against this background that the evaluation of the CJEU's interpretative approach is examined, in light of the national court's decision to refer to the CJEU, the reach of the Union's legislative efforts, and the shift from minimum to maximum to targeted maximum harmonisation.

THE CONSUMER CONCEPT IN THE NATION STATES, IN EU LEGISLATION AND AS INTERPRETED BY THE CJEU

i. The Emergence of the Consumer in the Nation States

Broadly speaking, the shift in understanding from status to contract[42] and the role of law in light of the liberal conception of the nation state and the market provided for a rather delayed recognition within the nation states of the need for specific protection for particular contracting parties. The formal understanding of contract law rather advanced contractual equality as an ideal, rejecting the scope for the categorisation of contracting parties into different groups that required specific levels of

---

reference to the Court, in order to avert the risk of an incorrect interpretation of EU law'.

38 In general, there are no time limits for a reference; the exception applies in relation to timelines for reviews of legality, per Art.263(6) TFEU.

39 The CJEU will review the question referred and, if necessary, reformulate the reference, requesting clarifications and confirmation from the national court, where necessary; Art.101 Rules of Procedure of the CJEU, OJ L265/25, 29.09.2012.

40 Reports on the private law cases before the CJEU have been published every year since 1995: Christian H. Kohler, 'Gemeinschaftsrecht und Privatrecht: Zur Rechtsprechung des EuGH im Jahre 1994' (1995) 3 *Zeitschrift für Europäisches Privatrecht* 482.

41 Consumer Rights Directive 2011/83/EU; hereinafter, CRD.

42 Henry S. Maine, 'From Status to Contract' in *Ancient Law* (Murray 1861).

protection and leaving little scope for the recognition of the 'consumer' as such. This understanding was based on the notion of a technical, apolitical private law, with limited or no social function, fundamentally reflected in freedom of contract.[43] The contrast came with the subsequent materialisation of contract law,[44] which gave rise across the national legal orders to mechanisms for the protection of specific contracting parties. As national markets began to emerge, tied to the political and economic strength of emerging nation states,[45] it was recognised that certain parties (predominantly individuals) who transacted for goods and services within those markets required additional levels of protection; within these confines, this protection could be offered by the state through a social protection lens.

Different conceptualisations of the consumer then became tied to 'notions of national citizenship', reflecting diverse national markets: 'national regulation and law would dictate the mode of national production, the extent and character of goods and services on offer within that market, as well as the terms and conditions under which such goods and services might or might not be purchased'.[46] As such, the rationales for the protection of the consumer and the scope of protection in general were (and indeed continue to be, to a certain extent) diverse within the Member States and between the national and European levels. Given the silence of Union law at the outset, the identity of the consumer emerged initially within the context of the nation state, initially concerned with

---

[43] Mark Freedland and Matthias Lehmann, 'Non-Discrimination and the "Constitutionalization of Contract Law"' in Gerhard Dannemann and Stefan Vogenauer (eds), *The Common European Sales Law in Context: Interactions with English and German Law* (OUP 2013) 168.

[44] Trends of materialisation of law were discussed in Weber's analysis of legal systems, Max Weber, *Economic and Sociology, Vol.II* (Günther Roth and Claus Wittig edn.) (Berkeley Press 1969); notwithstanding, the development of the discourse, between the formalists, promoting the maintenance of the autonomy of law, in respect of political and social concerns, and those promoting an understanding of law, incorporating concerns as to social justice arising in modern society, really came to the fore with critical legal scholarship.

[45] For a more detailed examination than is possible here, see Hans-Wolfgang Micklitz and Yane Svetiev, 'The Transformation(s) of Private Law' in Hans-Wolfgang Micklitz, Yane Svetiev and Guido Comparato (eds), *European Regulatory Private Law – The Paradigms Tested*, EUI Working Paper 2014/04, 69, 82 *et seq* and Saskia Sassen, *Territory, Authority, Rights: From Medieval to Global Assemblages* (Princeton University Press, 2008).

[46] Michelle Everson, 'Legal Constructions of the Consumer' in Frank Trentmann (ed.), *The Making of the Consumer: Knowledge, Power and Identity in the Modern World* (Bloomsbury 2006), 107.

the balancing of market power (and the private autonomy exercised therein) and attached to the party who was deemed to lack such power and autonomy.[47] The consumer identity therefore initially encompassed determinations of local preference, deriving from both 'consumer culture' and general culture,[48] or indeed the lack thereof.[49] The divergent understandings of consumer and consumer culture across national legal orders reinforced the notion that 'the consumer role model of a particular legal system can be seen as a mirror of this society's vision of its market and social system'.[50] Indeed, recent empirical research suggests that consumers in different national contexts continue to receive and understand information in different ways,[51] indicating that 'national cultural variation'[52] affects not only the conceptualisation of consumers but also the way in which consumers think and behave, including for example, how they process communications, their potential for trust and their exercise of rational thinking in decision-making.[53]

Moreover, as will be explored further below, the Member States have – where discretion allows it – transposed the concept of consumer as established in Union legislation into their national legal orders in diverse manners, either maintaining or providing for a higher level of protection than anticipated at the EU level. First, the definitions of the consumer concept established in Union legislation can be briefly set out.

---

[47] Hans-Wolfgang Micklitz, Norbert Reich and Peter Rott, *European Consumer Law* (2nd edn., Intersentia 2014), 1–6.

[48] Iris Benöhr, *EU Consumer Law and Human Rights* (OUP 2013) 14–16.

[49] This was the case, for example, with the central and Eastern European states, which lacked – largely in line with the socialist culture and tradition and at least before the 1990s – any real understanding of consumer culture. See the contribution of Józon herein.

[50] Brigitta Lurger, 'Old and New Insights for the Protection of Consumers in European Private Law in the Wake of the Global Economic Crisis' in Roger Brownsword *et al* (eds), *The Foundations of European Private Law* (Hart 2011), 106.

[51] Thomas Wilhelmsson, 'The European Average Consumer – a Legal Fiction?' in Thomas Wilhelmsson *et al* (eds), *Private Law and the Many Cultures of Europe* (Kluwer 2007).

[52] It might be seen that Hofstede's dimensions of national culture – Geert Hofstede, *Culture's Consequences: Comparing Values, Behaviours, Institutions and Organizations Across Nations* (2nd edn., Sage Publications 2001) – might be useful to cross-cultural analysis in the European context.

[53] Thomas Wilhelmsson, 'Harmonizing Unfair Commercial Practices Law: The Cultural and Social Dimensions' (2006) 44 *Os.Hall.L.J.* 461.

ii. The Consumer Concept in Union Legislation

In line with the Union's limited competences, briefly set out above, consumer protection legislation has been promulgated in response to specific problems arising at national and European levels, and legislated for against the background of the broader aims of European integration,[54] thus, like European private law, legislative efforts in respect of consumer law have been piecemeal, broadly reflecting a harmonisation of national consumer norms that could constitute a barrier to trade but which are deemed to be justified for reasons of consumer protection.

Union legislation provides neither for a consistent nor for a coherent concept of the consumer: this is true in respect of definitions found in legislation orientated at consumer protection and in legislation covering related regulated areas.[55] Usually, however, the consumer is defined as a natural person acting outside his trade or profession; it is therefore typically established as a negative conceptualisation.[56] Such a definition is used for example in Art.2, Doorstep Selling Directive (DSD),[57] and in Art.2(b), Unfair Contract Terms Directive (UCTD).[58] A slightly different understanding of what constitutes the relevant economic activity of the consumer was set out in the (now-abandoned) Proposal for a Common European Sales Law (pCESL), which referred to 'any natural person who is acting for purposes which are outside that person's trade, business, craft, or profession'. A different understanding of consumer is established in the most recent Package Travel Directive, which abandons

---

[54] Namely the removal of national barriers to trade and the promotion of the internal market (where national law might at once constitute barriers to trade and aim to promote the protection of consumer interests).

[55] The definitions in relevant pieces of legislation are set out in Table 7.1 below. See also, the introduction to the reasoning of AG Cruz Villalón in Case C-110/14 *Costea* EU:C:2015:271, Opinion of AG Cruz Villalón, para. 18, and the footnotes therein:

> The concept of consumer appears across many fields of EU law, beyond the specific instruments on the approximation of laws on consumer protection; examples are the fields of competition law, (9) judicial cooperation in civil matters, (10) the common agricultural and fisheries policies, (11) and other fields where measures to approximate laws exist. (12) In that regard, the many instruments of secondary law aimed at consumer protection do not provide an unambiguous conception of the term 'consumer' either. (13).

[56] Some provisions make reference to the notion of 'craft' while others do not; however, generally, the provisions provide for a negative definition of consumer.

[57] Directive 85/577/EEC.

[58] Directive 93/13/EEC.

the use of the consumer concept in favour of the notion of traveller.[59] It is worth noting that the previously applicable directive defined the consumer as 'any person who takes or agrees to take the package' (the principal contractor), or on whose behalf, the principal contractor agrees to purchase the package, per Art.2(4);[60] of key significance – a consideration to which we will return below – is that this definition was not limited to natural persons but could also be understood to include businesses and professionals. Each directive mentioned above – with the exception of the new Package Travel Directive – is of a minimum harmonisation reach.

In contrast to the piecemeal approach identifiable above, in the Proposal for the Consumer Rights Directive (hereinafter, pCRD),[61] the Commission initially intended to remedy the incoherence arising across European consumer law due to the piecemeal nature of the consumer *acquis* by adopting a maximum harmonisation approach. This approach would have removed the discretion of the Member States to maintain existing or indeed to establish higher levels of consumer protection. The initial draft of the pCRD, published in 2008, thus aimed at regulation 'in a systematic fashion, simplifying and updating the existing rules, removing inconsistencies and closing gaps'.[62] However, much of the criticism of the pCRD concerned its reach, the anticipated lack of flexibility with regard to its transposition and application in the national legal orders,[63] and in particular, the removal of the discretion for differentiated levels of protection. As enacted, the CRD is more limited in its scope; it is rather a directive of targeted maximum harmonisation.[64] Substantively, it repeals the Doorstep Selling Directive and the Distance Selling Directive[65] while amending parts of the UCTD and the Consumer Sales Directive.[66] Like Art.2(a) of the Unfair Commercial Practices Directive (UCPD), a directive of a maximum harmonisation nature,[67] which it leaves intact, the

---

59 See Package Travel Directive 2015/2302, recital 17 and Art.3(6).

60 Directive 90/314/EEC.

61 European Commission, 'Proposal for a Directive on Consumer Rights' COM(2008) 614 final.

62 Ibid.

63 Angus Johnston and Hannes Unberath, 'European Private Law by Directives: Approach and Challenges' in Christian Twigg-Flesner (ed.), *The Cambridge Companion to European Union Private Law* (CUP 2011), 89.

64 Art.4 CRD.

65 Directive 97/7/EC.

66 Directive 99/4/EC.

67 Directive 2005/29/EC as 'any natural person, who in commercial practices covered by this Directive, is acting for purposes which are outside his trade,

CRD provides in Art.2(1) that the consumer is 'any natural person who, in contracts covered by this Directive, is acting for purposes which are outside his trade, business, craft or profession'.[68] The directive in itself recognises – in recital 34, as per recital 18 UCPD – that there is a need for differentiation in levels of protection.[69] This is said to be the case in light of the existence of consumers who – for various reasons – are deemed to be more vulnerable than others, for example, those who are 'particularly vulnerable because of their mental, physical or psychological infirmity, age or credulity'.[70]

In related areas of regulation, the concept differs still more; for example, in respect of financial protection, the notion of consumer is conceived as applying to investors and clients of financial institutions.[71] Investors and shareholders might also qualify as consumers for the purposes of civil procedure. Another example can be found in the instruments on cross-border civil procedure; the consumer is defined in the Brussels I *bis* and Rome I regulations. In recital 18 to Brussels I *bis*, the consumer is understood – among other groups[72] – to be the 'weaker party' who 'should be protected by rules of jurisdiction more favourable to his interests than the general rules'; consumer contracts – the jurisdiction over which is established in Art.17 – are defined as those concluded by a person, 'the consumer, for a

business, craft or profession'. The UCPD does not refer explicitly – except in Recital 18 – to the notion of 'average consumer'; this conceptualisation was in fact included in the original version at Art.2(b).

[68] Similarly, this definition of consumer is also employed in private international law: Art.6, Rome I Regulation 593/2008.

[69] Note that, in respect of the UCPD, the notion of average consumer was initially included in the original draft of the directive but removed in the final version (with reference in recital 18); G Howells, 'Introduction' in Geraint Howells, Hans-Wolfgang Micklitz and Thomas Wilhelmsson (eds), *European Fair Trading Law: The Unfair Commercial Practices Directive* (Ashgate 2006). This has been recognised by the AG in Case C-110/14 *Costea* EU:C:2015:271, Opinion of AG Cruz Villalón, para. 18.

[70] The recital does not, however, as will be discussed below, refer explicitly to the notion of the 'average consumer'. For more on the vulnerable consumer, and the nature of this vulnerability, see Norbert Reich, 'Vulnerable Consumers in EU Law' in Dorota Leczykiewickz and Stephen Weatherill (eds), *The Images of the Consumer in EU Law: Legislation, Free Movement and Competition Law* (Hart 2016) 139.

[71] Consider, for example, the broad range of persons included in Art.4(1), Directive 2014/65/EU on markets in financial instruments, as well as the protection offered to consumers under the notion of 'payment service users' per Directive 2007/64/EC on payment services.

[72] Namely, employees and the insured.

purpose which can be regarded as being outside his trade or profession'.[73] Recital 23 to the Rome I Regulation also establishes that consumers fall within a category of 'weaker' individuals. The definition of the consumer contract is established in Art.6 for the purposes of the determination of the applicable law; this provision is slightly more comprehensive than Brussels I *bis* and defines consumer contracts as those 'concluded by a natural person for a purpose which can be regarded as being outside his trade or profession (the consumer) with another person acting in the exercise of his trade or profession (the professional)'.[74]

The applicable concept of the consumer also determines the level of protection, if any, offered in relation to 'mixed transactions', that is, those contracts in which a person enters into a transaction for both a personal and a professional reason. Again, the Union legislation diverges. The Product Liability Directive provides explicitly – and exceptionally, as most consumer protection legislation does not make specific reference to mixed transactions – that it applies to damages arising from defective products used 'mainly' for a private reason.[75] More recently, the Draft Common Frame of Reference (DCFR) has provided that a contract for primarily non-professional interests will be covered by consumer protection rules[76] while the CRD sets out at recital 17 that in respect of 'dual purpose' contracts, the CRD will apply so long as the 'trade purpose is so limited as not to be predominant'.

Four dimensions of the consumer concept can therefore be identified: whether the consumer is defined positively[77] or negatively,[78] whether the consumer is defined in relation to specific legislation or generally,[79] whether

---

[73] Regulation 1215/2012 on Jurisdiction and the Recognition and Enforcement of Judgments in Civil and Commercial Matters, recital 18, and Art.17.

[74] Regulation 593/2008 on the Law Applicable to Contractual Relations, recital 23 and Art.6.

[75] Directive 1985/374/EEC, Art.9(b)(ii).

[76] Consumer is deemed to be 'any natural person who is acting primarily for purposes which are not related to his or her trade, business or profession' at I.-1:105, DCFR.

[77] That is, where characteristics of a consumer are set out and the relevant party must be identifiable on this basis; Finland (Art.4, Consumer Protection Act), Sweden (for example, Art.2, Consumer Protection Act).

[78] Where the consumer is defined by his acting for purposes not related to his business or profession; an example can be identified in Estonian legislation in s.2(1) of the Consumer Protection Act.

[79] Consider specifically the French system, which does not define consumer law in itself but leaves the definition for the courts in respect of the relevant case before it; consider the law implementing the CRD, Loi n°.2014-344 du 17 mars 2014 relative à la consommation.

the definition of consumer extends to legal persons or is limited to natural persons[80] and, moreover, the manner in which mixed transactions are dealt with (that is, whether consumer protection laws apply only to those transactions falling entirely outside the professional activity of the relevant party[81] or whether it extends to those predominantly or 'mainly' outside of their professional activity[82]). These considerations will be explored in further depth, in terms of how they have engaged by the CJEU, below.

The literature has reflected on how these legislative provisions have been implemented in the Member States.[83] Two strands of analysis are identified herein as being particularly relevant to the evaluation of the interpretation of the consumer concept, shaping the way in which the evolution of

---

[80] Research Group on the Existing EC Private Law, *Contract II—Principles of the Existing EC Contract Law* (Sellier 2009) 59. Some Member States include legal persons in their definitions of consumer, if they acquire goods or services for private or final use, while others include employees (Germany: BAG, 25 May 2005, 5 AZR 572/04, NJW 2005, 3305 in relation to s.13 BGB, where the relevant purpose is not self-employed or commercial) and SMEs (the Netherlands, if under 49 employees). Moreover, in Belgium, for example, consumers are defined as 'toute personne physique ou morale qui acquiert ou utilise à des fins excluant tout caractère professionnel des produits ou des services mis sur le marché' (Art.1er, 7, de la loi du 4 juillet 1991 sur les pratiques du commerce et l'information et la protection du consommateur).

[81] For example, in Austria, the businessman starting a business is deemed to be a consumer (Art.3, KSchG; this can be compared to Germany, where persons starting a business or those who are self-employed are deemed to be professionals, per s.14 BGB, BGH 24 February 2005, BGHZ 162, 253).

[82] Research Group on the Existing EC Private Law, *Contract II—Principles of the Existing EC Contract Law* (Sellier 2009) 55. The French system also makes reference to the non-professional (Cass. Civ., 15 mars 2005, No. de pourvoi: 02-13285); generally, according to case law, the consumer will be a natural or legal person who concludes contracts not directly related to his profession (Cass.civ. 28 avril 1987, CP 1987. II. 20893; Cass.civ. 24 janvier 1995, Recueil Dalloz Sirey 1995, 327-329). In the UK, a business dealing outwith their own business purposes, can be deemed to be 'dealing as a consumer' (*R & B Customs Brokers Ltd* v *United Dominions Trust Ltd* [1988] 1 WLR 321. This can be compared with the approach of the Italian Corte di Cassazione; Cass. 25 guglio 2001, No.10127, I Contratti 2002, 338. The Swedish consumer sales law provides that contracts concluded for a 'mainly' private purpose will be covered by consumer protection law (s.1(1) Konsumentköplag 1990); in the German system, it is a matter for the domestic courts to assess where the predominance lies (OLG Celle, NJW-RR 2004, 1645).

[83] Hannes Rösler, 'Consumers and Consumer Protection Law' in Jürgen Basedow *et al* (eds), *Max Planck Encyclopedia of European Private Law* (OUP 2012) 371 and Martin Ebers, 'The Notion of Consumer' in Hans Schulte-Nölke *et al* (eds), *EC Consumer Law Compendium: Comparative Analysis* (Universität Bielefeld, 2008) 717–19.

European private law – broadly understood – has shaped – in its substantive and procedural dimensions[84] – and been shaped by the operation and application of the consumer concept.[85] On the one hand, the divergent understandings of consumer that emerged initially in the nation states have been met with those concepts advanced in the body of EU consumer protection instruments. Where this legislation has afforded a degree of discretion to the Member States by virtue of the reach of Union legislation – that is, depending on whether it is of a minimum, maximum or targeted maximum harmonisation character[86] – the scope for divergent levels of consumer protection have emerged within and beyond the national legal systems.[87] Moreover, the scope for the recognition of the experiences and expectations of consumers, particularly significant at the stage when the legislation is implemented and applied in the Member States, also depends on this reach.[88] On the other hand, and relatedly, the lack of common understanding of the consumer concept across the national legal orders, and the consequent existence of different levels of protection, has led the national courts to identify a lack of clarity in interpretation, or indeed potential conflicts between national and Union law, on the basis of which they have requested preliminary rulings from Luxembourg.

---

84 The connection has been made explicitly clear by AG Sharpston in Case C-497/13 *Faber* ECLI:EU:C:2014:2403, para. 62.

85 Reference can be made to Micklitz's outline of the three stages of the development of European regulatory private law: Hans-Wolfgang Micklitz, 'European Private Regulatory Law: A Plea for New Thinking', 15 *et seq* (on file with author). In practical terms, this relationship is also due to the fact that a considerable portion of the private law legislation deals with issues of consumer protection; this amounts to around 80 per cent according to Rösler, n.83, 370. Moreover, the legislative basis of the former derives in part from the latter per Arts.4(2)(f), 12, 114(3) and 169 TFEU.

86 The CRD aimed to generate a higher level of coherence; European Commission, 'Green Paper on the Review of the Consumer *Acquis*' COM(2006) 744 and Directorate-General for Internal Policies, Policy Department: Citizens' Rights and Constitutional Affairs, 'The Potential Impact of the Consumer Rights Directive on Member States' Contract Law' (PE 419.606, 2009), 14; the desire – in the legislature and CJEU – for coherence at the EU level arguably may come at the expense of national coherence; Weatherill references the CJEU's 'adventurous reading of EU measures' in this respect: Stephen Weatherill, 'Consumer Policy' in Craig and de Búrca, n.26, 865. Thus, it was considered that as a result of these divergences, the Member States' legislatures might have difficulties in delineating and implementing the CRD, one purpose of which was the promotion of coherence.

87 Discussed in greater detail below, in respect of the implementation of Union legislation in the Member States.

88 Wilhelmsson, n.51.

The rationales of the Member States for implementing Union legislation in a manner other than a word-for-word transposition diverge. For example, the national legislature may wish to maintain or establish a broad understanding of consumer. This may be done to promote coherence within the national system, that is, by advancing a consistent approach between national standards of consumer protection and the minimum standard envisioned by the invocation of EU consumer rights, via a definition that coincides with the national approach. On the other hand, as the examples above illustrate, the national legislature may have the intention of affording protection to a wider group than anticipated by the Union legislature. Where the Union legislature attributes this discretion to the Member States, a higher level of protection can be maintained or established. Thus, minimum harmonisation allows for both options. The trend towards maximum harmonisation, however, strictly understood, removes such latitude, limiting the scope for the Member States to establish and maintain a more stringent level of protection in the transposition of EU instruments.[89] As will be examined below, the CJEU has thus far facilitated the recognition of the divergences across Union legislation and the national systems by identifying three shifting categories of consumer and allowing, with limitations, for interpretations that are dependent on the context of the particular case before the national court.[90] More recently, the CJEU as well as legal scholars have begun to look to the development of an autonomous concept of the 'European consumer', bringing to the fore not only the significance of individual and group identity within and beyond the nation state, but also the scope for the transfer of national consumer concepts beyond the Member States to the Union level.

iii. The CJEU's Interpretation of the Consumer: References from National Courts

The interpretation of the consumer concept initially arose before the CJEU in relation to the application of the Misleading and Comparative Advertising Directive.[91] In the *Mars* case,[92] the CJEU introduced the

---

[89] This would seem to be the case in respect of Directive 2002/65/EC on the distance marketing of consumer financial services, with reference to recitals 13 and 29.

[90] Vanessa Mak, 'Standards of Protection: In Search of the 'Average Consumer' of EU Law in the Proposal for a Consumer Rights Directive' (2011) 19 *ERPL* 25, 29.

[91] Directive 84/450/EEC, subsequently amended by Directive 2006/114/EC.

[92] Case C-470/93 *Mars* [1995] ECR I-1923.

notion of the consumer as 'reasonably circumspect'; it subsequently developed this understanding, referring to the 'average consumer', who is 'reasonably well informed and reasonably observant and circumspect' in the *Gut Springenheide* case.[93] The 'average consumer' concept was defined as a Union standard that would allow the national court to make an objective determination as to whether a communication is misleading for consumers without engaging in a potentially subjective and extensive evaluation of the facts of the case and position of the relevant parties.

The CJEU, however, recognised that in certain circumstances, depending on the facts of the case, this standard of the average consumer does not suffice to afford the protection necessary. As noted above, the need for a differentiated level of protection – and thus, concept of consumer – has been developed in the Member States in light of the discretion afforded by Union instruments having a minimum and even targeted maximum harmonisation reach.[94] Indeed, the notion of the vulnerable consumer as the weaker party to the contract, thus in need of a high level of protection due to his or her vulnerabilities, emerged initially at national level. The vulnerable consumer requires a level of protection that goes beyond the provision of information, as he is not necessarily rational; indeed, even where he is deemed to be sufficiently well-informed, this lack of rationality potentially undermines the effectiveness of the protection available.[95] The position of these consumers is reflected in the recent – predominantly Spanish – cases concerning consumers who are subject to mortgage enforcement and parallel eviction proceedings.[96] Another example can be found in *Tomášová*, which concerned – in the context of a consumer

---

[93] Case C-210/96 *Gut Springenheide* [1998] ECR I-4657, judgment, para. 37. The CJEU has also developed a standard of the average non-consumer, as the recipient of comparative advertising, as 'reasonably well informed and reasonably observant and circumspect' in Case C-112/99 *Toshiba* [2001] ECR I-7945 and later in Case C-59/05 *Siemens* [2006] ECR I-2147.

[94] For example, recital 13 of the CRD provides: 'for instance, Member States may decide to extend the application of the rules of this Directive to legal persons or to natural persons who are not consumers within the meaning of this Directive, such as non-governmental organisations, start-ups or small and medium-sized enterprises', which might allow for a concept of consumer which extends protection beyond that defined in Art.2(1). See the references above.

[95] There is an evident behavioural law and economics dimension to the rationality discussion which goes beyond the scope of this chapter; see the 2011 special edition of the *Journal of Consumer Policy* (Volume 34).

[96] A key reflection of such a context is reflected in the judgment rendered in Case C-415/11 *Mohamed Aziz* EU:C:2013:164.

credit contract[97] – the validity of an arbitration clause, which provided for a seat of arbitration 400km (and largely inaccessible by public transport) from the place of residence of the consumer, a pensioner, with little higher education, and a small pension of 340 euros per month.[98] Thus, while the CJEU has predominantly referred to the 'average consumer', it has – along with the Union legislature[99] – also acknowledged the pertinence of differentiated concepts of consumer, and thus of levels of protection, depending on the nature of the activity in which consumers are involved and their characteristics as individuals. The activities that generate increased vulnerability would include, for example, the consumer being subject to doorstep selling;[100] these determinations seem to be matters of policy.[101] Moreover, the CJEU has acknowledged that the vulnerable or weaker consumer (who must of course be identified in light of his or her position to the other party to the contract) is a concept relevant to the procedural protection of consumers within the national systems;[102] in particular, this interpretation underpins the CJEU's development of the obligation on the national courts to exercise *ex officio* control of consumer protection, predominantly but not exclusively, in the context of

---

[97] For an initial amount of 250 euros, and an additional loan of 250 euros, in respect of which bailiffs ultimately collected more than 2000 euros. The case before the CJEU concerned the scope for state liability on the part of the Slovakian courts who had failed to engage of its own motion in an examination of the unfair character of the arbitration clause. The Court found that no state liability could be established, largely due to temporal considerations; that is to say, it was found that the *ex officio* obligation on the national courts could not be held to have been clearly established at the relevant time.

[98] Case C-168/15 *Tomášová* EU:C:2016:602.

[99] Thus, the UCPD, which broadly refers to the 'notional, typical . . . average consumer' as a 'benchmark', also sets out at recital 18 that the directive 'contains provisions aimed at preventing the exploitation of consumers whose characteristics make them particularly vulnerable to unfair commercial practices'.

[100] Case C-382/87 *Buet* [1989] ECR 1235, judgment, para. 13, in respect of the selling of education materials.

[101] Case C-168/05 *Mostaza Claro* [2006] ECR I-10421, judgment, para. 38 and Case C-137/08 *Pénzügyi Lízing* EU:C:2010:659, paras 46–47.

[102] See for example, Case C-453/10 *Pereničová and Perenič* EU:C:2011:788, Opinion of AG Trstenjak, para. 63; citing examples from German scholarship, i.e., if the gaps left by the exclusion of the term are too big (at fn.19), and with reference to the different language versions (German, French, English, Italian and Spanish), if the contract can continue in respect of its 'purpose and legal nature' without the unfair term. More recently, the CJEU has provided that if a term is found to be unfair, while it is reluctant to provide that national courts can adjust the term itself, it can replace it with default rules in order to ensure the continuation of the contract; Case C-26/13 *Kásler* EU:C:2014:282 judgment, paras 78 *et seq*.

contract terms regulation, that is, where consumers are largely faced with standard form contracts, which they cannot negotiate but either 'take or leave'.[103]

It is clear that for reasons set out in the paragraphs below, the application of the consumer protection regime may diverge depending on the relevant instrument, its purposes and overarching objective. The example of the protection in Arts.17–19 of the Brussels I *bis* Regulation can be examined with reference to the CJEU's judgments in *Benincasa*, *Kolassa* and *Hobohm*. The protective jurisdiction regime will only apply where the relevant party qualifies as a consumer per Art.17(1). The CJEU has held – in respect of the then-applicable Brussels Convention – that the consumer in then-Art.13 (now Art.17) must be 'a private final consumer, not engaged in trade or professional activities' . . . 'reference must be made to the position of the person concerned in a particular contract, having regard to the nature and aim of that contract, and not to the subjective situation of the person concerned'.[104] In *Hobohm*, the CJEU identified three criteria in respect of then-applicable Art.15 Brussels I Regulation (now Art.17), building on *Kolassa*.[105] The party claiming consumer status must contract outside his or her trade or profession, an actual contract between a professional and consumer must have been concluded and the contract must be one that can be characterised as one falling within Arts.15(1)(a)-(c).[106]

The CJEU has largely limited the concept of the consumer, whether the average, or vulnerable, to natural persons whose activities are for a purpose that fall outwith his trade or profession. This is true both in respect of substantive consumer protection and protection regimes established in cross-border civil procedure.[107] As a result, it has generally

103 Including, among others, Case C-472/10 *Invitel* EU:C:2012:242 and Case C-618/10 *Banco Español* EU:C:2012:349; Case C-137/08 *Pénzügyi Lízing* EU:C:2010:659, judgment, paras 56–57; Case C-484/08 *Caja de Ahorros* EU:C:2010:309, judgment, para. 37 (in the same case, the AG's approach is less consumer-orientated, making reference to the notion that the consumer is 'typically weaker' as opposed to consistently so; Opinion of AG Trstenjak, para. 38).

104 Case C-269/95 *Benincasa* EU:C:1997:337, paras 15–16.

105 Case C-375/13 *Kolassa* EU:C:2015:37, para. 23 in which the CJEU held that a direct contract did not exist, limiting in particular the application of the consumer protection regime in respect of Brussels I *bis* in the context of financial disputes.

106 Case C-297/14 *Hobohm* EU:C:2015:844, para. 24.

107 See, for example, *Benincasa*, n. 104, judgment, paras 17–19, Case C-180/06 *Ilsinger* [2009] ECR I-3961, para. 41 and Case C-419/11 *Česká Spořitelna*

rejected the possibility for extending the protection to legal persons;[108] this is particularly significant where the contract is a mixed agreement or a dual purpose one. As a general rule, where the contract is entered into within the course of a trade or profession, the protection afforded in the consumer instrument will therefore not apply.[109] This determination is made not only in light of the deemed lack of need for the application of consumer protection norms in such a context but of the desire – particularly, in respect of rules of cross-border civil procedure – for legal certainty and for strict interpretation of exceptions (as reflected in the special rules for consumers) to the general allocation of jurisdiction rule based on the domicile of the defendant.[110]

The situation is not clear, however, and again diverges depending on the relevant instrument, its aims and objectives. Three issues arise that will require further consideration by the CJEU. First, there is a lack of clarity as to the extent to which the contract must be disassociated from the trade or profession; for example, if there is only a marginal connection with the trade or profession, the CJEU has considered that the protection afforded in the relevant Union legislation might well apply. In the case of *Gruber*, the CJEU adopted a strict interpretation – in the cross-border civil procedure context[111] – of consumers in dual purpose contracts, such

EU:C:2013:165, paras 28 and 32, which set out the consumer as the weaker, private final consumer.

[108] Case C-541/99 *Cape v Ideal Service* [2001] I-9049, judgment, paras 12–16; the CJEU held that the notion of consumer only includes natural persons. In this case, the question of whether a businessperson acting outwith his profession or trade could be considered as a consumer was left unanswered by the CJEU although it did consider that the French understanding of consumer could be acceptable. Consider also Case C-361/89 *Patrice di Pinto* [1991] I-1189 (in which the AG considered that the concept of the consumer might cover some small business persons, where the relevant transactions fell outwith his normal business or profession, while the Court rejected this, interpreting the notion of consumer in a narrow way, such that a trader acting in respect of the sale of their business could not be considered to be a consumer; for the Court, a legal person, even if in a position similar to a consumer, cannot be so considered). In respect of credit agreements, this includes both the debtor consumer and a co-debtor: Case C-348/14 *Bucura* EU:C:2015:447, judgment, paras 33–39.

[109] Case C-45/96 *Bayerische Hypotheken* [1998] ECR I-1199, Judgment, para 23 (in this case, Directive 85/577).

[110] As etablished in Art.4, Brussels I *bis*. See also, Case C-96/00 *Gabriel* EU:C:2002:436, judgment, para. 39.

[111] See the discussion of the AG as to the contexts of the applicable concepts, and the dialogue between the Union legislature and the CJEU, from the *Gruber* case to recital 17 to the CRD, in Case C-110/14 *Costea* EU:C:2015:271, Opinion of AG Cruz Villalón, paras 35–47.

that the consumer concept could only apply if 'the trade or professional purpose is so *limited* as to be negligible in the overall context of the supply, the fact that the private element is predominant being irrelevant in that respect'.[112] In contrast, the reference to dual purpose contracts in recital 17 of the CRD differs in its wording, referring to contracts 'concluded for purposes partly within and partly outside the person's trade and the trade purpose is so limited as not to be predominant in the overall context'; for the AG this offers, where the situation allows it, a mechanism for 'an examination of the totality of the circumstances surrounding the contract at issue — beyond a purely quantitative criterion . . . and an assessment of the objective evidence available' as to whether the professional or private purpose is predominant in a given contract.[113]

Secondly, as noted above in relation to some Member States, consumer protection has been extended in limited circumstances to small business persons where the transaction is deemed to be alien to his or her normal profession or business.[114] Thirdly, in the context of the *ex officio* control of consumer law by the national courts, the CJEU has held that even if the buyer does not rely on his or her status as a consumer or specify whether the contract is one 'of sale to a private individual', even if it has been concluded in a manner not for the purposes of but related to his or her business, the national court is obliged to undertake an examination of its own motion and determine whether the party should be characterised as such within the meaning of the relevant directive. This reflects a more consumer-friendly approach in the CJEU's interpretation, transferred into an obligation on the national court to examine the potentially weak position of a party, who – as a result of his vulnerability – is unable to assert for himself his consumer status or the applicability of consumer law.[115]

The CJEU's interpretation has not stalled at the average or vulnerable consumer; indeed, the notion of the economically efficient, confident

---

[112] Case C-464/01 *Gruber* [2005] ECR I-0439, Judgment, para. 54, and at paras 34–40 for the purposes of Arts13–15 of the then-applicable Brussels Convention, while the burden of proof lies with the party wishing to rely on the regime of protection.

[113] Case C-110/14 *Costea* EU:C:2015:271, Opinion of AG Cruz Villalón, para. 44.

[114] For example, in France (Cour de cassation, 6 janvier, 1993, *JurisClasseur Périodique*, 27 janvier 1993, Actualités) and Italy (Tribunale da Roma, 20 ottobre 1999, *Foro Italiano* 2/2000). At Union level, in respect of the notion that small businesses and individual businesspersons might be entitled to the protection afforded to consumers, reference can also be made to the Green Paper on the Review of the Consumer Acquis, COM [2006] 744.

[115] C-497/13 *Faber* 2015:EU:C:357, Judgment, paras 32–48.

consumer[116] has recently emerged from Luxembourg. This understanding underpins the Commission's concept of the consumer who does not consider him or herself to be limited to the territorial or digital confines of his or her own Member State but who confidently contracts across borders: he or she is the confident, 'empowered consumer at the centre of the internal market' who is 'well-protected and able to benefit from the Single Market'.[117] As a result, the Union's policy preference has shifted away from protection alone towards the generation and promotion of consumer confidence.[118] In reality, not all consumers are weak or 'average', nor are they all confident or empowered; the former tends to reflect the consumer in reality who requires the protection afforded by consumer law, while the confident consumer tends towards the individual that the Commission and CJEU hopes to emerge on the other side of consumer law's application, in individual cases and in the abstract.[119] Indeed, the 'confident consumer' has been characterised as a 'political tool to convince Member States that mandatory standards in contract law were needed to strengthen consumer confidence in the Internal Market Project [thus] . . . the concept of the confident consumer now becomes a legal normative prerogative which changes the outlook of consumer law',[120] on the basis that 'an integrated market needs confident consumers'.[121] Along these lines, the CJEU has interpreted the consumer as an active participant in the internal market, playing a key role in 'raising the standard of living and the quality of life in its territory'.[122] While the CJEU goes back and forth, the notion of the confident consumer potentially affects – that is to say, lowers – the level of protection afforded to the consumer in favour of the facilitation of the

---

116 Brigitta Lurger, 'The CFR/Optional Code and the Various Understandings of Social Justice in Europe' in Wilhelmsson *et al*, n. 51, 193.

117 Proposal for a Regulation on a Consumer Programme (2011)COM 707 final, 2.

118 CRD, Recital 6.

119 This notion is also recognised by Leczykiewickz and Weatherill in Dorota Leczykiewickz and Stephen Weatherill, 'The Images of the Consumer in EU Law' in Dorota Leczykiewickz and Stephen Weatherill (eds), *The Images of the Consumer in EU Law: Legislation, Free Movement and Competition Law* (Hart 2016) 1.

120 Hans-Wolfgang Micklitz, 'The Visible Hand of European Regulatory Private Law' (2008) *EUI WP 2008/14*, 6 citing Dieter Hoffmann, 'Telling, v Miert' [1990] *Europäische Zeitschrift für Wirtschaftsrecht* 401.

121 With reference to 'The Internal Market After 1992: Meeting the Challenge', European Parliament Doc (SEC 92-final) 2277 (1992) and the White Paper on the Completion of the Internal Market; Hans-Wolfgang Micklitz, 'Social Justice and Access Justice' *EUI WP 2011/02*, 19.

122 Case C-168/05 *Mostaza Claro* [2006] ECR 1-10421, Judgment, para. 37.

internal market and the enforcement of rules that regulate and promote the market.[123]

The CJEU seems to acknowledge that there exist diverse conceptualisations of the consumer – and thus, differentiated levels of consumer protection – in two dimensions: between the Union conceptualisations and those established within the national legal systems and on the other, and to a lesser extent, between the EU legislative understandings. The exercise of its interpretative jurisdiction is shaped by a number of factors, including the determination of the national courts to invoke the preliminary reference procedure, the reach of the pertinent Union legislation (that is, whether the Union legislature advanced a minimum, maximum or targeted maximum harmonisation approach) and the area of law, including its aims and objectives, in which the relevant case arises.

REVISITING THE SCOPE FOR COOPERATION

While a skeleton definition of the consumer concept can be identified in Union legislation, and while the European Commission has implied that a coherent definition of the consumer would likely lead to greater consistency and a more rigid delineation of the scope of consumer law,[124] it must nevertheless be acknowledged that the choice not to identify a distinct or fixed understanding of the consumer concept seems to have been a conscious one on the part of the Union legislature. Instead, the task has been one which has fallen to the CJEU, an approach which – whether intended or not – seems to have provided scope for the AG and Courts to advance dynamic interpretations, in line with the aims and objectives identified by the Union legislature, the case referred by the national court, and more broadly, the CJEU's teleological interpretative approach.

The preliminary reference procedure has thus evolved as a mechanism by which the CJEU has been able to engage in this task. The exercise of the CJEU's interpretative jurisdiction is also shaped by the determinations of the Union legislature, notwithstanding that it has not gone so far as to provide for a single concept of the consumer: on the one hand, it is determined by the different concepts established in different pieces of Union legislation and, on the other, by the reach of this legislation and the discre-

---

[123] Thomas Wilhelmsson, 'The Abuse of the Confident Consumer as a Justification for EC Consumer Law' (2004) 24 *J.Con.Pol.* 317.

[124] European Commission, 'Green Paper on the Review of the Consumer Acquis' COM(2006) 744 and European Commission, 'Proposal for a Directive on Consumer Rights', COM(2008) 614 final, 15.

tion attributed by the EU to the legislatures of the Member States and the national courts in implementing, interpreting and applying EU concepts as transposed into the national systems.

Notwithstanding, the CJEU has adopted its own methodological approaches in the exercise of its interpretative jurisdiction. Mak, for example, identifies a comparative 'cross-directive' approach,[125] by virtue of which the CJEU has seemingly aimed at generating coherence and consistency between the provisions found in different EU consumer protection instruments. However, this approach is of course limited; the desire for coherence in itself cannot provide a legitimacy basis for its construction of a 'system' of European private law.[126] Thus, while in its interpretation of the consumer concept, the CJEU has, for example, held that 'in order to ensure compliance with the objectives pursued by the European legislature in the sphere of consumer contracts, and the consistency of European Union law, account must be taken, in particular, of the definition of "consumer" in other rules of European Union law',[127] it has also been quick to acknowledge that different conceptualisations may have been drafted for different purposes – 'the notion of consumer is not defined uniformly in all instruments, which belong to different spheres and have different objectives: it is a working, dynamic notion, which is defined by reference to the subject-matter of the legislative act concerned'[128] – and to reassert that interpretations of Union concepts must be rendered in line with the aims of the relevant legislation, that is, from a teleological perspective: '[t]he objective of consistency cannot, in any event, lead to the provisions of Regulation No 44/2001 being interpreted in a manner which is unconnected to the scheme and objectives pursued by that

[125] Vanessa Mak, 'Harmonisation through 'Directive-Related' and 'Cross-Directive' Interpretation: The Role of the ECJ in the Development of European Consumer Law' *Tilburg WP 2008/08*, 19 *et seq.*

[126] This goes against what Weatherill deems a 'militant cross-directive' approach; see Stephen Weatherill, 'Interpretation of the Directives: The Role of the Court' in Arthur S. Hartkamp *et al* (eds), *Towards a European Civil Code* (4th edn., Kluwer 2011) 185–203, at fn.79.

[127] In the context of the determination of whether Art.6(1)(d) of the European Enforcement Order, Regulation 805/2004 applied to a contract concluded between two persons acting outwith the context of their trade or profession, i.e., whether such a contract could be said to be a consumer one, the CJEU engaged the interpretation of 'weak' consumer rendered in respect of the UCTD, holding that the correction of the imbalance required did not exist in this case and that the contract could not be conceived as a consumer one; Case C-508/12 *Vapenik* EU:C:2013:790, paras 23–31.

[128] *Costea*, n. 55, Opinion of AG Cruz Villalón, para. 19.

regulation'.[129] The divergent interpretations rendered by the CJEU thus seem to be part and parcel of a balancing exercise wherein it weighs the needs of the consumer (where too low a level of protection leaves the consumer with a lack of information and unable to make effective free choices) with the operation of the internal market (in respect of which, too high a level of consumer protection undermines the scope for free movement). This undertaking – essentially constitutional in its nature – reflects an acknowledgement on the part of the CJEU that national consumer law transposing EU legislation and offering a higher level of protection in the Member States is, in respect of its compatibility with Union law, potentially deemed to be a 'legitimate objective' that might justify certain restrictions to the satisfaction of market objectives.[130] On the other hand however, there is evidence of a shift towards a 'frequent singularity and lack of differentiation' of the consumer concept.[131] Indeed, the CJEU's exercise of its jurisdiction in this purpose has been criticised as reflecting a 'one-sided' teleological approach;[132] for Schmid, the instrumentalisation of private law[133] dictates that the significance attributed to social justice and the 'the immaterial interests of consumers' (deriving from the national traditions)[134] on the one hand, and the promotion of the internal market, on the other, will never be equal, as preference is necessarily attributed to the facilitation of the internal market as promoting the *effet utile* of European law. Thus, to return to the CJEU's recognition of the desire for a degree of coherence, Schmid asserts that while consumer protection might be understood as an 'overarching interpretative meta-principle'[135] of EU law, the CJEU does not necessarily exercise its jurisdiction in efforts to seek to 'pursue[s] a coherent consumer model' or to advance

---

[129] Case C-45/13 *Kainz* EU:C:2014:7, para. 20, concerning the interpretation of Brussels I (Regulation 44/2001) and Rome II (Regulation 864/2007).

[130] Case C-120/78 *Rewe-Zentral* [1979] ECR 649, Judgment, para. 8, and Case C-441/04 *A-Punkt Schmuckhandel* [2006] ECR I-2093, Judgment, para. 27.

[131] Dorota Leczykiewickz and Stephen Weatherill, 'The Images of the Consumer in EU Law' in Leczykiewickz and Weatherill, n. 70, 8.

[132] Christoph Schmid, 'The ECJ as a Constitutional and a Private Law Court-A Methodological Comparison', (2006) 4 *ZERP Diskussionspapier*, 11–12.

[133] Christoph Schmid, 'The Thesis of the Instrumentalisation of Private Law by the EU in a Nutshell' in Christian Joerges and Tommi Ralli (eds), *European Constitutionalism Without Private Law: Private Law Without Democracy, Recon Report No.14* (Arena 2011) 26–7.

[134] Brigetta Lurger, 'Old and New Insights for the Protection of Consumers in European Private Law in the Wake of the Global Economic Crisis' in Roger Brownsword *et al* (eds), *The Foundations of European Private Law* (Hart 2011) 107.

[135] Schmid, n. 132, 22.

consumer protection but rather to promote coherence and consistency in the interests of furthering the internal market.

As set out above, the trend towards (targeted) maximum harmonisation has various consequences. Predominantly, it seems to operate to preclude the existence of national diversities and rather promotes single, Europeanised concepts of EU law – including that of the consumer – that are at least intended to be applicable across Union legislation and in the Member States in a uniform manner. This also affects the manner in which the CJEU renders its interpretations. One question that comes to the fore in respect of the consumer concept in targeted maximum harmonisation directives is whether this determination on the part of the Union legislature requires that the CJEU rejects divergent interpretations in favour of a restricted, yet-to-be-established European notion. It seems unclear what approach the CJEU should take. In respect of the consumer concept, both the Union legislature and the CJEU have recognised that the national and Union particularities must be taken into account.[136] For example, the CJEU has recognised that 'it must be determined whether social, cultural or linguistic factors' may provide for a particular national understanding of a product, and on this basis, a necessarily local-specific level of consumer protection, in the context of a case concerning potentially misleading trademarks,[137] while the Union legislature, at recital 18 of

---

[136] Fundamentally, in respect of the notion of average consumer, the CJEU sets out a kind of division of labour between the European and national levels; the determination is for the national courts in line with the principle of proportionality: Case C-220/98 *Estée Lauder* [2000] ECR I-117, Judgment, para. 30; this extends not only to the understanding of the consumer but the circumstances surrounding, see also, Case C-239/02 *Douwe Egberts* [2004] ECR I-07007, Judgment, para. 46:

> Finally, as regards the possible difficulty of establishing in certain cases the fraudulent nature of a certain statement, it should be recalled that it is for the national courts in all doubtful situations to form a view, taking into account the presumed expectations of an average consumer who is reasonably well informed and reasonably observant and circumspect.

[137] *Estée Lauder*, ibid., paras. 27–29: 'in particular, it must be determined whether social, cultural or linguistic factors may justify the term "lifting", used in connection with a firming cream, meaning something different to the German consumer as opposed to consumers in other Member States . . .'. This has long been recognised by the AGs of the CJEU: Case C-315/92 *Verband Sozialer Wettbewerb eV v Clinique Laboratoires and Estée Lauder Cosmetics* [1994] ECR I-317, Opinion of AG Gulmann, para. 18. See also Case C-581/13 *Intra-Presse* EU:C:2014:2387, judgment, paras 24 *et seq*., on the issue of language and translation.

the UCPD, has similarly acknowledged the significance of such factors.[138] However, both cases arose before the trend to targeted maximum harmonisation emerged.[139] While the CJEU itself has considered that even where European legislation provides for maximum harmonisation, 'a margin for manoeuvre' which 'authorises [Member States] to maintain or introduce particular rules for specific situations'[140] putatively exists, strictly speaking, a restricted interpretation of, for example, Art.2(1) CRD would indeed provide a kind of 'base line' whereby any understanding of 'consumer' established in any national legal tradition and providing for a higher degree of protection will fall foul of the European notion. The judgment rendered by the CJEU is binding not only in the Member State of the referring court but in all Member States, potentially having cross-border as well as cross-sectoral impact, that is beyond the substantive area of law concerned; furthermore, it is enforceable[141] with the force of *res judicata*.

If this is the case, not only a Europeanised concept but also a means of managing existing diversity (and potential future conflicts) must be identified.[142] Thus, for example, Wilhelmsson has advanced that in respect of the putative identification of a European concept of consumer in a multi-level context,[143] what is required is not only an acknowledgement of the existence of divergent understandings of consumer culture and their permeation across the national orders but also a broader and more transparent appreciation of the significance of national 'social, cultural

---

138 While the UCPD does not provide in itself for the notion of the 'average consumer', recital 18 refers to the CJEU's reference, in cases of advertising, to analyse the effect of such advertising 'on a notional, typical consumer . . . this Directive takes as a benchmark the average consumer, who is reasonably well-informed and reasonably observant and circumspect, taking into account social, cultural and linguistic factors, as interpreted by the Court of Justice'.

139 Of course, as noted above, the CRD itself continues to provide for a degree of discretion in recital 13 (see fn.87).

140 Case C-101/01 *Bodil Lindqvist* [2003] ECR I-12971, Judgment, para. 98.

141 CJEU Rules of Procedure, Art.91(1), OJ L 173 of 26.6.2013, p.65 and per Arts. 260, 266, 280 and 299 TFEU.

142 Mak sets out the difficulties that might be faced in national systems should any attempt to lower consumer protection become necessary: Vanessa Mak, 'Standards of Protection: In Search of the 'Average Consumer' of EU Law in the Proposal for a Consumer Rights Directive' (2011) 19 *ERPL* 25, 37–8.

143 Wilhelmsson highlights that the scope for the Europeanisation of such a concept and the identification of commonality at the Union level must be considered in light of the extent of the divergence between national notions of consumer; Wilhelmsson, n. 51, 245.

or linguistic factors' at the European level.[144] This understanding complements the one set out above; it suggests that neither the national nor the European consumer constitutes a mere legal concept but rather a dimension of identity deriving from culture and tradition. Identity or sense of belonging can be multiple, a notion supported by a pluralist, multi-level perspective of governance; this would suggest that it would be problematic to try to replace the diverse national understandings with a single, common, Europeanised concept in the context of European private law, at least without the development of a mechanism of cooperation – and particularly, dialogue between the courts – that could be engaged as a means of resolving the conflicts that potentially arise.

The preliminary reference procedure offers a mechanism for communication between the national courts and the CJEU. However, as is clear from this relatively brief analysis, it is a limited one; indeed, as de Witte has highlighted, a deep and considered dialogue, that is, the 'mutual exchange of arguments, [which] requires a series of subsequent references in different cases raising similar problems which is rather cumbersome and rarely happens'.[145] Its operation depends initially on the willingness of the national court to become so engaged, and on the CJEU to accept as admissible – either as is or in a revised form – the questions referred. Thus, the very nature of the preliminary reference procedure dictates that it is one that is initiated, proceeds and is concluded in line with the willingness of the participants to engage with each other. While this understanding has been shaped by the national courts, it has also been acknowledged by the CJEU itself: '[t]he system of references for a preliminary ruling is based on a dialogue between one court and another, the initiation of which depends entirely on the national court's assessment as to whether a reference is appropriate and necessary'.[146] This is an understanding to which both the AGs[147] and the Court[148] continue to attach significance.

---

144 Thomas Wilhelmsson, 'Introduction: Harmonization and National Cultures' in Wilhelmsson *et al*, n. 51, 15–16.

145 Bruno de Witte, 'The Closest Thing to a Constitutional Conversation in Europe: The Semi-Permanent Treaty Revision Process' in Paul Beaumont *et al* (eds), *Convergence and Divergence in European Public Law* (Hart 2002) 41; he gives the example of British sex equality references explored in Claire Kilpatrick, 'Community or Communities of Courts in European Integration? Sex Equality Dialogues Between UK Courts and the ECJ' (1998) 4 *ELJ* 121.

146 Case C-2/06 *Kempter* [2008] ECR I-411, Judgment, para. 42.

147 Case C-306/99 *BIAO* [2003] ECR I-1, Opinion of AG Jacobs, para. 44.

148 Case C-445/06 *Danske* [2009] ECR I-2119, Judgment, para. 65.

CONCLUSION

This analysis has focused on the interpretation of the consumer concept, a source of possible conflicts in interpretation, particularly in terms of the divergent concepts provided for in consumer law instruments and the understandings engaged by the national courts and the CJEU. Notwithstanding that, as briefly set out in the first section, the EU sphere might reflect a space ripe for communication, both cooperation and more specifically, dialogue, between the representatives of national and Union legal orders at the point at which they meet – that is, the courts in the preliminary reference procedure – exists in a superficial framework of communication but largely is missing in any deep sense of its understanding. Cooperation – whether between courts or institutions, or both – will not remove all scope for conflicting interpretations of norms,[149] whether these have been established at national or Union level, and it is advanced that it makes sense for the diversities in terms of application to make sense, against a balancing of the promotion of the internal market and the protection of consumer interests and in light of the shifting character of Union legislation. It is becoming clear that is it not possible to define the consumer only as the 'homo oeconomicus' as is inferred even from the CJEU's three broad categories of average, vulnerable and confident consumer; this finds support – as indicated above – not only from legal and political analysis but from social, cultural and economic studies.[150] The traditional, minimum understanding that can be identified from Union legislation and the CJEU's interpretations – the natural person acting for purposes which are outside his trade, business, craft or profession – is maintained in the Commission's most recent proposals.[151] The next step is the revision of the consumer *acquis*, the results of which will come after the 64 cases currently pending before the CJEU concerning consumer protection, is thus awaited.

149 Cesare Romano, 'Deciphering the Grammar of the International Jurisprudential Dialogue' (2009) 41 *NYU.J.Int.L.Pol.* 755.

150 Including behavioural analysis; see Bastian Schüller, 'The Definition of Consumer in EU Law' in James Devenney and Mel Kenny (eds), *European Consumer Protection: Theory and Practice* (Cambridge 2012).

151 Proposal for a Directive Concerning Certain Aspects of Contracts for the Supply of Digital Content (COM(2015)634 final) and Proposal for a Directive Concerning Contracts for the Online and Other Distance Sales of Goods (COM(2015)635 final).

Table 7.1 Definitions of 'consumer' in EU legislation

EU Instrument	Reach of Legislation and Status	Concept of the Consumer
Product Liability Directive 1985/374/EEC		Art.9: 'For the purpose of Article 1, "damage" means: (b) damage to, or destruction of, any item of property other than the defective product itself, with a lower threshold of 500 ECU, provided that the item of property: (ii) was used by the injured person mainly for his own private use or consumption.'
Doorstep Selling Directive 1985/577/EEC	Minimum harmonisation (Art.8) Repealed by CRD	Recital: For doorstep contracts, what is special, is the "surprise element", that is, "as a rule it is the trader who initiates the contract negotiations, for which the consumer is unprepared or which he does not expect; whereas the consumer is often unable to compare the quality and price of the offer with other offers." Art.2: '"consumer" means a natural person who, in transactions covered by this Directive, is acting for purposes which can be regarded as outside his trade or profession'.
Package Travel Directive 90/314/EEC	Minimum harmonisation (Art.8) Revised Package Travel Directive 2015/2302/EU	Art.2(4): '"consumer" means the person who takes or agrees to take the package ("the principal contractor"), or any person on whose behalf the principal contractor agrees to purchase the package ("the other beneficiaries") or any person to whom the principal contractor or any of the other beneficiaries transfers the package ("the transferee")'.

Table 7.1 (continued)

EU Instrument	Reach of Legislation and Status	Concept of the Consumer
Unfair Contract Terms Directive 1993/13/EEC	Minimum harmonisation (Art.8) Remains in force following CRD	Recital: '. . . whereas, in making an assessment of good faith, particular regard shall be had to the strength of the bargaining positions of the parties, whether the consumer had an inducement to agree to the term and whether the goods or services were sold or supplied to the special order of the consumer . . .'. Art.2(b): '"consumer" means any natural person who, in contracts covered by this Directive, is acting for purposes which are outside his trade, business or profession'.
Distance Selling Directive 1997/7/EC	Minimum harmonisation (Art.14) Repealed by CRD	Art.2(2): '"consumer" means any natural person who, in contracts covered by this Directive, is acting for purposes which are outside his trade, business or profession'.
Price Indication Directive 1998/6/EC	Minimum harmonisation (Art.10)	Art.2(e): '"consumer" shall mean any natural person who buys a product for purposes that do not fall within the sphere of his commercial or professional activity'.
Consumer Sales and Guarantees Directive 1999/44/EC	Minimum harmonisation (Art.8) Remains in force following CRD	Art.2(a): 'consumer: shall mean any natural person who, in the contracts covered by this Directive, is acting for purposes which are not related to his trade, business or profession'.
Regulation 44/2001 on Jurisdiction and the Recognition and Enforcement of Judgments in Civil and Commercial Matters (Brussels I)	N/A	Recital 13: 'In relation to insurance, consumer contracts and employment, the weaker party should be protected by rules of jurisdiction more favourable to his interests than the general rules provide for.' Art.15: 'In matters relating to a contract concluded by a person, the consumer, for a purpose which can be regarded as being outside his trade or profession . . .'

Universal Service Directive 2002/22/EC	N/A	Recital 7: 'Member States may . . . take specific measures for consumers in rural or geographically isolated areas . . . as well as ensure under the same conditions this access, in particular for the elderly, the disabled and for people with special social needs.' Definitions found in Framework Directive 2002/21/EC, Art.2(i): '"consumer"'means any natural person who uses or requests a publicly available electronic communications service for purposes which are outside his or her trade, business or profession'.
Insurance Mediation Directive 2002/92/EC	Minimum harmonisation, recital 19 Proposal for a revised directive on insurance sales (to be known as the Insurance Distribution Directive; COM/2012/0360 final – 2012/0175 (COD); http://eur-lex.europa.eu/legal-content/EN/TXT/?uri=CELEX:52012PC0360) agreed between Commission, Parliament and Council in July 2015 and adopted by the Parliament on 24.11.2015	No definition.
Regulation 805/2004 on Creating a European Enforcement Order for Uncontested Claims	N/A	Art.6(1)(d): a judgment on an uncontested claim can be certified as an EEO, for various reasons, and if it was made in the Member State of the debtor, as consumer, 'where it relates to a contract concluded by a person, the consumer, for a purpose which can be regarded as being outside his trade or profession'.

Table 7.1 (continued)

EU Instrument	Reach of Legislation and Status	Concept of the Consumer
Regulation 2006/2004 on Consumer Protection Cooperation	N/A	No definition.
Unfair Commercial Practices Directive 2005/29/EC	Maximum harmonisation directive, however, between June 2007 and June 2013, the Member States could apply national rules providing for greater protection, beyond the directive, insofar as it is necessary and proportionate (Art.3(5)) Remains in force following CRD	Recital 18: 'It is appropriate to protect all consumers from unfair commercial practices; however the Court of Justice has found it necessary in adjudicating on advertising cases since the enactment of Directive 84/450/EEC to examine the effect on a notional, typical consumer. In line with the principle of proportionality, and to permit the effective application of the protections contained in it, this Directive takes as a benchmark the average consumer, who is reasonably well-informed and reasonably observant and circumspect, taking into account social, cultural and linguistic factors, as interpreted by the Court of Justice, but also contains provisions aimed at preventing the exploitation of consumers whose characteristics make them particularly vulnerable to unfair commercial practices. Where a commercial practice is specifically aimed at a particular group of consumers, such as children, it is desirable that the impact of the commercial practice be assessed from the perspective of the average member of that group . . . The average consumer test is not a statistical test. National courts and authorities will have to exercise their own faculty of judgment, having regard to the case-law of the Court of

		Justice, to determine the typical reaction of the average consumer in a given case.' Recital 19: 'Where certain characteristics such as age, physical or mental infirmity or credulity make consumers particularly susceptible to a commercial practice or to the underlying product and the economic behaviour only of such consumers is likely to be distorted by the practice in a way that the trader can reasonably foresee, it is appropriate to ensure that they are adequately protected by assessing the practice from the perspective of the average member of that group.' Art.5: A commercial practice shall be unfair if . . . '(2) it materially distorts or is likely to materially distort the economic behaviour with regard to the product of the average consumer . . .'. Art.5(3): 'Commercial practices which are likely to materially distort the economic behaviour only of a clearly identifiable group of consumers who are particularly vulnerable to the practice or the underlying product because of their mental or physical infirmity, age or credulity . . .'
Regulation 1896/2006 creating a European Order for Payment Procedure	N/A	Art.6: relating to jurisdiction, in consumer contracts: '. . . the consumer, for a purpose which can be regarded as being outside his trade or profession, and if the defendant is the consumer . . .'.
Regulation 861/2007 establishing a European Small Claims Procedure	N/A	No definition.

Table 7.1 (continued)

EU Instrument	Reach of Legislation and Status	Concept of the Consumer
Regulation 593/2008 on the Law Applicable to Contractual Relations	N/A	Recital 23: 'As regards contracts concluded with parties regarded as being weaker, those parties should be protected by conflict of law rules that are more favourable to their interests than the general rules.' Art.6: 'concluded by a natural person for a purpose which can be regarded as being outside his trade or profession (the consumer) with another person acting in the exercise of his trade or profession (the professional)'.
Consumer Credit Agreement Directive 2008/48/EC	Maximum harmonisation (recital 9 and Art.22)	Art.3(a): '"consumer" means a natural person who, in transactions covered by this Directive, is acting for purposes which are outside his trade, business or profession'.
Timeshare Protection Directive 2008/122/EC	Maximum harmonisation (e.g. recital 11)	Art.2(1)(f): '"consumer" means a natural person who is acting for purposes which are outside that person's trade, business, craft or profession'.
Consumer Injunctions Directive 2009/22/EC	Directives providing for certain rules on civil procedure	No definition.
Consumer Rights Directive 2011/83/EU	Maximum (targeted) harmonisation (Art.4)	Recital 34: 'In providing that information, the trader should take into account the specific needs of consumers who are particularly vulnerable because of their mental, physical or psychological infirmity, age or credulity in a way which the trader could reasonably be expected to foresee. However, taking into account such specific needs should not lead to different levels of consumer protection.' Art.2(1): '"consumer" means any natural person who, in contracts covered by this Directive, is acting for purposes which are outside his trade, business, craft or profession'.

Regulation 1215/2012 on Jurisdiction and the Recognition and Enforcement of Judgments in Civil and Commercial Matters (Brussels I Recast)	N/A	Recital 18: 'In relation to insurance, consumer and employment contracts, the weaker party should be protected by rules of jurisdiction more favourable to his interests than the general rules.' Art.17: 'In matters relating to a contract concluded by a person, the consumer, for a purpose which can be regarded as being outside his trade or profession . . .'
ADR for Consumer Disputes Directive 2013/11/EU Regulation 524/2013 on Online Dispute Resolution for Consumer Disputes	Directives providing for certain rules on civil procedure	Art.4(a): '"consumer" means any natural person who is acting for purposes which are outside his trade, business, craft or profession'. Art.4(1)(a): provides for the same definition as Directive 2013/11/EU, wherein 'consumer' means any natural person who is acting for purposes which are outside his trade, business, craft or profession.
Consumer Credit Agreement Relating to Residential Immovable Property (Mortgage Credit) Directive 2014/17/EU	Minimum harmonisation (recital 7 and Art.2), except in relation to the provision of pre-contractual information through a European Standardised Information Sheet, and the calculation of the APR which should be done via a consistent EU standard per Annex I	Recital 3: reference to over-indebted consumers, i.e. 'consumers in the Union hold significant debt'. Recital 29: 'In order to increase the ability of consumers to make informed decisions for themselves about borrowing and managing debt responsibly, Member States should promote measures to support the education of consumers . . . It is particularly important to provide guidance for consumers taking out mortgage credit for the first time.' Recital 48: 'Personalised advice should be given to consumers; moreover, different consumers might need "additional assistance". . . creditors . . . should adapt the way in which such explanations are given to the circumstances in which the credit is offered and the consumer's need for assistance, taking into account the consumer's knowledge and experience of credit.'

Table 7.1 (continued)

EU Instrument	Reach of Legislation and Status	Concept of the Consumer
		The definition of consumer is taken from Directive 2008/48/EC, Art.3(a), wherein '"consumer" means a natural person who, in transactions covered by this Directive, is acting for purposes which are outside his trade, business or profession"'
Package Travel Directive 2015/2302/EU	Maximum harmonisation (Art.4)	Recital 17: 'The majority of travellers buying packages or linked travel arrangements are consumers within the meaning of Union consumer law. At the same time, it is not always easy to distinguish between consumers and representatives of small businesses or professionals who book trips related to their business or profession through the same booking channels as consumers. Such travellers often require a similar level of protection . . . Therefore, this Directive should apply to business travellers, including members of liberal professions, or self-employed or other natural persons, where they do not make travel arrangements on the basis of a general agreement. In order to avoid confusion with the definition of the term 'consumer' used in other Union legislation, persons protected under this Directive should be referred to as "travellers".' Art.3(6): '"traveller" means any person who is seeking to conclude a contract, or is entitled to travel on the basis of a contract concluded, within the scope of this Directive'.

Proposal for a Directive Concerning Certain Aspects of Contracts for the Supply of Digital Content (COM(2015)634 final)	Targeted maximum harmonisation (proposed Art.4)	The explanatory memorandum to the proposal explains that the Commission takes the view that 'consumers are not confident when buying online across borders'. Proposed Recital 4: 'Consumers are not confident when buying cross border and especially online. One of the major factors for this lack of confidence is uncertainty about their key contractual rights and the lack of a clear contractual framework for digital content.' Proposed Art.2(4): '"consumer" means any natural person who in contracts covered by this Directive, is acting for purposes which are outside that person's trade, business, craft, or profession'.
Proposal for a Directive Concerning Contracts for the Online and Other Distance Sales of Goods (COM(2015)635 final)	Targeted maximum harmonisation (proposed Art.3)	The explanatory memorandum to the proposal explains that the Commission takes the view that 'consumers are not confident when buying online across borders'. Proposed Art.2(b): '"consumer" means any natural person who, in contracts covered by this Directive, is acting for purposes which are outside his trade, business, craft or profession'.

8. European fundamental rights and private litigations: judicial dialogue and judicial governance

Aurelia Colombi Ciacchi

INTRODUCTION

The present chapter intends to contribute to the understanding of judicial dialogue and judicial governance in European private law. It focuses on the dialogue between the Court of Justice of the European Union (CJEU) – formerly: European Court of Justice (ECJ) – and national courts in preliminary reference proceedings. Therein, it concentrates on cases where European fundamental rights play a role, and the litigating parties are private actors.

'Private actors', for the purposes of this chapter, means all parties other than public authorities. 'European fundamental rights' means not only the rights enshrined in the Charter of Fundamental Rights of the European Union (CFREU) but also the rights laid down in international conventions binding on the EU or its Member States (such as the European Convention on Human Rights), as well as the rights acknowledged by the common constitutional traditions of the Member States.[1]

When a national court refers a case to the CJEU for a preliminary reference in adjudicating a private litigation, in respect of which some of the interests at stake are protected as European fundamental rights, six types of conflict come into consideration:

(a) conflict of *private* interests (of the litigating private parties);
(b) conflict of *societal* interests and policies at stake in the relevant case;

[1] Cf. Art.6(3) Treaty on the European Union (TEU): 'Fundamental rights, as guaranteed by the European Convention for the Protection of Human Rights and Fundamental Freedoms and as they result from the constitutional traditions common to the Member States, shall constitute general principles of the Union's law.'

(c) conflict between different European *fundamental rights*;
(d) conflict between a European fundamental right and a European *fundamental freedom*;
(e) conflict between *national laws*;
(f) conflict between national law and *EU law*.

This chapter intends to analyse some patterns of dialogue between national courts and the CJEU in dealing with these conflicts. The term 'judicial dialogue' is understood here in the same sense as explained by Fabrizio Cafaggi and his co-authors in their handbook on judicial interaction techniques in fundamental rights adjudication.[2]

Two cases will be taken as examples: *Angonese*[3] and *Sturgeon*.[4] For each of the two cases, this chapter will first assess the conflicts of fundamental rights, interests and policies at stake. Secondly, it will analyse the dialogue between the national courts and the European Court of Justice in taking a position on these conflicts. Thirdly, it will discuss how the judicial dialogue in the abovementioned two cases contributes to the governance of European society through European fundamental rights and private law.

This chapter is based on the assumption that the assessment and balancing of conflicting rights, interests and policies by national and supranational courts constitutes a form of judicial governance. The following section will explain this in more detail.

JUDICIAL GOVERNANCE

The term 'judicial governance' has been used by scholars from different backgrounds to describe fairly different phenomena. Giving a complete overview of the relevant literature would exceed the limited space and scope of this chapter. Therefore, the following paragraphs will only mention

---

[2] Fabrizio Cafaggi *et al.*, 'Judicial Interaction Techniques' – Their Potential and Use in European Fundamental Rights Adjudication', Final Handbook (European University Institute, Centre for Judicial Cooperation 2014), 38 *et seq.* This Handboook arose out of a project funded by the European Commission Fundamental Rights & Citizenship Programme (JUST/2012/FRAC/AG/2755): 'European Judicial Cooperation in the Fundamental Rights Practice of National Courts: The Unexplored Potential of Judicial Dialogue Methodology'.

[3] Case C-281/98 *Angonese* [2000] ECR I-4139.

[4] Joined Cases C-402/07 and C-432/07 *Sturgeon and Others* [2009] ECR I-10923.

some current uses of the term 'judicial governance', before explaining the understanding of this notion underlying the present chapter.[5]

In her monograph on 'judicial governance in the European legal community',[6] Frerichs analyses the jurisprudence of the European Court of Justice in the light of social science theories on multilevel governance. In particular, she adopts a sociological institutionalist theory viewpoint to explain how the Court of Justice adjudicates conflicts concerning the European economic and societal constitution. Frerichs views judicial governance in the EU as a social field that comprises, besides the Court of Justice, 'a whole bunch of private, public, national, supranational and transnational actors competing for the right interpretation of EU law in general and the European economic constitution in particular'. In this field, the Court of Justice acts as an arbiter of the transforming European political economy, which 'sometimes cannot but "govern" – in the Platonian sense – "beyond the law" as it is written'.[7]

Petersmann deals with 'multi-level judicial governance' when he describes how transnational disputes in Europe (especially on economic law) are adjudicated by different supranational courts on the basis of different legal methodologies and constitutional backgrounds.[8] In this context, he draws attention to the sometimes inadequate responses of supranational courts to the governance gaps created by globalisation.[9]

---

[5] This section of the chapter draws on Aurelia Colombi Ciacchi, 'Judicial Governance in Private Law through the Application of Fundamental Rights' (2014) *Austrian Law Journal* 120.

[6] Sabine Frerichs, *Judicial Governance in der Europäischen Rechtsgemeinschaft. Integration durch Recht jenseits des Staates* (Nomos 2008).

[7] Sabine Frerichs, 'Judicial Governance in the European Community of Law: Adapting the Economic Constitution to Social Change', paper presented at the 2004 Maastricht Forum on European Integration, European Institute of Public Administration (EIPA), Maastricht, 19 November 2004, available at http://www.uni-bamberg.de/fileadmin/uni/wissenschaft_einricht/gk_mse/Paper/frerichs-legal_perspectives.pdf.

[8] Ernst-Ulrich Petersmann, 'Judging Judges: From 'Principal-Agent Theory' to 'Constitutional Justice' in Multilevel 'Judicial Governance' of Economic Cooperation Among Citizens' (2008) 11 *Journal of International Economic Law* 827; Petersmann, 'Constitutional Problems of Multilevel Judicial Governance in Trade and Investment Regulation', *EUI Working Paper Law No.2012/8*, http://papers.ssrn.com/sol3/papers.cfm?abstract_id=2069916; Petersmann, 'Multilevel Judicial Governance in European and International Economic Law' in Samantha Besson and Andreas R. Ziegler (eds), *Le juge en droit européen et international / The Judge in European and International Law* (Schulthess 2013) 45 *et seq.*, and *EUI Working Paper No.2013/3*, http://papers.ssrn.com/sol3/papers.cfm?abstract_id=2244839.

[9] Petersmann, 'Judging Judges', ibid.

While Frerichs and Petersmann focus their judicial governance analyses on the adjudication by supranational courts, Whytock focuses on adjudication by domestic courts. He defines 'transnational judicial governance' as 'governance of transnational activity by domestic courts'.[10] In his analyses, he concentrates on the role of US courts as global governance actors in adjudicating private international law cases.

Mate speaks of judicial governance with reference to the adjudication by domestic courts. He focuses on the Supreme Court of India as policy-maker in a number of governance-sensitive issues. In fact, over the last 50 years, this Court has exercised judicial activism in its strongest form, asserting the power to invalidate constitutional amendments under the basic structure doctrine; control judicial appointments; govern in the areas of environmental policy; monitor and investigate government corruption; and promote electoral transparency and accountability.[11]

A general notion of judicial governance, comprising the activity of both national and supranational courts, is proposed by Schmid. He explicitly links judicial governance to judicial activism, i.e., 'the prominent phenomenon of courts assuming tasks which are, under the classic separation of powers doctrine, reserved to the executive and legislative power'.[12] Schmid does not criticise judicial activism as such. He starts from the assumption that adjudication is always embedded in a wider social context and is, therefore, always influenced by the political, economic and social circumstances under which it operates and which influence the minds of jurists and inform their decisions. Schmid deems such an influence not undesirable, but instead indispensable to adapting the law to its changing social environment.[13]

This chapter's approach to judicial governance is partly similar to

---

[10] Christopher A. Whytock, *Domestic Courts and Global Governance: The Politics of Private International Law* (Ph.D., Duke University, 2007, http://pqdtopen.proquest.com/pqdtopen/doc/304870759.html?FMT=ABS), 7; Whytock, 'Transnational Judicial Governance' (2016) 2 *St. John's Journal of International & Comparative Law* 55. Whytock understands 'governance' as 'processes and institutions that guide and restrain collective activity' (see *Domestic Courts and Global Governance* cited above, 7). Cf. also Whytock, 'Domestic Courts and Global Governance' (2009) 84 *Tulane L.R.* 67.

[11] Manoj Mate, 'The Rise of Judicial Governance in the Supreme Court of India' (2015) 33 *Boston University International Law Journal* 169.

[12] Christoph U. Schmid, 'Judicial Governance in the European Union' in Christian Joerges and Florian Rödl (eds), *Law and Democracy in Europe's Postnational Polity* (Routledge 2008) 85.

[13] Ibid. See also Christoph U. Schmid, *Die Instrumentalisierung des Privatrechts durch die Europäische Union* (Nomos 2010).

Schmid's approach. Both in this and in her previous publications,[14] the author of this chapter understands judicial governance as *societal policy-making* through adjudication at both national and supranational level. This governance analysis focuses on the *conflicting interests and policies* at stake in a certain private litigation.

Indeed, one of the most important goals in governing both private and public institutions and relationships is that the interests of all participants are well represented and realised. Governance as 'policy-making with or without politics'[15] implies accommodating and balancing different policy objectives and interests of different actors,[16] and taking decisions based on this balancing.

The interests and policies to be balanced and accommodated are both the economic and non-economic interests of individuals or collective entities, including human rights and basic societal values such as democracy, and efficiency goals. A large number of those interests are protected at a national, European or constitutional level as fundamental rights or constitutional principles.

The following paragraphs will attempt to analyse how judicial governance is realised through judicial dialogue on fundamental rights and policies in the *Angonese* and *Sturgeon* cases.

THE HARMONIOUS DIALOGUE: *ANGONESE*

In the *Angonese* case,[17] the object of controversy consisted in a piece of private regulation: a requirement for admission to a recruitment competi-

---

[14] Aurelia Colombi Ciacchi, 'Jenseits der 'Drittwirkung': Grundrechte, Privatrecht und Judicial Governance in Europa', in Andreas Furrer (ed.), *Europäisches Privatrecht im wissenschaftlichen Diskurs* (Bern: Stämpfli, 2006) 231; Aurelia Colombi Ciacchi, 'European Fundamental Rights, Private Law and Judicial Governance', in: Hans-Wolfgang Micklitz (ed.), *The Constitutionalisation of European Private Law* (Oxford University Press 2014) 102; Aurelia Colombi Ciacchi, 'Judicial Governance in Private Law through the Application of Fundamental Rights' (2014) *Austrian Law Review* 120.

[15] Ali Kazancigil, 'Governance and Science: Market-like Modes of Managing Society and Producing Knowledge' (1998) 50 *International Social Science Journal* 69.

[16] See also the definitions of governance by Beate Kohler-Koch, 'The Evolution and Transformation of European Governance' in Beate Kohler-Koch and Rainer Eising (eds), *The Transformation of Governance in the European Union* (Routledge 1999) 14; and Pearl Issalys, 'Choosing Among Forms of Public Action' in Pearl Eliadis, Margaret Hill and Michael Howlett (eds), *Designing Government: From Instruments to Governance* (McGill-Queen's University Press 2005) 154, 180.

[17] *Angonese*, n. 3.

tion, set by a private employer. A bank of the Italian province of Bolzano limited the eligibility for recruitment to candidates who could prove their Italian-German bilingualism through a special certificate, issued by the public authorities of the province of Bolzano after an examination which was held only in that province. Mr. Angonese, who was indeed perfectly bilingual, was excluded from the competition only because he was not in possession of such a certificate. He claimed before the Bolzano Court of First Instance that the requirement should be declared void and that the Cassa di Risparmio should be ordered to compensate him for his loss of opportunity.

The Bolzano Court held that the requirement in question might be void under Italian law on ground of it being contrary to Union law, since it penalised job candidates not resident in Bolzano: in that it made it considerably more difficult for workers coming from outside that province to obtain the requested bilingualism certificate in good time. Therefore, the Bolzano Court referred to the ECJ the question of the compatibility of this requirement with the freedom of movement for workers enshrined in Art.48 of the EC Treaty, and its compatibility with Regulation No 1612/68 on freedom of movement for workers within the EU. The ECJ, having considered the latter Regulation not to be applicable to the present case, held that Art.48 of the EC Treaty precluded an employer from setting such a requirement.

In *Angonese*, like in many other employment-related cases, two fundamental rights and/or interests conflict with each other: the employer's fundamental right to private autonomy and freedom of contract[18] on the one hand, and the candidate's interest in not being unjustly discriminated against in an employment selection procedure, on the other.

Mr. Angonese's interest, however, could only be qualified as a subjective right if it could be subsumed under one of the legally recognised discrimination grounds. The legal qualification of the factual discrimination suffered by Mr. Angonese is much more problematic than what would appear at first sight. The relevant EU law provision in this case was the freedom of movement for workers, entailing the abolition of any discrimination based on nationality. However, Mr. Angonese himself

---

[18] On party autonomy or freedom of contract as an EU fundamental right, see Aurelia Colombi Ciacchi, 'Party Autonomy as a Fundamental Right in the European Union' (2010) *European Review of Contract Law* 303; Aurelia Colombi Ciacchi, 'Freedom of Contract as Freedom from Unconscionable Contracts' in Mel Kenny, James Devenney and Lorna Fox O'Mahony (eds), *Unconscionability in European Private Financial Transactions. Protecting the Vulnerable* (Cambridge University Press 2010) 7.

was *not* discriminated against on grounds of his nationality. He was an Italian citizen resident in the province of Bolzano since his birth. He was not a national of any EU Member State other than Italy. He was only a resident of Bolzano. He had left Italy to study abroad, but he had neither lost his Italian nationality, nor had he acquired the nationality of another country. The only 'discrimination' that he actually suffered consisted in the allegedly unjust discrimination *between different means to prove* his bilingualism. However, the discrimination between means of proof is not a legally recognised discrimination ground.

One might argue that the bank had a legitimate private interest in limiting the means of proof of bilingualism in its employment selection procedure. Indeed, an accurate assessment of one's bilingualism on an individual basis costs time and therefore money. The bank could have been mainly motivated not by the interest in excluding non-locals from the competition, but by the interest in a quick and cheap selection procedure that profited from the high-quality standards of the official proof of bilingualism carried out by the closest state actor. Thus one might argue that the bank's exercise of private autonomy in the *Angonese* case was in principle a legitimate one. Moreover, the conditions privately set by the bank did not infringe upon any fundamental rights of Mr. Angonese; since Mr. Angonese did not possess a nationality other than his Italian one, his right to non-discrimination on grounds of nationality was not infringed in the present case.

For these reasons, the harmonious dialogue between the referring national court and the ECJ in the *Angonese* case was enriched by two loudly protesting voices: both the private bank and the Italian Government intervened and contended that the question raised by the national court was artificial and had no connection with Community law.

These protesting voices remained unheard. The judicial dialogue in this case continued perfectly harmoniously both in the ascending and in the descending phase,[19] until the end of the litigation and thereafter. The referring national court held that the controverted condition of eligibility for employment could be null and void on the grounds of incompatibility with Community law. The ECJ confirmed the incompatibility of the condition in question with the fundamental freedom of movement for workers and

---

[19] On the different phases of the judicial dialogue centred around a preliminary reference procedure, including the ascension of the case to the national court(s) to the CJEU, and the subsequent descent of the case to the national deciding court, see Fabrizio Cafaggi's description of the method used in the Workshop on Judicial Cooperation in European Private Law, held in April 2013 at the EUI, in this volume.

the prohibition of discrimination on grounds of nationality enshrined in the Treaty. No other judicial actors seem to have raised any dissenting voices in this or similar cases decided after the *Angonese* judgment.

Despite of the lack of infringement of any fundamental right or otherwise legally recognised subjective rights of Mr. Angonese, the harmony of the judicial dialogue and the content of the judicial governance in this case were perfectly legitimate. Indeed, in the *Angonese* case, not only the fundamental rights of the litigating parties, but also the fundamental rights *of a countless number of other individuals*, as well as important European societal policies, were at stake. The condition in question objectively impaired the freedom of movement of workers in the EU. The condition was objectively discriminatory vis-à-vis all potential candidates who were not already in possession of the Bolzano certificate, and therefore also vis-à-vis *potential candidates coming from other EU Member States*.

Neither the national court nor the ECJ expressly balanced all fundamental rights, interests and policies at stake in the *Angonese* case against each other. However, an implicit balancing of these rights, interests and policies clearly resulted in the prevalence of the fundamental freedom of movement of workers and the correlated prohibition of discrimination on ground of nationality enshrined in the Treaty.

The judicial governance dimension of the *Angonese* case is evident. Unlike ordinary private law adjudication, where the focus lies on the conflicting rights *of the litigating parties*, in the *Angonese* case, the focus lies on EU societal governance policies that go clearly beyond the rights of the individual litigating parties.[20]

However, from the personal perspective of the author of this chapter, the most interesting judicial governance aspect in *Angonese* does not concern the balancing of conflicting fundamental rights and societal policies. It rather concerns the position taken by the *Angonese* judgment in the wider cross-national judicial dialogue on the direct horizontal effect of fundamental rights and freedoms. This issue will be dealt with in the following section.

---

20 With regard to all cases in which the ECJ pursued policies going beyond the protection of the rights of the litigating parties, Schmid speaks of 'instrumentalisation' of private law for EU integration purposes: Schmid, *Die Instrumentalisierung*, n. 13.

ANGONESE AND THE CROSS-NATIONAL JUDICIAL DIALOGUE ON THE HORIZONTAL EFFECT OF FUNDAMENTAL RIGHTS

The *Angonese* case is a perfect example of the direct horizontal effect of fundamental freedoms and fundamental constitutional principles (such as non-discrimination) on private relationships. One might argue that with this decision the ECJ took a position in the cross-national judicial dialogue on the horizontal effect of fundamental rights, freedom and constitutional principles, reinforcing the direct horizontality doctrine.

For the purposes of this chapter, 'direct horizontal effect' means that some entitlements and obligations within a private relationship directly descend from a fundamental right or constitutional principle, without the intermediation of a classic private law rule. On a theoretical level, this may imply that the fundamental right or constitutional principle in question is not only binding upon public authorities, but to some extent also upon private parties. Vice versa, for the purposes of this chapter, 'indirect horizontal effect' means that a private law remedy is based on a private law rule which is interpreted and applied in the light of a fundamental right or constitutional principle. On a theoretical level, this may imply that the fundamental right or constitutional principle in question is only binding upon public authorities who have the duty to ensure and protect it.[21]

Between the late 1940s and the end of the 1970s, the national courts of different EU Member States, including Italy and Germany, applied constitutionally protected fundamental rights and principles (such as the equality principle) *directly* in adjudicating litigation on labour relationships.[22] In the 1970s, the ECJ also began to apply fundamental

---

[21] On the definition of 'horizontal effect' and the distinction between 'direct' and 'indirect' horizontal effect of fundamental rights and freedoms see Colombi Ciacchi, 'European Fundamental Rights,' n. 14, 102 at 104 *et seq*., with further references.

[22] In Italy, see Trib. Firenze, 23 March 1948, Mon. trib. 1949 no. 18: the Court held that the stipulation of a too low remuneration in an individual labour contract was invalid on ground of violation of Art.36 of the Italian Constitution, which establishes the right to a remuneration sufficient to ensure a free and dignified existence for employees and their families. In Germany, see ArbG Bamberg, 7 November 1950, RdA 1951, 118: the Court found a dismissal from employment due to the employee's membership of the Communist Party invalid on ground of violation of the fundamental right to freedom of expression of political opinions enshrined in Art.5(1) of the German Constitution. On the direct and indirect horizontal application of fundamental rights to the adjudication of private litigation in nine European countries see Gert Brüggemeier, Aurelia Colombi Ciacchi and

principles enshrined in the Treaty, such as the prohibition of discrimination, *directly* in adjudicating litigations on labour relationships.[23] One might therefore argue that a harmonious judicial dialogue, or at least a harmonious judicial interaction on this issue, existed between the ECJ and the national courts of the said Member States until the end of the 1970s.

This harmony was partially troubled in the 1980s by the change of the prevalent opinion in Germany. In order to understand this change, one has to consider the history of the German judicial dialogue on the horizontal effect of fundamental rights on labour relationships. In the early 1950s, Germany was one of the first European countries to embrace the doctrine of direct horizontal effect of fundamental rights and constitutional principles on labour relationships. This doctrine was mainly developed by Nipperdey, who was not only a scholar[24] but also the President of the German Federal Labour Court (*Bundesarbeitsgericht, BAG*) from 1954 until 1963. Not unrelatedly, the first *BAG* decision on the direct horizontal effect of fundamental rights goes back to 1954.[25]

However, in its famous *Lüth* decision of 1958,[26] the German Federal Constitutional Court (*Bundesverfassungsgericht, BverfG*) did not embrace Nipperdey's doctrine. Instead, it embraced the doctrine of *indirect* horizontal effect of fundamental rights theorised by Dürig, who was one of

---

Giovanni Comandé (eds), *Fundamental Rights and Private Law in the European Union. Volume 1: A Comparative Overview* (Cambridge University Press 2010).

[23] Case C-36/1974 *Walrave and Koch* [1974] ECR 1405; Case C-43/1975 *Defrenne* v. *Sabena* (I) [1976] ECR 455. For a recent account on horizontal effect of EU fundamental rights see Matteo Fornasier, 'The Impact of EU Fundamental Rights on Private Relationships: Direct or Indirect Effect?' (2015) 23 *European Review of Private Law* 29.

[24] Hans C. Nipperdey, 'Gleicher Lohn der Frau für gleiche Arbeit', Recht der Arbeit 1950, 121; Hans C. Nipperdey in Ludwig Enneccerus and Hans C. Nipperdey, *Allgemeiner Teil des Bürgerlichen Rechts* (14th edn, Mohr 1954); Hans C. Nipperdey, 'Die Würde des Menschen' in Karl A. Bettermann, Franz L. Neumann, Hans C. Nipperdey and Ulrich Scheuner (eds), *Die Grundrechte. Handbuch der Theorie und Praxis der Grundrechte* Vol. II: *Die Freiheitsrechte in Deutschland* (Duncker & Humblot 1954) 111, 143; Hans C. Nipperdey, *Grundrechte und Privatrecht* (Scherpe 1961).

[25] BAG 3 December 1954, BAGE 1, 185; NJW 1955, 606. For a discussion of this case in English see Phillip Beckmann, Aurelia Colombi Ciacchi et al., 'Germany', in Brüggemeier, Colombi Ciacchi and Comandé, n. 22, 253, 289–90.

[26] BVerfG 15 January 1958, BVerfGE 7, 198. For a discussion of this case in English see Gert Brüggemeier, 'Constitutionalisation of Private Law – The German Perspective', in Tom Barkhuysen and Siewert Lindenbergh (eds), *Constitutionalisation of Private Law* (Brill/Nijhoff 2006) 59, 68 et seq.

the leading commentators on the German Constitution.[27] Since the *Lüth* case did not concern labour law, the *BAG* continued to apply the direct horizontal effect doctrine to labour relationships until the 1980s. The disharmony in the internal German judicial dialogue on this issue ceased in 1985, when the *BAG* aligned its jurisprudence to that of the *BVerfG* and definitively rejected the direct horizontal effect doctrine in respect of individual labour relationships.[28] Moreover, in the course of the last 30 years, the *BAG* has increasingly established the indirect horizontal effect doctrine for what concerns collective labour agreements.[29]

The current German approach[30] substantially converges with the prevalent opinion in England, which also supports a merely indirect horizontal effect of fundamental human rights on contractual relationships.[31]

---

[27] Günter Dürig, 'Grundrechte und Zivilrechtsprechung' in Theodor Maunz (ed.), *Vom Bonner Grundgesetz zur gesamtdeutschen Verfassung*, Festschrift zum 75. Geburtstag von Hans Nawiasky (Beck 1956) 176.

[28] BAG 27 February 1985, BAGE 48, 123. For an overview of the scholarly debate on the direct and indirect horizontal effect of fundamental rights in labour relationships between 1950 and 1985 see Dieter Fabisch, *Die unmittelbare Wirkung der Grundrechte im Arbeitsrecht* (Peter Lang 2010) 223.

[29] BAG 25 February 1998, BAGE 88, 118, 123; BAG 18 March 2009, BAGE 130, 43. However, the different sections of the Court take different positions on this issue. For an overview see Felix Hartmann, *Negative Tarifvertragsfreiheit im deutschen und europäischen Arbeitsrecht* (Mohr Siebeck 2014) 92; Matteo Fornasier, 'Die Wirkung der europäischen Grundrechte im Arbeitsverhältnis', in Clemens Latzel and Christian Picker (eds.), *Neue Arbeitswelt* (Mohr Siebeck 2014) 25, with further references.

[30] For recent accounts on the horizontal effect of fundamental rights and freedoms in Germany see Detlev W. Belling, Antje Herold and Marek Kneis, 'Die Wirkung der Grundrechte und Grundfreiheiten zwischen Privaten' in Badó Attila and Detlev W. Belling (eds), *Rechtsentwicklungen aus europäischer Perspektive im 21. Jahrhundert – European Perspectives on Legal Developments in the 21st Century* (Universitätsverlag, 2014) 53; Dirk Looschelders and Mark Makowsky, 'The Influence of Human Rights and Basic Rights in German Private Law', in Verica Trstenjak and Petra Weingerl (eds), *The Influence of Human Rights and Basic Rights in Private Law* (Springer 2016) 295 et seq. with further references.

[31] Simon J. Whittaker, 'Introductory' in Hugh Beale (gen. ed.), *Chitty on Contracts*: Volume 1, *General Principles* (31st edn, Sweet & Maxwell 2012) 68 *et seq.*; Alison L. Young, 'The Human Rights Act 1998, Horizontality and the Constitutionalisation of Private Law' in Katja Ziegler and Peter Huber (eds), *Current Problems in the Protection of Human Rights* (Hart Publishing 2013) 69 et seq. For a recent comparison of the German and English horizontal effect approaches see Justin F. Krahé, 'The Impact of Public Law Norms on Private Law Relationships – Horizontal Effect in German, English, ECHR and EU Law' (2015) 2 *European Journal of Comparative Law and Governance* 124, with further references.

However, these German and English approaches clash with the prevalent position of courts and scholars in other European countries, such as Italy and France, where fundamental rights undoubtedly have *direct* horizontal effect on labour relationships.[32]

As a result, the *Angonese* decision fully harmonises with the previous ECJ jurisprudence and with the Italian-French case law, while it clashes with the currently prevalent judicial approaches in Germany and England. This comparative law dimension of the ECJ jurisprudence on the horizontal effect of fundamental rights and freedoms does not seem to have been discussed by commentators before. Were the ECJ judges who decided the *Angonese* case aware of the conflict of views between judiciaries of different Member States on the direct application of fundamental rights and freedoms on labour relationships? Even if they were unaware of it, *Angonese* represents a strong voice in the supranational and cross-national judicial dialogue on this issue.

THE HERMENEUTICAL DIALOGUE: *STURGEON*

The judicial dialogue in the *Sturgeon* case runs along patterns of conflict that are remarkably different from the ones in *Angonese*. In *Sturgeon*, the main legal conflict concerns different interpretations of a piece of EU secondary law: Regulation No 261/2004 on air passenger rights.[33] Two airlines (Condor and Air France) were sued before national courts in Germany and Austria by a number of passengers claiming compensation under Art.7 of the Regulation, after having arrived at their destination more than 20 hours later than scheduled. These passengers had been informed by airport personnel that their flights had been 'cancelled'. However, the airlines refused compensation arguing that the flights were not cancelled but simply delayed, and that Regulation No 261/2004 only allowed for compensation in cases of flight cancellation. Furthermore,

---

32 Christoph Herrmann and Chiara Perfumi, 'France', in Brüggemeier, Colombi Ciacchi and Comandé, n. 22, 190, 206 et seq.; Chantal Mak, Maria D. Sanchez Galera, Sabine Wünsch, F. Jorge Ramos and C. Kraus, 'Italy', in Brüggemeier, Colombi Ciacchi and Comandé, ibid., 325, 341.

33 Regulation (EC) No 261/2004 of the European Parliament and of the Council of 11 February 2004 establishing common rules on compensation and assistance to passengers in the event of denied boarding and of cancellation or long delay of flights, and repealing Regulation (EEC) No 295/91, OJ L 46, 17.2.2004, 1–8. For a comprehensive analysis of the EU law on air passenger rights see Francesco Rossi dal Pozzo, *EU Legal Framework for Safeguarding Air Passenger Rights* (Springer 2014).

the airlines maintained that the late arrival of the flights was attributable to technical faults on the aircraft, which were covered by the concept of 'extraordinary circumstances' within the meaning of Art.5(3) of Regulation No 261/2004, and that they were thus released from the obligation to pay compensation.

The national courts referred a number of questions to the ECJ for a preliminary ruling. Complexly, they asked whether and under which circumstances a flight delay could be regarded as a cancellation for the purposes of the obligation to pay compensation under Regulation No 261/2004. Moreover, they asked whether technical problems with a plane and the resulting changes to the flight schedule represented extraordinary circumstances in the sense of Art.5(3) of this Regulation.

The ECJ began answering these questions by stating that under Regulation No 261/2004 cancellation and delay are two quite distinct categories: if a flight departs later than scheduled but all other elements pertaining to this flight remain unchanged, there is a delay and not a cancellation. In this regard, neither the length of the delay nor the terminology used by the airport personnel can play any role. So far, the Court's interpretation confirmed the correctness of the interpretation of the term 'cancellation', as defended by the airlines. Then, however, the Court brought forward a new, revolutionary interpretation of Regulation No 261/2004: it established the principle according to which the passengers who suffered a delay longer than three hours also have a right to compensation. The Court beautifully constructed the existence of this right by acknowledging the need to interpret the Regulation beyond its wording, so as to consider both the reasons for the adoption of the Regulation laid down in its preamble, and the objectives pursued by the rules in question.

Scholars familiar with the doctrines of interpretation of the law can easily recognise in this judgment all hermeneutical criteria discussed in the literature: the historical, the literal, the systematic, the teleological, and the evolutionary argument. The most revolutionary interpretation is the evolutionary one, which may even contradict the wording of a legislative rule. This interpretation (which is called in German literature '*richterliche Rechtsfortbildung*',[34] i.e., 'further construction of the law by the judiciary'),

---

[34] For a classic account see Wolfgang Fikentscher, *Methoden des Rechts in vergleichender Darstellung, V* (Mohr Siebeck 1977) 353 and passim. On the evolution of the concept of *richterliche Rechtsfortbildung* during the last decades, see Christian Fischer, *Topoi verdeckter Rechtsfortbildungen im Zivilrecht* (Mohr Siebeck 2007) 38 with further references. For a recent collection of papers on this topic see Daniel Effer-Uhe, Adam Sagan, Christian Deckenbrock, Clemens Höpfner, Matthias Kilian, Alexander Morell (eds), *Richterliche Rechtsfortbildung*

was actually applied in the *Sturgeon* judgment, although not explicitly mentioned by the ECJ. The Court only explicitly mentioned the teleological argument. However, the teleological argument can only apply where the legislative wording is open to different interpretations. In the *Sturgeon* case, despite the elegant attempts of the ECJ to demonstrate the contrary, the wording of Arts.6 and 7 of Regulation No 261/2004 were not open to different interpretations. This wording very clearly limited the scope of application of the compensatory remedy to flight cancellations.

The interpretation given by the ECJ was thus a *richterliche Rechtsfortbildung* that created a new right: the right to compensation in cases of long delay. This right, the existence of which is perfectly logical and legitimate, could not be introduced through the legislative process because of the successful lobbying of airlines and national governments protecting the airlines' interests. It needed therefore to be introduced through judicial governance.

The *Sturgeon* case is indeed a wonderful example of judicial governance. At first sight, the conflict of interests looks relatively simple: on the one hand, the airlines' economic interests, and on the other hand, the air passengers' interest in receiving adequate compensation for the economic and non-economic losses suffered as a consequence of long delays to flights. However, after a closer look, another interest at stake in this litigation appears to be the most important and weighty one: the interest in equal treatment. This interest justified the evolutionary interpretation given by the ECJ to Regulation No 261/2004. Indeed, from the principle of equal treatment, the ECJ deduced the need to provide equal remedies to all air passengers who, without any fault on their part, have reached their destination more than three hours later than scheduled as a consequence of a problem not extraneous to the airline's sphere of control.

The interest in equal treatment is protected in the framework of the general equality principle, which enjoys the status of a fundamental right or constitutional principle by most Member States' constitutional orders. Although the ECJ in *Sturgeon* did not explicitly balance all conflicting fundamental rights and constitutional principles at stake, it seems that the reference to the principle of equal treatment enabled the Court to tip the balance in favour of the consumers.

---

und kodifiziertes Richterrecht. Jahrbuch Junger Zivilrechtswissenschaftler 2014 (Boorberg Verlag 2016).

CONCLUSION

The Court of Justice in *Sturgeon* realised judicial governance in its strongest form: the creation of a new legal rule substantively opposite to the one that resulted from the weighing of interests and policies previously carried out within the legislative process. This is precisely the judicial governance conceptualised by Schmid as judicial activism: 'courts assuming tasks which are, under the classic separation of powers doctrine, reserved to the executive and legislative power'.[35]

For this reason, the *Sturgeon* decision has been sharply criticised[36] and has scattered further judicial and scholarly dialogue in several Member States on the right to compensation for air passengers in cases of delay.[37] Some airlines have disapplied the *Sturgeon* principles and tried to challenge them before the courts. Accordingly, German and English courts have submitted further questions for preliminary ruling. These were jointly decided by the CJEU in 2012 in the *Nelson* judgment,[38] which confirmed the *Sturgeon* principles.

Compared with *Sturgeon*, the *Angonese* judgment appears at first sight as a less revolutionary voice in the supranational judicial dialogue. In both cases, however, the European Court's judicial governance has helped protect fundamental interests of European citizens substantively, which without the Court's interference would have remained outweighed by the powerful private governance of corporate actors such as airlines and banks. Judicial governance is almost never a politically neutral exercise.[39]

---

35 Schmid, in Joerges and Rödl, n. 12, 85 et seq.

36 See e.g. Koen Lenaerts, 'The Court's Outer and Inner Selves: Exploring the External and Internal Legitimacy of the European Court of Justice' in M. Adams, H. de Waele, J. Meeusen and G Straetmans (eds), *Judging Europe's Judges: The Legitimacy of the Case Law of the European Court of Justice* (A&C Black 2014) 13: 'if courts go beyond the duty of saying "what the law is", they lack legitimacy as they intrude into the political process'.

37 For a recent comparative study on air passenger rights, including contributions from a large number of EU member states, see Michel Bobek and Jeremias Prassl (eds), *Air Passenger Rights: Ten Years On* (Hart Publishing 2016).

38 Joined Cases C-581/10 and C-629/10 *Nelson and Others* EU:C:2012:657.

39 See Colombi Ciacchi, 'Judicial Governance in Private Law, n. 14, 120 with further references.

9. On the transformations of European consumer enforcement law: judicial and administrative trialogues, instruments and effects

Fabrizio Cafaggi[1]

INTRODUCTION

The enforcement of consumer law is characterized by a combination of judicial and administrative regimes that involve European and national institutions.[2] The principle of sincere cooperation, enshrined in Art.4(3) TEU, imposes the engagement of institutional dialogue based on loyalty.[3] Increasingly, the Charter of Fundamental Rights (CFR) and, in particular Art.47 CFR, plays a role in shaping enforcement both before courts and before administrative authorities exercising enforcement power. The separation between rights (at EU level) and remedies (at Member State level) has disintegrated, driven by the principles of equivalence and effectiveness.[4]

---

[1] This chapter has benefited from the collective work within the ACTIONES project. The author is grateful for numerous conversations and exchanges with Paola Iamiceli, Federica Casarosa, Marc Clement, Mateusz Grochowski, Stephanie Law, Chantal Mak, Madalina Moraru, Francesco Patti, and Raffaele Sabato. Many thanks also to Julio Baquero Cruz and Hans Micklitz for useful conversations on the CJEU case law. Responsibility is mine.

[2] Within judicial enforcement, both civil and criminal should be considered. In this contribution judicial enforcement is limited to civil mechanisms; it does not deal with criminal adjudication.

[3] See Case C-34/13 *Kušionová* EU:C:2014:2189. In particular, according to the Court's settled case-law relating to the principle of sincere cooperation, now enshrined in Art.4(3) TEU, while the choice of penalties applicable to infringements of EU law remains within their discretion, Member States must ensure in particular that they are effective, proportionate and dissuasive (see, to that effect, the judgment in Case C-565/12 *LCL Le Crédit Lyonnais* EU:C:2014:190, para.44 and case-law cited).

[4] See Norbert Reich, *General Principles of EU Civil Law* (Intersentia 2014) 89, in which Reich distinguishes between eliminatory, hermeneutical, and remedial functions of the principle of effectiveness.

Fundamental rights and in particular the right to fair trial and to effective judicial protection are increasingly influencing both administrative enforcement and the scope of judicial review.[5] The role of Art.47 CFR in shaping the relationship between the two forms of enforcement is still to be determined.[6] Clearly, a much more frequent and significant reference is made to this provision by the courts than by administrative enforcement authorities. To a more limited extent, administrative enforcement has been influenced by the principle of good administration (Art.41 CFR), which also includes the right to effective remedies.

The role of national courts as enforcers of EU law has long been recognized.[7] However, the modes of interaction between administrative and judicial enforcement was initially neglected; in recent years, increasing attention has been devoted to the coordination of different enforcement mechanisms, including private justice.[8] This contribution examines the weaknesses of institutional design concerning the interaction between courts and administrative authorities exercising enforcement powers, broadly defined.[9] Institutional dialogue between European and domestic enforcement bodies has been an important driver of legal innovation in

---

5 See in relation to competition, ECtHR, Case *Menarini Diagnostics S.r.L. v Italy*, Judgment of 27 September 2011, App.No.43509/08.

6 See Koen Lenaerts, 'Effective Judicial Protection in the EU' (Available at: http://ec.europa.eu/justice/events/assises-justice-2013/files/interventions/koenlenarts.pdf; Last Accessed: 04/06/2016); Marek Safjan and Dominik Dusterhaus, 'A Union of Effective Judicial Protection' (2014) 33 YEL 15, connecting the *Rewe* principles and Art.47 CFR. They suggest that the interplay can result in four different scenarios: 'superposition, coexistence, infusion and exclusivity'. Steve Peers *et al* (eds), *The EU Charter of Fundamental Rights: A Commentary* (Hart, Oxford; 2014) and therein Herwig Hoffman *et al*, 'Commentary on Art.47: Right to an Effective Remedy and to a Fair Trial' 1197.

7 See Joseph H.H. Weiler, 'The Transformation of Europe' (1991) 100 Yale L.J. 2403; Walter Van Gerven, 'Of Rights, Remedies and Procedures' (2000) 37 CMLR 501; and A. Sweet Stone, *The Judicial Construction of Europe* (OUP 2004).

8 See Fabrizio Cafaggi and Hans-Wolfgang Micklitz, *New Frontiers of Consumer Protection – The Interplay between Private and Public Enforcement* (Intersentia 2009); Olha O. Cherednychenko 'Editorial – Public and Private Enforcement of European Private Law: Perspectives and Challenges' (2015) 23 481; and Hans-Wolfgang Micklitz, 'The Transformation of Enforcement in European Private Law: Preliminary Considerations' (2015) 23 ERPL 491.

9 It builds on the analysis carried out almost ten years ago. See Fabrizio Cafaggi, 'The Great Transformation: Administrative and Judicial Enforcement in Consumer Protection: A Remedial Perspective' (2009) 21 *Loyola Consumer Law Review* 496.

European consumer law.[10] The different levels of enforcement are not separate but rather interact continuously and often strategically. Dialogue can occur between national and European courts, among administrative bodies and their networks, and between courts and administrative authorities.[11] The practical effects of the dialogue on the national legal systems depends on several variables: (1) the actors involved (whether courts, independent administrative authorities, legislators, governments); (2) the role of the Court of Justice of the European Union (CJEU), in particular the width of its rulings; (3) the role of the European Commission; and (4) the instruments of dialogue between administrative and judicial authorities.

Administrative dialogue between European networks and national administrative authorities has played an important role in shaping enforcement practices in consumer law. Clearly the outstanding example is the Consumer Protection Cooperation (CPC) network, where national competent consumer authorities cooperate to address intra-community infringements.[12] The network, created by the CPC regulation, is com-

---

[10] See Opinion 2/13, EU:C:2014:2454, para.176:

> In particular, the judicial system as thus conceived has as its keystone the preliminary ruling procedure provided for in Art.267 TFEU, which, by setting up a dialogue between one court and another, specifically between the Court of Justice and the courts and tribunals of the Member States, has the object of securing uniform interpretation of EU law (see, to that effect, judgment in *van Gend & Loos*, EU:C:1963:1, p. 12), thereby serving to ensure its consistency, its full effect and its autonomy as well as, ultimately, the particular nature of the law established by the Treaties (see, to that effect, Opinion 1/09, EU:C:2011:123, paragraphs 67 and 83).

[11] See Takis Tridimas, 'The ECJ and the National Courts: Dialogue, Cooperation and Instability' in Anthony Arnull and Damian Chalmers (eds), *The Oxford Handbook of European Union Law* (OUP 2015) 403; Bruno de Witte, 'The Preliminary Ruling Dialogue: Three Types of Questions Posed by National Courts' in Bruno de Witte *et al* (eds), *National Courts and EU Law: New Issues, Theories and Methods* (Edward Elgar Publishing 2016) 21; Koen Lenaerts, Ignace Maselis, and Kathleen Gutman (eds), *EU Procedural Law* (OUP 2014) 70; Hans-Wolfgang Micklitz, 'The ECJ Between the Individual Citizen and the Member States – A Plea for a Judge-Made European Law on Remedies' in Bruno de Witte and Hans-Wolfgang Micklitz (eds.), *The European Court of Justice and the Autonomy of the Member States* (Intersentia 2011) 347, and section 3.2 therein.

[12] Regulation 2006/2004 has established a network of national competent authorities in the field of consumer intra-community enforcement in order to coordinate activities especially related to cross-border infringements. The CPC network is in charge of market surveillance:

> Article 1: Objective This Regulation lays down the conditions under which the competent authorities in the Member States designated as responsible for the

plemented by sector-specific networks in the fields of telecom, energy, transport, banking and financial regulation, as well as other areas.[13] Such complementarity often generates the need for coordination among domestic authorities involved in enforcing consumer protection, giving rise to overlapping competences. The problem of coordination between general and sector-specific consumer enforcement exists at national level where different regulatory architectures are in place but is reflected at European level where several networks may be competent for consumer protection in regulated markets. The instruments, the effects, and the impact of this type of dialogue differ, depending on the power conferred on each European network and the instruments used to monitor national authorities when exercising their enforcement powers. Coordination instruments of administrative enforcement have come under scrutiny, especially in relation to electronic commerce, and their shortcomings have resulted in proposals for reform. The reform of Regulation 2006/2004 on consumer protection cooperation – now under examination in relation to e-commerce – addresses some of the current design shortcomings, which will be analysed in this chapter.[14] The proposal strengthens the

---

> enforcement of the laws that protect consumers' interests shall cooperate with each other and with the Commission in order to ensure compliance with those laws and the smooth functioning of the internal market and in order to enhance the protection of consumers' economic interests;
>
> Article 9(1): Competent authorities shall coordinate their market surveillance and enforcement activities. They shall exchange all information necessary to achieve this.

See Cristina Poncibò, 'Networks to Enforce European Law: The Case of the Consumer Protection Cooperation Network' (2012) 35 *Journal of Consumer Policy* 175.

13 The comparison is limited to dialogue amongst administrative independent authorities but forms of dialogue and cooperation exist also among branches of the national executives dealing with consumer safety in relation to both products and processes: for example the Rapid Alert System for Dangerous Non-Food Products (RAPEX) system (Information available at: http://ec.europa.eu/consumers/consumers_safety/safety_products/rapex/index_en.htm; Last Accessed: 27.06.2016). In the area of unfair commercial practices competent authorities are at times independent authorities, at times governmental agencies.

14 See European Commission, 'A Comprehensive Approach to Stimulating Cross-border e-Commerce for Europe's Citizens and Businesses' SWD(2016) 163 final 9:

> Assessment of the implementation of the CPC Regulation as a cross-border enforcement instrument of the EU consumer acquis has identified several gaps. Mutual assistance mechanisms are insufficient and the response to widespread infringements across the EU is inefficient, especially when those occur in the

investigative and sanctioning powers of national authorities, particularly in light of the exponential growth of e-commerce in cross-border infringements.[15] Coordination concerns investigative and sanctioning powers. It can result in simultaneous action or in 'delegation' to one competent authority.[16] The role of the European Commission would also

---

> digital environment. The detection of such infringements is very often difficult and slow. Finally, national enforcement plans do not give sufficient priority and resources to enforcement actions that relate to cross border markets.

A proposal for a new regulation was published in May 2016. See European Commission, 'Proposal for a Regulation on Cooperation between National Authorities Responsible for the Enforcement of Consumer Protection Laws' COM(2016) 283 final.

15 See the CPC Proposal at Recital 9, which provides that:

> Competent authorities should be in a position to open investigations on their own initiative if they become aware of intra-Union infringements or widespread infringements by means other than consumer complaints. This is particularly necessary to ensure effective cooperation among competent authorities when addressing widespread infringements

and at Recital 14, which provides:

> As regards consumer redress, the competent authorities should choose proportionate, just and reasonable measures that would prevent or reduce the risk of recurrence or repetition of infringements, taking into account in particular the anticipated benefits to consumers and the reasonable administrative costs likely to be associated with the implementation of those measures. Where the consumers concerned cannot be identified or where they cannot be identified without disproportionate cost to the trader responsible, the competent authority may order that the restitution of profits obtained through the infringement be paid to the public purse or to a beneficiary designated by the competent authority or under national legislation.

16 See CPC Proposal Regulation, Explanation of main proposals:

> To ensure compliance with Union consumer law the competent authorities may empower one authority to take enforcement measures on behalf of consumers in other Member States concerned by the infringement. The competent authorities may also act simultaneously in all or some of the Member States concerned.

Recital 21:

> If a trader responsible for the widespread infringement or the widespread infringement with a Union dimension fails to cease the infringement voluntarily, the competent authorities of the Member States concerned should designate one competent authority in a Member State to take the enforcement action adapted to preserve the rights of consumers residing in the other Member States concerned by the infringement.

be strengthened.[17] The coordination established by the new Regulation should not operate with prejudice to the existing forms of coordination between sector-specific regulators.[18]

Judicial dialogue takes place vertically between the CJEU and the ECtHR or national courts and horizontally between European and domestic courts. The role of the CJEU is highly relevant and its outcome depends on several factors, among which are included: (1) the content of its rulings; (2) their effects on the country of the referring court, and in particular the 'resistance' exerted by the different national tribunals to overcome their previous jurisprudence; and (3) the impact of the decision on other countries.

Dialogues often become trialogues or tetralogues. Participants can be voluntary or involuntary, passive or active, actors (often this is the case for parliaments and executives). The dialogue is often iterative and does not coincide with the life cycle of a single case. Trialogues occur between national courts, national regulatory authorities, and the CJEU. Trialogues also occur when courts are trying to promote legislative changes by asking the CJEU to evaluate the conformity of national legislation with EU law, for example, in the determination of whether EU legislation precludes national existing legislation or a specific interpretation of that legislation. Hence in these instances, the trialogue is between the national court, the national legislator, and the CJEU. Thirdly, a trialogue takes place when, in the field of EU consumer law, both the ECtHR and the CJEU have not rendered perfectly coinciding judgments: the domestic judge, strained between the two, has to find the 'right' or balanced solution. Here the trialogue is purely judicial. The 'games' enshrining the trialogue are different in each case and players may have different roles. We shall examine when and how trialogues or tetralogues are embedded within a strategic environment and their effects on consumer enforcement.

---

17 CPC Proposal Regulation art. 10: 'The Commission may adopt implementing acts setting out the conditions for the implementation and exercise of the minimum powers of competent authorities referred to in Article 8. Those implementing acts shall be adopted in accordance with the examination procedure referred to in Article 48(2).'

18 See the CPC Proposal at Recital 29, which provides:

> This regulation complements sectoral Union rules providing for cooperation among sectoral regulators and sectoral Union rules on the compensation of consumers for harm resulting from infringements of those rules. This Regulation is without prejudice to other cooperation systems and networks set out in sectoral Union legislation. This Regulation furthers cooperation and coordination among the consumer protection network and the networks of regulatory bodies and authorities established by sectoral Union legislation.

This chapter addresses and compares the different forms of institutional dialogue that have characterized judicial and administrative enforcement in consumer law and the potential role of Art.47 CFR on the right to effective judicial protection.[19] It shows that there is an erosion of the principle of procedural autonomy, in respect of which fundamental rights and general principles play an increasing role in defining the architecture of consumer enforcement. It concludes by analysing how judicial and administrative enforcement of consumer law may be recombined in the light of the Charter's impact. The shift from the multilevel approach to the dialogical approach forces us to rethink how national and European enforcers interplay, creating a body of rules strained between uniformity and diversity. The perspective of strategic interaction offers additional and more convincing explanations to the conventional multilevel literature and especially to the concrete operations of enforcement mechanisms.

THE GEOMETRY OF DIALOGUE AND ITS EFFECTS ON ENFORCEMENT

Vertical judicial dialogue is based on cooperation in the shadow of the supremacy and effectiveness of EU law. It is diffused since it encompasses both high and lower courts.[20] The power of lower courts to ask for preliminary references has been a key instrument towards institutional cooperation. Had the dialogue been limited to the highest courts and the CJEU, the development of EU law and its enforcement would have been radically different. This is particularly clear in consumer law, where lower courts have been remarkably active; of course, high courts, including supreme administrative courts, have also made preliminary rulings but often with different objectives.

Vertical judicial dialogue occurs mainly via preliminary rulings proposed

---

[19] For an overview see Sybe de Vries, 'Ulf Bernitz, and 'Stephen Weatherill (eds.), *The EU Charter of Fundamental Rights as a Binding Instrument: Five Years Old and Growing* (Hart 2015); see also, Chantal Mak, 'Rights and Remedies – Article 47 EUCFR and Effective Judicial Protection in European Private Law Matters' in Hans-Wolfgang Micklitz (ed.), *The Constitutionalization of Private Law* (OUP 2014) 236. For a comparative analysis related specifically to private law, see Verica Trstenjak, 'General Report' in Verica Trstenjak and Petra Weingerl (eds), *The Influence of Human Rights and Basic Rights in Private Law* (Springer 2016) 3.

[20] National courts are considered to be the primary agents for the enforcement of EU law by the CJEU. See Anne-Marie Slaughter, Alec Stone Sweet, and Joseph H.H. Weiler (eds.), *The European Court and the National Courts—Doctrine and Jurisprudence: Legal Change in its Social Context* (Hart 1998).

by national jurisdictional bodies to the CJEU.[21] Member States' judiciaries differ as to the intensity and motivation to engage the CJEU.[22] The CJEU has defined by way of interpretation the structure, the procedural details, and the incentives to engage in dialogue.[23] National courts have the power and/or duty to submit a preliminary reference when the interpretation of EU law to be applied domestically is uncertain or when issues related to EU law validity arise.[24]

High courts have a duty to submit the preliminary references and national law cannot preclude them from doing so.[25] The CJEU has speci-

---

[21] The function of judicial dialogue on the basis of preliminary references is summarized by the CJEU in its Opinion 2/13, EU:C:2014:2454, para.176, n. 10.

[22] Note the differences between countries. Germany, Italy and Spain rank among the first countries to submit preliminary references. See CJEU Annual Report 2015 – Judicial Activity, especially table 19 (Available at: http://curia.europa.eu/jcms/upload/docs/application/pdf/2016-04/en_ap_jur15_provisoire2.pdf; Last Accessed: 06.07.2016).

[23] See the Guidelines issued by the CJEU on the procedure to be followed under Art.267; Recommendations to National Courts in Relation to the Initiation of Preliminary Ruling Proceedings, Official Journal C 338, 06.11.2012.

[24] See Case C-689/13 *Puligienica Facility Esco SpA (PFE) v. Airgest SpA* EU:C:2016:199, paras. 32, 33:

> As the Court has repeatedly held, national courts have the widest discretion in referring questions to the Court involving interpretation of relevant provisions of EU law (see, to that effect, judgment in *Rheinmühlen-Düsseldorf*, 166/73, EU:C:1974:3, para.3), that discretion being replaced by an obligation for courts of final instance, subject to certain exceptions recognised by the Court's case-law (see, to that effect, judgment in *Cilfit and Others*, 283/81, EU:C:1982:335, para. 21 and operative part). A rule of national law cannot prevent a national court, where appropriate, from using that discretion, (see to that effect, judgments in *Rheinmühlen-Düsseldorf*. . ., para. 4; *Melki and Abdeli*, C-188/10 and C-189/10, EU:C:2010:363, para. 42, and *Elchinov*, C-173/09, EU:C:2010:581, para. 27) or complying with that obligation.
> 33 Both that discretion and that obligation are an inherent part of the system of cooperation between the national courts and the Court of Justice established by Art.267 TFEU and of the functions of the court responsible for the application of EU law entrusted by that provision to the national courts.
> 34 As a consequence, where a national court before which a case is pending considers that a question concerning the interpretation or validity of EU law has arisen in that case, it has the discretion, or is under an obligation, to request a preliminary ruling from the Court of Justice, and national rules imposed by legislation or case-law cannot interfere with that discretion or that obligation.

[25] See ibid., para. 31:

> Article 267 TFEU must be interpreted as precluding a provision of national law, in so far as that provision is interpreted to the effect that, where a question

fied that even when the domestic rule is at the same time unconstitutional and contrary to EU law, national courts cannot be obliged to first refer the question to the domestic constitutional court and cannot be precluded from submitting the preliminary reference.[26] The possibility to make a preliminary reference exists even when fundamental rights are protected at the same time by national constitutions and by the Charter.[27] National constitutional courts have resisted this rule and have often affirmed the necessity to first submit the question of constitutionality to the domestic court; nevertheless, the CJEU has been firm and has consistently provided for the application of the rule.

The CJEU has interpreted Art.267 TFEU broadly, affirming its power to recast the preliminary questions within the boundaries of the national body's request.[28] Patterns of dialogue differ depending on how open-ended the rulings are: whether they are rulings of outcome, principle or deference.[29] The CJEU can: (1) provide the solution to the conflict with

---

> concerning the interpretation or validity of EU law arises, a chamber of a court of final instance must, if it does not concur with the position adopted by decision of that court sitting in plenary session, refer the question to the plenary session and is thus precluded from itself making a request to the Court of Justice for a preliminary ruling.

[26] See Case C-188/10 *Melki and Abdeli* EU:C:2010:363. See also, Case C-112/13 *A v. B* EU:C:2014:2195, para.38.

[27] See *A v. B*, ibid., para.41.

[28] See Case C-470/12 *Pohotovosť* EU:C:2014:101, para.27:

> It should be noted in that respect that, according to settled case-law, questions on the interpretation of European Union law referred by a national court in the factual and legislative context which that court is responsible for defining, and the accuracy of which is not a matter for the Court to determine, enjoy a presumption of relevance. The Court may refuse to rule on a question referred for a preliminary ruling by a national court only where it is quite obvious that the interpretation of European Union law that is sought bears no relation to the actual facts of the main action or its purpose, where the problem is hypothetical, or where the Court does not have before it the factual or legal material necessary to give a useful answer to the questions submitted to it (see, for example, Joined Cases C-222/05 to C-225/05 *van der Weerd and Others* [2007] ECR I-4233, para.22 and the case-law cited).

In some instances the reference to the principles of equivalence and effectiveness has been brought in by the CJEU even if national courts had not mentioned it in their preliminary reference. In other instances (Case C-34/13 *Kušionová* EU:C:2014:2189), the CJEU has integrated the preliminary ruling bringing in Art.47 of the Charter.

[29] See Takis Tridimas, 'The ECJ and the National Courts: Dialogue, Cooperation and Instability' in Anthony Arnull and Damian Chalmers (eds), *The Oxford Handbook of European Union Law* (OUP 2015) 403.

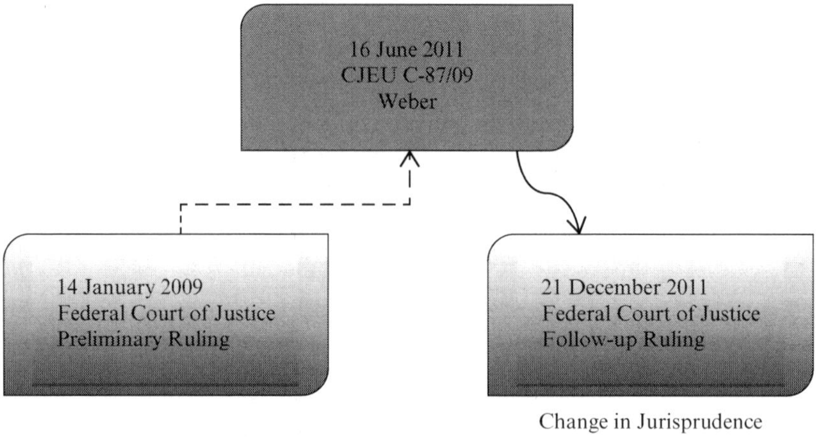

Figure 9.1 Graphical representation of judicial dialogue related to the CJEU decision in Case C-65/09 Weber and Putz EU:C:2011:396

detailed and specific rules (prescriptive); (2) offer guidance but leave the concrete solution to the national court (promotional); or (3) state the EU principle but defer to the national court to identify the appropriate rule and the solution (deferential).[30] Depending on the type of ruling the dialogue may end or continue with the same or with different courts to clarify the consequences of the application of EU law in the national legal systems, see for an example, Figure 9.1.

National courts, especially the high courts, engage also in horizontal dialogue by making references to the decisions of other Member State courts.[31] It is becoming ever more frequent that European comparative law is used in domestic judicial activities.[32] Judicial networks proliferate but they do not engage in a stable and formalized review of practices. However, unlike in administrative dialogue among independent regulatory authorities, no formalized peer review of national judicial activity

---

[30] See ibid., 408–9.

[31] These references are generally made to support the conclusion reached. Rarely does the art of distinguishing build on references to other national courts.

[32] European University Institute, Centre for Judicial Cooperation, 'European Judicial Cooperation and Fundamental Rights: Some Practical Guidelines' and the Handbook (Available at: http://www.eui.eu/Projects/CentreForJudicialCooperation/Documents/JUDCOOPdeliverables/JUDCOOPdeliverables/JUDCOOP%20Guidelines%20-%20Multilingual%20version.pdf; Last Accessed: 16.05.2016).

takes place among national judiciaries.[33] It will be important to design a more structured governance system that integrates judicial and regulatory networks in consumer enforcement.[34] This is all the more relevant given that the reform of Regulation 2004/2006 related to the CPC is now in process.[35]

Often the dialogue includes both trajectories. That is to say, there is first vertical dialogue between one national court and the CJEU and then the preliminary ruling triggers dialogue among national courts over the application of the principle set by the European court. This horizontal dialogue may push back the question to the CJEU for further clarification.[36] Dialogue is therefore recursive and the influence between European and national courts is reciprocal even under the principle of the supremacy of EU law.[37]

Administrative dialogue has operated mainly horizontally, between national regulatory authorities and both the European regulatory networks and the European Commission.[38] Cooperation and consensus, rather

---

33 For proposals to introduce forms of peer review and other instruments usually associated with the open method of coordination in European private law see Walter van Gerven, 'Bringing (Private) Laws Closer to Each Other at the European Level' in Fabrizio Cafaggi (ed.), *The Institutional Framework of European Private Law* (OUP 2006) 37 and Fabrizio Cafaggi, 'Introduction' in Fabrizio Cafaggi (ed.), *The Institutional Framework of European Private Law* (OUP 2006).

34 See Fabrizio Cafaggi, 'The Making of European Private Law: Governance Design', in Fabrizio Cafaggi and Horatia Muir Watt (eds), *Making European Private Law: Governance Design* (Edward Elgar Publishing 2008) 289.

35 See European Commission, 'A Comprehensive Approach to Stimulating Cross-border e-Commerce for Europe's Citizens and Businesses' SWD(2016) 163 final 9.

36 European University Institute, Centre for Judicial Coöperation, 'European Judicial Cooperation and Fundamental Rights: Some Practical Guidelines' and the Handbook (Available at: http://www.eui.eu/Projects/CentreForJudicialCooperation/Documents/JUDCOOPdeliverables/JUDCOOPdeliverables/JUDCOOP%20Guidelines%20-%20Multilingual%20version.pdf; Last Accessed: 16.05.2016).

37 See Charles F. Sabel and Jonathan Zeitlin (eds), *Experimentalist Governance in the EU* (OUP 2010) and Maartje De Visser, *Network-Based Governance in EC Law* (Hart 2009).

38 This is not to say that dialogue between the CJEU and administrative bodies does not exist. It operates via judicial bodies exercising judicial review. Courts exercising judicial review may ask preliminary questions concerning the enforcement of administrative authorities. The principle of effectiveness applies also to administrative bodies; the CJEU has provided guidance on how administrative bodies should implement the principle of effectiveness when national rules preclude the effective application of EU law. In the field of consumer credit agreements, Directive 2014/17 has regulated cooperation among administrative authorities

than voting, encompass the primary decision-making tools. Dialogue between administrative enforcers is governed by different mechanisms from those of judicial dialogue, deploying primarily but not exclusively soft law;[39] hierarchy does not play a significant role even in the area of financial markets, where European agencies have been conferred legal powers to solve conflicts and to sanction national authorities.[40] National administrative authorities define their practices in accordance with the guidelines issued by the European networks and revise their applications in peer review procedures.[41]

(Art.36) and conflict resolution when disputes arise (Art.37). Worth mentioning is the latter provision conferring on the EBA the power to decide in cases of conflict: Art.37 on the settlement of disagreements between competent authorities of different Member States. The competent authorities may refer the situation to the EBA where a request for cooperation, in particular the exchange of information, has been rejected or has not been acted upon within a reasonable time, and request the EBA's assistance in accordance with Art.19 of Regulation 1093/2010. In such cases, the EBA may act in accordance with the powers conferred on it by that provision and any binding decision made by the EBA in accordance with that provision shall be binding on the competent authorities concerned regardless of whether those competent authorities are members of the EBA or not. See for example, Case C-453/00 *Kühne & Heitz* [2004] ECR I-0837. In order to establish what obligations derive from EU law with regard to review of a final administrative act on the ground that it is contrary to EU law, the referring court considers at length the contributions of the judgment in *Kühne & Heitz*. In that judgment the Court held that the principle of sincere cooperation imposes on an administrative body an obligation to review a final administrative decision, where an application for such review is made to it, in order to take account of the interpretation of the relevant provision given in the meantime by the Court where (a) under national law, it has the power to reopen that decision, (b) the administrative decision in question has become final as a result of a judgment of a national court ruling at final instance, (c) that judgment is, in the light of a decision given by the Court subsequent to it, based on a misinterpretation of EU law which was adopted without a question being referred to the Court for a preliminary ruling, and (d) the person concerned complained to the administrative body immediately after becoming aware of that decision of the Court.

39 Especially in the field of financial regulation, the use of hard law has partly replaced soft law. See Niamh Moloney, *EU Securities and Financial Markets Regulation* (OUP 2014).

40 However recently EU Directives have conferred on European agencies – such as the EBA – the power to solve conflicts among national administrations when cooperation amongst them fails; see Arts.36 and 37, Directive 2014/17/EU on credit agreements for consumers relating to residential immovable property and amending Directives 2008/48/EC and 2013/36/EU and Regulation 1093/2010.

41 For example, in the field of sanctions where enforcement is decentralized, the Commission, as well as the networks, has issued guidelines in the area of financial regulation. See European Commission, 'Communication by the Commission,

One of the most relevant issues about administrative enforcement concerns sanctioning; sharing the definition of sanctioning practices, often quite diverse at national level, has involved networks to quite a significant extent. Country reports reveal considerable differences in the sanctioning practices, even when on paper the approach might appear to be similar. The proposed regime in the new CPC regulation empowers the designated authority to enforce consumer violations in other MS.[42] Such power is currently unavailable in judicial enforcement of consumer law.

In consumer law, dialogue between administrative authorities and European courts is only indirect. Judicial dialogue affects administrative enforcement when national courts engaged in judicial review ask for preliminary rulings from the CJEU in respect of the scope of judicial review and the activities of administrative authorities.[43] The CJEU has provided guidance on how national courts should review the decisions of administrative authorities dealing with consumer protection in regulated markets, for example, on the determination of tariffs and of the way in which consumer interests should be taken into account.[44]

The CJEU can address both procedural and substantive rules concerning how administrative enforcers proceed when examining the unfairness of contractual terms and trade practices.[45] In particular, it can provide

---

Reinforcing Sanctioning Regimes in the Financial Services Sector' COM(2010) 716 final.

42 See CPC Proposal Regulation Art.18:

> The competent authorities concerned may designate one competent authority to take enforcement measures on behalf of the other competent authorities in order to **bring about the cessation or to prohibit the widespread infringement, to ensure compensation of consumers or to impose penalties** . . . . Once the competent authority has been designated to take enforcement measures by the other competent authorities concerned, it shall become competent to act on behalf of the consumers of each such Member State as if they were its own consumer.

43 Case C-206/11 *Köck* EU:C:2013:14, Case C-28/15 *Koninklijke KPN and Others v. ACM,* EU:C:2016:692 and Case C-119/15 Biuro.

44 See *Koninklijke*, ibid., paras.60 and 61.

45 See Case C-119/15 *Biuro* concerning the use of list of unfair contract terms by administrative authorities. The CJEU was asked about the compatibility of an abstracto review system of unfair contract terms and Art.47 CFR. The Court stated:

> 26 In the absence of a provision in Directives 93/13 and 2009/22 providing explicitly for a scheme of effective judicial protection for the seller or supplier, they must be interpreted in the light of Article 47 of the Charter.
> 27 It follows that the interpretation of Directives 93/13 and 2009/22 in the light of Article 47 of the Charter must take account of the fact that any person

the Member States with guidance on how to coordinate administrative and judicial enforcement. For example, the scope of judicial review of administrative authorities may: (1) simply focus on the exercise of power by the administrative enforcer and remand to the administrative authority when its decision is not compliant with law; or (2) directly issue an injunction that stops the practice when the effectiveness of consumer protection so requires replacing administrative authorities.[46] The former solution might delay the enforcement of consumer protection but may also ensure a clearer allocation of tasks between administrative enforcers and courts exercising review power.

STRATEGIC JUDICIAL INTERACTIONS BETWEEN CONFLICT AND COOPERATION

Judicial dialogue often occurs between institutions seeking multiple objectives. Some objectives are openly stated while others remain undeclared. Strategic interaction among courts occurs when players pursue additional objectives that lie behind the legal question proposed to the CJEU for the resolution of the specific dispute.[47] Obviously, it is important to clarify that not all interactions are strategic and that not every preliminary reference has strategic implications. A strategic feature emerges when repeat

---

whose rights guaranteed by EU law might be infringed is entitled to an effective judicial remedy. This concerns not only consumers who feel that they have been wronged by an unfair term of a contract they have concluded with a seller or supplier, but also a seller or supplier, such as Biuro Partner, who argues that the contract term in dispute cannot be held to be unlawful and sanctioned by a fine solely because an equivalent term has been entered in the national registry of unlawful standard contract terms, without that seller or supplier having been a party to the proceedings culminating in the entry of such a term in that register.

[46] See AG Trstenjak's Opinion in *Köck*, n. 43, para.62, concluding that Member States can confine judicial review to the examination of the administrative enforcer without exercising direct power and grant remedies to the consumer. The conclusion is that Member States can opt for a strict boundary and limit the scope of judicial review, or for a more flexible division and allow the reviewing court to grant the remedy when effectiveness so requires. In the Italian practice, the administrative courts reviewing the decisions of the Competition Authority (AGCM) in relation to unfair commercial practices have scrutinized the enforcement power and specified the content of effectiveness and proportionality of sanctions.

[47] For a model of game theoretic strategic interaction between the Spanish courts, the Spanish government and the CJEU, see the contribution of Gomez and Lyczkowska in this book.

interactions between the courts occur in order to change legislation or to modify the current interpretation of the law.[48] To qualify as strategic the interaction does not necessarily have to take place between identical courts. For strategic interaction to materialize, it is sufficient that lower courts from the same countries or even from different states submit questions logically connected in order to achieve a common objective. Clearly, the strategic nature is reinforced when the same national court proposes sequential preliminary references on similar issues to the CJEU.[49]

In this analysis, we would like to highlight both the technical and the strategic aspects, and suggest that in many instances dialogue between the national and the European courts is used strategically to promote legislative change or to foster new interpretations of national law both substantive and procedural in addition to the solution of the specific question.[50] Such changes concern national procedural rules that condition the effectiveness of remedies and, as a result, the enforceability of individual and collective consumer rights.

The strategic interaction can take place between three or more actors giving rise to trialogues or tetralogues. When legislative change is the objective, the interaction occurs between domestic courts, the national legislator or the government, and the CJEU. When jurisprudential change is the goal, the relevant trialogue is between lower and higher courts of a Member State and the CJEU.[51] At times, the interaction takes place between high courts, e.g., constitutional and supreme courts, or especially in the field of fundamental rights, between constitutional courts, the ECtHR and the CJEU.[52] Tetralogues can involve lower and high

---

[48] As for example in the references made by the Spanish courts.

[49] See for example the Budapest First instance court (in Case C-472/11 *Banif Plus Bank* EU:C:2013:88 Case C-32/14 *ERSTE Bank* EU:C:2015:637) or the Castelon Appeal Court (in Case C-169/14 *Sánchez Morcillo and Abril García* EU:C:2014:2099).

[50] See the publications stemming from the JUDCOOP project (Available at: http://www.eui.eu/Projects/CentreForJudicialCooperation/Documents/JUDCOOPdeliverables/JUDCOOPdeliverables/JUDCOOP%20Guidelines%20-%20Multilingual%20version.pdf; Last Accessed: 16.05.2016).

[51] In Spain this has often been the case in the area of loan agreements when lower courts wanted to change the interpretation offered by *Tribunal Supremo* and in some instances by *Tribunal Constitucional*. See for example: C-240-244/98 *Océano Grupo* EU:C:2000:346; C-168/05 *Mostaza Claro* EU:C:2006:675; C-40/08 *Asturcom* EU:C:2009:615; C-618/10 *Banco Español de Crédito* EU:C:2012:349; C-472/11 *Banif Plus Bank* EU:C:2013:88; C-413/12 *ACICL* EU:C:2013:800 and so on.

[52] Examples concern conflicts between constitutional and supreme courts or supreme courts and the Councils of State.

courts, the legislator and the CJEU or national courts and administrative enforcers, the national legislator, and the CJEU.

Legislative change has not been the exclusive objective of judicial interaction. Rather changes of judicial interpretations have more often been the primary objectives of preliminary references. Often lower courts have raised questions whose impact has gone well beyond the solution of the specific dispute before them: they have asked for guidance on the powers of civil judges, on the relationship between different remedies, and most recently, on the function of collective and individual redress. One of the most recent developments concerns the solution of interpretive disputes among domestic judges in relation to the interpretation of EU law.[53] Traditionally, this function (*nomofilachia*) belongs to the highest court. However, conflicts, (1) between courts and (2) between the national judiciary and the legislator, have been indirectly solved by the CJEU by virtue of its examination of the compatibility of national legislation with EU law, or its current judicial interpretation.[54]

Strategic interactions in vertical judicial dialogue can be driven by preliminary references. The use of the preliminary reference procedure particularly by the Spanish, Slovak, and Hungarian courts in consumer litigation illustrates that lower courts have been at the forefront of legal innovation in the field of consumer enforcement law, promoting changes in procedural law to ensure fair outcomes in litigation concerning con-

---

[53] See Case C-381/14 *Sales Sinués* EU:C:2016:15, Opinion of AG Szpunar:

30 As is clear from the documents before the Court, it is the divergent interpretation and application by the national courts of Art.43 of the Code of Civil Procedure in the context of the collective injunctive proceedings brought by ADICAE which render the analysis of the questions referred for a preliminary ruling even more complex, the matter not having been decided by the highest national courts.
31 On the one hand, certain courts appear to take the view that there is an issue of civil procedural precedence, in accordance with Art.43 of the Code of Civil Procedure, and have stayed individual proceedings pending the delivery of a final judgment in the collective proceedings, on the basis of the connection between the subject-matter of the individual actions and that of the collective actions.
32 On the other hand, certain other courts appear to believe there to be a situation of *lis alibi pendens* as regards the individual actions vis-à-vis the collective actions, on the view that the cause of action and the parties are the same, and are removing from the register individual actions on the basis of Art.222(3) of the Code of Civil Procedure. It is apparent from the documents before the court that such courts are in the minority (footnotes omitted).

[54] As has been the case in the references cited herein.

sumer credit, mortgage loans and foreclosure proceedings in times of financial crisis.[55] This litigation has reduced the impact of the financial crisis onto small real estate owners and has reallocated its burden between banks and borrowers.[56] The finding of contractual unfairness related to interest rates, penalties for default, and contractual termination has been the mechanism by which banks and credit institutions have been precluded from using domestic legislation that would facilitate the foreclosure of homes offered as securities. Interestingly, to a greater extent than in administrative regulation, judicial intervention has influenced the subsequent determination of interest rates, and the processes of renegotiation between banks and consumers, both individually and collectively, in light of new credit legislation that was passed to address problems arising out of the financial crisis.[57]

The Spanish legislation and pre-existing judicial practice allowed the banks to foreclose; if the contractual term on which basis foreclosure was executed turned out to be unfair, it only permitted the granting of pecuniary indemnification without restitution of the house.[58] The CJEU in *Aziz* responded to the preliminary reference made by the first instance court of Barcelona in such a way that required a change in the Spanish procedural rules that precluded the assessment of unfairness. The final outcome of the case is unclear given that it was reformed in appeal after the referring first instance court decided according to the indications given by the CJEU.[59] In any case, its impact has been enormous, empowering judges to

---

55 For a comparative analysis, see the contributions to Hans-Wolfgang Micklitz and Irina Domurath (eds), *Consumer Debt and Social Exclusion in Europe* (Ashgate 2015).

56 See the contribution of Gomez and Lyczkowska herein.

57 National regulatory authorities in the field of consumer law have not engaged the CJEU often. The dialogue between national regulators and the European judiciary is underdeveloped when compared with judicial dialogue.

58 See Case C-415/11 *Mohamed Aziz* EU:C:2013:164 and Hans-Wolfgang Micklitz, 'Unfair Contract Terms – Public Interest Litigation Before European Courts' in Evelyn Terryn *et al* (eds), *Landmark Cases of EU Consumer Law: In Honour of Jules Stuyck* (Intersentia 2013) 633.

59 See the preliminary reference to the CJEU and the observations made by the Commission in *Aziz*. Interestingly after the CJEU's decision, the case was decided by the first instance court in Barcelona, which went along with the CJEU position. The case was then appealed and the Court of Appeal in Barcelona took a much more restrictive approach. First, at para.26, it provided:

> Y tampoco es preciso renunciar al principio de la demanda o principio dispositivo, que inspira el principio de congruencia e informa también el ordenamiento procesal de todos los países de nuestro entorno. Creemos que es inconcebible que el principio dispositivo pueda considerarse derogado por exigencia de la

evaluate the potential unfairness of contractual terms in loans and other contracts financing the purchase of homes and other consumer goods, see Figure 9.2.

The outbreak of preliminary references related to mortgage and foreclosure in Spain has occurred in an institutional environment favourable to the strategic use of judicial dialogue.[60] Not only has the occurrence of legislative change been significant, but both its quality and impact have also been the subject of CJEU scrutiny. The sequence of Spanish references shows that the CJEU, after inducing legislative changes, has had the opportunity to scrutinize the adequacy of procedural changes made by the Spanish legislator to pursue effective consumer protection via adequate procedural rules; this has given rise to a trialogue, or a tetralogue if we include the Spanish Constitutional Court. The nature of the institutional trialogue among lower courts, the Spanish legislator and the CJEU, in *Aziz,* thus shows both the willingness and the limits identified

---

> efectividad del derecho comunitario porque ese dispositivo o de la demanda informa también el derecho comunitario a través de la Carta de Derechos Fundamentales de la Unión Europea, y particularmente del reconocimiento en la misma del derecho de propiedad privada (artículo 17), que incluye el derecho de disponer de los derechos y del derecho a la tutela efectiva (artículo 47), que incluye el derecho de acción. Y también incluye el derecho a un proceso equitativo, que exige entre sus presupuestos que se trate de un proceso congruente y en el que se respete la contradicción efectiva.

Thereafter, at para.41:

> En resumen, el ámbito de los poderes de oficio del juez civil en el enjuiciamiento de cuestiones relacionadas con la Directiva comunitaria 1993/13 no supone una práctica derogación del principio dispositivo sino exclusivamente el reconocimiento al juez de la facultad de pronunciarse sobre todas aquellas cuestiones relevantes para la suerte de la pretensión ejercitada por el consumidor o frente al consumidor. Eso se traduce en las siguientes facultades: a) Cuando el consumidor es parte demandada en un proceso en el que se ha ejercitado una pretensión dimanante de un contrato de consumo: la posibilidad de apreciar de oficio la nulidad de todas aquellas estipulaciones relevantes desde la perspectiva de la acción ejercitada por el predisponente, con la posibilidad de desestimar su pretensión. b) Cuando el consumidor es parte demandante, en un proceso instado a su instancia, la posibilidad de que la pretensión ejercitada pueda ser estimada con fundamento en razones distintas a las esgrimidas en la propia demanda, esto es, incluso en el caso de que esas razones pudieran llegar a fundar causas de pedir distintas no invocadas. En este caso, el límite está, al menos en principio, en las propias peticiones de la demanda, con la excepción a la que se hace referencia en el apartado siguiente.

The case is now pending before the *Tribunal Supremo*.

60 See the contribution of Gomez and Lyczkowska herein.

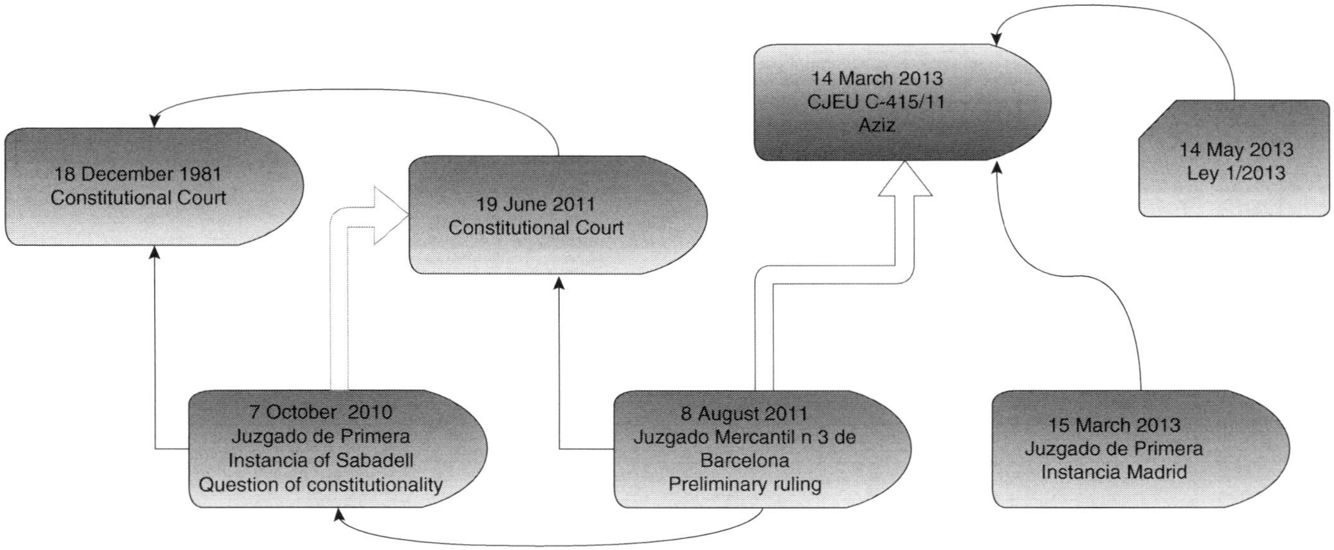

Figure 9.2 *Graphical representation of judicial dialogue related to CJEU decision in Case C-415/11 Mohamed Aziz EU:C:2013:164*

by the CJEU in examining national procedural laws applied to consumer litigation under the umbrella of Art.47 CFR.[61] The issue brought to the attention of the CJEU in *Sanchez Morcillo I and II* was the violation of the principle of equal arms in exercising the right to appeal in foreclosure proceedings, in the case where the contract might have included unfair terms. The Spanish judge from the appeal court of Castellon proposed the preliminary reference after the Spanish Constitutional Court's rejection of the constitutionality question concerning the general civil procedure law (*Ley de enjunciamento civil*, hereinafter LEC).[62] The preliminary ruling in *Sanchez Morcillo I* identified the conflict between domestic and EU law.[63]

---

61 The trialogue is between the lower courts, the Spanish Constitutional Court and the CJEU. In fact, the dialogue includes also the Spanish legislator which changed the procedural law in order to grant right to appeal to the consumer following Case C-169/14 *Sánchez Morcillo and Abril García* EU:C:2014:2099.

62 See ibid., in which the preliminary reference stated:

> Must Article 7(1) of [Directive 93/13], read in conjunction with Articles 47, 34(3) and 7 of the [Charter] be interpreted as precluding a procedural provision of the kind laid down in Article 695(4) of [the amended LEC], applicable to appeals against a decision determining the outcome of an objection to enforcement proceedings in relation to mortgaged or pledged goods, which allows an appeal to be brought only against an order terminating the proceedings, disapplying an unfair term or rejecting an objection based on an unfair term, the immediate consequence of which is that more legal remedies on appeal are available to the seller or supplier seeking enforcement than to the consumer against whom enforcement is sought?

In para.23 the CJEU explained what was the objective of the preliminary ruling:

> In its request for a preliminary ruling, the referring court asks, in essence, if Article 7(1) of Directive 93/13, read in conjunction with Articles 47, 34(3) and 7 of the Charter, must be interpreted as precluding a national provision of the kind at issue in the main proceedings, by which the consumer, as a mortgage debtor against whom enforcement proceedings are brought, may bring an appeal against the decision rejecting his objection to the enforcement only when the court of first instance has not upheld an objection based on the unfairness of the contractual term upon which the enforcement is based, while the seller or supplier, may, by contrast, appeal against any decision terminating the proceedings regardless of the ground of objection on which that decision is based.

63 The answer given by the Court was:

> In light of those considerations, the answer to the question referred is that Article 7(1), of Directive 93/13, read in conjunction with Articles 7 and 47 of the Charter, must be interpreted as not precluding a national provision of the kind at issue in the main proceedings, by which the consumer, as a mortgage debtor against whom enforcement proceedings are brought, may bring an

As a result, the Spanish legislation was changed but the same judge submitted a new preliminary reference concerning the second legislative reform to which the CJEU gave a negative answer, holding that the reformed Spanish legislation was not in conflict with EU law.[64]

These instances of Spanish judicial activism have been partly justified by the inertia and immobility of the competent administrative regulators. The references to the CJEU came after a line of cases, from *Océano* to *Mostaza y Claro, Asturcom, Pannon* and *Penzugyi*, by virtue of which the CJEU empowered the national courts to raise *ex officio* questions that the parties, and especially consumers' lawyers, had failed to include in their pleadings.[65] The content and the limits of this power have been delineated over time and the potential conflicts, which arise

---

appeal against the decision rejecting his objection to the enforcement only when the court of first instance has not upheld an objection based on the unfairness of the contractual term upon which the enforcement is based even though sellers or suppliers may, by contrast, appeal against any decision terminating the proceedings regardless of the ground of objection on which that decision is based.

64 Ibid.

65 Including, inter alia, Case C-240/98 *Océano* [2000] ECR I-4941, and the cases that followed, including, inter alia, Case C-227/08 *Martin Martin* EU:C:2009:792, Case C-137/08 *VB Pénzügyi Lízing* EU:C:2010:659, Case C-243/08 *Pannon GSM* [EU:C:2009:350, Case C-453/10 *Pereničová and Perenič* EU:C:2012:144, Case C-618/10 *Banco Español de Crédito* EU:C:2012:349, Case C-470/12 *Pohotovost'* EU:C:2014:101, Cases C-482, 484, 485 and 487/13 *Unicaja Banco and Caixabank* EU:C:2015:21, Case C-497/13 *Faber* EU:C:2015:357, Case C-32/14 *ERTSE* EU:C:2015:637, Case C-169/14 *Sánchez Morcillo* EU:C:2014:2099. In *Banco Español* it was provided:

> 42 It is in the light of those principles that the Court has therefore held that the national court is required to assess of its own motion whether a contractual term falling within the scope of Directive 93/13 is unfair, compensating in this way for the imbalance which exists between the consumer and the seller or supplier (see, to that effect, Case C-168/05 *Mostaza Claro* [2006] ECR I-10421, para.38; Case C-243/08 *Pannon GSM* EU:C:2009:350, para.31; Case C-40/08 *Asturcom* EU:C:2009:615, para.32; and Case C-137/08 *VB Pénzügyi Lízing* [EU:C:2010:659, para.49).
> 43 Consequently, the role attributed to the national court by EU law in this area is not limited to a mere power to rule on the possible unfairness of a contractual term, but also consists of the obligation to examine that issue of its own motion, where it has available to it the legal and factual elements necessary for that task (see Case C-243/08 *Pannon GSM* [2009] ECR I-4713, para.32).

On this evolution see Verica Trstenjak, 'Procedural Aspects of European Consumer Protection Law and the Case Law of the CJEU from the Perspective of Insurance Law' (2013) 21 ERPL 451, and Hans-Wolfgang Micklitz, 'The in respect of the conventional allocation of powers between litigants and judges, have been revised accordingly. Clearly, transformations of national procedural systems which aim to ensure the effective judicial protection of consumers occur at a different pace following preliminary rulings from the CJEU.[66] National judges have been provided with new powers and responsibilities to monitor unfair market practices, thus changing certain national procedural rules. The public policy rationale, usually deployed in national legal systems to legitimize judicial intervention, has been widened and complemented by the principle of effectiveness broadening the power to assess *ex officio* EU law effects on procedural rules beyond the pure metric of equivalence between domestic and EU law.[67]

How has judicial vertical dialogue on consumer enforcement had an impact on legal systems other than that of the referring court? Judgments are binding on all the Member States but their impact differs according to the specific legal framework where they apply. The impact of a CJEU ruling on various Member States depends on systemic factors. Different impacts of the CJEU have occurred across the Member States because some have chosen judicial, while others have opted for administrative, enforcement.[68]

A plurality of enforcement mechanisms with different procedural rules might lead to EU consumer protection case law having diverse effects across the Member States. Clearly the *ex officio* case law that has stimulated changes in procedural laws for those countries that have privileged

---

Transformation of Enforcement in European Private Law: Preliminary Considerations' (2015) 23 ERPL 491.

[66] The impact on the legal system where the referring court is located is generally much stronger than elsewhere notwithstanding the binding nature of the judgments in all Member States.

[67] See Hanna Schebesta, 'Does the National Court Know European Law? A Note on Ex Officio Application after Asturcom' (2010) 18 ERPL 847, Simon Whittaker, 'Who Determines What Civil Courts Decide? Private Rights, Public Policy an EU Law' in Dorota Leczykiewicz and Stephen Weatherill (eds), *The Involvement of EU Law in Private Law Relationships* (Hart 2013) 89, 117 *et seq.*, Arthur S. Hartkamp, 'Ex officio Application in Case of Unenforceable Contracts or Contract Clauses: EU Law and National Law Confronted' in Louise Gullifer and Stefan Vogenauer (eds), *English and European Perspectives in Contract and Commercial Law: Essays in Honour of Hugh Beale* (Hart 2014) 470 and Anna Mancaleoni, 'The Obligation on Dutch and Italian Courts to Apply EU Law of Their Own Motion' (2016) 24 ERPL 529.

[68] In relation to unfair contract terms the majority stand on the judicial side, while in relation to unfair trade practices a greater number have chosen the administrative side in addition to judicial enforcement.

judicial enforcement has had little impact on those deploying primarily administrative control where *ex officio* powers to investigate were already provided for. But even the changes of procedural laws in countries other than those of the referring courts have been uneven and not always consistent.

The use of preliminary references is therefore bringing about important changes in national procedural rules, highlighting the limits of dissociating substance from procedure and the shortcomings of administrative enforcement in consumer law.[69] However, judicial dialogues and trialogues have institutional limitations that render the process of change unstable and not always harmonious. Improvements on the instruments of dialogue can provide for a higher level of stability and legal certainty across Member States.

INSTITUTIONAL DIALOGUE AND THE REGULATORY FUNCTIONS OF CONSUMER ENFORCEMENT

Judicial and administrative dialogues have reinforced the regulatory functions of consumer law in policing market behaviour, regulating market access, and granting consumers the possibility to switch between different operators thereby increasing competition and expanding consumer choice.[70] The regulatory function of consumer law operates through contract, civil liability, and property within the domain of private law but it is also characterized by the use of administrative law.[71] The regulatory functions influence both the institutional and the substantive facets of dialogue. The complementarity of different instruments pursuing regulatory

---

[69] See Walter Van Gerven, 'Of Rights, Remedies and Procedures' (2000) 37 CMLR 501; V. Trstenjak and E. Beysen, 'European Consumer Protection Law: curia sempter dabit remedium?' (2011) 48 CMLR 95, p 120, and Hans-Wolfgang Micklitz, 'The ECJ Between the Individual Citizen and the Member States – A Plea for a Judge-Made European Law on Remedies' in Bruno de Witte and Hans-Wolfgang Micklitz (eds), *The European Court of Justice and the Autonomy of the Member States* (Intersentia 2011) 347, and section 3.2, especially.

[70] See, for an analysis of the regulatory functions of European private law, Fabrizio Cafaggi and Horatia Muir Watt (eds), *The Regulatory Functions of European Private Law* (Edward Elgar Publishing 2009) and more broadly, Cafaggi and Muir Watt, n.34.

[71] See Cafaggi and Muir Watt, ibid., and Stephen Weatherill, *Contract Law of the Internal Market* (Intersentia 2016) 129.

functions makes the conventional public-private divide obsolete in relation to both substantive and remedial law.

Consumer contracts, most of the time standard contracts, regulate a large number of exchanges, having an impact on the markets where those services and goods are traded. By regulating a large number of exchanges, standard contract forms regulate the market of that commodity, including provisions related to information, safety, quality and, increasingly, environmental and social protections.[72] Such regulatory functions of consumer contract law refer both to regulated and 'non-regulated' markets. This distinction might be further specified. All markets are regulated, but the instruments and objectives differ depending on the nature and accessibility of the services provided, the degree of market liberalization and competitiveness, and the necessity or opportunity to engage in price regulation. By regulated markets, we refer to markets that have been at least partly liberalized and are subject to specific control by independent sector-specific regulatory authority in addition to the ordinary control exercised by judicial bodies and competition authorities.

Regulated markets differ from the other markets because consumer protection is ensured by the intervention of specialized authorities entrusted with mechanisms of a more intrusive nature to police contracts and monitor trade practices.[73] On the one hand, in regulated markets, liberalization has broadened the scope of contract laws; on the other hand, a strong interplay between administrative and judicial control has taken place.[74] Consumer protection in liberalized markets often concerns consumers' choices. In some instances, consumers are offered the choice between acting in a fully liberalized market where choices among different suppliers may be broader but also more complex or to stay within regulated markets where regulators steer and nudge. Consumer protection concerns free choices among different and competing options in the marketplace.

Enforcement reflects these functions since – primarily through injunc-

[72] On the regulatory function of standard contract forms and boilerplates see Hugh Collins, *Regulating Contracts* (OUP 1999), the contributions in Omri Ben-Shahar, *Boilerplate: The Foundation of Market Contracts* (Cambridge University Press 2007) and in particular, the contribution of Stephen J. Choi and Mitu Gulati, 'Contract as Statute', 145 and Kevin E. Davis, 'The Role of Non-Profits in the Production of Boilerplates', 120.

[73] See Weatherill, n. 71, 129.

[74] See Hans-Wolfgang Micklitz, 'Regulatory Strategies on Services Contracts in EC Law' in Cafaggi and Muir Watt, n. 70, 16.

tions and findings of invalidity – it sanctions unlawful market behaviour. Moreover, new remedies that promote cooperation between enforcers and infringers, primarily in the area of administrative enforcement, also reinforce the regulatory function of consumer law. On the one hand, *ex ante* requests from traders and professionals may be made in order to verify the fairness of contractual clauses or trade practices.[75] On the other hand, traders that have violated the law may offer commitments in order to avoid sanctions, where they are accepted by the administrative enforcers and ensure compliance with the relevant standards. Consumer enforcement addresses market failures arising from non-compliance with principles and rules.

In energy, telecom, transport, and financial markets, administrative enforcement assumes specific features that are partially reflected in the dialogue between administrative authorities and the European regulatory networks.[76] The scope of regulation is broader because it encompasses areas like price control and the legal instruments that allow for switching between operators.[77] Often sector-specific regulators oversee both compliance with competition and also consumer protection. Administrative enforcement is not limited to regulated markets and has been enhanced by Member States' choices to move away from exclusive judicial oversight. Administrative dialogue occurs between

---

[75] See for example Art.37 of the Italian *Codice del consumo*, in France the *Commission des clauses abusives* (Art L 822-4 *Code de la consummation*) and the *Commission d'examen des pratiques deloyales commerciales.* The situation is similar in Belgium. In the UK, Part 8 of the Enterprise Act 2002 provides for the enforcement procedures of the Competition and Markets Authority. In the Netherlands, *ex ante* control is exercised by private bodies.

[76] The access by administrative authorities to the channels of judicial dialogue may be limited due to the limitation posed by Art.267, TFEU. See Case C-394/11 *Belov* EU:C:2013:48, excluding that the Bulgarian Commission for Protection against Discrimination is a court or a tribunal pursuant to Art.267 TFEU; from a different perspective, see Joined Cases C-58/13 and C-59/13 *Angelo Alberto Torresi* (C-58/13) *and Pierfrancesco Torresi* (C-59/13) *v Consiglio dell'Ordine degli Avvocati di Macerata* EU:C:2014:2088, concluding that 'in this instance, there is indeed a case pending before the Consiglio Nazionale Forense and it is called upon to give a ruling within proceedings intended to result in a decision that is of a judicial nature'.

[77] See Hans-Wolfgang Micklitz, 'The Public and the Private – European Regulatory Private Law and Financial Services' (2014) 10 ERCL 473; Olha O. Cherednychenko, 'Editorial – Public and Private Enforcement of European Private Law in the Financial Services Sector' (2015) 23(4) ERPL 621 and Giuseppe Bellantuono, 'Public and Private Enforcement of European Private Law in the Energy and Telecommunications Sectors' (2015) 23 ERPL 649.

sector-specific, general regulators, branches of the executives, and courts exercising judicial review.

The regulatory function of consumer enforcement influences not only its institutional aspects but also its substantive ones. By expanding the use of collective redress and privileging injunctions over compensatory remedies, both administrative and judicial enforcement stimulate forward-looking measures to prevent violations, deter infringements, and steer market behaviour.[78] Control over the unfairness of terms and over trade practices can foster regulatory objectives such as warranting access to services, increasing market transparency, and ensuring market stability.[79] This is generally the case when enforcers do not simply prohibit conduct and activities but engage traders in a process of change supported by legally-binding commitments.[80]

Such regulatory functions influence both the instruments and the objectives of enforcement. Even when courts decide individual cases, they clearly bear in mind the potential effects of judgments on a large number of consumers facing similar issues.[81] As provided by the CJEU in *Invitel*, the effects of injunctions go beyond the litigants to the individual dispute and apply *ultra partes* to all consumers who have signed or will sign contracts

---

[78] The relationship between individual and collective redress has developed through several stages. The EU has promoted the development of effective collective redress that was initially deployed only by a few Member States. More recently, the CJEU has had the opportunity to define the interaction between individual and collective remedies affirming the principle of complementarity. While the benefits of collective redress are fully acknowledged, it is clear, in the realm of unfair contract terms, that individual protection cannot be sacrificed. It remains to be seen whether this position will have a more general impact on consumer protection. See Case C-381/14 *Sales Sinués* EU:C:2016:252.

[79] In several recent cases the role of transparency and information regulation via contract has been expanded by the CJEU. Even when the unfairness concerns the main subject matter of the contract, the CJEU has indicated that transparency scrutiny can bring similar results. A lack of transparency concerning unilateral changes of consumer prices over time or interest in consumer credit agreements has been subject to judicial intervention. The CJEU has scrutinized clauses and practices related to price changes by credit institutions, gas, energy and telecom suppliers.

[80] For a clear illustration see the unfair trade practices evolution documented in the recent report issued by the Commission services: European Commission, 'Guidance on the Implementation and Application of Directive 2005/29/EC on Unfair Commercial Practices' SWD(2016) 163 final.

[81] See Case C-472/10 *Invitel* EU:C:2012:242, para.37; Case C-76/10 *Pohotovost'* EU:C:2010:685, para.44.

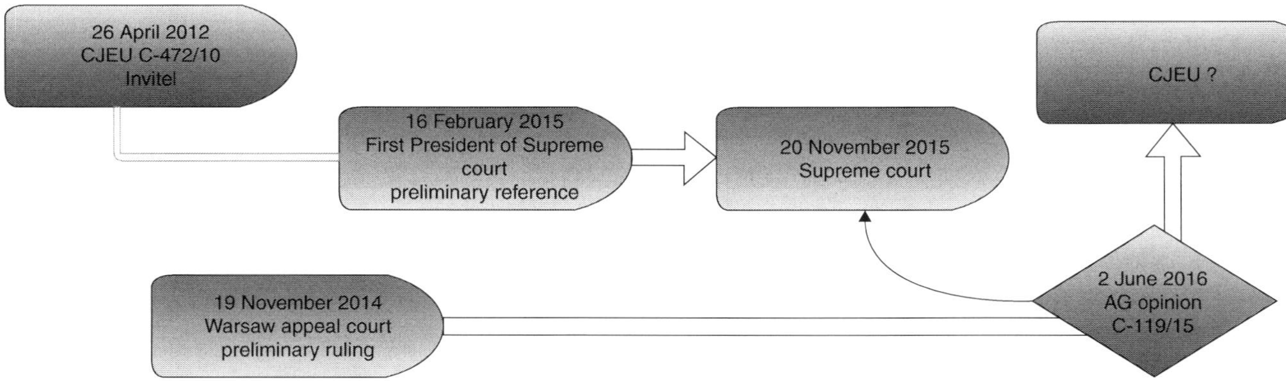

Figure 9.3 Graphical representation of judicial dialogue related to CJEU decision (AG Opinion) in Case C-119/15 Biuro

including such terms.[82] Signalling effects of judicial decisions play a significant role in consumer enforcement and constitute part of judicial dialogue. This is even more relevant for the enforcement of consumer law by administrative authorities. Enforcement decisions at the EU and the national level both solve individual disputes and signal to market actors the expected conduct. This is not only true for unfair contract terms and trade practices, but also for the selection of remedies and the definition of compensation for mass economic and personal harms. As such, enforcement significantly contributes to market regulation and in particular to consumer regulation.

THE EFFECTS OF INSTITUTIONAL DIALOGUE IN PRIVATE LAW: A SHORT DETOUR

Judicial dialogue, having the impact of generating changes to procedural law, has contributed to defining the scope of consumer legislation and its spillover effects into other areas of EU private law beyond consumer protection and to areas of consumer protection not covered by EU legislation. The definition of professionals and consumers for the purposes of applying EU law has been central to judicial dialogue.[83] It is important to note that the scope of CJEU intervention has been expanded to areas not directly

---

[82] See *Invitel* ibid., para.44:

In the light of those considerations, the answer to the first question is that Article 6(1) of the Directive, read in conjunction with Article 7(1) and (2) thereof, must be interpreted as meaning that:

- it does not preclude the declaration of invalidity of an unfair term included in the GBC of consumer contracts in an action for an injunction, provided for in Article 7 of that directive, brought against a seller or supplier in the public interest, and on behalf of consumers, by a body appointed by national legislation from producing, in accordance with that legislation, effects with regard to all consumers who concluded with the seller or supplier concerned a contract to which the same GBC apply, including with regard to those consumers who were not party to the injunction proceedings;
- where the unfair nature of a term in the GBC has been acknowledged in such proceedings, national courts are required, of their own motion, and also with regard to the future, to take such action thereon as is provided for by national law in order to ensure that consumers who have concluded a contract with the seller or supplier to which those GBC apply will not be bound by that term.

See also Fabrizio Cafaggi and Stephanie Law, 'Effect of Collective Proceedings' in Terryn *et al*, n. 58, 653.

[83] See Dorota Leczykiewicz and Stephen Weatherill (eds), *The Images of the*

within the scope of EU legislation, for example, when Member States have broadened the applicability of EU law in their national legislation to contracts and agreements beyond those falling within the scope of the legislation being transposed.[84] Similarly, a spillover effect has occurred when national courts have inferred broader implications from CJEU judgments concerning specific areas of EU law.[85] This evolution opens up the space for scrutinizing the grey area of the impact of judicial dialogue onto spillover effects of EU law in national legal systems.[86] Moreover, the potential spillover effects in domestic legal orders go beyond EU legislation. How should the *ex officio* power in national consumer legislation be applied in areas of consumer law not directly legislated for at EU level?[87] For example, can the *ex officio* powers, justified as aiming to promote a high level of consumer protection, be extended to areas where similar objectives are pursued, such as social housing, health, education? How does the principle of effectiveness work in relation to the objective of protecting weaker parties outside the realm of the consumer? How does the right to effective judicial protection enshrined in Art.47 of the Charter apply to other areas of private law connected to those of consumer protection?

Spillover effects of institutional dialogue concern different policy areas of individual Member States and their intensity and scope differ across

---

Consumer in EU Law: Legislation, Free Movement and Competition Law (Hart 2016).

84 This is the issue discussed in Case C-377/14 *Radlinger and Radlingerová* EU:C:2015:769, Opinion of AG Sharpston, para.43:

> It is the credit agreement itself that falls within the scope of Directive 2008/48 rather than the resulting debts or the creditor's claims. However, credit agreements secured by a mortgage are expressly excluded from the scope of Directive 2008/48 (Art.2(2)(a)). The Commission states in its submissions that the national transposition provisions are broader in scope than Art.2 of Directive 2008/48, as they also cover credit agreements secured by a mortgage. That position is not inconsistent with the aims of Directive 2008/48. Member States are entitled to maintain or introduce, in accordance with EU law, national legislation corresponding to some or all of the provisions of Directive 2008/48, that covers credit agreements outside its scope.

85 See, for example, the judgment of the Italian Supreme Court (*Corte di cassazione*), n. 14828/2012, where a general contract law provision is interpreted in the light of the CJEU judgment rendered in the *Pannon* case (Case C-243/08 *Pannon* [2009] ECR I-4713) with reference to the court's duty to ascertain the unfairness of an abusive clause.

86 On the spillover effects see Angus Johnston, "Spillovers' from EU Law into National Law: (Un)intended Consequences for Private Law Relationships' in Leczykiewicz and Weatherill, n.67, 357.

87 See above for an example in the Italian case law, at n.81.

Member States. The extent to which procedural changes determined by judicial dialogue in consumer law are spilling over into other Member States, given the binding effects of CJEU judgments, is unclear. The current research shows that changes in procedural law and the law of remedies are not consistent across national legal systems.[88] As such, it is clear that the impact of individual judgments is not homogeneous.

EUROPEAN JUDICIAL AND ADMINISTRATIVE ENFORCEMENT OF CONSUMER LAW RECOMBINED IN THE LIGHT OF INSTITUTIONAL TRIALOGUES

The transformations in European consumer law enforcement mechanisms have been staggering.[89] They concern the relationship between administrative and judicial systems, the allocation of tasks between EU and national levels, and substantively, the interaction between rights and remedies, the new balance between individual and collective redress, and the shifting focus from compensation towards prevention and deterrence.[90] Within the judicial enforcement, changes are primarily driven by national courts 'supported' by the CJEU, whereas administrative enforcement is reinforced by legislation and by soft law, including recommendations issued by the European Commission and guidelines drafted by the European networks.[91] These transformations are reshaping the role of national courts

---

[88] See ACTIONES project of the Centre for Judicial Cooperation at the European University Institute (Information available at: http://www.eui.eu/Projects/CentreForJudicialCooperation/Projects/ACTIONES/ACTIONES.aspx; Last Accessed: 27.06.2016).

[89] See Hans-Wolfgang Micklitz, 'The Consumer: Marketised, Fragmentised, Constitutionalised' in Leczykiewicz and Weatherill, n.83, 21.

[90] See for an analytical framework Cafaggi, n.9. More recently and with references to private law, see Franziska Weber and Michael Faure, 'The Interplay between Public and Private Enforcement in European Private Law: Law and Economics Perspective' (2015) 23 ERPL 525, revisiting the conventional law and economics perspective defined by A. Mitchell Polinsky and Steven Shavell, 'An Economic Theory of Public Enforcement of Law (2000) 38 J.Econ.Lit. 45.

[91] The powers of the European Commission will be strengthened by the new CPC regulation. See CPC proposal Regulation recital 16:

> The Commission must be better able to coordinate and monitor the functioning of the mutual assistance mechanism, **issue guidance, make recommendations and issue opinions to the Member States** when problems arise. The Commission also must be better able to effectively and quickly assist competent authorities

and administrative authorities, increasing the interplay between civil and administrative enforcement. In this chapter the analysis has focused on the relationship between administrative and civil enforcement, but similar if not more important interactions characterize the interplay between administrative and criminal enforcement, where principles like *ne bis in idem* are contributing to the definition of the dual-track regimes.[92]

A consistent trend is identifiable in the clear growth of administrative enforcement.[93] This is certainly the case for consumer protection in regulated markets but similar patterns also inform general market regulation (for example, in the case of unfair trade practices).[94] The growth of administrative enforcement has been partially recalibrated by the intervention of the ECtHR and the CJEU with regard to the criminal nature of the administrative sanctions and the impact of *ne bis idem.*[95] The use of administrative sanctions of criminal nature in consumer protection is relatively limited but significant. The effectiveness of administrative enforcement has been questioned, especially in respect of trans-border violations of consumer law. As noted above, the Regulation 2006/2004 is currently under reform in order to strengthen the powers of individual authorities and their modes of coordination for cross-border violations.

As to judicial enforcement, significant changes to procedural rules driven by the principle of effectiveness and by the public policy nature of consumer protection rules have been stimulated by dialogue between national courts and the CJEU.[96] The principle of effectiveness linked to the objective of higher consumer protection is leading to a reallocation of

---

to resolve disputes over the interpretation of their obligations of the competent authorities stemming from the mutual assistance mechanism.

92 Case C-617/10 *Åkerberg Fransson* EU:C:2013:280 and *Grande Stevens v Italy*, App.Nos.18640/10, 18647/10, 18663/10, 18668/10 and 18698/10.

93 Fabrizio Cafaggi and Hans-Wolfgang Micklitz, *New Frontiers of Consumer Protection – The Interplay between Private and Public Enforcement* (Intersentia 2009), Cherednychenko, n.8.

94 See European Commission, 'First Report on the Application of Directive 2005/29/EC' COM(2013) 139 final, 26: 'Most systems, however, combine elements of public and private enforcement. Penalties range from injunction orders, damages, fines and criminal sanctions, and administrative; in most Member States there is a combination of all of these.'

95 *Åkerberg Fransson*, n.92 and *Grande Stevens v Italy*, n.92e.

96 See cases at n.67. See Stephen Whittaker, 'Who Determines What Civil Courts Decide? Private Rights, Public Policy an EU Law' in Leczykiewicz and Weatherill, n.83, 89; and Micklitz, n.8.

power between judges and parties.[97] This is reflected in the expansion of the *ex officio* power to assess terms and practices of unfairness, to broaden the scope of existing remedies, and to redefine the allocation of burden of proof. These powers have been extended to different branches of the judiciaries and to new players, including the Spanish *secretario judicial*.[98]

Administrative enforcement does not replace judicial enforcement but it increases the menu of sanctions and remedies for violations of consumer law.[99] It also introduces different approaches focusing on commitments and engaging traders in cooperative behaviour after infringement. These features will be reinforced by the proposed regulation amending Regulation 2006/2004, in which new powers concerning monitoring and sanctioning, well beyond the conventional array, are explicitly defined. In particular, the possibility for the competent authority to order compensation is explicitly stated together with the power to order the restitution of profits when the identity of harmed consumers is unknown.[100] Cooperative

---

[97] See Safjan and Dusterhaus, n. 6; E. Cannizzaro, 'Effettività del diritto dell'Unione e rimedi processuali nazionali' (2013) *Il Diritto dell'Unione Europea* 663 and R. Conti, 'l'effettività del diritto comunitario ed il ruolo del giudice' (2007) *Europa e dir priv.* 479.

[98] See Case C-503/15 *Panicello,* in which the power of *secretario judicial* to assess unfairness of contract clauses is considered in the light of Art.47 CFR.

[99] Administrative authorities often negotiate with enterprises for modifications of practices that can generate sanctions if they persist in using them.

[100] See Art.8 of the proposed Regulation amending Regulation 2006/2004, n.14, which provides that:

> The Competent authority shall:
>
> . . .(g) adopt interim measures to prevent the risk of serious and irreparable harm to consumers, in particular the suspension of a website, domain or a similar digital site, service or account;
>
> (h) start investigations or procedures to bring about the cessation or prohibition of intra-Union infringements or widespread infringements of its own initiative and where appropriate to publish information about this;
>
> (i) obtain a commitment from the trader responsible for the intra-Union infringement or widespread infringement to cease the infringement and where appropriate to compensate consumers for the harm caused;
>
> (j) request in writing the cessation of the infringement by the trader;
>
> (k) bring about the cessation or the prohibition of the infringement;
>
> (l) close down a website, domain or similar digital site, service or account or a part of it, including by requesting a third party or other public authority to implement such measures;
>
> (m) impose penalties, including fines and penalty payments, for intra-Union infringements and widespread infringements and for the failure to comply with any decision, order, interim measure, commitment or other measure adopted pursuant to this Regulation;

administrative enforcement develops strategies which differ from the more conventional criminal-like sanctions that include fines and prohibitions. The reform develops this approach and generalizes the power to seek or accept requests of undertakings by the enterprises accused of consumer violations. This approach has not yet found significant recognition in judicial enforcement in the use of injunctions where case management is still rather rudimentary.

The differences between the powers of civil courts and administrative enforcers remain quite significant even following the increase of *ex officio* powers in the domain of civil proceedings.[101] Procedural rules differ and the framework of litigation is different. Administrative authorities can start investigations themselves and have a much wider power to seek evidence than civil judges.[102] Judges responsible for private enforcement are instead 'constrained' by the perimeter of litigation defined by the parties and can only exceptionally expand it when public policy and the right to effective judicial protection so requires.[103] Whereas the enforcement relationship between administrative bodies and infringers is usually a repeat game, in civil proceedings rarely is the same court responsible for deciding cases for repeat violations by the same infringer.[104] Furthermore,

---

(n) order the trader responsible for the intra-Union infringement or widespread infringement to compensate consumers that have suffered harm as a consequence of the infringement including, among others, monetary compensation, offering consumers the option to terminate the contract or other measures ensuring redress to consumers who have been harmed as a result of the infringement;

(o) order the restitution of profits obtained as a result of infringements, including an order that those profits are paid to the public purse or to a beneficiary designated by the competent authority or under national legislation;

(p) publish any final decisions, interim measures or orders, including the publication of the identity of the trader responsible for the intra-Union infringement or widespread infringement;

(q) consult consumers, consumer organisations, designated bodies and other persons concerned about the effectiveness of the proposed commitments in ceasing the infringement and removing the harm caused by it.

101 See the text at n.33 *et seq.*

102 See for example Art.27, Italian *Codice del consumo*. These powers are likely to increase if the new proposed regulation is approved.

103 See Joined Cases C-430–431/93 *Van Schijndel* [1995] ECR I-4705.

104 Administrative authorities using their sanctioning powers can not only consider the duration of the violation as one of the factors determining the choice of sanctions but also the repeat nature of the violation which is taken into account by criminal courts and much less by civil courts. This is not to say that civil remedies and in particular fines cannot be used to penalize persistent non-compliance with judicial orders to stop the unfair practice or other infringements affecting

even if the deciding court were the same, unlike administrative enforcers or criminal judges, they do not decide the case on the basis of previous conduct sanctioned in past proceedings.[105] These features make the use of cooperation between enforcer and infringer more feasible in administrative than in civil enforcement. As to the available remedies, administrative authorities have a wide array of sanctions and remedies mainly aimed at policing market behaviour and at prohibiting repeat violations. Administrative enforcers monitor compliance with the sanctions and, in case of non-compliance, fine the infringers to a much larger extent than judges in private enforcement.[106] Costs of monitoring compliance with sanctions in judicial proceedings are borne by the parties, often wary of effective monitoring instruments before the infringement.

Administrative enforcers are constrained by the principle of legality and, when applying sanctions of a criminal nature, by the principle *nulla poena sine lege*. The combination of fines and injunctions is determined by the seriousness and duration of the violation and must be consistent with the principles of proportionality and deterrence.[107] Both administrative and judicial enforcers have to follow the principles of effectiveness, proportionality, and dissuasiveness.

The relative weight of different enforcement mechanisms varies within consumer law with an impact on institutional dialogue. In some areas administrative enforcement prevails, while in others judicial enforcement predominates. The reports of the European Commission and scholarly research show that administrative enforcement in areas like unfair commercial practices is more diffused.[108] Litigation is limited and in particular, compensatory remedies are hardly ever sought either by individual consumers or by consumer organizations. This is not the case in relation to unfair contract terms, where invalidity and injunctions ordered by civil judges have been playing a very significant role compared to that of administrative enforcers.

Sanctioning is a key element of enforcement policies and is determined

---

consumer welfare. See Directive 22/2009/EC on injunctions for the protection of consumers' interests.

[105] In the area of unfair trade practices, national legislations explicitly impose to consider previous violations when the amount of the fine is determined. See for instance Art.27, Italian *codice del consumo*.

[106] With the reform, administrative enforcers will be able to order compensation for consumers and profit restitution, widening both the array of remedies and the functional scope of administrative enforcement.

[107] See Directive 2005/29/EC and Art.24, Directive 2011/83/EU.

[108] See European Commission, 'First Report on the Application of Directive 2005/29/EC' COM(2013) 139 final.

by the interaction between judicial and administrative enforcement. The definition of principles is primarily a matter of EU law, with Art.47 CFR gaining importance in the determination of what constitutes effective judicial protection. The principles of effectiveness, proportionality and dissuasiveness have now been integrated into EU legislation and should guide judicial and administrative enforcement.[109] Differences between administrative and judicial enforcement concern the type of sanctions and their objectives.

Administrative enforcers focus on the infringer. Sanctioning in consumer administrative enforcement is guided by multiple variables, including: (1) the seriousness of the violation; (2) the number of consumers potentially involved; (3) the magnitude of harm or risk created by the conduct; (4) the duration of the infringement; and (5) the past conduct of the infringer and the repetition of the violation. Relevance, especially in unfair trade practices, is attributed to the gains made by the trader when engaging in the practices and to its shares.

Judicial enforcement focuses on the injured and differs depending on whether redress is individual or collective. Compensation is certainly one of the main goals, but preventive measures are also used both in criminal and civil judicial enforcement. If, as is stated in the proposed Regulation, compensation will be available also within administrative enforcement; hence the conventional approach that distinguishes between *ex ante* (administrative) and *ex post* (judicial) control will disappear, expanding the functions of administrative enforcement.[110]

---

[109] See Elise Poillot, 'The European Court of Justice and General Principles Derived from the Acquis Communautaire', (2014) 1 *Oslo Law Review* 67.

[110] See the proposed Regulation, n.14 above, Art.18, 'Enforcement measures in coordinated actions', which provides:

> 1. The competent authorities concerned may invite the trader responsible for the infringement to propose commitments to cease the infringement and where appropriate to compensate or take other measures facilitating compensation of consumers that have suffered harm. The trader may also, on its own initiative, propose commitments to cease the infringement and to compensate consumers.
> 2. Where the trader proposes commitments, the competent authorities concerned, may, where appropriate, publish the proposed commitments on their websites or, as appropriate, on the Commission website to seek the views of other parties concerned and to verify whether the commitments are sufficient to cease the infringement and to compensate consumers.
> 3. The competent authorities concerned may designate one competent authority to take enforcement measures on behalf of the other competent authorities in order to bring about the cessation or to prohibit the widespread infringement, to ensure compensation of consumers or to impose penalties. When designating a competent authority to take enforcement measures the competent authorities

The evaluation of sanctioning has become a priority both for the European and national regulators. Indicators for the evaluation of effectiveness are on the agenda of the European Commission in many areas, from financial markets to competition. The possibility to evaluate different enforcement mechanisms and their effectiveness is often undermined by the lack of coordination instruments and the different rationales that drive each enforcement mechanism. What is still missing in the current institutional framework is a clear legislative indication concerning how effectiveness, proportionality and dissuasiveness should be applied to combined administrative, criminal and civil sanctions. Should proportionality be separately defined in relation to each enforcement mechanism or should it apply across enforcement mechanisms? Should the level of fines be correlated to that of compensation when civil actions for damages are brought? Should the content and the effects of injunctions be commensurate to civil penalties or to criminal fines?

We contend that these principles apply not only within but also between enforcement mechanisms. Some scattered evidence, which implicitly shows that national regulators operating in the field of competition and telecoms are incorporating the potential outcome of the flow of suits for damages, exists; however, beyond the example of the voluntary redress scheme, there are currently no clear indications about the application of the principle of proportionality to multiple sanctions and remedies across enforcement mechanisms.

---

shall take into consideration the location of the trader concerned. Once the competent authority has been designated to take enforcement measures by the other competent authorities concerned, it shall become competent to act on behalf of the consumers of each such Member State as if they were its own consumers.
4. The competent authorities may decide to take enforcement measures simultaneously in all or some Member States concerned by the widespread infringement. In such a case, the competent authorities shall ensure that those enforcement measures are launched simultaneously in all Member States concerned.
5. The instruction of a designated body to take enforcement measures pursuant to paragraphs 1 to 4 shall only be possible if the competent authorities concerned give their consent to such instruction and where such instruction does not lead to disclosure of information which is subject to the rules on professional and commercial secrecy set out in Article 41.

INSTITUTIONAL TRIALOGUES AND PATTERNS OF CHANGE

Dialogue is a remarkable driver of effective enforcement but its current design is far from perfect. Cooperation among national courts involved in consumer enforcement has not been formalized and stabilized. Cooperation among consumer administrative authorities has been institutionalized but differences in national practices, including sanctioning policies, persist; these differences cause significant misalignment among Member States. The most problematic facet of the current system is the lack of effective coordination between administrative and judicial enforcers, which undermines dialogue and institutional cooperation.[111] This is true at European level, between the regulatory networks and the CJEU and, at national level, between independent administrative authorities and the judiciaries, where clear general rules about parallel proceedings or the binding force of judgments and administrative acts are not in place, save for a few exceptions in respect of competition violations and financial regulation. Failure to coordinate can generate divergent responses to the same violations, creating legal uncertainty about remedies. Such shortcomings are all the more relevant considering the increasing role played by administrative enforcement in consumer law. The proposed reform of Regulation 2006/2004 does not address these shortcomings and in particular the coordination with judicial enforcement.

In this perspective, it would be extremely useful if national administrative enforcement bodies with jurisdictional powers could request preliminary rulings from the CJEU, both concerning their own power and their relationship with judicial enforcement. When Member States decide to adopt administrative enforcement, the competent authorities should be able to engage in a dialogue with the CJEU in respect of their power and the potential hurdles to the principle of effectiveness that are generated by the application of administrative procedural rules. Dialogue between administrative networks and national courts should be promoted in order to improve coordination among consumer enforcement mechanisms. The CJEU could play an important role, providing guidance about the factors to be considered in the allocation of enforcement powers according to the principle of effectiveness, the right to effective judicial protection (Art.47 CFR), and the principle of good administration. The principles of effectiveness, proportionality and dissuasiveness (should) guide both the legislators, administrative enforcers, and the courts in defining the appropriate

[111] See Cafaggi, n.9.

sanctions. The CJEU should scrutinize their correct application and provide guidance.[112]

The role to be played by Art.47 CFR in shaping the relationship between the two forms of enforcement is still to be determined. Clearly, a much more frequent and significant reference is made to this provision in the judicial system than by regulatory authorities. Administrative enforcement at national level, unlike judicial enforcement, has so far hardly been influenced by the reference to Art.47. When exercising administrative enforcement powers, the national authorities should be subject to Art.47 and warrant a right to an effective remedy. Otherwise, the principle of procedural autonomy could be used to avoid the duty to conform with the right to effective judicial protection when administrative rather than judicial enforcement is chosen. To a more limited extent, consumer enforcement by administrative authorities has been influenced by the general principle of good administration. Whether Art.47 CFR will produce a set of integrated principles concerning both judicial and administrative enforcement is yet to be seen.

To conclude, there seems to be two main forms of dialogue in consumer protection, which have an impact on enforcement in national systems: vertical judicial dialogue for civil law enforcement between the CJEU and national courts and administrative horizontal dialogue within European networks for administrative enforcement. This picture is likely to change. Increasingly, forms of vertical dialogue in administrative enforcement are used in regulated markets, while horizontal dialogue among courts is left to informal instruments; systematic peer review of national judicial practices is not yet in place in respect of the latter. The instruments and the impact differ; however, in both instances, dialogue plays a major role in innovation, and possibly one which goes beyond assuring the uniformity of enforcement practices in consumer law. The role of the CJEU in promoting new forms of dialogue can be relevant and its intensity associated with different forms of judgments.[113] However, it is of fundamental significance that the European Commission increases its coordinating role when reporting about the implementation of directives and regulations,

---

112 See Fabrizio Cafaggi and Paola Iamiceli, 'The Principles of Effectiveness, Proportionality and Dissuasiveness in the Enforcement of Consumer Law' (on file with the authors), discussing how judges should apply the principles to remedies and sanctions when deciding consumer cases. See also the ReJus project, led by Fabrizio Cafaggi and funded by the European Commission's Directorate-General for Justice and Consumers.

113 See the distinction made by Tridimas and its implication for judicial dialogue, set out in the text referenced at n.11 herein and in the introduction at n.48.

engaging both courts and administrative enforcers. The new design that will emerge with the reform of Regulation 2004/2006 should duly take into account the need to defining principles for the coordination of different forms of enforcement including criminal enforcement and alternative dispute resolution. Both principles – defining structural coordination, related to the proceedings, and functional coordination, related to the nature and objectives of the remedies available to redress consumers – should be clearly stated, leaving the Member States with the choice of how to operationalize these principles and distribute relevant weight between the different mechanisms of enforcement within the framework of effective judicial protection under Art.47 CFR.

Index